Fantasy Femmes of Sixties Cinema

ALSO BY TOM LISANTI
AND FROM MCFARLAND

*Glamour Girls of Sixties Hollywood:
Seventy-Five Profiles* (2008)

*Hollywood Surf and Beach Movies:
The First Wave, 1959–1969* (2005)

*Drive-in Dream Girls: A Galaxy of B-Movie
Starlets of the Sixties* (2003)

BY TOM LISANTI AND LOUIS PAUL

*Film Fatales: Women in Espionage Films
and Television, 1962–1973* (2002)

Fantasy Femmes of Sixties Cinema

Interviews with 20 Actresses from Biker, Beach, and Elvis Movies

TOM LISANTI

Foreword by CHRIS NOEL

McFarland & Company, Inc., Publishers
Jefferson, North Carolina, and London

The present work is a reprint of the illustrated case bound edition of Fantasy Femmes of Sixties Cinema: Interviews with 20 Actresses from Biker, Beach, and Elvis Movies, first published in 2001 by McFarland.

LIBRARY OF CONGRESS CATALOGUING-IN-PUBLICATION DATA

Lisanti, Tom, 1961–
　　Fantasy femmes of sixties cinema : interviews with 20 actresses from biker, beach, and Elvis movies / by Tom Lisanti ; foreword by Chris Noel.
　　　　p.　　cm.
　　Includes bibliographical references and index.
　　Contents: Joan O'Brien — Diane McBain — Joan Staley — Jill Haworth — Pamela Tiffin — Francine York — Joy Harmon — Eileen O'Neill — Julie Parrish — Jean Hale — Irene Tsu — Chris Noel — Lana Wood — Celeste Yarnall — Judy Pace — Salli Sachse — Deanna Lund — Karen Jensen — Linda Harrison — Tisha Sterling — More groovy gals.

　　ISBN 978-0-7864-6101-1
　　softcover : 50# alkaline paper

　　1. Motion picture actors and actresses—United States—Biography. 2. Actresses—United States—Biography.　I. Title.
PN1998.2.L57　2010
791.43'028'0820973—dc21　　　　　　　　　　　　　　00-64008

British Library cataloguing data are available

©2001 Tom Lisanti. All rights reserved

No part of this book may be reproduced or transmitted in any form or by any means, electronic or mechanical, including photocopying or recording, or by any information storage and retrieval system, without permission in writing from the publisher.

On the cover: Celeste Yarnall

Manufactured in the United States of America

McFarland & Company, Inc., Publishers
　Box 611, Jefferson, North Carolina 28640
　www.mcfarlandpub.com

To my parents, Vincent and Joan,
for all those wonderful summer evenings at the drive-in.

Acknowledgments

A number of people had a hand in helping me put together this book. First and foremost, I relay my thanks to the lovely ladies who let me interview them and who shared their lives in Hollywood with me: Jean Hale, Joy Harmon, Linda Harrison, Jill Haworth, Karen Jensen, Deanna Lund, Diane McBain, Chris Noel, Joan O'Brien, Eileen O'Neill, Judy Pace, Julie Parrish, Salli Sachse, Joan Staley, Tisha Sterling, Pamela Tiffin, Irene Tsu, Lana Wood, Celeste Yarnall and Francine York. I also wish to thank Mitchell Bard, Brendon Boone, Shelley Fabares, Laurel Goodwin, Sue Ane Langdon, Carol Lynley and Dale Sheets for their brief comments.

This book and my writing career would never have come to pass if it weren't for the encouragement from my pool buddies and fellow authors Louis Paul and Heidi Stock (a groovy gal in her own right). Thanks to Mark Tolleson for his editing prowess. He now knows more about "sixties gals" than he ever could have imagined. Thank you to my longtime friends John Covelli and Teresa DeTurris with a special thank you to Teresa for her legal help. My gratitude goes to my colleague Barbara Cohen-Stratyner for her input and advice, to my former boss Robert Marx at the New York Public Library for the Performing Arts for giving me the support and flexibility to write this book, and to Bob Taylor, the curator of the Billy Rose Theatre Collection, for giving me unlimited access to the collection.

I also wish to thank my family—my mother Joan Lisanti, Joe and Beth Lisanti, Lorraine and Richie Nicolo (I spelled it right!) and Donna and Mike Cates. A big hurrah to my number one fan on Long Island, Vincent Page.

Kudos to my friends who have prodded me along with their helpfulness and encouragement—top billing must go to my LA friend Shaun "Floyd Smoot" Chang and (in alphabetical order) Keith Aden, Bill Benish, Anne and Chris DeMarco, Jeff Failla, Scott Hannibal, Pete Kaiser, Tom Kazar, Phil Lindow, Jeremy Megraw, Alan Pally, Tim Roberts, Mitchell Soble and Kevin Winkler.

And last but certainly not least, special thanks to a great guy named Ernie DeLia.

Table of Contents

Acknowledgments vii
Foreword by Chris Noel 1
Preface 3
Introduction 5
*Elvis, Beach, Biker and Alienated Youth Films:
A Brief Summary* 17

Joan O'Brien 27
Diane McBain 40
Joan Staley 53
Jill Haworth 67
Pamela Tiffin 79
Francine York 92
Joy Harmon 108
Eileen O'Neill 120
Julie Parrish 132
Jean Hale 146
Irene Tsu 158
Chris Noel 170
Lana Wood 184
Celeste Yarnall 197

Judy Pace   211
Salli Sachse   224
Deanna Lund   234
Karen Jensen   247
Linda Harrison   259
Tisha Sterling   271
More Groovy Gals   282

Bibliography   295
Index   299

Foreword

The sixties were the highlight of my life. While my high school friends had gone off to college, I hit New York City, where director Sandy Howard cast me in his first film. I then went to California. I had always dreamed of Hollywood. How exciting to be under contract to MGM and to become a working movie actress! I learned my craft from successful, important actors. Having not attended acting school, I studied by paying attention, being disciplined and working hard. Some of us worked mightily at being the best we could be in one of the most demanding and desired of all careers. Though we were competitive with each other, we also liked one another. Actress Eileen O'Neill and I are best friends today—almost like sisters.

Author Tom Lisanti has the heart to understand, appreciate and applaud us "Ol' Sixties Cinema Gals." We enjoyed doing Elvis, beach and teenage movies. These films were innocent fun. Nudity, violence or foul language weren't necessary in these films. It wasn't until the late sixties that we encountered this.

I loved our sixties film culture. I didn't go to movies or work in films that caused nightmares from any violence or horror. I experienced that visiting our troops in Vietnam. Going back and forth from the glamour of filmmaking to the stark reality of war later gave me nightmares. I wish for all the children of the world never to have nightmares of fright and violence, whether from war or films. That is one reason I still like Elvis, beach and teenage movies. They make me happy!

Chris Noel

Preface

Why a book on sixties actresses who are known only by cult movie fans or have been long forgotten? That is the question I have been asked most since I began working on *Fantasy Femmes of Sixties Cinema*. I just felt these actresses had long been overlooked in film history. Though none of them became superstars, they appeared in some of the most popular films of the decade, worked in genres aimed at the teenage audience, and guest-starred on some of the most beloved TV shows of our time. But nobody was writing about them. There were no interviews in genre film magazines and they were rarely mentioned in film history books—not even ones that focused on the sixties.

The second question I've been asked is why I didn't focus on better-known actresses. The answer is simple—stars such as Ann-Margret, Jane Fonda, Faye Dunaway, Raquel Welch, Stella Stevens, Sandra Dee, and Connie Stevens have been written about *ad nauseam*. There are biographies, autobiographies, chapters in books and numerous magazine articles on these actresses. I never tried to contact any of them because they were not the people I wanted to write my book about. I wanted to interview and write about the lovely young women who graced Elvis, beach, biker and alienated youth movies.

I became familiar with most of the women profiled in this book by going to the drive-in with my family in the late sixties and early seventies, and by watching WABC-TV's 4:30 movie every afternoon. I would rush through my paper route to get home in time for "Elvis Week," "Beach Party Week," "Biker Movie Week," etc. As a teenager during the seventies, I was enthralled by the music, the attitude, the clothes and especially the actresses of the sixties. I became a fan of most of them and followed their careers into the seventies and eighties. Often I would wonder, "Whatever became of...?" When nobody answered my question, I decided to find out the answers myself. Hence this book.

Biographical information and acting credits were accumulated through research on the Internet, at the Academy of Motion Pictures Arts and Sciences' Margaret Herrick Library, the Museum of Television and Radio and especially the Billy Rose Theatre Collection at the New

York Public Library for the Performing Arts. I've tried to be as inclusive as possible regarding film and TV credits. The reader should note, however, that it is extremely difficult to document variety, talk and game show appearances.

The actresses are listed in a somewhat chronological order based on when they started acting professionally. The last chapter of this book contains summaries on actresses who declined to be interviewed or could not be located but deserved mention in this book nonetheless.

Tom Lisanti

Introduction

Elvis Presley musicals, beach movies, biker flicks and alienated youth films were just some of the genres aimed at young audiences during the swinging sixties. And though science fiction, fantasy and horror films weren't exclusive to the decade, where else could you see talking marauding gorillas, giant rampaging teenagers, suave secret agents and bikini-clad robots?

The talented actresses interviewed for this book could be found in these films twisting on the shores of Malibu, careening down the highway on a chopper, being serenaded by Elvis or taking on the establishment as hip college coeds. As cult fantasy figures, they contributed greatly to that period of filmmaking aimed at the teenage audience who frequented the drive-ins of America. They frolicked, screamed, watusied and protested their way into sixties movie history in such "groovy" films as *Teenage Millionaire, For Those Who Think Young, Get Yourself a College Girl, Psychomania, The Girls on the Beach, Dr. Goldfoot and the Bikini Machine, Tickle Me, Village of the Giants, The Ghost and Mr. Chicken, Out of Sight, The Haunted House of Horror, The Trip, The Mini-Skirt Mob, Three in the Attic, Wild in the Streets,* and *Paradise, Hawaiian Style.*

But these actresses weren't limited to teenage genre films. They appeared in some of the sixties' best and most popular films, as well: *Exodus, The Alamo, Cape Fear, The Nutty Professor, Cool Hand Luke, Tony Rome, In Like Flint, Planet of the Apes, Bob & Carol & Ted & Alice* and *Cotton Comes to Harlem,* among others. Their male co-stars ranged from Elvis Presley, Frankie Avalon and Fabian to Peter Fonda, Dennis Hopper and Bruce Dern to Jerry Lewis, Don Knotts and Vincent Price. They also worked with some of Hollywood's biggest stars (John Wayne, Steve McQueen, Paul Newman, Charlton Heston, Frank Sinatra, Sean Connery) and an eclectic array of directors (John Ford, Roger Corman, Otto Preminger, Irwin Allen, William Asher, Billy Wilder).

Though filming on the beach, getting close to Elvis, and riding a chopper sounds exciting, being a working young actress during the sixties was not all fun and games. Actresses working during that time saw the demise of the studio system, the relaxing of censorship with the beginnings of screen nudity, and the rise of the male buddy pictures. All of these had an adverse affect on the women profiled in this book. They were the first generation of actors to have no choice but to go freelance without a studio's support. They were the first to have to make the decision to do screen nudity or not. And they were the first to encounter a time in Hollywood where roles for women were diminishing at an alarming rate.

Some actresses also felt frustrated because they perceived that these genre roles were the *only* things they could get on the big screen. Shelley Fabares remarks, "During the mid-sixties, Elvis and beach movies were the kind of films that were available to actresses of my age. Our whole society changed with the advent of the Beatles, the drug culture, campus unrest, what have you. Around 1967, films and particularly television shows began to focus on alienated youth, runaways, drug addicts, etc. But I was not seen as someone like that and wasn't considered for those types of roles." Julie Parrish concurs: "Hollywood was still doing beach and Elvis films during the mid-sixties. I didn't know how to go about trying to get better roles. Women were not supposed to think back then, so I went on whatever my agents sent me on. There weren't many good dramatic roles for people in my age bracket anyway at that time."

During the early to mid-sixties, the studio system was still in place. Being part of the contract system was good and bad for actors. The studios nurtured and protected their contract players. A number of them did not come from professional acting backgrounds but were discovered in beauty pageants and while modeling. The studios sent them to classes to learn their craft and provided work in films and on television.

Sometimes it was a truly positive experience. "Dick Zanuck allocated a great deal of money to the acting school at 20th Century–Fox," says Linda Harrison. "We had a voice coach, an acting coach and a dance instructor. We were completely taken care of from head to toe and inside and out. It was just like the old studio talent schools but probably even better." Judy Pace states, "You didn't turn down the opportunity to be under contract when you were African-American. Columbia Pictures signed me and it was wonderful working there. Though sometimes it was lonely being the only black person on the lot, other than the shoe-shine boy."

But other times, the studio experience was not so pleasurable. Pamela Tiffin remarks, "Sometimes the studio made you do films you didn't want to do. I tried not to do *The Pleasure Seekers* and was suspended by 20th Century–Fox. No studio could hire me until I gave in." Recalling her days at MGM, Joan Staley says, "Allegedly I was supposed to be MGM's answer to Marilyn Monroe, which was nice, but to *do* that, you had to work. I asked them to at least let me do an episode of *Dr. Kildare* but I never got one. They told me they were saving me for films. I said, 'Please don't save me—work me!' One of the political mistakes I think I made was that I didn't play the glamour game. In those days under the contract system, if you wanted to be a star you had to look like a star—Yvette Mimieux always did. I was stupid for not having realized that."

Being a contract player also meant dealing with the whims of the studio's publicity departments. Every actress had to do cheesecake and publicity shots. They were also required to go on tour to promote their films. And studio-arranged dates became a norm for single actresses.

Introduction

Linda Harrison, contract player at 20th Century–Fox (courtesy of Linda Harrison).

There was nothing the studios liked more than having their up-and-coming contract players photographed at parties and premieres or mentioned in the next day's newspaper columns by Hedda Hopper or Louella Parsons—especially if they were trying to protect the reputations of their actors.

Chris Noel remembers, "I went out with Richard Chamberlain on a date arranged by MGM when we were filming *Joy in the Morning*. Richard was invited to a party at Rock Hudson's and the studio didn't want him to go alone. I knew Rock was gay and there was a lot of talk about Richard. But I didn't have a problem with it."

Other actresses were not so accommodating. "While filming *State Fair*, the publicists wanted to link me romantically to director Jose Ferrer, who was separated from his wife," recalls Pamela Tiffin. "The publicists at 20th Century–Fox were so cynical and wanted to go in that direction. But I told them no. A number of times I heard them discuss Gene Kelly, Marilyn Monroe and others in derogatory ways. I felt I was in enemy territory and I could be next." However, for those who did play Hollywood's publicity game, fame was the reward. How else can you explain why Raquel Welch became a superstar and some of her more talented peers did not?

Actresses of the sixties always had to compromise when it came to their families. They felt they were caught between the moralistic fifties and liberated seventies when it came to being working mothers. The studios didn't help much either. They expected their contract players to be married to their profession, which came first above everything else—including a family. Gone were the days where Joan Crawford would pose with her "perfect" family for *Photoplay* with the studio's blessings. With the film studios fighting to get people away from their television screens and into the theaters, they invested a lot in their contract players and wanted them to appear to be available gods and goddesses to the audience. When an actress didn't fit the mold of being single and available, it caused problems.

For example, the producers of *The Oscar* spent a lot of money touting Jean Hale as their new discovery. But Jean's sex goddess image of the silver screen crashed head-on with her off-screen role as a new mother when she had to go on tour to promote the film. The studio wouldn't allow Hale's daughter to accompany her because they were adamant about promoting her as a glamorous siren. "They conceded only after I promised to hire a nanny and agreed not to have photos taken with her," says Jean, incredulously. "I sat in first-class while my child and my sister, acting as nanny, sat back in coach. When we disembarked from the plane, the photographers were snapping away at Stephen Boyd and me. Looking past them, I saw my daughter crying. I wanted to reach out to her desperately but I couldn't. It broke my heart."

Actresses with families had to choose between their children and their careers so much that a number of them (Hale, Joy Harmon, Joan O'Brien, Joan Staley, Linda Harrison and Judy Pace, among many others) abandoned acting to concentrate on their families. It just became too difficult for them to juggle both in an industry that didn't support them in any way. Joan O'Brien opines, "You couldn't be in both places at once and, as the expression goes, 'You can't serve two masters and serve them well.' This is basically the reason why I quit acting. I needed to devote my time to my children." However, some actresses did do both out of necessity. Joan Staley, Deanna Lund, Celeste Yarnall and Diane McBain had to keep working to support their children. But as Staley so aptly puts it, "No matter how you looked at it, there was always guilt associated with being a working mother."

If it was tough for white actresses to do both, it was even more difficult for black actresses. Judy Pace says, "As a

Publicity photo of Judy Pace.

colored actress, as a Negro actress, as a black actress, and as an African-American actress, if you are not able to give 999 percent of your energy to your career—since the roles are so limited and the chances are so sparse—you cannot participate. You are almost automatically taken out of the running. If a black actress passed on an audition, the next one could be a month or two down the road.

You had to be able to react immediately whenever the opportunity presented itself. I couldn't, so I stopped acting."

The studios' attitude towards television also changed during the sixties. Contract players were not allowed to do television in the early to mid-fifties. At that time, the studios combated the boob tube with big-budgeted color spectaculars filmed in CinemaScope or Panavision and featuring all-star casts to tempt the audience to leave their couches and return to the movie theaters. Box office grosses were at an all-time low.

Columbia Pictures was the first studio to recognize the money to be made in television and began producing television programs in 1952 via Screen Gems. In 1955, Warner Bros. entered the fray. Bill Orr, Warner Bros.' executive producer for TV, told the authors of *Warner Bros. Television*, "We got into television because—if you can't lick 'em, join 'em." Overnight they created new stars in James Garner, Clint Walker and Edd "Kookie" Byrnes, to name just a few. Instead of barring their contract players from doing television, they began to require it. Warners' roster of actors could be seen weekly on *Cheyenne, Sugarfoot, Bronco, Maverick, 77 Sunset Strip, Hawaiian Eye, The Roaring Twenties, SurfSide 6*, etc.

Since this was new territory, some studios acted cautiously. MGM (*Dr. Kildare, The Lieutenant*) and 20th Century–Fox (*Adventures in Paradise, Bus Stop, Peyton Place*) produced only a handful of shows between them in the early sixties. Universal didn't go full scale into TV production until MCA, which owned Revue Productions, bought Universal Studios and gave Revue a new name: Universal Television.

All the studios wondered whether the public would pay to see their favorite actor or actress on the big screen when they could see them for free at home. According to Warner Bros. contract player and *SurfSide 6* regular Diane McBain, "It was a big question mark back then if it was a good idea to do television. Some people crossed over to the big screen easily and others didn't. I'm not sure how it worked out for me to be honest because I did both with an equal amount of felicity. I didn't know if I should be doing *SurfSide 6* or not. But I had to do TV because of my contract. We all did. I wasn't like Jim Garner who fought with the studio. He took them all on."

By the mid-sixties, most TV shows were produced in vivid color and the small screen saw an influx of mod science fiction and fantasy programs—*Bewitched, I Dream of Jeannie, The Man from U.N.C.L.E., The Wild Wild West, Lost in Space, Batman, Star Trek, The Monkees, Land of the Giants*. "Television in those days was kind of peeking out from the shelf," comments Eileen O'Neill. "Up until that time, TV shows were more traditional. Then all of a sudden, shows like *Batman* were trying to be more bizarre and zany and different. I think that it was the sign of the times. The mid-sixties were mod, with hippies and flower children who were breaking away from tradition. It was an expression and a breakthrough. Good or bad, it had to happen."

The actresses profiled in this book were perfect for these types of shows. From playing the villain's "henchgirl" on *Batman* to being romanced by Captain Kirk on *Star Trek* to playing the damsel in distress on *The Man from U.N.C.L.E.*, these sixties gals always came through with poise and confidence.

The issue of nudity first reared its head during the sixties. Prior to this decade, the worst thing that most aspiring

Eileen O'Neill had the perfect look for the mid-sixties influx of mod fantasy television programs. Here she is on *Batman* with Walter Slezak as Clock King and Adam West as the Caped Crusader.

actresses had to worry about were doing cheesecake photos. Featuring the actresses in sexy outfits or bathing suits, these photographs were used in newspapers and magazines to promote the careers of many rising young stars. For actresses of the sixties, the required attire was the bikini and stiletto heels—every young Hollywood hopeful, at one point in her career, had to pose wearing this outfit.

Doing pin-ups became standard even if an actress felt she then wouldn't be taken seriously.

Pamela Tiffin remarks, "When doing cheesecake, you became the puppet for the photographer's fantasies. I did a movie called *The Lively Set* [1964], which

I hated, and the studio made me do publicity photos wearing a bathing suit and high heels. I thought this was ridiculous! But their still photographers were these clean-cut World War II veterans who had a certain vision of what they thought was sexy. You'd have to hold your head one way while posing the rest of your body another way. They took the conventions of female beauty and pandered it to man's lowest common denominator."

Lana Wood had similar experiences and says, "I loved acting but I wish that I had been allowed to just do the acting and go home. I wasn't good at doing the publicity and the cheesecake that came with it. I'd go out to do a talk show or make a public appearance and they'd say, 'Couldn't you wear something shorter and low cut?' I'd reply, 'That isn't who I am. I'm *Lana Wood* and I don't dress like that!'"

Deanna Lund begrudgingly played a bikini-clad robot in *Dr. Goldfoot and the Bikini Machine* (1965) and also posed for photos in a bikini. She comments, "Bikini roles were a vicious trap to get into. I turned down a role as one of the Flint girls in *In Like Flint* because of it. I not only turned down bikini roles but also roles that required nudity. This was starting to become an issue for actresses during the sixties and I wanted to stay clear of doing topless scenes."

Nudity became an issue in part due to *Playboy* magazine. During the fifties, Marilyn Monroe was the first *Playboy* Playmate; later sex symbols such as Jayne Mansfield, June Wilkinson and Anita Ekberg were photographed topless for the magazine. These ladies made a career of exuding sex so it didn't hurt their careers to be featured semi-nude in print.

As the decade progressed, a number of aspiring actresses posed as *Playboy* Playmates in hopes of getting some attention. Stella Stevens is probably the most famous of the Playmates. Other young starlets to disrobe for the magazine included Teri Hope, Joan Staley, Mara Corday, Yvette Vickers, Marilyn Hanold and Marianne Gaba. When asked if she felt posing for *Playboy* hurt her career, Joan Staley responds, "I don't know if I consider *Playboy* a mistake. In a naïve sort of way it was exciting. It gave me a name recognition factor. That helped. But the pictorial also got me a lot of unwanted offers of a personal nature. Obviously *Playboy* was quite well read, but I didn't realize *how* well read by people in the industry. It made it difficult sometimes when I'd go on an interview. There were some compliments that it was a nicely done layout but there were some people who attempted to take advantage of it."

During the sixties, Hugh Hefner was still getting Hollywood hopefuls to pose as Playmates. But soon a number of well-known European actresses (including Elke Sommer, Ursula Andress, and Catherine Deneuve) also began turning up semi-nude in the pages of *Playboy*. Then in 1965, former teenage actress Carol Lynley appeared in a layout titled "Carol Lynley Grows Up." Lynley was taken to task by the Hollywood press and particularly Louella Parsons. She called Lynley "young and foolish." Lynley remarks, "To this day, I can't believe the hoopla that surrounded that pictorial. My agent suggested it because it would be good for my career. I'm very liberal so I agreed. It was very tame—before they started to show pubic hair. I firmly believe there is no evil in nudity."

Lynley was followed by Sharon Tate, Sherry Jackson, Carroll Baker, Julie Newmar and Barbara McNair. With these "legitimate" actresses willing to take it off, it put a burden on others to follow suit, especially as censorship was beginning to relax. Diane McBain states, "There was a balancing act between the kinds of values we had in the fifties and the values we were now being forced to accept as actors in the sixties. And a lot of that had to do with nudity. Because that was something we never had to consider up until that point. I certainly considered it and even did something about it. I did a layout for *Playboy*. I went home that night and said, 'You know, Diane, someday you're going to have kids. They're going to see this stuff and you're not going to like that.' So I called up my manager and asked him to kill the layout."

Karen Jensen comments, "Looking back, I think actresses who did nude scenes or disrobed for *Playboy* received a lot of attention. It started and in some cases furthered a lot of careers. Maybe it did put some pressure on the rest of us but you have to make choices in life. I never wanted to do it because I never would have wanted my family to see me nude in a magazine or on film."

Every actress in this book had to deal with the nudity issue. Judy Pace has a very lengthy nude scene in *Cotton Comes to Harlem* (1970). "It wasn't a hard decision to do this," Judy says matter-of-factly. "I didn't think it was a big deal. Remember this was in late 1969. Film nudity had just become almost the norm by that time. The nude scene was story-dictated so that's why I did it." When Francine York was offered a role that required her to appear topless in a scene with George Peppard in *Cannon for Cordoba,* she accepted it: "I have beautiful breasts so I thought, 'What the hell!'"

But a number of actresses weren't as free-spirited and turned down roles that required them to appear nude. Eileen O'Neill says, "I passed on a role in the Joseph L. Mankiewicz film *There Was a Crooked Man...* starring Kirk Douglas and Henry Fonda because I did not advocate doing nude scenes on film. To me, nudity was for the man in your life and not for the world to see. This role was mine and if I had done it things probably would have gone in a different direction for me."

Sometimes an actress had to forgo her convictions to survive. Celeste Yarnall passed on small roles that required nudity in *Bob & Carol & Ted & Alice* and *Winning,* but she accepted the lead role as *The Velvet Vampire* even though there was a topless scene. She explains, "I had separated from my husband at that time. So when this role was offered to me, I decided to take it because I needed the money. At this point in my life, my mortgage payment depended on it so I really didn't have much choice. When you have a child to support, sometimes you have to make some compromises."

By 1967, the business of Hollywood began to shift. The independent filmmaker was on the rise while the studio system was collapsing. Beginning with Sidney Lumet and Robert Altman—and continuing with Francis Ford Coppola, Bob Rafelson, Peter Bogdanovich, Martin Scorsese, etc., these directors were anti-establishment in every way, from using less cumbersome movie equipment to casting. Occasionally these directors used actresses from the studio system but for the most part they cast new talent from the stages of New York and elsewhere. "We all received a backlash from the 'artsy' independent filmmakers," remarks Diane McBain. "For instance, Sidney Lumet wouldn't test any 'Hollywood' actresses when casting *The Group*. In their experimental filmmaking and acquiescing to the Hollywood standard, these filmmakers managed to break loose

Pamela Tiffin poses in bathing suit and high heels, the obligatory dress for sixties cheesecake shots.

from established mores that maybe needed to be broken loose from—like the image of beauty—but were devastating to me personally. Everybody in Hollywood was so gorgeous and beautifully dressed in movies. Even when they woke up out of a dead sleep, they were beautifully made-up. That was a bit silly. But at the same time, I was a part of this."

The studio contract system was also

crumbling by 1967. Actors had no choice but to go freelance and to rely totally on their agents to help get them work. Judy Pace comments, "I think once the studio system collapsed and we all had to go freelance, actors were on their best behavior. You had to be to get work. It was now tougher to get acting roles and you didn't want a bad reputation because no one would hire you. The days of the prima donna movie stars were over." Karen Jensen remarks, "It was nice being under contract because it was comfortable and safe. You had a steady paycheck and I really liked that. When I went freelance, life was shakier but more exciting. I never knew when the next job was coming."

That was especially true for actresses. Not only were the male buddy films taking over Hollywood due to the success of *Butch Cassidy and the Sundance Kid* (1969), but roles for women were decreasing at a disturbing rate. And, horror of horrors, the sixties generation of actresses were fast approaching their (gulp!) thirtieth birthdays. While the roles began to dry up for them—there was always someone younger and prettier right behind them—their male counterparts (John Saxon, Michael Callan, Troy Donahue) continued acting at a steady pace.

Eileen O'Neill remarks, "During the sixties, they always felt that a woman's career was over by the time she hit thirty. If you hadn't made it by then, you were dead because at that point if you were thinking about getting married and being a mother nobody wanted you. God bless people today like Meryl Streep, Sally Field and Goldie Hawn who got married, had children, produced their own movies and still had the audiences like them. These are the women who broke down those barriers. During the sixties, those barriers still existed. In that respect, the business has grown up and become a profession."

But Judy Pace points out that "the age factor for black actresses is not the same for Caucasian actresses. We don't age the same way—look at Lena Horne. We can play teenagers when we're thirty. I was in my mid-twenties and still playing high school students on *Peyton Place* and *The Mod Squad*. When I was heading into my forties, I was playing 20-year-olds."

Looking back at all the hurdles sixties actresses had to face, it is surprising that they went as far with their careers as they did. A number of them are still active in the acting profession today. But one still wonders why none of these lovely talented ladies became superstars. When commenting on why her co-star from *Valley of the Dragons* Danielle de Metz did not become a star, Joan Staley recited a verse from a plaque (given to her by director Hal Needham) that hangs in her office. It is from an uncredited writer and may help answer why the actresses in this book didn't make it to the top of the Hollywood heap. "Nothing in the world can take the place of persistence. Talent will not. Nothing is more common than unsuccessful men with talent. Genius will not. Unrewarded genius is almost a proverb. Education alone will not. The world is full of educated derelicts. Persistence and determination alone are omnipotent."

Elvis, Beach, Biker and Alienated Youth Films: A Brief Summary

When the sixties began, film companies were still targeting young people with holdover genres from the fifties—juvenile delinquent, rock 'n' roll and hot rod/biker films. The juvenile delinquent films began with the major studios, which released *The Wild One* (1953), *Blackboard Jungle* (1955) and *Rebel Without a Cause* (1955). Soon the small independent film companies, most notably American International Pictures (AIP), began out-producing the majors by releasing low-budget teen exploitation films (aimed directly at the youth market) to drive-ins across the country. *Crime in the Streets* (1956), *Reform School Girl* (1957), *Teenage Doll* (1957), *The Cool and the Crazy* (1958) and *High School Confidential!* (1958) were just some of the films released. Other films tried to ape the success of *The Wild One* by featuring motorcycles and hot rods—*Hot Rod Rumble* (1957), *Motorcycle Gang* (1957), *Dragstrip Riot* (1958) and *Hot Rod Gang* (1958). And with rock 'n' roll emerging as the teenagers' music of choice, the juvenile delinquent theme was combined with it for a string of rock 'n' roll films beginning with *Rock Around the Clock* (1956), *Shake, Rattle and Rock* (1956), and *Don't Knock the Rock* (1957).

The juvenile delinquent films began to peter out by 1960 but a few holdovers remained including *The Girl in Lover's Lane* (1960) with Brett Halsey and Joyce Meadows, *High School Caesar* (1960) with John Ashley and *The Choppers* (1961) with Arch Hall, Jr. A few years later, Lee Philips and Jean Hale starred in *Psychomania* (1963), about a killer stalking coeds on a college campus. Bert I. Gordon turned H.G. Wells' story *The Food of the Gods* into a teen exploitation film, *Village of the Giants* (1965), starring Beau Bridges, Joy Harmon and Tisha Sterling as teenagers who grow to giant proportions and terrorize the inhabitants of a small town. Rock 'n' roll films continued during the sixties with *Twist Around the Clock* (1961), *Teenage*

Millionaire (1961) and *Get Yourself a College Girl* (1964) in which the musical acts received top billing over the actors. When *A Hard Day's Night* starring the Beatles premiered in 1964, it changed the face of rock musicals. The Beach films also featured plenty of rock acts. The King of Rock 'n' Roll, Elvis Presley, became a film genre of his own, though his hip-swaying, hard-rocking musical style of the fifties was tuned down considerably during the sixties. The biker film re-emerged during the mid-sixties as motorcycle gangs such as the Hell's Angels began riding the country's highways. This new generation of motorcycle films contained rock music and drug use and were more psychedelic than their fifties counterparts. And though teenagers weren't portrayed as juvenile delinquents, in the alienated youth films of the late sixties, they were "good kids gone bad" as they took drugs, practiced free love, dodged the draft and fought the establishment.

THE ELVIS PRESLEY FILM

The Elvis Presley Film became a genre of its own with the lush musical *Blue Hawaii* (1961). Prior to this, Elvis starred in *Love Me Tender* (1956), his first movie. The film and the title song warbled by Elvis were phenomenal hits. He next appeared as a truck driver who becomes a singer in *Loving You* (1957), as an ex-con who becomes a rock star in *Jailhouse Rock* (1957) and as a juvenile who gets involved with a street gang and mobsters down New Orleans way in *King Creole* (1958). Critics agree that Elvis was at his best in these films and proved that he really *was* the King of Rock 'n' Roll. In 1958, Elvis was drafted and he didn't return to the big screen until late 1960 in Paramount's *G.I. Blues,* followed by *Flaming Star* (1960) and *Wild in the Country* (1961). But *Blue Hawaii* (produced by Hal B. Wallis for Paramount), with Elvis as a returning G.I. who becomes a guide for a tourist agency where his girlfriend (Joan Blackman) works, was the box office smash. The soundtrack sold over six million dollars worth of LPs. *Blue Hawaii* featured excellent location photography, pretty girls vying for the King's attention and lots of songs—things that were to become synonymous with the Elvis Presley film. Each of Elvis' subsequent films featured plenty of beautiful women (including Shelley Fabares, Laurel Goodwin, Diane McBain, Chris Noel, Joan O'Brien, Julie Parrish, Joan Staley, Irene Tsu, Celeste Yarnall and Francine York, among others) and lots of songs sung by the King amid luscious scenery. In most of his films (a majority produced by Wallis), Elvis gets the girl, loses her to his rival and then wins the girl again for the fade-out. Though the plots were threadbare, the films were fun. Among the King's better films were *Follow That Dream* (1962), *Girls! Girls! Girls!* (1962), *Fun in Acapulco* (1963), *It Happened at the World's Fair* (1963), *Roustabout* (1964), *Girl Happy* (1965) and *Spinout* (1966). Most critics feel his best sixties film was *Viva Las Vegas* (1964), which teamed Elvis with the red-hot Ann-Margret. The combination of the King and the girl with the red mane lit the screen on fire. Elvis played a racecar driver who loses all his money before he can enter the Las Vegas Grand Prix. He gets a job as a waiter in a hotel where Ann-Margret works as a swimming instructor and before long the duo are singin', dancin' and romancin'. Throw in Cesare Danova as Elvis' suave Italian rival who also falls for Ann-Margret and the complications begin.

With the box office receipts falling by 1966, producer Hal Wallis tried to regain the luster of *Blue Hawaii* by casting Elvis as a pilot starting up a charter helicopter service to fly tourists between islands in *Paradise, Hawaiian Style* (1966). And though the Hawaiian locations were stunning, the songs more than passable, and the girls (including Suzanna Leigh, Marianna Hill, Irene Tsu and Julie Parrish) gorgeous to look at, Elvis fans have been vehemently divided on this film. In *Elvis in Hollywood*, author Paul Lichter calls it "a really poor film featuring a very poor soundtrack." The mainstream media found it pleasant but no more. *Paradise* co-star Julie Parrish comments, "I don't think any of Elvis' later movies are all that good so I can't really judge *Paradise, Hawaiian Style*. But I have had fan mail saying it is their favorite Elvis film. I don't know if they are just saying that. I love *Jailhouse Rock* and *King Creole*. They were before he started his association with Hal Wallis. The Colonel [Colonel Tom Parker, Elvis' manager] and Wallis were just making money off of Elvis, who was much better than his material. He didn't deserve to have that done to him."

By the following year, the Elvis Presley film was becoming passé. Young people were tuning in, dropping out and doing acid. Musical acts like the Jefferson Airplane, Grateful Dead, the Doors, Janis Joplin and many others were dominating the airwaves. Elvis Presley was not considered as cool as he once was. And films like *Clambake* (1967) with Shelley Fabares and *Speedway* (1968) with Nancy Sinatra didn't help. In *Live a Little, Love a Little* (1968), Elvis played a magazine photographer who has a psychedelic pill-induced dream and almost gets to bed a fashion model (Celeste Yarnall). This was the hippest Elvis was allowed to be on camera and the last of the standard Elvis Presley films, though he appeared in three more movies (*Charro!*, *Change of Habit* and *The Trouble with Girls*) before calling it quits in 1969.

THE BEACH FILM

The Beach genre began in 1959 with Columbia Pictures' release of *Gidget*, based on Frederick Kohner's novel about his daughter and her adventures hanging out with the local surfers. The film stars Sandra Dee as Gidget, Cliff Robertson as the Big Kahuna and James Darren as Moondoggie. With its excellent surfing footage and surfer lingo, the film became a huge hit with young audiences and the cult of surfing (first relegated to Southern California) slowly began to spread nationwide. In late 1960, MGM released *Where the Boys Are*, about four Chicago coeds (Dolores Hart, Yvette Mimieux, Paula Prentiss and Connie Francis) who, along with thousands of other college students, descend on Fort Lauderdale, Florida, for spring break. But the beach genre really took off in 1963. Producers Samuel Z. Arkoff and James H. Nicholson of American International Pictures were about to launch a new cycle of teenage delinquent films reminiscent of the JD movies of the mid-fifties. However, per director William Asher's suggestion, they decided to gamble on a new formula aimed at the teenage market. Instead of portraying teens as dope smoking, jive-talking, motorcycle-riding juvenile delinquents, they presented them as clean-cut, Coca-Cola–drinking, beach-loving, surfboard-riding, wholesome kids. They also capitalized on the surf sound that was beginning to hit the airwaves. Songs by the Beach Boys, Jan and Dean, the Surfaris, the Pyramids and Dick Dale

Publicity shot from *Paradise, Hawaiian Style* (Paramount, 1966) with Elvis Presley surrounded by (*clockwise from upper left*) Julie Parrish, Suzanna Leigh, Marianna Hill, Donna Butterworth, Linda Wong and Irene Tsu (courtesy of Julie Parrish).

& His Del-Tones were extolling the joys of Southern California living (and surfing, in particular). This greatly helped AIP's first Beach film 1963's *Beach Party*, starring singing sensation Frankie Avalon with Mouseketeer cast-off Annette Funicello, become a box office smash. The combination of the chemistry between Frankie and Annette, the Malibu shoreline, the surfing footage, a zany supporting cast (Harvey Lembeck, John Ashley, Jody McCrea and Candy Johnson) and authentic surf rhythms provided by Dick Dale & His Del-Tones made the film a must-see for the Clearasil set. The adult guest stars, including Bob Cummings, Dorothy Malone and Morey Amsterdam, made it appealing to older audiences as well. Arkoff and Nicholson then released in quick succession *Muscle Beach Party* (1964), *Bikini Beach* (1964), *Beach Blanket Bingo* (1965) and *How to Stuff a Wild Bikini* (1965), all starring Frankie and Annette, who became synonymous with the beach.

AIP began raking in millions due to the success of *Beach Party* and its sequels and the major studios quickly took notice. They began releasing their own beach films pairing different young and upcoming stars. From United Artists came *For Those Who Think Young* (1964) with James Darren and Pamela Tiffin. Columbia released *Winter a-Go-*

Go (1965), a variation on the formula as the film's young people (James Stacy, Beverly Adams, Julie Parrish, etc.) traded in their surfboards for skis. And Paramount produced *Beach Ball* (1965), the most blatant rip-off of *Beach Party*, starring Edd "Kookie" Byrnes and Chris Noel. Other films include *Surf Party* (1964), *The Girls on the Beach* (1965), *A Swingin' Summer* (1965), *One Way Wahine* (1965), *Wild Wild Winter* (1966) and *It's a Bikini World* (1967). Besides the beach milieu, the other thing that these films had in common were a great line-up of sixties rock stars. Among the performers featured were the Beach Boys, the Supremes, the Four Seasons, James Brown, Little Stevie Wonder, Gary Lewis & the Playboys, Lesley Gore, the Turtles, the Righteous Brothers—the list goes on and on.

Beach film aficionados consider *Ride the Wild Surf* (1964) as arguably the best of the genre. Three surfers (Fabian, Tab Hunter and Peter Brown) travel to Hawaii for the yearly surfing event at Waimea Bay. While waiting for the big waves to roll in, the boys get involved with, respectively, a blonde Shelley Fabares (as a vacationing coed), Susan Hart (as a local beauty with an overprotective mother) and Barbara Eden (as an auburn-haired tomboy). *Ride the Wild Surf* features spectacular on-location photography, an excellent cast, the hit title song performed by Jan and Dean, and awesome surfing footage. Remembers Shelley Fabares, "Art and Jo Napoleon produced *Ride the Wild Surf*. They went to Hawaii with cinematographer Joseph Biroc, who shot the incredible surfing scenes. It really was wonderful! Then Art and Jo wrote the script around it. It was like, 'The guy in the green trunks rides the wave all the way in. He'll be the hero.' [*Laughs*] They actually matched the costumes to the footage that they had."

The beach films also had their offshoots. Hot-rod films were sort of companion pieces to the beach movies with dragsters replacing surfboards as the focal passion. Appearing on screens throughout the drive-ins of America were *The Lively Set* (1964) with James Darren, Pamela Tiffin, and Doug McClure; *Fireball 500* (1966) with Frankie, Annette, and Julie Parrish; and *Thunder Alley* (1967) with Fabian, Annette, and Diane McBain. Some producers combined the beach formula with the horror and sci-fi genres: *The Horror of Party Beach* (1964), *Pajama Party* (1964) with Tommy Kirk as a Martian who crashes a beach party and *The Beach Girls and the Monster* (1965). Due to the popularity of the James Bond movies, the spy craze hit its peak during the mid-sixties, and to attract a young audience it was combined with the beach genre. *Dr. Goldfoot and the Bikini Machine* (1965) starred Vincent Price as a mad scientist who plots to take over the world with his beautiful bikini-clad robots (including Susan Hart, Deanna Lund and Salli Sachse). And in *Out of Sight* (1966), Jonathan Daly poses as a secret agent who helps beach bunny Karen Jensen prevent Big D (John Lawrence) from sabotaging the upcoming rock music festival.

THE BIKER FILM

By 1966, the beach films had become passé for various reasons. The Sunset Strip in Hollywood was populated by hippies and motorcycle gangs. The counterculture was in full swing. Young people were turning on, tuning in and dropping out. They fought the establishment in every way—from protesting the U.S.

Chris Noel and Edd "Kookie" Byrnes having a *Beach Ball* (Paramount, 1965).

presence in Vietnam to taking hallucinogenics to practicing free love. Of course Hollywood took notice, and soon bikers, hippies, radicals and flower children began dominating the big screen, especially in films by exploitation and independent film companies. Young people weren't buying the beach films because there was nothing meaningful in them. The innocence of the early sixties was being replaced by the cynicism of the late sixties. AIP sensed this change first and began catering to young people with biker and alienated youth films. The sixties biker genre began when Roger Corman's *The Wild Angels* roared onto the big screen in 1966 with Peter Fonda and Nancy Sinatra. It is a graphic and violent look at the Hell's Angels motorcycle gang. The mainstream media blasted the film for its violence and its glorification of hoodlums. However, it became a cult artistic triumph, receiving praise from some film critics for its *cinéma vérité* realism. Grossing over $6 million at the box office, *The Wild Angels* spawned a flock of imitation biker films featuring hard rockin' soundtracks, on-location color photography and enough violence and sex to appeal to the under 25 male audience for whom these films were intended. The outlaw bikers portrayed in these films represented freedom and nonconformity—traits respected by disenchanted young people raised on *The Adventures of Ozzie and Harriet* and *Father Knows Best*. Among the better-known films were *Devil's Angels* (1967), *Hell's Angels on Wheels* (1967), *The Born Losers* (1967), *The Glory Stompers* (1967), *Hell's Chosen Few* (1968), *The Mini-Skirt Mob* (1968), *Hell's Belles* (1969), *The Cycle Savages* (1969) and *C.C. and Company* (1970). The latter starred Joe Namath as a renegade member of the Heads who saves singer Ann-Margret from the clutches of biker leader William Smith. Many of the biker films starred actors on the way up (Jack Nicholson, Tyne Daly, Bruce Dern, Don Stroud, etc.) or former teen stars of beach and Elvis movies (Diane McBain, Jeremy Slate, Chris Noel, Jody McCrea, Salli Sachse, etc.). "Doing a biker film was very different than doing a beach movie," remarks Sachse. "All that familiarity and innocence of the beach movies was gone. This was also new territory for me—riding a motorcycle and playing a bad girl. I had more fun playing a beach girl because I felt more comfortable on the sand and around the water."

Most biker films featured the motorcycle gangs as the villains but a few focused on hero cyclists. *The Savage Seven* (1968) starred Adam Roarke as a gang member who falls in love with an Indian waitress (Joanna Frank) despite the protestations of her brother (Robert Walker, Jr.). They join forces when the town's crooked businessmen plot against both of them. Directed by Richard Rush and featuring songs by Cream and Iron Butterfly, *The Savage Seven* is considered one of the best of its genre. In *Angels Die Hard!* (1970) starring Tom Baker and William Smith, it's redneck townspeople versus a biker gang who are trying to peacefully honor the memory of a fellow biker killed after being released from the local jail. And *Angel Unchained* (1970) starred Don Stroud as a biker who leaves his gang to join a hippie commune that is being harassed by local rednecks. By the early seventies, the returning Vietnam veteran (either as hero or villain) began becoming the central character of some biker films—*Satan's Sadists* (1969), *Chrome and Hot Leather* (1971) and *The Hard Ride* (1971). Since biker films were made cheaply they usually turned a profit. The cycle lasted into the mid-seventies.

THE ALIENATED YOUTH FILM

A counterpoint to the biker film was the alienated youth film. For the most part, these movies focused on teenagers, college students and hippies who rebel against authority. By far the best of these films was the classic *Easy Rider* released by Columbia in 1969. It combined bikers,

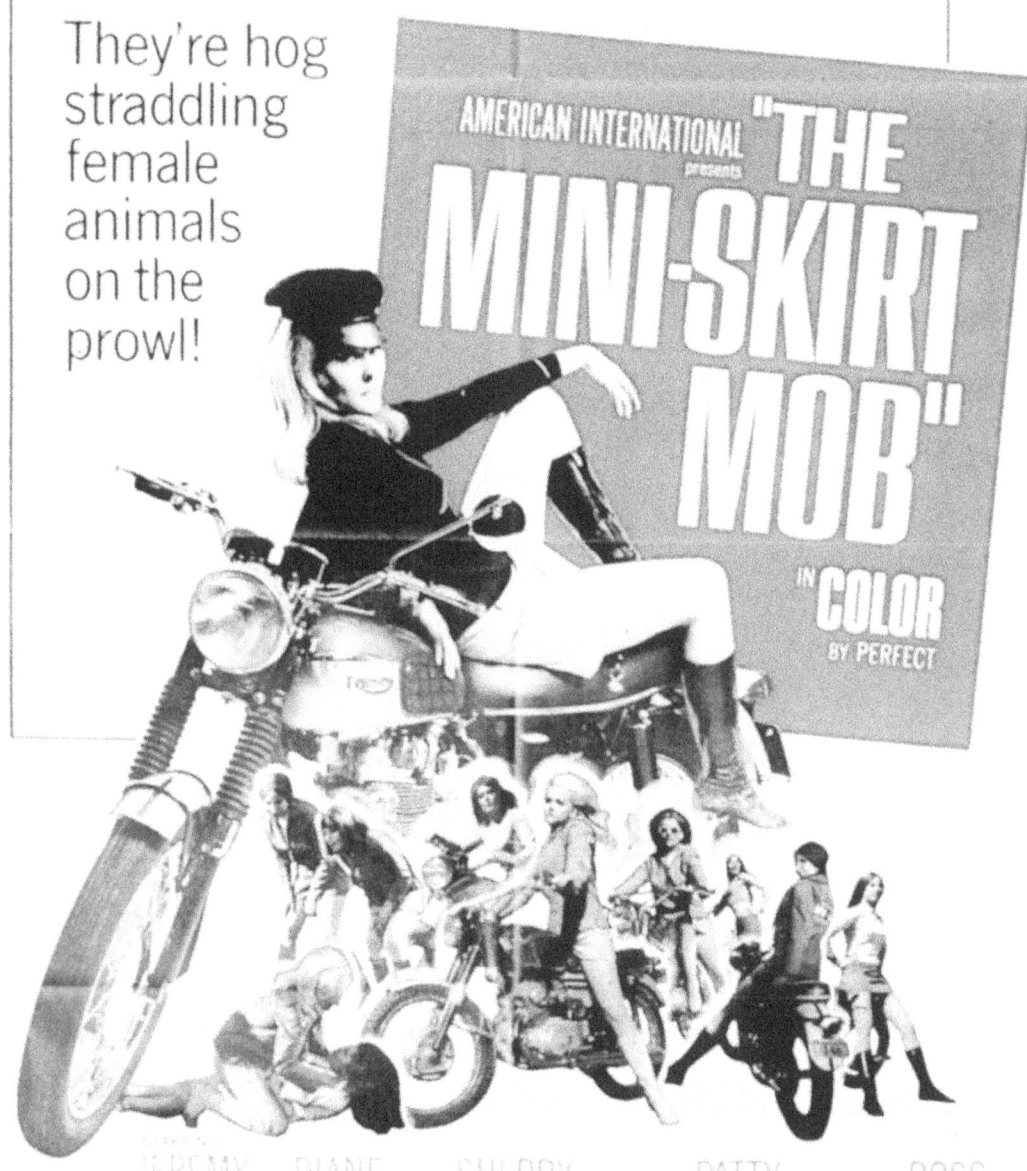

Three in the Attic (AIP, 1968) featured Maggie Thrett, Yvette Mimieux and Judy Pace as college coeds who discover they are making it with the same guy.

hippies, and rock 'n' roll to great effect. Peter Fonda and Dennis Hopper played hippie cyclists who travel the back roads of the U.S. looking for the "real America." During the course of their journey they smoke marijuana, visit a commune, get arrested, hook up with an alcoholic lawyer (Jack Nicholson) and, when heading for Florida, are shot and killed by some local rednecks. Watching the film more recently, Leonard Maltin found it "dated but quite worthwhile, highlighted by fine Laszlo Kovacs photography, a great rock soundtrack, and Nicholson's star making performance."

Most of the other alienated youth films were maligned by young people who really were trying to change government policy for the good of the country. They felt these films exploited them and their attentions and that there was too much emphasis on free love and drug-taking. As students in the U.S. were trying to get the voting age lowered from 21 to 18, AIP released *Wild in the Streets* (1968) starring Christopher Jones as a rock star elected president when the voting age is lowered to 14. He then imprisons everyone over the age of 35 in detention camps.

As with beach and biker films, the alienated youth film had their "ministars," including Jones, Mimsy Farmer, Patty McCormack, Tisha Sterling, Kevin

Opposite: Poster art for *The Mini-Skirt Mob* (AIP, 1968).

Coughlin, Judy Pace and Michael Margotta. *Psych-Out* (1967) starred Susan Strasberg as a deaf girl who journeys to Haight-Ashbury in search of her missing brother (Bruce Dern) and who is aided by hippies Dean Stockwell and Jack Nicholson. It contains a great soundtrack with songs performed by the Strawberry Alarm Clock and the Seeds, among others. *The Trip* (1967), featuring Peter Fonda as a TV director who takes LSD for the first time, was a colorful and psychedelic experience just as the ads proclaimed. Other films in this genre include *Riot on Sunset Strip* (1967), *The Love-Ins* (1967), *Maryjane* (1968), *The Young Runaways* (1968), *Born Wild* (1968), *Three in the Attic* (1968) and *Free Grass* (1969). By the late sixties, alienated youth movies began addressing the Vietnam issue and campus protests in *Alice's Restaurant* (1969), *Getting Straight* (1970), *The Strawberry Statement* (1970), *Up in the Cellar* (1970) and *Drive, He Said* (1971), among others. The returning Vietnam veteran was looked at sympathetically in *The Ballad of Andy Crocker* (1969) with Lee Majors and Jill Haworth and *Norwood* (1970) with Glen Campbell. But, unfortunately, the "psycho Vietnam vet" films such as *The Ravager* (1970) and *Welcome Home, Soldier Boys!* (1972) became the norm until later in the decade.

Joan O'Brien

Lovely blonde actress Joan O'Brien was a former teenage singer on TV's *The Bob Crosby Show* before making her film debut in *Handle with Care* (1958). Her second film, *Operation Petticoat* (1959) with Cary Grant, made her a star. Joan was a sensation as nurse Dolores, whose bounteous proportions made life difficult for the men of the submarine *Sea Tiger* trying to pass her in the submarine's close quarters. She immediately became a well-respected and sought after actress co-starring opposite such stalwart stars as John Wayne, Audie Murphy, George Montgomery and Jerry Lewis. But to genre fans she is most remembered for her popular drive-in films where she could be counted on to look fabulous and give a pleasant performance. In *It Happened at the World's Fair* (1963) she plays a prim nurse romantically pursued by pilot Elvis Presley amid the excitement of the Seattle World's Fair. The following year's *Get Yourself a College Girl* ("a harmless piece of fluff," quips Joan) features O'Brien as a dance instructor at an all-girls school who teaches her students how to groove. A Sam Katzman quickie, the film is memorable for its impressive lineup of rock acts including the British invaders the Dave Clark Five and the Animals, plus Astrud Gilberto and the Standells—all of whom received billing over the film's actors. "I think I would rather be remembered for other parts I played which I thought were a lot meatier and more flattering," states Joan. "But if these films make people happy, they can remember me any way they want to."

Joan O'Brien was born on February 14 in Cambridge, Massachusetts. When she was a young girl, her parents David and Rita O'Brien relocated the family to Southern California. At eight years old she began taking dancing classes; her singing ability was discovered while doing recitals and community shows. "The first time they heard me open my mouth to sing, they wouldn't let me dance any more," recalls Joan. While attending Chaffey Union High School in Ontario, California, she was discovered by Cliffie Stone and began appearing on his local TV program *Hometown Jamboree* with Tennessee Ernie Ford, Tommy Sands and Molly Bee. This led to a successful four-year run (beginning in 1954)

Joan O'Brien (*center*) teaches her students, including Nancy Sinatra (*far left*) and Mary Ann Mobley (*third from left*), the art of the Watusi in *Get Yourself a College Girl* (MGM, 1964).

on *The Bob Crosby Show*. Joan became a huge national television star and received more fan mail than Bob himself.

When *The Bob Crosby Show* was cancelled in 1958 due to slipping ratings, Joan was urged by her MCA agents to give acting a try. They presented her to all the major studios as a beauty who could not only sing and dance but act as well. Her talent so impressed the powers-that-be at MGM that they signed her to a multiple picture deal. "This was the ideal arrangement to have," says Joan. "It meant that MGM had to use me in three films within a certain period of time. But I also had loanout rights to work at any other major Hollywood studio if I so chose to." First up for Joan was the black-and-white programmer *Handle with Care* co-starring Dean Jones. As law students, Jones and O'Brien took the mayor of their small town to court after revealing that he had been skimming tax money. "It was a wonderful experience for me doing my first film with Dean Jones. He was a very sweet young man devoted to his family. I didn't have to worry about his ego or any of those things—he was just terrific."

Joan next braved a horrible cold and a temperature of 103 degrees to audition for the role of Lt. Dolores Crandall in *Operation Petticoat*. "I was sicker than a dog when I did my test," remembers Joan, chuckling. "If it had been for any film but *Operation Petticoat* I wouldn't

Publicity shot of the shapely O'Brien in *Operation Petticoat* (1959).

have been there. When I read the screenplay by Stanley Shapiro and Maurice Richlin, I laughed myself silly. Usually when I read a script, it doesn't read that funny to me. And I thought, 'If this is funny on paper, it has to be hilarious on film.' I also really wanted this because I wanted to play opposite Cary Grant."

Joan beat out 12 other notable actresses for the part and was told that "Cary had seen my screen test and had personally selected me. I was greatly complimented by that."

Set during WWII, *Operation Petticoat* starred Grant as commander of the submarine *Sea Tiger* and Tony Curtis as his conniving, wheeler-dealer second-in-command. When a Philippine island is threatened by a Japanese attack, Curtis sneaks several islanders onto the sub along with five beautiful nurses including O'Brien, Dina Merrill and Madlyn Rhue. One of the film's running gags was the fact that the men had trouble passing the well-developed, accident-prone Joan in the sub's tight passageways, resulting in Grant's character issuing the order that "when Lt. Crandall walks through any part of this boat, see that she gets free passage." Joan is hilarious as Dolores—underplaying to perfection. Lt. Crandall was a character that, if played by a Jayne Mansfield or a Mamie Van Doren, would have become a caricature. Instead, O'Brien portrays her naively, making the character truly believable. *New York Magazine* described Joan as "luscious" while *Variety* commented, "O'Brien offers solid support." When told Tina Louise turned the role down due to the "boob jokes," O'Brien says incredulously, "I can't even imagine a young actress at the stage of her career or mine at that particular time refusing a role opposite Cary Grant. First of all, I've never seen a bad Cary Grant film. The man had impeccable taste. Second, I was not concerned with the humor or the so-called boob jokes in the film because it was all tastefully done. There was nothing vulgar about it and in fact the writers went on to receive an Academy Award nomination for their screenplay."

Skillfully directed by Blake Edwards (whom Joan describes as being "a pixie—very quiet and gentle with sparkling eyes and a little smile—but always carrying a big stick"), *Operation Petticoat* went on to become one of the biggest hits of 1959 due to the expert playing of Cary Grant. When asked if Grant helped the novice actress with her performance, Joan replies laughing. "Help me? He tried to upstage me all the time. I didn't realize it until Madlyn Rhue called me over to the side one day and said, 'Do you know what's happening here?' I replied, 'No, what's happening?' She said, 'Every time you do a scene with Cary he's upstaging you and we're looking at the back of your head.' Cary had a way of doing that but I don't know if it was deliberate on his part. I think he always knew where he was while in front of the camera. Once I caught onto that, I felt I was on a more equal footing with him. I'd get in there—and it was kind of fun—forcing him to meet me halfway. I'd then turn sideways so the camera would pick up more of me. Cary and I quickly became chums and I think we had good screen chemistry together. During the film's long set-ups, we would sit and talk. I learned a lot about him in terms of his values and what he thought about life in general. He was a very warm, down-to-earth, straightforward guy. With his legendary screen image, I thought he might be difficult or hard to work with. But he wasn't."

During the film's arduous two-month shoot on location in Key West, Joan and the cast would escape the pressures of filming by jumping into a boat and heading to a tiny island with no trees. "We'd go out there and spend the day swimming, snorkeling and picnicking," Joan remembers fondly. "We all just kicked back, relaxed and had a great time. We'd burn to a crisp and come back like red lobsters." Regarding her other co-stars, Joan says, "I learned and saw a side of Dina Merrill that probably very few people knew. She is a warm, lovely girl, beautifully mannered and well-bred but not stuffy at all. Madlyn Rhue and I became extremely close friends and I was a bridesmaid at her wedding. Tony Curtis is a really cute guy and has big, beautiful blue eyes. He was a riot—jumping all around and doing pranks. I remember he got his first Rolls-Royce while we were making *Operation Petticoat* and he was like an excited little kid with a new toy."

O'Brien's agents next wrangled her an interview for a role in John Wayne's epic film *The Alamo* (1960). The small part of Sue Dickinson interested Joan because "I thought it would be a nice thing to play a historic character and this role had the big dramatic ending as she and two children are the sole survivors of the massacre. I could envision that whoever portrayed Sue would get a big play on the screen." Meeting Wayne, whose image was bigger than life itself, terrified Joan, who was summoned to his office alone without her agents. "John Wayne was a huge guy—a giant," comments Joan. "But he made me feel very much at home. I remember he put his feet up on his desk and looked down at me from his big leather chair. He just talked to me like a regular person. I thought, 'Gee, he's not hard to take.' Then he told me that Loretta Young had offered to do the part for free. Right away he had me because I thought, 'If Loretta Young offered to do it for nothing, I should be so happy to do this and get paid.' He was very flattering and said to me, 'You remind me of a younger Lana Turner.' He thought I was right for the part and I knew I had nothing to lose by taking it."

The Alamo was Wayne's personal undertaking and obsession. His plans for this film began in 1946 while he was under contract to Republic Studios. But it wasn't until he broke free from Republic in 1951 and formed his own production company (Batjac) that pre-production began. Wayne directed the film himself and agreed to star as Col. Davy Crockett per his terms with United Artists, who backed the film along with private investors. Others in the cast included Richard Widmark as James Bowie, Laurence Harvey as Col. William Travis, Richard Boone as Gen. Sam Houston and, in an effort to draw the teenage audience, Frankie Avalon as Smitty. *The Alamo* finally began shooting on September 9, 1959, in Brackettville, Texas. Describing the location, Joan says, "This dusty little town had one gas pump, one little café where they only spoke Spanish, and one movie house that only showed Spanish films. There was nothing to do in that town and I went stir crazy. This shoot was long, laborious and exhausting." The film was shot in 91 days at a cost of $12 million. Though it received an Academy Award nomination for Best Picture, it received mixed reviews. While critics praised the camerawork and Wayne's direction of the rousing battle scenes, they felt the film's more intimate moments were sluggish and not historically accurate (which they weren't). But Wayne never intended to make a truly factual movie. As Frank Thompson wrote in an *American Cinematographer* article defending Wayne's film, "*The Alamo* was made to celebrate heroism, not history."

Despite her discomfort with the location, Joan has pleasant memories of working with the cast of *The Alamo*. "Laurence Harvey was a complete crack-up," states Joan. "He had a sense of humor that was really fun. He was the only one in the cast who could get away with calling the Duke Dukie. Wayne would tell him what to do and Laurence Harvey would always say, 'Okay, Dukie.' Also, every afternoon about three o'clock you'd see Larry—that's what we called him—walking around with a paper cup in his hand. He'd have this French wine flown in by the case while we were on location. And he got me hooked on it! It was really good. Richard Widmark, on the other hand, was a very intense, serious guy. He would come over to me occasionally and give me suggestions on how to play the scene. I don't think that he felt that John Wayne was all that great of a director."

As for her opinion of John Wayne, O'Brien muses, "He was just getting his feet wet as a director with *The Alamo*. He knew how to stage scenes and what to do with the camera, the lighting, and positioning his actors. But he wasn't very good getting an emotional draw from an actor. Which is unusual because when an actor directs, they usually handle other actors extremely well. I didn't feel any frustration with him because I felt that my character was truly defined. He also seemed at times somewhat abrupt and impatient with some individuals. I think one of the reasons for that was *The Alamo* was a project of *enormous* magnitude. He not only starred in it but also produced and directed it. He had a lot riding on this film. And when you also have money invested in it, sometimes it is very difficult to be charming. However, Wayne was never rude with me."

Joan made such an impression in *The Alamo* that she was cast in another Wayne western, *The Comancheros* (1961). However, it wasn't the studio or Wayne who requested her but Wayne's daughter. "Aissa Wayne played my child in *The Alamo*," recalls Joan. "She asked for me to play her mom again. My agents called me and asked if I would be interested in doing this role which was a bit more than a cameo. I said, 'Sure, I'll do it.' I liked Aissa and thought it would be good to be in another John Wayne movie. I was also excited to get the chance to work with director Michael Curtiz because he had such a reputation for being a fine director, which he was. He was also a very volatile, explosive, energetic kind of a man. I thought he would scare me to death but he didn't. He was all business and knew what he was doing. One day when we were shooting outside, he said, 'Oh, Miss O'Brien, you are such a natural actress!' I thought that was really nice and quite a compliment from someone of his stature."

Nineteen sixty two was Joan's busiest movie year as she had four films in release. *Variety* found O'Brien "appealing" as a widow seeking revenge on the hired gun who killed her husband in the Audie Murphy oater *Six Black Horses* and "pleasant" as Kenneth More's romantic interest in the British comedy *We Are in the Navy Now*. Joan next journeyed to the Philippines for the George Montgomery–directed adventure film *Samar*, based on a true story about Spanish political prisoners who were exiled to the Filipino penal colony in the 1870s. She played the wife of Gilbert Roland, who ran the colony more as a community than a prison. When Spanish officials demand that he explain his actions, he joins prisoner George Montgomery in torching the prison and escaping on a trek through the treacherous jungles. "I wasn't overly pleased with *Samar*," states Joan. "George wasn't much of a director. I had a little personal problem with him right up front, which I straightened out nicely and neatly right away. He came on to me the minute I arrived in Manila. And at that time he was still married to Dinah Shore. I said to him, 'Are you kidding me? You didn't bring me all this way to make a pass at me! I can be on the next plane back to the States tomorrow if you don't knock it off. And this will cost you a lot of money trying to get someone to replace me.' He backed off immediately. I also did not enjoy the location shooting at all. The places we were filming had no sanitation, no rest rooms, no running

The newly rich Jerry Lewis lives it up with bride O'Brien in the comedy *It's Only Money* (Paramount, 1962).

water, no anything. If I had to go to the bathroom, I had the choice of going into the ocean or climbing up to these village houses built on stilts where maybe one of them had a chamber pot. It was quite an experience!"

Returning to Hollywood, Joan tried her hand at physical comedy opposite the wild and woolly Jerry Lewis in one of his funniest films, *It's Only Money*. He plays a bungling would-be detective searching for Mae Questal's long-lost nephew and heir to her fortune. Questal's crooked lawyer (Zachary Scott) realizes Jerry is the missing relative and tries to dispose of him in a number of ways—most hysterically by mowing him down with a platoon of electrically operated lawnmowers. Joan is delightful as Questal's nurse, who also suspects that Jerry may be the nephew and tries to help him. Describing the experience of working with the comic genius, Joan says, "Jerry Lewis was *totally* off the wall and we had a lot of fun working on this film. He had me laughing so hard and so long during some scenes we had to stop and start over. We wasted a lot of time and money just cutting up and laughing. He was such a practical joker and had all of us including our director, Frank Tashlin, in stitches. You never knew what Jerry was going to do next. You could play the same scene with him ten times and it wouldn't come out the same way twice. But Jerry could be serious also. He was very generous and gave me a book that I still have called *You're Better Than You Think*. Inside he inscribed, 'And you really are, Joannie.' I was going through a period of time with a bad marriage and feeling down and depressed. I was unhappy about a lot of things. Jerry really set my head straight. He said, 'Do you want to see some people who really have problems? Then come with me to visit my kids with Muscular Dystrophy who are wired up. Yours are nothing in comparison.' He also gave me some insight on how to appreciate myself a lot more as an individual."

O'Brien finished out her contract with MGM by appearing in two films aimed at the youth market. First up was *It Happened at the World's Fair* (1963). Elvis Presley (whom Joan describes as being "very sweet, kind and gentle") stars as a grounded bush pilot who pursues her prim nurse at the Seattle World's Fair. Complications ensue when six-year-old Vicky Tiu is unexpectedly left in his care. Shot on location during the actual World's Fair, Joan describes the first day of filming as "a madhouse. When I arrived at the World's Fair, I saw Elvis, whom I had never met before, over the heads of all these people. You talk about crowds! It was unbelievable. People everywhere! After we finished the first morning's sequences, they had an electric car for Elvis and me to use. They had to set up barricades and use hundreds of policemen to hold back the crowds just to get us out of there. We then went for lunch to some building that had this huge empty exhibition hall. They dropped us off, locked the door and posted more policemen outside."

Joan got to know Elvis very well during the film's shoot. He told her all about his stint in the service and his experiences in Europe. And he was still at the point where he hadn't become disenchanted making movies though he did have some problems during the shoot, according to Joan. "I don't know if it carried over to other films that he did—but Elvis would get hung up on his dialogue like he had a speech impediment. It kept happening over and over. He began getting uptight and breaking out into a sweat. I started feeling really sorry for him because it was embarrassing. So finally Norman Taurog [the director] said, 'Let's just wrap it up for today. Go home and forget about it and we'll come back tomorrow and shoot this.' And that's what we did. It was the right thing to do."

Though Joan was a professional singer, to her chagrin, she did not get to sing with Elvis in *It Happened at the World's Fair*. Only a few of his co-stars (Juliet Prowse, Ann-Margret, Nancy Sinatra, etc.) would get the opportunity. "If I would have been using my noodle at the time, I would have had my agents push that for me and probably something would have come of it," says Joan matter-of-factly. "But at the same time it might have been too much of a departure from my character. I was playing an uptight nurse and it might have looked a little weird to break into song. And I also think Elvis' representatives might not have been happy about it because it would have taken away from him a little. They had a product to sell and the fans flocked to his films to see and hear Elvis." Though Elvis did serenade Joan throughout the film, she found these scenes to be "tedious and hard because he had all the action and I felt awkward. It was very difficult for me—I don't know about other actresses—to be aware of the camera, pay attention to him, and try to look all dreamy-eyed and in love. I felt like I had egg on my face most of the time."

O'Brien as a nurse and Elvis Presley as a pilot share a tender moment in *It Happened at the World's Fair* (MGM, 1963).

Critical reaction to *It Happened at the World's Fair* was mixed. *Variety* called it "a tedious romp through the Seattle Fair of 1962" though they did find Joan to be easy "on the eyes" while the *New York Herald Tribune* commented that the movie was an "inoffensive bit of escapist fluff." Joan opines, "I think this was a better vehicle for Elvis on some standpoints. The premise of Elvis caring for a cute little girl was unique and different. It showed a side of him that was the real thing—a very sweet gentleman. A child-like attitude even emerged from him which I enjoyed watching. I also like the fact the film was relatively uncluttered. It didn't have all these women falling out of the sky and dancing to bongo drums. From that standpoint I think *It Happened at the World's Fair* was a better-than-average Elvis film. But as far as Elvis' acting ability, *Love Me Tender* [1956] and *King Creole* [1958] were better showcases for him. I think Elvis had dramatic talent that if developed would have made him an extremely fine actor. But he really just wanted to play his guitar and face those live audiences."

Joan's last film appearance was in *Get Yourself a College Girl* (1964). O'Brien plays a dance instructor at a staid all-girls school. ("I went up to the Beverly Hills Dance Academy and worked out like a fiend trying to learn all the latest dances like the Watusi and the Monkey for this film. I trained so hard I must have lost close to ten pounds over a

weekend.") When one of the students (Mary Ann Mobley) is found to be a writer of hit rock songs, the headmistress wants to expel her. O'Brien gets her a reprieve and chaperones Mobley, Nancy Sinatra and Chris Noel on a Sun Valley ski vacation where arrogant song publisher Chad Everett woos Mobley. They also meet up with a senator who is seeking re-election by courting the youth vote. "I think I did *Get Yourself a College Girl* because I just needed a job," says Joan with a laugh. "It was not the caliber of film I had been in previously though I had fun making it. I was working with a nice bunch of girls—Mary Ann Mobley, Chris Noel and Nancy Sinatra. They were all just darling. I couldn't say I was fond of one more than the other—although Nancy and I had some very long discussions about life and marriage. And she talked about her dad a great deal. I really enjoyed working with her very much. Mary Ann was sweet as Southern pie. And Chris Noel was just a beautiful girl with blonde hair and big blue eyes. The producers wanted me to look older than the other girls who were playing students so I wore my hair up. I had the most horrible hairdo during this film. It looked like I had a bird's nest on it. I hated it!"

With four young aspiring actresses working together, it is only natural to expect the fur to fly: Hollywood in the early sixties was a starlet-eat-starlet world. However, it was the film's male co-star Chad Everett who surprisingly proved the diva. "My career up to that point exceeded anything that those girls did," Joan says. "They were all newcomers and had done next to nothing so there was no axe to grind. There was no competition. That probably accounts for the reason why we all got along so well. Chad Everett, on the other hand, was very reserved and rather cold. He was very handsome and he knew it. He just loved looking at himself in the mirror. Most young actors do. They are by far more narcissistic than women can ever be. Chad changed years later, after he grew up!"

Joan's extensive television appearances ranged from *The Lawrence Welk Show* to *The Untouchables* to *The Dick Van Dyke Show*. Her last acting gig was an episode of the long-forgotten sitcom *Valentine's Day* starring Tony Franciosa (whom Joan describes as being "handsome, graceful and just great to work with"). O'Brien, however, didn't give up show business completely. She toured with the Harry James Orchestra as their singer, playing universities and supper clubs all over the U.S. "The greatest audiences in the world are college students, military personnel and convicted criminals," opines Joan, laughing. "All I had to do is walk out on the stage in Chino State Prison and the men went wild." But Joan soon gave up singing to concentrate on raising her two children, Russell and Melissa Anne. She found that she could not be both an actress and a good mother because "there is no way that any woman can devote the time, the effort and the energy that it takes to work as an entertainer without neglecting her children. There's no way to juggle both. I know. I tried. It just can't be done. I really felt that the so-called 'failures' that I had in my personal life regarding my two marriages were a direct result of the instability and unpredictability of the lifestyle associated with show business." Joan then entered the business world and had a very successful management career working for the Hilton Hotel chain.

Opposite: Poster art for *Get Yourself a College Girl* (MGM, 1964).

Chris Noel, Mary Ann Mobley and Joan O'Brien in *Get Yourself a College Girl* (MGM, 1964).

Today, Joan O'Brien is happily remarried and resides in Northern California. "I had a charmed life as far as my work was concerned," says Joan. "I worked every medium that there is—theater, television and motion pictures. I even made recordings. There isn't anything I haven't done in the industry and I didn't have one bad experience. Mine were all good ones."

Film Appearances

1958   **Handle with Care** (MGM) d. David Friedkin.
1959   **Operation Petticoat** (Universal) d. Blake Edwards.
1960   **The Alamo** (United Artists) d. John Wayne.
1961   **The Comancheros** (20th Century–Fox) d. Michael Curtiz.
1962   **Six Black Horses** (Universal) d. Harry Keller.
       Samar (Warner Bros.) d. George Montgomery.
       It's Only Money (Paramount) d. Frank Tashlin.
       We Are in the Navy Now/We Joined the Navy (Great Britain; Dial) d. Wendy Toye.
1963   **It Happened at the World's Fair** (MGM) d. Norman Taurog.
1964   **Get Yourself a College Girl** (MGM) d. Sidney Miller.

Television Appearances

The Bob Crosby Show [series regular] 9/14/53 to 8/30/57 CBS.
Shower of Stars (with host Jack Benny) 1/10/57 CBS.

The Liberace Show [series regular] 10/13/58 to 12/31/58 ABC.
Bat Masterson "One Bullet from Broken Bow" 1/21/59 NBC.
M Squad "The Take Over" 2/27/59 NBC.
Markham "We Are All Suspect" 8/1/59 CBS.
Riverboat "The Fight Back" 10/18/59 NBC.
Bat Masterson "Shakedown at St. Joe" 10/29/59 NBC.
Perry Mason "The Case of the Singing Skirt" 3/12/60 CBS.
The Tennessee Ernie Ford Show 4/21/60 NBC.
The Alaskans "Kangaroo Court" 5/8/60 ABC.
Bronco "La Rubia" 5/17/60 ABC.
Wagon Train "The Luke Grant Story" 6/1/60 NBC.
The Chevy Mystery Show "Enough Rope" 7/31/60 NBC.
The Deputy "Meet Sergeant Tasker" 10/1/60 NBC.
The Islanders "The Terrified Blonde" 10/16/60 ABC.
Bat Masterson "High Card Loses" 11/10/60 NBC.
The Westerner "The Courting of Libby" 11/11/60 NBC.
Spirit of the Alamo (special) 11/14/60 ABC.
Wagon Train "The Candy O'Hara Story" 12/7/60 NBC.
Bachelor Father "Dear Bentley" 12/15/60 NBC.
The Untouchables "The Tommy Karpeles Story" 12/29/60 ABC.
Cheyenne "Incident at Dawson Flats" 1/9/61 ABC.
Bringing Up Buddy "The Singer" 1/23/61 NBC.
Adventures in Paradise "Wild Mangoes" 5/8/61 NBC.
Whispering Smith "The Idol" 9/18/61 ABC.
Bachelor Father "Kelly's Graduation" 9/21/61 CBS.
SurfSide 6 "Jonathan Wembley Is Missing" 11/13/61 ABC.
G.E. Theater "Tippy-Top" 12/17/61 CBS.
The Outlaws "A Bit of Glory" 2/1/62 NBC.
The Tall Man "The Impatient Brides" 2/3/62 CBS.
Follow the Sun "Annie Beeler's Place" 2/11/62 ABC.
Bus Stop "The Ordeal of Kevin Brooke" 2/25/62 ABC.
Rawhide "The Pitchwagon" 3/2/62 NBC.
The Dick Van Dyke Show "The Foul Weather Girl" 1/9/63 CBS.
The Lieutenant "Man with an Edge" 3/21/64 NBC.
The Virginian "Dark Challenge" 9/23/64 NBC.
The Man from U.N.C.L.E. "The Green Opal Affair" 10/27/64 NBC.
Perry Mason "The Case of the Lover's Gamble" 2/18/65 CBS.
Valentine's Day "Instant Father" 4/2/65 ABC.

Also:
The Lawrence Welk Show.

Diane McBain

Pretty, blonde Diane McBain began her acting career at a time when Hollywood was searching for a nymphet who could recapture Carroll Baker's earlier success as the thumb-sucking, pouty *Baby Doll*. Sandra Dee, Tuesday Weld, Sue Lyon, Carol Lynley, Yvette Mimieux and McBain vied to fill that casting slot. As described by author Marianne Sinclair in *Hollywood Lolitas*, "All were childish blondes in their early to late teens, with the vacant blue eyes of babies and the flawless porcelain complexion of dolls. These girls were alike as puppies—or piglets—in the same litter, adorable clones who very briefly crystallized a certain ideal of the young girl." However, whereas most of these actresses embodied the naïve, put-upon good girl, Diane excelled as the sophisticated bitch who never got her man in such films as *Parrish*, *Claudelle Inglish*, *A Distant Trumpet* and *Spinout*. Diane brought a vulnerability to these characters and she was able to get the audience to identify with them. However, playing these parts had a down side for McBain. "These roles typed me almost forever as the bad girl," says Diane, disappointed. "I wanted to play the ingenue. I could never understand why everyone wanted to play the bitch. Because when you go into society, people view you as they see you on the screen. It's terrible to be thought of as this messy, horrible person when you're not!" McBain later essayed even more villainous roles in *Thunder Alley*, *Maryjane* and, most memorably, *The Mini-Skirt Mob*. Diane is still a strikingly beautiful woman and remains active today.

Diane McBain was born on May 18 in Cleveland, Ohio. Her family relocated to Glendale, California, when Diane was just a child. Soon she began modeling, and before she reached her sixteenth birthday her face was known throughout the U.S. from TV commercials and magazine ads. Talent agent Sollie Biano spotted her in a play during her senior year of high school and brought her to the attention of Warner Bros. "The studio started using me for small roles in their Westerns," remembers Diane. "I guess they were keeping an eye out on me to see if I would do well. When I was about to graduate from high school, they offered me the role of Richard Burton's granddaughter in *Ice Palace* [1960]. And believe

Diane McBain as a spoiled heiress and Troy Donahue as a poor tobacco farmer share a romantic moment in *Parrish* (Warner Bros., 1961) (courtesy of Diane McBain).

it or not, but I didn't even know who Richard Burton was! [*Laughs*] I think the only film of his that I'd seen was *The Robe* [1953]. But I hadn't paid much attention. He was an English actor and I was a teenybopper so I didn't know much about him. When I met him, he was very charismatic. When acting with him, he looks at you as if you're the only person in the world. He was very powerful and a rather overwhelming actor."

Diane's excellent performance impressed the powers-that-be at Warners so much that they signed her to a seven-year contract. She immediately began doing guest stints on their popular TV series including *Maverick*, *The Alaskans*, *Sugarfoot* and *Hawaiian Eye*. In 1960 she became a regular on the series *SurfSide 6*, an imitation of the studio's popular detective series *77 Sunset Strip*. McBain played kooky socialite Daphne Dutton, who owned the yacht docked next to the houseboat where private eyes Troy Donahue, Van Williams and Lee Patterson lived and operated. "I liked doing *SurfSide 6* very much," remarks Diane. "It was a lot of fun. The guys were all great to work with."

In *Parrish* (1961), McBain plays tobacco farmer Dean Jagger's spoiled, willful daughter, who loses teen dream Troy Donahue to the much nicer Sharon Hugueny. The film, directed by Delmer Daves ("They called Daves the director with the velvet whip. He was very tender and soft but he let you know how he felt in no uncertain terms"), also starred Claudette Colbert, Connie Stevens and Karl Malden. At the time, *Parrish* was derided by the critics but was a hit at the box office. Today, it is a camp favorite and was described by authors Edward Marguiles and Stephen Rebello in *Bad Movies We Love* as being "just another unintentionally hilarious hothouse teen soap opera." However, Diane defends the film and Troy Donahue. She comments, "I like *Parrish*. It was fun to do. I played my first movie bad girl in this film and it typed me almost forever. Troy Donahue was a star at that time and that's what they wanted. Troy and I got along very well. He's a good guy. Perhaps Connie Stevens and I should have been rivals but we were friendly. We had known each other from when I was working at the Glenville Center Theatre when I was doing a play. She was dating one of the actors I was working with. She was pretty feisty and let the studio know when she was unhappy about things. I was one of those folks who liked to go along. I didn't like to fight. I just wanted to work."

Though Diane enjoyed working with the cast, she felt the wrath of Claudette Colbert, who played her governess. "This was Claudette Colbert's swan song in the film business," says Diane. "I'm sure she wanted to make a good impression. I was a novice actress. Even though I had done some things in television, I still was quite green. I didn't sleep a wink the night before the first day of shooting. When it came time for me to say my lines, I just froze. I couldn't remember any of the lines I learned. In all honesty, I ruined the scene. It was pure terror for me. Colbert and the director got very upset with me. I think she looked upon me with some sort of disdain. I was very aware that she was not happy and she had every right to be unhappy. I swore that I would never let that happen again. And I haven't. It was the only time."

In Karl Malden's bio, he suggests that the young actors in *Parrish* weren't properly prepared to handle their roles. Diane agrees "because the pressure was just so tremendous. And I know it wasn't just myself having this trouble. Troy, Connie, Sharon Hugueny and I all struggled because we were trying to keep up with such movie legends. We weren't quite ready and they could have helped us a lot more than they did. It was my first time working with stars of such huge magnitude. The studio system worked in many ways but one of the ways it didn't sometimes was that a lot of us came into acting from unprofessional stages. The stage I worked at was an Equity waiver situation because it was sort of community theater. Most people didn't launch their careers there. I did television too but I didn't get much direction. I had to wing it a lot. Most of the directors were not terribly helpful in terms of acting. They certainly were helpful in wanting to make you comfortable so you could do your job but they didn't offer any good advice on how to play a scene."

Her next film, *Claudelle Inglish* (1961), features McBain in a star-making role as a slutty farm girl who meets a tragic end after using a slew of men. The *NY Daily News* commented, "Diane McBain is a breathtakingly beautiful blonde who gives promise of becoming a good actress" and *Variety* remarked, "McBain delivers an earnest portrayal of an unappealing character." "This was a very coveted role," states Diane. "It came down to Shirley Knight and me for the part." Diane had a banner 1963 by proving her versatility as a farm owner in the western *Black Gold* with Phil Carey, a nurse in *The Caretakers* with Robert Stack and Joan

Crawford (whom Diane describes as being "a royal bitch"), and an uptight health nut in *Mary, Mary* with Debbie Reynolds. Theater owners in *Motion Picture Herald* took note of her good work and voted her a "Star of Tomorrow" for 1963.

Diane's comments regarding Joan Crawford stem from the fact that Crawford was one of the film's investors. That was probably the only way she could do movies in those days because she was an old lady compared to the nubile young things of the time. In *The Caretakers*, McBain plays a nurse and was supposed to be the romantic interest of the head psychologist (Stack). "The first day I met Joan Crawford, a gay friend of mine had taken me to lunch at a big Hollywood restaurant," recalls Diane. "He insisted I wear my beautiful picture hat. After that, I walked on the set wearing my hat and Joan Crawford saw me and immediately grew long green tentacles. And from that point on, the woman basically undermined everything I did on the movie. Instead of standing next to me in our scenes, Crawford would always stand in another place in the room so we would never be in the same shot together. When they got into the cutting room she had me chopped out of all of these scenes. She was very clever. The only scene that remained was when she was teaching karate and I was with a group of girls. I had no idea until the movie came out. Everyone with me at the premiere was appalled. Everything everybody has ever said about her is absolutely true! She was a challenge!"

In McBain's last film for Warner Bros., the Western *A Distant Trumpet* (1964), she was back to her conniving ways by competing with Suzanne Pleshette for cavalry officer Troy Donahue. As usual, McBain doesn't get her man. "I was excited at the prospect of working with legendary director Raoul Walsh. But we had so many problems doing this film. Walsh was getting old and might have been a little senile at the time. He would shoot footage and there wouldn't be any connecting scenes. So the actors had to kind of do some rewriting on the set to straighten things out for him. We all got along very well. I especially liked Suzanne Pleshette but she cursed like a truck driver. She had the dirtiest mouth of any woman I met up to that point. In the early sixties, before the sexual revolution, women just didn't speak like that."

Diane's contract with the studio ended amicably in 1964. "They wanted me to accept a small role in *Sex and the Single Girl*. I was doing leads and thought this wasn't a good idea." McBain next found herself competing with Shelley Fabares and Deborah Walley for race car driver Elvis Presley in *Spinout* (1966). Diane plays an author who sets her sights on Elvis as the model for a book she is writing about the perfect male. "I play the more mature character in the film. I felt I needed to come across a little older than Shelley and Deborah's characters. I wind up with Carl Betz, who plays Shelley's dad, at the end. Shelley is a lovely person. Deborah and I became close friends and later formed a production company called Pied Piper Productions. We were trying to make a feature film but in the meantime we produced children's theater and other things."

In what seems to be a consensus among Elvis Presley's co-stars, McBain too only has praise for him. "Elvis was extremely good-looking, very sexy and a major gentleman. I had not been a fan of Elvis so I didn't know what to expect. I was really impressed by him. He was a joy to work with, especially in the scenes when he'd sing to you. Can you think of anything nicer than to be serenaded by Elvis?"

In *Spinout* (MGM, 1966), McBain (*left*) vies with Shelley Fabares for Elvis Presley's attention.

Though McBain appeared on numerous television series during the sixties including *77 Sunset Strip*, *Burke's Law*, *Kraft Suspense Theater*, *The Man from U.N.C.L.E.*, and *The Wild Wild West*, her favorite show was *Batman*. She gave an amusing performance as Pinky Pinkston in the memorable episodes "A Piece of the Action" and "Batman's Satisfaction" in which Adam West and Burt Ward as Batman and Robin tangle with Van Williams and Bruce Lee as the Green Hornet and Kato. "This was such a fun, zany show to work on," recalls McBain fondly. "As Pinky, I had pink hair, a pink outfit and a pink dog. I enjoyed playing this role so much. It was one of my few forays into comedy." In the episode, Roger C. Carmel is the villainous Col. Gumm, who is using Pinky's stamp company to deal counterfeit stamps. "Everybody was great to work with. Bruce Lee, however, was always off by himself. I respected him as a fellow actor but never expected him to become such a phenomenal star. In person, he didn't exhibit great charisma."

It was at this point in her career that McBain started to appear in low-budget drive-in films. Producer Samuel Z. Arkoff cast her in AIP's *Thunder Alley* (1967), *Maryjane* (1968) and *The Mini-Skirt Mob* (1968). "I never signed a contract with AIP," states McBain matter-of-factly. "Each film was done on an individual basis. I met Samuel Z. Arkoff somewhere down the line but I don't remember much about him. I don't mean to sound so disrespectful. He did, after all, provide work for me." With the studio system breaking up, the independent studios and filmmakers began to flourish. In the sixties,

McBain as Pinky Pinkston on the ABC-TV series *Batman* with Roger C. Carmel (*pointing gun*) as the villainous Colonel Gumm and Neil Hamilton (*right*) as Commissioner Gordon.

they were more exploitative and were all trying to copy *The Wild Angels* or *Beach Party* or *Easy Rider*. Diane began appearing in these types of films because "those were the sort of scripts I was being offered."

Diane teamed with Fabian in the drive-in classics *Thunder Alley* and *Maryjane*. In the former, Fabian plays a stock car racer suspended from racing after he causes the death of another driver. He goes to work for promoter Jan

Murray's "thrill circus" and falls for his daughter Annette Funicello. McBain plays Fabian's thrill-seeking ex-girlfriend who uses rival race car driver Warren Berlinger to get back at Fabian. Though directed by Richard Rush, *Thunder Alley* is a standard programmer. "I don't remember much about this film," says Diane laughing. "Most of my off screen time was spent watching them film *In the Heat of the Night* [1967] with Sidney Poitier next door."

Directed by Maury Dexter, *Maryjane* was a sort of *Reefer Madness* for the 1960s, written by comedian Dick Gautier and *Hollywood Squares* host Peter Marshall. ("I guess we all dabble," quips Diane.) A camp classic, it took itself so seriously that the producers urged theater owners to have special screenings for local clergymen to inspire anti-drug sermons. In the film, Fabian plays a high school art teacher who discovers that his students (including Kevin Coughlin, Michael Margotta and Patty McCormack) are smoking marijuana. When Fabian tries to help good kid Margotta, he is rebuffed and framed for possession. Fellow teacher Diane, to whom he is attracted, bails him out of jail. However, she turns out to be the school's main dope supplier! McBain is a gas as the prim schoolteacher by day and pothead by night. "This is such a silly movie and is totally unrealistic," comments Diane. "But I did enjoy working with Fabian again. He's very nice."

Though Diane would seem to be per-

Maryjane (AIP, 1968) featured Fabian and McBain as high school teachers who get involved with their pot-smoking students.

Diane McBain as the leader of *The Mini-Skirt Mob* (AIP, 1968) puts a stranglehold on her rival Sherry Jackson. *Below:* Motorcycle Mama! McBain in *The Mini-Skirt Mob*.

fectly cast as a beauty queen, she was excellent as the vicious leader of *The Mini-Skirt Mob*, the ultimate sixties drive-in movie. "I wasn't an obvious choice to play this part," agrees McBain. "I think I was just the person with the recognizable name. That's what the producers were looking for." Described as "hog straddling female animals on the prowl," the Mini-Skirts included Patty McCormack and Sandra Marshall with Jeremy Slate, Harry Dean Stanton and Ronnie Rondell as their boyfriends. "After I agreed to do this movie, I went out and learned how to ride a motorcycle. A *big* motorcycle. When I arrived on the set, they gave us these tiny scooters. It was the silliest bike you ever saw. I thought it was ridiculous to have this Mini-Skirt Mob on these small bikes. I knew then I was in trouble," she says with a laugh.

The Mini-Skirt Mob, also directed by Maury Dexter, is an exciting variation on the typical biker films released in the late sixties. It was beautifully shot on location in the Arizona desert by cinematographer Arch R. Dalzell and features a winning musical score by Les Baxter. Spurned by her former boyfriend (Ross Hagen), McBain seeks revenge against him and his new bride (Sherry Jackson). She enlists her fellow cyclists to make life hell for the newlyweds. Their idyllic honeymoon is turned into a wild, beer-swilling melee after the Mini-Skirts crash it. The brawl ends with a wild motorcycle chase with Rondell swerving off a cliff. The gang also causes the death of McCormack who, tiring of McBain's sadistic ruthlessness, tries to help the newlyweds escape. The film climaxes with McBain and Slate catching up with the fleeing couple. While Slate tries to run down Hagen, the women scuffle. McBain ends up hanging over the side of a cliff with one hand held by Jackson. As Hagen goes to get help from the police, Jackson delivers her own brand of justice and lets McBain fall to her death.

"What attracted me to do this film was the role of Shayne," says Diane. "I thought it would be fun to play such a sadistic killer because women don't usually get to play these sort of roles. The part also required me to do my own stunts. I rode my own motorcycle. I actually hung off the mountain attached to a cable. And I did the fight scenes with Sherry. We had been roommates at one time so we were fairly friendly. We had no problems doing those scenes. Actually, all the actors got along nicely, which was great because we shot it on location. Patty McCormack was very nice. Jeremy Slate was friendly and professional with me but we didn't get close or anything. He often plays the tough guy because he has those distinct features. Harry Dean Stanton was such a character, very intense with a spark in his eye. It always looked like he was keeping some funny little secret." Though she has the highest regard for her co-stars, *The Mini-Skirt Mob* is not a film McBain is very proud of because "I didn't think it is a very realistic movie. Girl gang members didn't wear mini-skirts! It was just AIP's way to cash in on the popularity of mini-skirts and biker films."

Despite her disappointment, McBain and *The Mini-Skirt Mob* received some very decent reviews. *Citizen News* raved, "Diane McBain is superb as the troublemaking Shayne." *Variety* found the film to have "slickness and polish as directed by Maury Dexter." And *Boxoffice Magazine* commented, "Creamy thighs straddling motorcycles should offer the big draw for the summer drive-in trade." Most critics, however, were in agreement that the controversial ending was sending out the wrong message to young viewers. "The ending sort of soothes people's feelings for retribution against someone so vile," opines McBain. "I think in today's movies you would find that happening and no one blinks an eye. But for 1968 it was a bit shocking. On the set, Maury did talk about doing the ending differently. But they didn't have much of a budget. He felt he could legitimize Sherry's character playing judge and jury with the evilness in my character, who certainly deserved what she got. I personally think any movie that tends to teach people the wrong message needs to be looked at. You need to say, 'Is this really a legitimate way to end this movie or can we do it a little bit differently to send a slightly better message and still have a dramatic ending?' If an immoral ending is really appropriate, then it should be done."

McBain continued her dalliance in drive-in fare with *I Sailed to Tahiti with an All-Girl Crew* (1969), whose title pretty much sums up the film. Produced and directed by Richard L. Bare, Diane co-stars with Gardner McKay, Pat Buttram and Edy Williams. "This was a comedy and was fun to do," recalls McBain. "However, I did not find working with Gardner McKay very pleasurable. He was a bit arrogant and not particularly friendly. Years later I saw him again at Tippi Hedren's home. At the time he was teaching classes at UCLA and was much more humble. I got along much better with Richard Bare. He directed many episodes of *Green Acres*. I was always surprised when I would end up working with him. He liked that I could play the bad girl and cast me again in *Wicked, Wicked* [1973]. That film was a big disappointment. He and I were a little bit at odds on that particular shoot."

Filmed on location in Hawaii, *I Sailed to Tahiti with an All-Girl Crew* featured beautiful women and breathtaking scenery. "Two things stand out for me about this film," remembers McBain. "The first being that the water in this lagoon was a beautiful bluish green and was like a sheet of glass. It was spectacular. The second thing was that in one of the scenes, the boat gets stuck and Edy Williams and the rest of the girls have to jump in the water and push the back of the boat. As they're all kicking their legs to make the boat move, all of Edy's falsies came floating out from the top of her bikini. It was hysterical!"

McBain ended the sixties playing supporting roles. *The Sidehackers* (a.k.a. *Five the Hard Way*, 1969) is a violent biker film about a cyclist (Ross Hagen) who shuns his gang to settle down. As his girlfriend, McBain is the victim this time, viciously raped and murdered by the vengeful gang. *The Delta Factor* (1970) is based on a novel by Mickey Spillane. Christopher George (whom McBain describes as being "a sweetheart to work with") plays an adventurer forced to team with a CIA agent (Yvette Mimieux) to rescue an imprisoned scientist. Diane played an informer who helps George. She states, "I took this part even though it hurt my ego that I would be playing a supporting role to Yvette, whom I'd always been compared with. After we shot the film, the director Tay Garnett came to me and said, 'You know, Diane, I'm really sorry that I didn't hire you in the lead role. We had a lot of problems with Yvette. You turned out to be a much more professional actress.' That made me feel a bit better."

During the seventies and eighties, McBain took time out from her career to raise her son. She continued working intermittently in film and television. "It was

Diane McBain ca. 2000—still lovely as ever (courtesy of Diane McBain).

very hard for actresses to juggle a career and a family back then," remarks Diane. "During the seventies, I was very busy with my family and being a mom. I had to put my career aside for him. Many actresses had done that before and got away with it. But I didn't. I wasn't established enough in Hollywood to put it aside. It was a bad choice. Now it wouldn't be a problem. You can even take your child on the set and breast-feed. You couldn't do that 25 years ago. I tried. I took my baby on the set when I did an *ABC Wide World of Mystery* in England. I asked if I could and they were very reluctant. I took him and breast-fed him on the soundstage. I was probably one of the first actresses to do that. It was not an acceptable thing at the time." Her films during this period include *Savage Season* (1970), *The Deathhead Virgin* (1974) and, her favorite, *Red Fury* (1984), a Western about a little Mexican boy who wanders into a white town in the Old West and is discriminated against by many of the townspeople. On television, Diane could be seen in two episodes of *Dallas* ("Larry Hagman did not particularly impress me").

In 1982, Diane was making a comeback on the daytime drama *Days of Our Lives* as the outrageous Foxy Humdinger when she was brutally raped by two men outside her West Hollywood apartment. Unfortunately, the men were never caught. To help others and herself deal with the aftermath of being raped, she has worked as a counselor for rape victims and battered women.

Today's Diane McBain is as beautiful, talented and charming as ever. With her son Evan Andrew Burke now a grown man ("He does creative support construction for the studios. His credits include *Godzilla*"), McBain has returned to acting. However, the Hollywood of today is a lot different from what Diane remembers. "Hollywood today is very sad," remarks Diane wistfully. "I guest-starred on *Dr. Quinn, Medicine Woman* and it was like going back to the sixties because they have that same sort of family atmosphere. Everybody likes each other and nobody competes with each other. In the sixties, everybody worked together to produce a good movie. I liked it much better then when creative people were working on films and not the suits. Now these guys come down to the sets to pronounce and make changes and they don't know anything about being creative. I guess you can't argue with it because movies are making money but it is still sad."

Though Diane should find great success in her return to the business, to most drive-in film fans she will always be remembered for her performance as the fierce motorcycle gang leader in *The Mini-Skirt Mob*. Though it is not her favorite film, Diane has retained her sense of humor regarding the notoriety this drive-in classic has brought her. "I love the fact that there are a lot of people out there who enjoy *The Mini-Skirt Mob* and my other AIP movies, for whatever reasons. That I have fans in that respect is great. I even mention that I'm a cult movie actress and sometimes make a joke out of it. On the other hand, wouldn't it have been wonderful if I didn't have to make movies like that!?"

Film Appearances

1960   Ice Palace (Warner Bros.) d. Vincent Sherman.
1961   Parrish (Warner Bros.) d. Delmer Daves.
          Claudelle Inglish (Warner Bros.) d. Gordon Douglas.
1963   Black Gold (Warner Bros.) d. Leslie H. Martinson.
          The Caretakers (United Artists) d. Hall Bartlett.

	Mary, Mary (Warner Bros.) d. Mervyn LeRoy.
1964	A Distant Trumpet (Warner Bros.) d. Raoul Walsh.
1966	Spinout (MGM) d. Norman Taurog.
1967	Thunder Alley (AIP) d. Richard Rush.
	The Karate Killers (MGM; edited episodes of The Man from U.N.C.L.E.) d. Barry Shear.
1968	Maryjane (AIP) d. Maury Dexter.
	The Mini-Skirt Mob (AIP) d. Maury Dexter.
1969	The Sidehackers/Five the Hard Way (Crown International) d. Gus Trikonis.
	I Sailed to Tahiti with an All-Girl Crew (World Entertainment) d. Richard L. Bare.
1970	The Delta Factor (Continental) d. Tay Garnett.
	Savage Season/Temporado Salvaje (U.S./Mexico; Commonwealth United) d. Myron J. Gold
1973	Wicked, Wicked (MGM) d. Richard L. Bare.
1974	The Deathhead Virgin (U.S./Philippines) d. Norman Foster.
	Donner Pass: The Road to Survival (TV-movie) d. James L. Conway.
1981	Legend of the Wild (Jensen Farley Pictures)
1984	The Red Fury d. Lyman D. Dayton.
1986	Fly from the Hawk (Spain) d. Cecil Barker.
1995	Puppet Master 5: The Final Chapter (Direct-to-video) d. Jeff Burr.
1998	Besotted (unreleased) d. Holly Hardman
1999	Invisible Mom II (Direct-to-video) d. Fred Olen Ray.
	The Christmas Path (TV-movie) d. Mark Malis.

Television Appearances

Maverick "Passage to Fort Doom" 3/8/59 ABC.
77 Sunset Strip "Six Superior Skirts" 10/16/59 ABC.
Maverick "A Fellow Brother" 11/22/59 ABC.
77 Sunset Strip "The Starlet" 2/26/60 ABC.
The Alaskans "Behind the Moon" 3/6/60 ABC.
Bourbon Street Beat "The Missing Queen" 3/14/60 ABC.
Sugarfoot "Return to Boot Hill" 3/15/60 ABC.
Bourbon Street Beat "Wall of Silence" 3/28/60 ABC.
The 22nd Annual Academy Awards (special) [costume model] 4/4/60 ABC.
77 Sunset Strip "Fraternity of Fear" 5/6/60 ABC.
The Lawman "The Judge" 5/15/60 ABC.
Bourbon Street Beat "Ferry to Algiers" 6/6/60 ABC.
SurfSide 6 [series regular as Daphne Dutton] 10/3/60 to 9/24/62 ABC.
77 Sunset Strip "Leap, My Lovely" 10/19/62 ABC.
Hawaiian Eye "Pursuit of a Lady" 12/11/62 ABC.
Hawaiian Eye "Pretty Pigeon" 1/22/63 ABC.
77 Sunset Strip "Nine to Five" 3/8/63 ABC.
77 Sunset Strip "5" (Parts 1,2,3 & 5.) 9/20, 9/27, 10/4, & 10/18/63 ABC.
Kraft Suspense Theater "My Enemy, This Town" 2/6/64 NBC.
Burke's Law "Who Killed Marty Keslo?" 2/28/64 ABC.
Arrest and Trial "Tigers Are for Jungles" 3/22/64 ABC.
Wendy and Me (pilot) 9/14/64 ABC.
Burke's Law "Who Killed Mr. Cartwheel?" 10/21/64 ABC.
Burke's Law "Who Killed the Tall One in the Middle?" 11/25/64 ABC.
Kraft Suspense Theater "One Tiger to a Hill" 12/3/64 NBC.
Bob Hope Chrysler Theater "Double Jeopardy" 1/8/65 NBC.
Burke's Law "Who Killed Nobody Somehow?" 3/31/65 ABC.
You Don't Say! [celebrity panelist] 5/3 to 5/7/65 NBC.
The Dean Jones Show (pilot) 7/2/65.
The Wild Wild West "The Night of a Thousand Eyes" 10/22/65 CBS.
The Man from U.N.C.L.E. "The Deadly Toys Affair" 11/12/65 NBC.
Batman "The 13th Hat" 2/23/66 ABC.
Batman "Batman Stands Pat" 2/24/66 ABC.
The Wild Wild West "The Night of the Vicious Valentine" 2/10/67 CBS.
Batman "A Piece of the Action" 2/23/67 ABC.
Batman "Batman's Satisfaction" 2/24/67 ABC.
The Dating Game [celebrity contestant] 2/25/67 ABC.
The Man from U.N.C.L.E. "The Five Daughters Affair" 3/31 & 4/7/67 NBC.
Dateline: Hollywood 8/22/67 ABC.
Love, American Style "Love and the Roommate" 11/7/69 ABC.

Mannix "Blind Mirror" 1/24/70 CBS.
Land of the Giants "Panic" 1/25/70 ABC.
To Rome with Love "To Go Home Again" 1/25/70 CBS.
The Mod Squad "Kicks Incorporated" 1/12/71 ABC.
ABC Wide World of Mystery "Tight as a Drum" 2/11/74 ABC.
The Barbary Coast "Sauce for the Goose" 10/20/75 ABC.
Marcus Welby, M.D. "The Highest Mountain" 2/17 & 2/24/76 ABC.
Cross-Wits [celebrity panelist] 4/12 to 4/16/76 Synd.
The Life and Times of Grizzly Adams "Once Upon a Starry Night" 12/78 NBC.
Charlie's Angels "Disco Angels" 1/31/79 ABC.
Hawaii Five-O "The Moroville Covenant" 3/29/80 CBS.
Charlie's Angels "Angels on the Line" 2/14/81 ABC.
Eight Is Enough "Yet Another Seven Days in February" 5/2/81 ABC.
Dallas "Denial" 1/15/82 CBS.
Dallas "Head of the Family" 1/22/82 CBS.
Days of Our Lives [recurring role as Foxy Humdinger] 1982 to 1983 NBC.
Matt Houston "The Rock and a Hard Place" 1/2/83 ABC.
Airwolf "Sins of the Past" 10/27/84 CBS.
Crazy Like a Fox "Bum Tip" 2/24/85 CBS.
Knight Rider "Ten Wheel Trouble" 3/24/85 NBC.
General Hospital [series regular as Claire Howard] 1988 ABC.
Jake and the Fat Man "I Know That You Know" 12/12/90 CBS.
Sabrina, the Teenage Witch "A Halloween Story" 10/25/96 ABC.
Dr. Quinn, Medicine Woman "Point Blank" 2/28/98 CBS.

Also:
Police Story.

Joan Staley

Blonde Joan Staley was one of the busiest actresses on television in the early sixties. This former *Playboy* Playmate was a regular on the summer variety series *The Lively Ones* with Vic Damone and the sitcom *Broadside* as Machinist's Mate Roberta Love. Staley also had recurring roles on *The Tab Hunter Show*, *The Beachcomber* and the last season of *77 Sunset Strip* and she guest-starred on numerous series including *The Dick Van Dyke Show*, *Burke's Law*, *The Munsters*, *Batman* and *Laredo*, among others. On the big screen, she appeared in *The Ladies' Man* with Jerry Lewis, the classic *Cape Fear* with Robert Mitchum and the fantasy film *Valley of the Dragons* (as a cave girl). In 1964, she quipped to her agent and friends, "Elvis has worked with every other Joan in the business but *I* knew him back in Memphis. When is it going to be my turn?" Joan got her chance and got to slap the King in *Roustabout*. But her most memorable film role was in 1966 as the heroine in the Don Knotts comedy *The Ghost and Mr. Chicken*. This was the one film where Staley's beauty and acting talent were used to their full advantage. She retired from acting shortly thereafter to work with her husband with his talent management company, International Ventures.

Joan Staley was born Joan McConchie on May 20 in Minneapolis, Minnesota, to James and Jean McConchie. At the time, her father was in civilian ministry and her mother was an accomplished musician who played violin, piano, organ and viola. Joan began taking violin lessons at three years old while other kids her age were barely out of diapers. "My mom took me to a concert and afterwards she said I begged her to take lessons. She thought it was nice and my interest would pass. Soon after, I joined Carl Moldiam's Baby Orchestra in L.A. It was a quite famous string orchestra featuring very young children." At the ripe old age of five, Joan became one of the youngest members of Peter Meremblum's Junior Symphony, whose members included Diana Lynn and André Previn, and she played the Hollywood Bowl at age six.

Joan made her film debut at eight years old as a musician in *The Emperor Waltz* (1948). "That was the only way my mother would agree to let me do it," remembers Joan. "To appear as a musician was okay but as an actor—no. She made sure that I wouldn't have any lines. It's not that she didn't want me to act but she didn't want me to go through what young actors go through. The producers assured her that I would only be playing music. Bing Crosby and Joan Fontaine are stranded and they hear music drifting over from this little village. They pan through this town and I am on this fire truck. It was only a few days' work but I remember it vividly."

Though an accomplished violinist, as Joan got older her interests turned to singing (she has an extraordinary two-and-a-half octave voice range) and then acting. Her father was stationed in France during Joan's high school days and she appeared in some operettas (*Adele* and *Die Fledermaus*) as well as straight comedies like *Harvey*. After returning to the U.S., she was briefly enrolled in Chapman College in Orange, California, before relocating to Memphis with her new husband Chuck Staley. "I was singing and doing backup on some records for Sam Phillips," says Joan. "I also sang on television on *Wink Martindale's Dance Party*." Joan returned to Los Angeles and began working as a secretary during the day. To keep herself busy at night, she got involved with a theater group. "We performed at the Music Box Theatre, which was on the corner of Hollywood and La Brea," recalls Joan. "We did eight shows a week. I played roles in *Brigadoon* and *Wonderful Town*. That was where the acting actually started. I was out trying to be an actor at this point. I loved the expression, I loved what we were doing, and I loved the singing and the acting. My name started getting mentioned in newspaper reviews. That's when I came to realize that here I am in the town where this is done. My

Publicity photo of MGM contract player Joan Staley (courtesy of Joan Staley).

first television role was a one-liner on *Perry Mason*."

In 1958, Joan's career took a turn when she was approached by an acquaintance named Lawrence Schiller, a photographer with *Life* magazine. However, he asked Staley if she'd be interested in posing for *Playboy*. "It was a rather daunting suggestion but honestly we needed the money for rent so I agreed with the understanding that we'd do it once only," reveals Joan. "Larry and I were alone in the studio for the actual centerfold shot. Somebody came in to do my hair and makeup and then left. Over the years, other people claim to have been there but they weren't. Larry set it up and we shot it. I had just finished some TV shows at CBS—those were the prehistoric days of live television—where they had just built the new CBS Television City. After we did the shots for the centerfold, we went over to CBS to shoot some of the sidebar shots. He also photographed me on the set on a show I was doing with Joan Blondell. As a result, Larry was barred from CBS for at least a year because he used the CBS logo eye without permission even though the logo appeared on a 35mm Mitchell film camera, not a TK 41 camera used for live television. It was an insider's joke."

Joan was Miss November of 1958. Her centerfold is very tame even for the standards of the late fifties. Though she posed totally nude, her shot is of her standing holding onto a script (covering her breasts) in one hand and pulling a curtain to hide the rest of her with the other. She was happy with the layout except for the fact that they padded her bio. And surprisingly, Joan met Hugh Hefner *after* her photos were published. "I met him at a cocktail party in Los Angeles," recalls Joan. "We chatted and that was it. He was very gracious and a gentleman. I got to know him better years later and have had some nice conversations with him. I honestly believe that during the time of my layout, Hefner really was elevating the girl-next-door. Now we may not approve of his method but he took the girl-next-door and made her that same person that you used to look to the silver screen as unattainable. Hef said, 'No, no, no. She lives right next door.' It is an elite sorority. The end of 1999 is the forty-fifth anniversary. I am one of the oldest living Playmates." [*Laughs*]

"I never considered posing for *Playboy* a mistake," continues Joan. "However, the suggestion of the casting couch was still very prevalent in Hollywood by those who chose to use it. It did make that a little more difficult because there were assumptions made that if you posed for *Playboy* you would be more willing to accept other invitations, which was not the case. I was very nervous at those times. You'd try to talk or laugh your way out of it without injuring the person personally because you are honestly auditioning and want the part. I had some guys who had buttons underneath their desks, which would literally lock the doors. I discovered this on one of my first film interviews with a man who is dead now—he has already met his reward—who did that to me. I tried to talk my way out of this but he got up and came toward me—that frightened me. I went for the door and the door was locked. There were secretaries on the other side—I pounded on the door—none of them came. I think I was very naïve in not expecting and realizing that I'd get more of that behavior than I did."

Whatever the effect *Playboy* had—good or bad—Joan became one of the busiest actresses on the small screen. Between 1959 and 1963 she could be seen playing a variety of different roles including a researcher in an unsold pilot with Carroll O'Connor. ("I felt intimidated and uncomfortable around O'Connor. He was rather gruff. Years later when I saw him at a benefit he was nicer.") She also had a recurring role as a model on *The Tab Hunter Show* during the 1960-61 season and played Charly, one of Vic Damone's two sidekicks on his successful 1962 summer music series *The Lively Ones*. One reason Joan stayed so busy was that she was now divorced and had a young daughter named Sherrye to support. "I was a single mother for a long time and I was very worried what that was doing to my daughter," comments Joan. "There were times where I had to leave for interviews and to go to work. There was guilt but I think it is the kind any single mother has." Joan's talent and dedication got her noticed and she was voted a Hollywood Deb Star in 1962. And in between pursuing acting roles and raising her daughter, she even found time to play left field for a girls' baseball team called the Deb Stars.

Joan's career was not limited to television, however. She began appearing in small roles on the big screen in *Ocean's Eleven* (1960), *Midnight Lace* (1960) and *Dondi* (1961). In *Breakfast at Tiffany's* (1961) starring Audrey Hepburn (whom Joan describes as being "a very nice and a gracious, gracious lady"), Staley played a model. Unfortunately, however, her big scene was cut because of director Blake Edwards' mistake. Joan recalls that "Blake came to me and said, 'Joan, I discovered I have you in two places at the same time. We have to cut one of them out.' I pleaded, 'Please don't cut the bedroom scene.' But he did. It was awfully hard to find me in the other scene—the party sequence—because there was a lot of people in it. When the film was initially reviewed, the photo that accompanied it in either *Time* or *Newsweek* was of me with my foot dangling over the bed and somebody tickling it. The one word caption under the picture was 'salacious.' And that was the scene that was cut out."

Joan received more screen time in the Jerry Lewis comedy *The Ladies' Man* (1961). She played one of a bevy of beauties (including Pat Stanley, Madlyn Rhue, Marianne Gaba, Daria Massey, Sheila Rogers and Francesca Bellini) who live in a rooming house where clumsy, heartbroken college grad Lewis gets a job as a handyman. The film, directed by Lewis, is amusing but the enormous, multi-level set was the real star. As Lewis descends the main staircase on his first day of work, the camera pulls back revealing the magnitude of the magnificent set with its hallways, twisting staircases, bedrooms and huge dining room. "I was just agog over the set," recalls Joan. "It was so monstrous that everyone had his or her own chair in one line across the stage. Jerry was trying to shoot like live television, following the actors through doorways and that sort of thing, which was very difficult because he was shooting from the front. But he did an amazing job. It was also the first time I had seen a television monitor and a camera mounted on the same crane. Due to union rules, this was never allowed. As a director, Jerry communicated extremely well with the actors as to what he wanted. I think not all of us—whether it was medication he was on or the excitement of his directing his second film—can stay on the set for hours at a stretch and continue on for another 12. We went from straight time to overtime to Golden time and continued on to the second day because he was trying to get a shot. You get to the point of fatigue well beyond exhaustion. But Jerry did a fantastic job in trying to keep everyone in the huge cast feeling specific and individual. It was difficult to be around that many females [*laughs*]. Maybe it isn't for a guy but there were *tremendous* egos. Everyone had their own dressing room with fresh flowers and sometimes you'd get little presents.

"Jerry Lewis *is* Jerry Lewis," continues Joan. "There is no switch that turns him on or off. He is what he is. I think every great comedy performer has a dark side. And I think it is part of that dark side that lends itself to the pathos that you have to have in order to be a strong comedic actor, especially in the type of humor that Jerry does. I worked on *The Ladies' Man* for many weeks. Jerry Lewis was kind enough to let me off after about six weeks because I had an offer for a TV pilot."

Joan's first movie lead was as the cave girl Deena in *Valley of the Dragons* (1961), directed by B-movie vet Edward Bernds. Based on Jules Verne's *Off on a Comet*, Cesare Danova and Sean McClory played

Valley of the Dragons (Columbia, 1961) with Staley (left) and Cesare Danova.

two nineteenth century adversarial adventurers who are swept up onto a passing comet during a windstorm. There they find a world inhabited by prehistoric beasts and cave people. Once separated, Danova wanders among the River People and is attracted to a beautiful blonde (Staley). McClory finds his way to the River People's hostile neighbors, the Cave People, and a curvaceous brunette (Danielle de Metz). The adventurers get the two tribes to unite to fight off more life-threatening creatures including attacking dinosaurs and dragons, all courtesy of stock footage from *One Million B.C.* (1940) and *The Lost World* (1960). Due to this, Joan wore the exact same costume Carole Landis wore in *One Million B.C.* "We filmed mostly on a soundstage and in one of the canyons in Hollywood for entrances and exits out of the cave," recalls Joan. "I had never done anything that had so much earth in it. They were manmade boulders, which I had to climb up. I remember looking at the fake rocks on the set and wondering if they were going to photograph like they're real. Itty-bitty lizards were used so most of the acting was reacting. The giant lizards were intercut later on. The technical angle of this film was fascinating to me. I got to know how they edited in the process shots."

Joan won the role of Deena without an interview: Her agent put her up for the role and the producers chose her. When asked why she accepted a lead role in a B-movie, Joan replies, "People can talk a lot about choosing scripts and I think 90 percent of that is hype because there is a point in any Hollywood career where heat breeds more heat. The more you work, the more your name is in the trades for acting. The more people cast you, the more buzz is created about you. I didn't have publicity at that time. It wasn't until later on that I realized that I could pay my rent and hire a publicist. I had to do it the old-fashioned way by working.

"I had fun doing *Valley of the Dragons*," says Joan. "Cesare Danova was delightful and Sean McClory had a wonderful sense of humor." Though Joan enjoyed her co-stars, the one thing she found problematic was that she didn't have any words to say in the script. Being a cave girl, her character didn't speak English. "Let's face it, a role like Deena did not require a Sarah Bernhardt. I tried to make her believable and as interesting and charming as possible. I had to devise sounds my character would speak. It was difficult because you didn't want it to be 'ooga ooga.' I talked it over with Edward Bernds. I told him, 'I feel like an idiot saying this—does it sound strange?' He answered, 'Try and pick sounds that you would try to teach a child a word for. If you were talking to a child, would you say apple or *ap*-ple to try to get them to hear the sounds?' I found that very helpful. Bernds was such a patient man. He knew what he wanted and he got it."

In 1961, Joan was signed to a contract by MGM. However, she did not make one film there. Though she attended their talent school and took advantage of their speech, acting and singing classes, the studio never used her in a movie or their TV shows. After leaving MGM, Joan's career picked up steam. She appeared next in the classic tale of suspense *Cape Fear* (1962). Robert Mitchum

Robert Mitchum as the menacing Max Cady with Staley as a waitress in the bowling alley scene from *Cape Fear* (Universal, 1962).

starred as Max Cady, a con who is released from prison after serving a six-year term for rape and assault. He shows up in the hometown of the former prosecutor (Gregory Peck) who sent him to jail and begins a campaign of terror against Peck and his family. Staley has the small role of a waitress in the memorable bowling alley scene as Cady sits at the snack bar intently eyeing the Peck family. Mitchum proved to be an inspiration to the young actress when he gave up his close-ups in their scene so Joan would have more screen time. "In the middle of the shot, Mitchum looked right into the camera and said to the director, J. Lee Thompson, 'You know, everybody knows what the hell this stupid face looks like. Stop this and give the shot to Joan. She's just starting.' That was the end of the shot and he wouldn't do any more. Now, he had no reason to do that other than he was just being nice. I was feeding him lines off-stage and my mouth went down to the floor. Lee said, 'Okay. Let's re-set for the reverse.' I don't know that I did the scene as well as I could because I remember during the whole thing I kept thinking, 'I can't believe he's doing this.' And there was a 'But *why* is he doing this?'" [*Laughs*]

"Robert Mitchum was a pussycat and was very nice," raves Joan. "He had such a natural ease about him. There was such a difference working with actors who came from the studio system of the forties and fifties. There was a separateness—which did not come from them—but was present around them. They had an air that they carried that was ingrained into them by the training they got by the studios and the separation from reality that they enjoyed due to the studio publicity departments. It was a more confident world that they lived in."

Joan continued working on the big screen with roles in the gangster drama *Johnny Cool* (1963), the Paul Newman-Joanne Woodward comedy *A New Kind of Love* (1963) and *Roustabout* (1964) with Elvis Presley as a reckless singer named Charlie Rogers. "My little snotty comments to my agents about every Joan in town working with Elvis except me helped me land this film," Joan recalls. *Roustabout* incidentally featured another Joan—Joan Freeman, who played Elvis' main love interest. Staley had a supporting role as a waitress who's in love with the King. After getting into a brawl with three college guys at the start of the film, Elvis heads off on his motorcycle for parts unknown, deserting Staley. Joan's distinction amongst Elvis' leading ladies is that her character actually slaps Elvis. "I asked him if he wanted me to pull up," recalls Joan. "He said, 'no.' I said, 'Are you sure? I could leave a welt.' He replied, 'That's okay.' So I belted him. [*Laughs*] The slap you hear in the film was not put in afterwards—that was the slap. Elvis was fun to work with. He was just a nice, nice man." *Roustabout* is a notable Elvis film due to the fact that he co-starred with screen legend Barbara Stanwyck, who played the owner of a carnival Elvis winds up working in.

While doing films, Joan was also kept busy on television. Her many appearances on *Burke's Law* helped her get on the cover of *TV Guide* with actresses Eileen O'Neill and Sharon Hillyer (flanking series star Gene Barry). Joan co-starred (with Kathy Nolan, Sheila James and Lois Roberts) in the sitcom *Broadside*, the flip side to the popular *McHale's Navy*, during the 1964-65 TV season. The comedy series centered on four WAVEs working as machinist's mates on a South Pacific island during WWII complete with a stuffy Commanding Officer (Edward Andrews) and his befuddled

Staley as Madge, the forlorn jilted girlfriend of Elvis Presley in *Roustabout* (Paramount, 1964).

Though she has just bailed him out of jail that doesn't stop Elvis Presley from deserting Joan Staley early on in *Roustabout* (Paramount, 1964).

lieutenant (Dick Sargent). Staley played Roberta "Honey Hips" Love, a former stripper who joined the Navy. To get this role, Joan had to sign a long-term contract with Universal. "We had some wonderful people in *Broadside* but there was one thing wrong with it—we didn't have a straight man. In order for comedy to work, you need that straight man to play off of. If everybody is playing a banana, it won't work. Dick Sargent's character was the closest we had to a straight man but I think we needed more. It also didn't help to be placed up against *The Rifleman* on Sunday nights." Though *Broadside* was not a critically acclaimed series (Frank Judge of the *Detroit News* quipped, "The Navy should sue"), according to Joan, "At times there was some incredible comedy in it."

Though the series was cancelled after one season, Joan remained under contract. Joan starred in Universal's Audie Murphy Western *Gunpoint* (1966) and in the Don Knotts comedy *The Ghost and Mr. Chicken* (1966). In the former, Joan plays a saloon singer who is kidnapped by an outlaw gang while Murphy, the town's sheriff, organizes a posse and comes to her rescue. The film was intended just to fill the bottom of a double-bill. However, it is distinguished with the pleasant singing voice of Joan (accompanied by Laurindo Almeda on guitar) and beautiful on-location photography in St. George, Utah. Joan jokes, "Today it is a resort town but back then it was, as *Reader's Digest* would say, 'a poke and plum town'—you poke your head out the window and you are plum out of town."

Joan enjoyed working with Robert Pine (who played the young hero) and a great bunch of character actors. She found Audie Murphy to be "an unusual man. I wondered if he really ever felt comfortable as an actor. He always seemed to be as if he was in a different place. He was a little distant and I never quite felt at ease with him." Joan also discovered the perils of filming a Western. She did all of her own horseback riding that was filmed on the flat lands. "It was exciting to be riding at full gallop with a camera car beside you," exclaims Joan. "I remember one scene I was supposed to be without reins and they hooked a wire around my thumb. It was so tight I thought it was going to take my finger off. In another scene, we shot on these cliffs and I suddenly became apprehensive about the height and I couldn't come down after we got the shot. The wranglers brought the horses down but left me sitting there on some smooth rock cropping. I was petrified and could not move. I remember the director [Earl Bellamy] saying, 'If you can't walk down, bump your butt down and just slide!' I was so mortified. But that's how I came down—inch by inch."

The Ghost and Mr. Chicken featured Joan's most famous film role as the damsel in distress. ("The part called for a brunette. I wore a wig that was made for Claudia Cardinale for a movie she made a few months prior to this.") A funny spoof of haunted house movies, it stars Don Knotts as Luther Heggs, a timid typesetter for his hometown newspaper, who dreams of being a reporter and winning the heart of Alma Parker (Staley). He gets his chance when he writes an article on the local haunted house, which has remained vacant for 20 years following some gruesome murders. His piece gets such strong reaction from the townsfolk that Luther's envious rival (Skip Homeier) suggests that he spend the night in the house. A terrified Luther does and he finds a hidden staircase, an organ that plays by itself and a bloodstained portrait. The town throws Luther a celebratory picnic in his honor but the son of the murdered couple and the house's owner Nick Simmons (Philip Ober) sues Luther and the newspaper for libel. During the course of the trial, Alma disappears and Luther inadvertently saves her and proves that Simmons was the killer. One of the film's clever running gags is that throughout the film somebody off-camera keeps saying 'Attaboy, Luther!' When asked about this, Joan reveals, "This was added in during post-production except for one live one in the crowd scene. It sounds like one of Don's ideas because it's off-the-wall and it worked so well."

The Ghost and Mr. Chicken remains one of Joan's most treasured working experiences due to Don Knotts. "I think Don is an incredible comedy actor," remarks Joan. "He is probably the greatest professional I ever worked with. He is an extremely sweet, gentle human being who is very diligent and works his proverbial off. Don is so prepared when he comes onto a set yet he is very flexible. He is open to changes and improv as long as it doesn't destroy the direction in which you are going. He is very careful in what you are doing and why we are going there." When asked to compare Knotts with Jerry Lewis, Joan opines, "A lot of Jerry Lewis' comedy was, 'throw it up against the wall and see what sticks.'

If it happened, he'd run with it. Don knows what works—he knows what he does best."

Joan got the role of Alma due to the film's director Alan Rafkin, who had directed Joan on some *Broadside* episodes. He suggested her for the lead to the producers. This helped Joan break free of just playing the kook, which Universal typed her as. She campaigned mightily for the role that Jean Seberg played in *Moment to Moment* (1965) but didn't get it because "I was seen as only being able to play sexy parts." *The Ghost and Mr. Chicken* proved to the studio that she could also play it straight successfully. "It was an *awesome* responsibility to play opposite Don Knotts," says Joan. "My character was not a comedic role. She couldn't be funny because everybody else in the film was a banana. My favorite scene is when mine and Don's characters meet to have lunch and he orders soup. That was the hardest sequence to keep a straight face through with his slurping and standing. And when you hear the crew behind the camera start to crack up, it does not help. The crew would start to snicker, Don would throw me a look, and I would lose it and be on the floor laughing."

As expected of a Don Knotts comedy, *The Ghost and Mr. Chicken* received mixed reviews. *Variety*, however, praised the film and particularly Joan: "Of the younger players, Miss Staley's dimpled

Don Knotts as a reporter (with Staley as his girlfriend) is honored by his townsfolk after surviving a night in the local haunted house in *The Ghost and Mr. Chicken* (Universal, 1966).

Joan Staley with her husband Dale Sheets on New Year's Eve 1995 (courtesy of Joan Staley).

cheek, pleasant voice, and expressive eyes promise more for the future." Alas, it was not meant to be as this was Joan's final film appearance. The film also turned out to be one of Universal's most profitable films in 1966. According to Joan's husband, former MCA executive Dale Sheets, "The film was budgeted at $700,000 and out-grossed everything at the studio at that time." The film grossed millions, mostly from drive-ins in the South and Midwest. It was not a hit in the big cities. Joan quips, "Contrary to everybody's belief, the country does not revolve just around New York and Los Angeles. There is a *whole* lot more people in between."

The Ghost and Mr. Chicken was Joan's last film for a number of reasons.

After the film's release, Joan was injured in a horseback riding accident. She broke her back and was out of commission for six months. She returned to work at Universal, who used her in a number of their series including *McHale's Navy, The Munsters, Ironside, Laredo,* and *Mission: Impossible.* She was also loaned out to Fox to play Annie Oakie opposite Cliff Robertson as Shame on a two-part episode of *Batman.* ("I wanted to do *Batman* badly because it was such a funny spoof and I knew it worked. The show was fun to do and I became huge in my daughter Sherrye's eyes because I got to work with Batman and Robin!") Soon after, Universal did not pick up Staley's option. Losing the contract did not bother Joan as much as it could have because she and Dale were making plans to wed. They've been married since 1967. "Dale contributed three children [Linda, Patti and Vickie] from a previous marriage and I had a daughter named Sherrye," states Joan. "And then we had three more together [Stephanie, Greg and Dina]. We don't have any stepchildren, we just have kids. Dale's ex-wife is a singer named Anita Gordon who dubbed Pamela Tiffin's singing voice in *State Fair* [1962]. Anita is a nice lady so we are all close. Now we have ten grandchildren and one great-grandchild."

After leaving Universal in 1969, Dale formed International Ventures Incorporated, a theatrical personal management company. Their first client was the late, great Mel Tormé. Their current list includes Vic Damone, Roger Williams, clarinetist Ken Peplowski (Benny Goodman's protégé), comic-impressionist Paul Boland, country vocalist Marlise, the Tormé family estate and Tennessee Ernie Ford Enterprises, whose television shows are enjoying a major revival on PBS. "I pretty much stopped acting around that time and joined him,' says Joan. "We had made one agreement that there would be no overnight locations. He had previously been married to someone in the business and it is very difficult to manage two careers. I don't know if the marriage we have could have withstood an acting career. The focus changes when you get married and both partners have to work at it 3000 percent. And if you're going to be the equal support emotionally of another human being, you have to be there and not on the road or on location. And that means working and sharing and doing everything that is necessary. It is what they used to call an old-fashioned marriage and that's what you have to give it—old-fashioned work, love and dedication." Joan is also a consumer activist and was the national director of FIT (Fight Inflation Together) for two years.

When asked if she misses acting, Joan replies in conclusion, "If a part was offered to me, of course I'd take it. I dedicated a lot of years to it and once you have it in your blood, the feeling never goes away. But would I give up what I do now for it—never."

Film Appearances

1948	The Emperor Waltz (Paramount) d. Billy Wilder.
1960	Ocean's Eleven (Warner Bros.) [uncredited bit] d. Lewis Milestone.
	Midnight Lace (Universal) [uncredited bit] d. David Miller.
1961	Gun Fight (United Artists) d. Edward L. Cahn.
	The Ladies' Man (Paramount) d. Jerry Lewis.
	Dondi (Allied Artists) d. Albert Zugsmith.
	Breakfast at Tiffany's (Paramount) d. Blake Edwards.
	Valley of the Dragons (Columbia) d. Edward Bernds.
1962	Cape Fear (Universal) d. J. Lee Thompson.
	Belle Sommers (Columbia) d. Elliot Silverstein.
1963	A New Kind of Love (Paramount) d. Melville Shavelson.
	Johnny Cool (United Artists) d. William Asher.
1964	Kisses for My President (Warner Bros.) d. Curtis Bernhardt.
	Roustabout (Paramount) d. John Rich.
1966	The Ghost and Mr. Chicken (Universal) d. Alan Rafkin.
	Gunpoint (Universal) d. Earl Bellamy.

Television Appearances

Studio One "A Funny Looking Kid" 5/19/58 CBS.
Playhouse 90 "The Great Gatsby" 6/26/58 CBS.
Perry Mason "The Case of the Corresponding Corpse" 9/20/58 CBS.
77 Sunset Strip "Secret Island" 12/4/59 ABC.
The Steve Allen Show 1/4/60 NBC.
Perry Mason "The Case of the Gallant Grafter" 2/6/60 CBS.
Bonanza "The Stranger" 2/27/60 NBC.
The Tab Hunter Show [recurring role as Elaine] 9/18/60 to 9/10/61 NBC.
Hawaiian Eye "Girl on a String" 11/16/60 ABC.
77 Sunset Strip "Once Upon a Caper" 2/10/61 ABC.
Checkmate "A Matter of Conscience" 2/18/61 CBS.
Bringing Up Buddy "The Aunts Have a Baby" 5/8/61 CBS.
The Asphalt Jungle "The Professor" 5/28/61 ABC.
The Lawless Years "The Miles Miller Story" 6/30/61 NBC.
The Dick Powell Show "Amos Burke: Who Killed Julie Greer?" 9/22/61 NBC.
The New Breed "Death of a Ghost" 10/17/61 ABC.
Bonanza "Burma Rarity" 10/22/61 NBC.
The Untouchables "Hammerlock" 12/21/61 ABC.
Frontier Circus "Lippizan" 12/28/61 CBS.
Father of the Bride "The Wedding" 2/2/62 CBS.
The Beachcomber [recurring role as Linda] 2/20/62 to 9/62 Synd.
The Adventures of Ozzie and Harriet "The Client's Daughter" 3/29/62 ABC.

Tales of Wells Fargo "To Kill a Town" 3/31/62 NBC.
Alcoa Premiere "All Clients Are Innocent" 4/17/62 ABC.
The 87th Precinct "Girl in the Cage" 4/30/62 NBC.
Hawaiian Eye "Location Shooting" 5/9/62 ABC.
The Dick Van Dyke Show "Jealousy!" 5/9/62 CBS.
Perry Mason "The Case of the Lonely Eloper" 5/26/62 CBS.
The Lively Ones [series regular as Charley] 7/26/62 to 9/13/62 NBC.
Alcoa Premiere "Whatever Happened to Miss Illinois?" 11/22/62 ABC.
The Adventures of Ozzie and Harriet "An Old Friend of June's" 12/13/62 ABC.
Dick Powell Theater "Colossus" 3/12/63 NBC.
Stoney Burke "Kelly's Place" 4/15/63 ABC.
The Real McCoys "The Partners" 5/26/63 CBS.
Alcoa Premiere "Five, Six, Pick Up Sticks" 5/30/63 ABC.
Burke's Law "Who Killed Wade Walker?" 11/15/63 ABC.
77 Sunset Strip [series regular as Hannah] 12/6/63 to 2/7/64 ABC.
The Joey Bishop Show "Ellie Gives Joey First Aid" 12/28/63 NBC.
The New Phil Silvers Show "Beauty and the Least" 1/11/64 CBS.
The Jack Benny Show (episode title unknown) 3/3/64 CBS.
Burke's Law "Who Killed Don Pablo? 5/1/64 ABC.
Kraft Suspense Theatre "Charlie, He Couldn't Kill a Fly" 5/7/64 NBC.
Broadside [series regular as Machinist's Mate Roberta Love] 9/20/64 to 9/5/65 ABC.
Kraft Suspense Theatre "Kill Me Only on July 20th" 6/17/65 NBC.
Laredo "Anybody Here Seen Billy?" 10/21/65 NBC.
The Virginian "Beyond the Border" 11/24/65 NBC.
Perry Mason "The Case of the Double-Entry Mind" 12/26/65 CBS.
The Clumbsies (unaired pilot) 1966 ABC.
McHale's Navy "The Wacky Wac" 1/18/66 ABC.
Gypsy [talk show guest] 2/1/66 Synd.
The Munsters "Cyrano de Munster" 2/24/66 CBS.
Gypsy [talk show guest] 4/12/66 Synd.
The Jean Arthur Show "A Slight Case of Music" 11/14/66 CBS.
Batman "Come Back, Shame" 11/30/66 ABC.
Batman "It's the Way You Play the Game" 12/1/66 ABC.
Rango "Gunfight at the K. O. Saloon" 2/3/67 NBC.
Pistols 'n' Petticoats "Harold's Double" 3/11/67 CBS.
Mission: Impossible "The Council" 11/19 & 11/26/67 CBS.
Adam-12 "Tell Him He Pushed Back a Little Too Hard" 3/29/69 ABC.
Adam-12 "Air Drop" 9/27/72 ABC.
Dallas "Mama Dearest" 12/31/82 CBS.

Also:

Climax, Maverick, Wagon Train (3), *SurfSide 6* (2), *Naked City, The Munsters* and *Ironside* (2).

Jill Haworth

Jill Haworth is a saucy, petite blonde with a wonderfully throaty voice and just a trace of an English accent. She was discovered in 1959 by producer-director Otto Preminger (or, as he was referred to, "Otto the Ogre") and appeared in his films *Exodus*, *The Cardinal*, and *In Harm's Way*. "When you make three films with Otto Preminger, you've made three films with *Otto Preminger* and no one dicks around with you after that," says Jill with a laugh. After appearing in the horror film *It!*, Jill temporarily abandoned movies for Broadway when Hal Prince cast her over Liza Minnelli and many other actresses in the coveted role of Sally Bowles in the hit musical *Cabaret*. Jill enjoyed great success as Sally and remained with the show for over two years. Returning to films, she played a hippie in *The Ballad of Andy Crocker* and a swinging Londoner in the horror opus *The Haunted House of Horror*. Haworth continued in the horror genre begrudgingly through the mid-seventies before returning to the stage. More recently, she has concentrated on doing voiceovers and was coaxed out of retirement in 1999 to play an ex-hippie mother in the independent film *Mergers & Acquisitions*.

Jill Haworth (pronounced Hahworth) was born in Sussex, England, on August 15. To get away from her unpleasant home life, she began taking ballet lessons at the prestigious Sadler Wells Ballet. Soon after, producer-director Otto Preminger came to England on a worldwide search for an unknown to play the role of the ill-fated Jewish girl in *Exodus* (1960). Haworth was asked to audition after Preminger saw her picture in a modeling magazine. "I had no interest in acting," reveals Jill. "I only auditioned just to get out of going to school. When it came down to the screen test, I remember competing against Christine Kauffman and three other actresses. I won the role and two weeks later I'm in Israel and people are asking me, 'How does it feel to be Jewish?'"

Exodus, based on the novel by Leon Uris, is Preminger's ambitious epic about the founding of Israel starring Paul Newman, Eva Marie Saint, Ralph Richardson, Peter Lawford, Lee J. Cobb and Sal Mineo. Though beautifully photographed and featuring an Academy Award–winning

Jill Haworth in *The Haunted House of Horror* (AIP, 1969).

score by Ernest Gold, the film is long (213 minutes) and ponderous with surprisingly little action. The supporting cast does well but Newman (as a Haganah leader) and Saint (as a nurse who joins the rebellion) are miscast. Jill disagrees: "I thought Newman was wonderful in the role. He is half Jewish. Personally, he is shy and very quiet. And he's an absolute gentleman."

Everybody agreed, however, that Jill gave an impressive performance as a noble young refugee who becomes a victim of Jewish-Arab hatred in Palestine. Her scenes with Mineo as a concentration camp survivor are touching and well-acted. Jill was voted Best Juvenile Actress by *Film Daily*, was nominated for a Golden Globe for "Most Promising Newcomers—Female" and was featured on the covers of *Life* and *Look* magazines. "Truthfully, I didn't know what I was doing," says Jill. "But my friendship with Sal Mineo helped me a lot in terms of my acting. We became more than just friends and remained very close until his death. Sal was the most gentle man I ever met in my life. He was also an incredible actor. His scenes with Lee J. Cobb and David Opatoshu are phenomenal."

Jill surprisingly never had any trouble with director Otto Preminger, who was also nicknamed Otto the Ogre because of the way he mistreated his actors. Though she saw him yell at other actors and fire crew members at the drop of a

Sal Mineo and Haworth as the ill-fated young Jewish couple in *Exodus* (United Artists, 1960).

hat, he was for the most part always respectful to Jill. "I experienced Mr. Preminger's ill temper a number of times but thankfully it was never directed towards me. He would fire prop men usually in public with 200 extras standing around. He kept you constantly on edge and the atmosphere on his sets was always very tense. Mr. Preminger would yell at people to get what he needed from them. That was part of his power. You never knew when he would lose his cool. All the actors would be in such a state, praying it wasn't their turn to get yelled at. You had to hit your marks and say your lines until he was satisfied. And, damn, sometimes it would take up to 35 takes and you'd hope you'd be able to get through it.

"I remember that he threw me off the set at my burial," continues Jill. "As they began throwing dirt on me, I panicked because I felt like I was being buried alive. I couldn't stop crying so Mr. Preminger asked me to leave the set. He once paid me the greatest compliment. I was having dinner with him and his soon-to-be wife Hope who was pregnant. Mr. Preminger said to me that he hoped they were having a girl and that she would be just like me. He could be very sweet."

After Jill's success in *Exodus*, Preminger signed her to an exclusive contract. He had an influence on her life as well as her career. "He insisted I live in New York to become more Americanized," remembers Jill. "I even had to dress a certain way. My mother was *always* coming to my defense. He wouldn't let me live in Hollywood because he didn't want me to become a 'starlet a-go-go.' During this time, I had no idea what was

"The Sixth Finger," an episode of the ABC-TV series *The Outer Limits*, featured David McCallum (*right*) as a man who becomes a super-intelligent being and Haworth as the girl who loved him.

going on. Remember, I was just a teenager so I was literally befuddled and bewildered. Mr. Preminger turned down *Lolita* [1962] but for some reason let me do three French movies and an episode of *The Outer Limits*." That episode was the classic "The Sixth Finger" and Jill's first excursion into the macabre ("I played the village idiot," jokes Jill). Haworth played the love interest of a dim-witted young coal miner (David McCallum) who volunteers to be used in an experiment to accelerate human evolution. After being transformed into a superior being of the future with a bulging cranium, sixth finger and mental prowess, he wants to rule the world but is returned to normal by his loving girlfriend.

Working for Preminger again in *The Cardinal* (1963), Jill is wasted in the small role of Lalage Menton, a novitiate nun who helps a priest (Tom Tryon) care for his dying pastor (Burgess Meredith) in one of the film's many vignettes. Again, Haworth was featured as part of an eclectic ensemble, which included John Huston as an outspoken cardinal, Carol Lynley as Tryon's ill-fated sister and Dorothy Gish as Tryon's mother. "I liked working with Tom Tryon," comments Jill. "He was very nice. I even liked John Huston and Burgess Meredith. I remember I had to wash Burgess' feet in one scene and he kept laughing because I was tickling him. The only person I did not like was Carol Lynley. I just did not understand people who couldn't get over themselves." Acting-wise, Jill fared better with *In Harm's Way* (1965). Preminger's WWII epic is set in Hawaii before and after the bombing of Pearl Harbor and focuses on the personal and professional conflicts of Navy men and their women. Preminger got expert performances from his all-star cast including John Wayne, Patricia Neal, Burgess Meredith, Paula Prentiss and Tom Tryon. Haworth plays her first sexy adult role as Ensign Annalee Dorne—a nurse engaged to a stuffy young lieutenant (Brandon DeWilde). She commits suicide after being raped by hard-drinking officer Kirk Douglas.

"My favorite scene is with Patricia Neal when she was plucking her eyebrows and I was off to get raped," Jill says chuckling. "I liked her a lot. She was a very experienced actress and knew what she was doing, unlike myself. I adored Brandon DeWilde. We were the youngest members of the cast so we would hide out together in the hotel—mostly trying to avoid my tutor. We were so excited when Bob Dylan came to the set one day. He was a big John Wayne fan. I also liked Kirk Douglas. Our first scene together was the rape scene. He was very nice to me and made it very easy." Jill, however, detested John Wayne, whom she describes as "the *meanest, nastiest* man with the worst attitude I ever worked with."

Jill's venom against the Duke stems from the scene where she meets Wayne and Douglas on a cruiser. Jill explains, "In the scene, Wayne had to walk up to Kirk Douglas and myself and hit his mark. I had to just stand there because it was a dolly shot. Wayne kept over-stepping the mark, causing his shadow to come down on me. I was like stone and didn't move a muscle. And that *son of a bitch* kept blaming me! This was my last shot of the film and I wasn't going to end this picture with Mr. Preminger yelling at me for something that wasn't my fault. Mr. Preminger never said a word to Wayne. Thankfully Kirk Douglas spoke up and said, 'I think John is off his mark.' It took another 15 takes before Wayne got it right."

As for working with Preminger, Jill comments, "I think he was a brilliant producer. He broke the blacklist by giving

Dalton Trumbo screen credit for writing *Exodus*. He made these epic films with thousands of extras and always came in on time and under budget. His crews came from all over the world to work with him and he'd fire some of them twice a day. But they still came back to work with him." After her contract to Preminger ended amicably in 1965 ("He had nothing for me to do"), Jill began working in episodic television. Though she appeared in such acclaimed series as *Twelve O'Clock High*, *The Rogues*, *Burke's Law*, *The F.B.I.* and *Run for Your Life*, Jill found her directors to be less than inspiring. "With television it was only hit your mark, say your lines, and hope the lighting guy gets you. There was no direction in terms of giving a performance."

Recalling some of her TV work, Jill comments, "I *loved* doing *The Rogues*. It was great getting the opportunity to work with David Niven and Charles Boyer. And I was smart enough to turn down *Hawaii Five-0* because Jack Lord had a horrible reputation. I also guest-starred on the last *Rawhide* episode with Brendon Boone and Charles Bronson. I adored Bronson. If it weren't for him, I'd have been on a plane back to New York. Nobody else talked to me. Clint Eastwood was the star of the show and he barely said two words to me off camera." Though most actresses enjoyed the Western genre, this series left a bad taste in Jill's mouth. Not only was she treated shabbily by Eastwood, the crew also ignored her. "During one scene, they left me alone in a four-horse buggy. The horses somehow got spooked and took off. I couldn't stop them and there were no stuntmen around to help me. So I jumped and luckily got only a few scrapes. In another scene, I wound up standing in this man-made pond in waist-deep water for about six hours doing retakes. I caught pneumonia and was in bed for close to two months!"

Jill returned to her native England in 1966 to co-star opposite Roddy McDowall in *It!*—her first movie excursion into the realm of horror. She plays an innocent young girl lusted after by disturbed museum curator Roddy McDowall who (à la Norman Bates) keeps his mummified mommy around the house. If that's not bad enough, he brings to life a Hebrew statue called the Golem and uses it to do away with his enemies. Despite the premise, director Herbert J. Leder did a decent job in creating suspense. "I only did this film because I needed the money," divulges Jill. "I hated everything about this movie—particularly what they did to my hair. They gave me an atrocious hairstyle for it. But I did like Roddy McDowall. He was very nice to work with. And with Roddy, what you see is what you got. He even brought me the poster for *It!* on the opening night of *Cabaret*. I couldn't believe they were going to release it. He signed it and put an S-h before the *It!* This film really was a piece of shit."

During the filming of *It!*, Jill was introduced to director Hal Prince, who was on his way to Germany to do research for his new show *Cabaret* (the musical version of Christopher Isherwood's *Goodbye to Berlin* stories). "Hal Prince asked if I could sing," recollects Jill, "and I responded, 'Louder than Merman.'" She flew to New York to audition and won the part on the spot. "Getting the opportunity to sing and dance in a Broadway musical was a chance of a lifetime. I was pretty brave accepting this role but I really had no idea what I was getting myself into. I learned so much about acting doing *Cabaret*. It was a fabulous experience. Hal Prince was wonderful to me. I

It! (Warner Bros., 1966) with Aubrey Richards, Haworth and Roddy McDowall as a crazy museum curator who revives the Golem.

enjoyed working with him thoroughly. But my favorite was Lotte Lenya. When I heard I would be working with her, I was terrified; I thought she would be this tough German woman, like the part she played in *From Russia with Love* [1963]. But she was great, and we became very good friends. We even shared the star's dressing room together."

Cabaret, starring Jill Haworth, Jack Gilford, Lotte Lenya, Bert Convy and Joel Grey, opened in New York on November 20, 1966. Jill recalls, "Everybody was terrified for me that night—my mother, Sal Mineo, Hal Prince, everybody! I didn't have time to be scared because I was concentrating on hitting my marks, singing my songs and hoping the damn sets wouldn't crash down on me."

Jill played the part of Sally Bowles well and received a Drama Critics Circle nomination for Most Promising Newcomer. Most of her reviews were in the line of George Oppenhiemer in *Newsday*, who described Jill as "a charmer, who can sing, dance, and act," and Norman Nadel in the *New York World Tribune*, who remarked that Jill succeeded as Sally because she had a "spontaneous kind of charm [and the] abundance of heart she throws into her performance." The exception was Walter Kerr of *The New York Times*, who maliciously commented, "Haworth ... is worth no more to the show than her weight in mascara." Haworth remained with *Cabaret* for two years and four months because "I wanted to spite Kerr. No, the real reason was because the cast and crew became like family to me. They were all marvelous to work with."

After leaving *Cabaret*, Jill co-starred in *The Ballad of Andy Crocker* (1969), the first made-for-TV movie to address the Vietnam War. Haworth played a California hippie who picks up a Vietnam veteran (Lee Majors) at the airport. Still attired in his uniform, Majors is taken by Jill to a party where he is abruptly ejected because the other partygoers are uncomfortable doing drugs around him. Returning to his hometown, things get worse for Majors who finds his girlfriend (Joey Heatherton) married to someone else, his business almost bankrupt due to his partner, and hostility from some of his former friends. This film made a powerful statement about the problems Vietnam veterans faced returning to society. It took a compassionate view of the vets and was not a "psycho Vietnam vet" film with violence and gore, which was to become the norm in the early seventies.

Jill returned to England later in 1969 to do her second thriller *The Haunted House of Horror* (a.k.a. *Horror House*)—or as the critics nicknamed it, "Haunted House a-Go-Go." ("My agents at ICM thought this would be a good career move. It wasn't!") Mini-skirted Jill and perennial teenager Frankie Avalon are part of a bunch of young swingers who hold a séance in a supposedly haunted house. One of them turns up murdered and the survivors begin suspecting each other. When Scotland Yard begins snooping, the teens return to the scene of the crime to flush out the killer. "Frankie didn't want to do this film either but he was under contract to [AIP]. But we just made the best of the situation and had a fabulous time working together. He has a great sense of humor. And you *needed* one doing this film. They housed us with the crew in this old, supposedly haunted hotel in Southport, England. The conditions were horrible. There weren't any private bathrooms and you even had to take your own toilet paper to use the john! Frankie and I just kept laughing. Sometimes you need to laugh to get through unpleasant things."

Speaking of unpleasant things, Jill's characters faced a number of disturbing situations in her horror films to come. She is strangled by a maniac in *Horror on Snape Island* (1972), pitchforked to death in *Home for the Holidays* (1972) and is accosted by her mutated boyfriend and goes into a catatonic state of shock in *The Mutations* (1973), directed by Jack Cardiff. "I never wanted to do horror movies," admits Jill. "But when acting is your livelihood, you sometimes have to accept unwanted roles just to survive. I remember in *Horror on Snape Island* my character stumbles upon five dead bodies and I had to say with a straight face, 'Ooh, the police aren't going to like this.' The crew just kept laughing every time I said it. And I was never paid for doing *The Mutations*. Jack Cardiff was a lovely man but Donald Pleasence spooked me. He and Tom Baker would always wander off into a pub and the crew would have to go look for them. They used real freaks who lived together on a ranch in Florida to play the mutations from Donald's mad experiments. There was a guy named Popeye who popped his eyeballs out and a lizard woman. I thought they were being exploited but they seemed to be enjoying themselves—and they got paid!"

Though Jill dismisses her horror movies, James O'Neill (writing in *Terror on Tape*) praised the uncut version of *Horror of Snape Island* (a.k.a. *Tower of Evil*) as being "A gory, ahead-of-its-time slash flick ... complete with nude sex scenes; bloody, imaginative murders; a

Haworth and Frankie Avalon played swinging London teenagers out for kicks in *The Haunted House of Horror* (AIP, 1969).

disfigured, Jason-like killer, and a twist ending."

Home for the Holidays was directed John Llewellyn Moxey, who achieves pure terror with this made-for-TV film as he did with *The Night Stalker*. The film (from a script by Joseph Stefano) stars Walter Brennan as a dying old man who summons his four daughters back home after he begins to suspect that his new wife (Julie Harris) is poisoning him. With the Christmas season upon them, the reunited siblings (played by Haworth, Sally Field, Eleanor Parker and Jessica Walter) are brutally butchered one by one. "We were the most disparate group of sisters ever to hit the screen," jokes Jill. "None of us looked anything alike. Sally Field and I had star billing and we got along famously. She is a serious actress and was taking classes at the Actor's Studio. She also had a great sense of humor and a mouth worse than mine. Julie Harris is a great actress and it was an honor to work with her. Jessica Walter was very serious about her acting. And Eleanor Parker *always* had to make a grand entrance onto the set. Cross-reference everything I said about John Wayne and that's my opinion about Eleanor."

On television during the seventies, Jill also had the opportunity to work for a young director named Steven Spielberg on an episode of *The Psychiatrist*, starring Roy Thinnes. "I never imagined Spielberg would become such a phenomenal director from working with him on this show," remarks Jill. "I played a woman married to an impotent Indian who could only get it up if we went back to the teepee. All I knew was that Spielberg was the only person on the set not doing drugs because I was the only *other* person not doing drugs. Remember that this was during the days of *Easy Rider*."

After a few intermittent film and theater roles in the late seventies and eighties (she received rave reviews for the national tours of *Bedroom Farce* and *Butterflies Are Free*), Jill quietly dropped from the limelight. Her last screen credit is the comedy *Strong Medicine* (1981). She returned to London in the early eighties to work in the theater and on programs for the BBC. Today Jill lives comfortably with her gracious and proper mother on New York's Upper East Side.

She still acts, but mostly doing voiceovers for television and commercials. However, she recently completed a role in *Mergers & Acquisitions* after an 18-year retirement.

Mergers & Acquisitions (2000) is an independent production starring Brian Vander Ark (lead singer of The Verve Pipe), Steven Chester Prince, Lee Tergesen of *Oz* and Martha Byrne of *As the World Turns*. The role in the film that enticed Jill to return to the big screen was that of Mrs. Richards, an out-of-control ex-hippie (described as being "a few sandwiches short of a picnic") with two sons—Larry, an uptight wealthy banker (Vander Ark), and Del, a free-spirited magazine writer (Prince). The film was produced, directed and written by Mitchell Bard, whose previous films include the award-winning short *Soup or Salad?* and the feature *The Dry Season*.

Mergers & Acquisitions (Lopsided Pictures, 2000) features Jill Haworth as an eccentric ex-radical who returns to her home with a black eye after struggling with the police during a sit-in at town hall (photo by and courtesy of Liz Hanellin).

Regarding Jill's performance, Bard exclaims, "I think Jill is fantastic! The feedback regarding Jill has all been positive. She really threw herself into the role. The film has a weird mix. Steven Prince gives a very natural performance. A lot of the other characters that surround him are a bit over-the-top—his boss, his brother and the operative who is trying to take over the magazine. The mother also falls into this category. Though the mother is losing her mind, there is humor at the expense of the fact that she is losing it. It required some fearlessness on the part of Jill to throw herself into this. And I have to say, considering it's been so long since Jill has been in front of the camera, I think that Jill showed a lot of courage. She just said, 'Okay. This is a big character and I'm going to play it big.' I think she did very well." Jill remarks, "I was so nervous about doing this film. I read for it on a Saturday and was called that Monday night to report to the set the next day. Looking back, it was a totally different but *wonderful* experience for me. They shot my scenes in a couple of days at this house on Long Island. Mitchell Bard treated me wonderfully! I hope to do more independent films."

Film Appearances

1959   The Thirty-Nine Steps (Great Britain, 20th Century–Fox) [uncredited bit] d. Ralph Thomas.
1960   Exodus (United Artists) d. Otto Preminger.
1962   À cause, à cause d'une femme (France) d. Michael Deville.
        Les Mystères de Paris (France/Italy, Unidex) d. Andre Hunebelle.
1963   Your Shadow Is Mine (France/Italy, Continental) d. Andre Michel.
        The Cardinal (Columbia) d. Otto Preminger.
1965   In Harm's Way (Paramount) d. Otto Preminger.
1966   It! (Great Britain, Warner Bros.) d. Herbert J. Leder.
1969   The Ballad of Andy Crocker (TV-movie) d. George McCowan.
        The Haunted House of Horror/Horror House (Great Britain, Tigon/AIP) d. Michael Armstrong.
1972   Tower of Evil/Horror on Snape Island (Great Britain, Grenadier Films) d. Jim O'Connolly.
        Home for the Holidays (TV-movie) d. John Llewellyn Moxey.
1973   The Mutations (Great Britain, Columbia) d. Jack Cardiff.
1981   Strong Medicine (Film Forum) d. Richard Foreman.
1988   Light Years (France, Miramax) [voice only] d. René Laloux.
2000   Mergers & Acquisitions (Lopsided Pictures) d. Mitchell Bard.

Television Appearances

The Outer Limits "The Sixth Finger" 10/14/63 ABC.
Twelve O'Clock High "The Sound of Distant Thunder" 10/16/64 ABC.
Twelve O'Clock High "To Heinie, with Love" 2/5/65 ABC.
The Rogues "Mr. White's Christmas" 4/4/65 NBC.
Burke's Law "Who Killed the Card?" 5/5/65 ABC.
Twelve O'Clock High "The Hot Shots" 10/18/65 ABC.
The Long Hot Summer "Home Is a Nameless Place" 10/21/65 ABC.
The F.B.I. "To Free My Enemy" 10/24/65 ABC.
Twelve O'Clock High "Runway in the Dark" 11/1/65 ABC.
Run for Your Life "The Savage Season" 11/8/65 NBC.
Rawhide "Duel at Daybreak" 11/16/65 CBS.
Girl Talk [talk show guest] 6/8/66 Synd.
Password [celebrity contestant] 2/20 to 2/24/67 NBC.
The 22nd Annual Tony Awards (special) [performer] 4/21/68 CBS.
Pay Cards! [celebrity contestant] 9/30/68 Synd.
Match Game [celebrity panelist] 10/14 to 10/18/68 NBC.
The Dating Game [celebrity contestant] 3/8/69 ABC.

The Donald O'Connor Show [talk show guest] 4/4/69 Synd.
The Most Deadly Game "Witches' Sabbath" 10/17/70 ABC.
Mission: Impossible "My Friend, My Enemy" 10/24/70 CBS.
The Virginia Graham Show [talk show guest] 12/24/70 Synd.
Bonanza "The Reluctant American" 2/14/71 NBC.
Four in One: The Psychiatrist "The Longer Trail" 2/24/71 NBC.
The 25th Annual Tony Awards (special) [performer] 3/31/71 CBS.
The F.B.I. "A Gathering of Sharks" 1/14/73 ABC.
Baretta "Under the City" 11/3/76 ABC.
Vega$ "The Eleventh Event" 1/17/79 ABC.

Pamela Tiffin

"Mine was a kind of Cinderella story," says Pamela Tiffin. "I was discovered while visiting friends on the Paramount lot." An exquisite brunette, this former model became one of the early sixties' most popular actresses. She won critical raves for her performances in her first two films, *Summer and Smoke* and *One, Two, Three*. But Hollywood typed Pamela as the marriage-minded ingenue out to trap herself a husband in a string of drive-in films aimed at the youth market—*Come Fly with Me*, *For Those Who Think Young*, *The Lively Set*, and *The Pleasure Seekers*. With her sultry looks and seductive, whispery voice, Pamela instilled in her romance-seeking characters an endearing flightiness which helped make these films better than expected. Her reward was more mature roles in *The Hallelujah Trail* with Burt Lancaster and *Harper* with Paul Newman. Though Pamela proved she had the talent and poise to become a superstar, she fled to Rome in 1967 to escape an unhappy marriage. As a sexy blonde, she starred opposite some of Italy's top leading men (including Marcello Mastroianni, Vittorio Gassman and Franco Nero) but her films were rarely released in the U.S. As early as 1972, fans were writing to movie magazines asking, "Whatever became of Pamela Tiffin?"

Pamela Tiffin was born Pamela Tiffin Wonso on Oct. 13 in Oklahoma City. She is the only child of retired architect Stanley Wonso and his late wife Grace. She began modeling at age 13 ("to save money for my college education") and, after graduating from high school, she relocated to New York to pursue her career. Soon she became a *Vogue* cover girl and one of New York's top fashion models, earning up to $1,500 a week. While on Thanksgiving vacation in 1960, she went with her mother to visit friends in Los Angeles, which led to a chance encounter with movie producer Hal B. Wallis. "Two boys that I knew rented horses to the movies," remembers Pamela. "I accompanied them to the Paramount lot and we had lunch in the commissary. I got the thrill of my life because I saw John Wayne. He was enormous and sauntering—I was dazzled. An associate of Hal Wallis spotted me and brought me to Mr. Wallis' office, where they offered me a screen test for *Summer and Smoke*

Horst Buchholtz and Pamela Tiffin as the kooky, young lovers (who drive James Cagney to exclaim, "I'd rather be in hell with my back broken!") in *One, Two, Three* (United Artists, 1961).

(1961). I told them it wouldn't work out because I didn't know how to act. I didn't want to embarrass myself. Mr. Wallis said, 'I think you can act. Recite something.' So the only thing I could think of was *The Raven* and *The Gettysburg Address*. It was a very peculiar scene in that little office of his. I finally agreed to a screen test because I liked Tennessee Williams' work. After I returned to New York, they notified me that I got the part." Unbeknownst to Tiffin, while she was in Hollywood director Billy Wilder had spotted her in a lingerie ad in *The New York Times Magazine* and had his agent trying to track her down in New York.

Debuting in *Summer and Smoke* as a sweet young girl who innocently steals doctor Laurence Harvey away from spinster Geraldine Page, Tiffin awed the critics with her natural beauty and talent. But it was her superior performance that same year in Billy Wilder's frenetic comedy *One, Two, Three* that brought her real attention. Pamela won raves as the impetuous, scatterbrained Scarlett Hazeltine who (while on vacation in West Berlin) sneaks across the border and marries a Communist (Horst Buchholtz) to the consternation of her guardian (James Cagney). Her antics elicited from Cagney's character (Coca-Cola's man in West Berlin) the comment, "I'd rather be in hell with my back broken." Pamela's performance earned her two Golden Globe nominations from the Hollywood Foreign Press for "Best Supporting Actress" and "Most Promising Newcomers—Female." Theater owners in *The Motion Picture Herald* voted her a "Star of Tomorrow." James Cagney compared Pamela's beauty and comic flair to that of Carole Lombard, Kay Kendall and Lucille

Ball. And Billy Wilder commented to *Esquire*, "She's another Audrey Hepburn ... she comes off on the screen even better than she looks and in this case that's saying a lot."

"James Cagney was gracious, kind, and warm," recalls Pamela. "He even went out of his way to help me with my acting. I thought Horst Buchholz was really attractive but he's naughty and irrepressible. He loves to act, the way Jim Carrey loves to act. They are compelled and cannot stop themselves. Cagney didn't like Horst's style. An 'old hoofer' as he called himself, Cagney saw all the tricks actors used to get time and attention. That's what he saw Horst doing and he didn't like it. But Horst wasn't arrogant—he was enthusiastic! If you are a director, you want someone that eager. However, in that context, Mr. Wilder and I.A.L. Diamond [fresh from winning the Academy Award for writing *The Apartment*] had written the script and you change no word. It was like musical notation. Somehow I knew and understood a written article and preposition had to be that one. Horst didn't. Mr. Wilder saw that Horst was always trying to improve on the script and he didn't like it. But I didn't get involved. I just minded my own business like my parents taught me." Most critics feel Tiffin gives her best performance in *One, Two, Three* and Pamela agrees. "Mr. Wilder made me feel very comfortable. I didn't feel like I was acting. I felt I *was* Scarlett. The best directors are unobtrusive."

Pamela began her third movie, *State Fair* (1962), before her first two films were released. A remake of the 1945 classic, it stars Tiffin, Pat Boone, Bobby Darin, Ann-Margret, Tom Ewell and Alice Faye. "The studio [20th Century–Fox] wanted us to do this," states Tiffin. "Though I didn't see the original or the musical version, I knew they were supposed to be lovely and charming. So it was pointless to do another *State Fair*. I thought, 'I wouldn't want to go see it.' But the studios had scripts and contract players, so to keep everyone honored and busy that's what they did. Pat Boone played my brother and he seemed to be very comfortable in the role. I had just returned from Europe doing *One, Two, Three* so playing this country girl Margie seemed light years away from Scarlett.

"While doing *State Fair*, the one person I didn't understand was Bobby Darin," continues Pamela. "He played my romantic interest. He was a wonderful actor and singer. But at the time, I thought he was just a tough, cocky guy from New York. Mother was worried about his entourage—they were direct and flirtatious. She didn't want me near the music business crowd. I feel guilty because I decided I just didn't like Bobby Darin. Who in the world was I not to like him? He was friendly and I wasn't as friendly as I should have been."

In real life, Pamela mirrored the sweet ingenues she convincingly played on screen. She lived quietly in New York and attended college classes between films. She was never fodder for the movie columnists at the time, unlike some of her contemporaries (i.e., Tuesday Weld, Sandra Dee, Connie Stevens and Carol Lynley). In 1962, Pamela met and married *Esquire* editor Clay Felker. She prepared to retire from acting but her husband encouraged her to keep working. "After I married, I had in my mind that I was not going to do any more movies," comments Pamela. "I was going to be Clay's wife and have babies. I was very romantic. I had dreams of moonlight and roses all the time. But I was under contract to Hal Wallis, the Mirisch Brothers and 20th Century–Fox, so I had to keep working.

The beach film *For Those Who Think Young* (United Artists, 1964) starring James Darren and Pamela Tiffin as United Artists' answer to Frankie and Annette.

I was never smart enough to plan a career and say 'this is a good movie' or 'that's a good script.' I was passive. And in my passivity, of course, people took advantage of me. I never wanted to do teenage movies. I wanted to do more Tennessee Williams and work with Billy Wilder again."

"I tried to get better roles," continues Pamela. "Believe it or not, John Sturges wanted me to play a Japanese woman in a movie called *A Girl Named Tamiko* [1962] for Hal Wallis. I spent hours in makeup and did look Japanese. I thought, 'I'm under contract, I'll do whatever they want, but this is rather ridiculous!' Luckily they got France Nuyen to replace me. I auditioned for Otto Preminger for the role of the priest's sister in *The Cardinal* [1963]. Carol Lynley got that part. Preminger frightened me to death. I knew he would. He kept yelling, 'No! No! No!' I thought, 'This isn't for me because I can't do anything right for him.' Another film that I didn't get was *The Group* [1966]. Jessica Walter got the part that I wanted. They told me I was *too* funny. I was devastated. But Sidney Lumet [the director] did write me a kind note. A lot of people told me I was best for comedy, not drama. They were probably right."

Despite Pamela's accolades, the best Hollywood could offer her was the ingenue role in a series of popular though forgettable films aimed at the youth audience. She was quickly becoming the brunette Sandra Dee. In *Come Fly with*

Me (1963), Pamela, Dolores Hart and Lois Nettleton portray stewardesses out to land rich husbands while working the New York to Paris and Vienna routes. As the innocent virgin, Pamela lands pilot Hugh O'Brian. "I remember Hugh O'Brian was always busy being a playboy," says Pamela with a laugh. "He played a playboy in the movie and lived it fully in real life! Dolores Hart and I had some nice conversations. She is a warm, decent and vulnerable woman. Dolores had some unhappy experiences in love matters. And if I'm not mistaken, she was ending one up at the time. She told me the story and was still very upset about it. She said she was going to enter a convent. And at that time I couldn't understand it. I said, 'Oh, but you don't want to, Dolores!' Now I understand it. So there she is." Even in romantic drivel like this, Pamela was still receiving good notices. *Variety* raved, "Sometimes one performance can save a picture, and in *Come Fly with Me*, it's an engaging and infectious one by Pamela Tiffin."

In 1964, Pamela reluctantly teamed with James Darren in the beach movie *For Those Who Think Young* and the hot rod film *The Lively Set*. *For Those Who Think Young* was the first of the many *Beach Party* knock-offs released between 1964 and 1966. Directed by Leslie H. Martinson, the film had a major tie-in with Pepsi-Cola. In fact, the title itself was Pepsi's slogan at that time. In the film, set at Oceancrest College, rich boy James Darren pursues poor-but-proud coed Pamela Tiffin, whose uncles (Paul Lynde and Woody Woodbury) are putting her through school. When not surfing or lounging on the beach, Darren, Tiffin and their friends (Bob Denver, Nancy Sinatra, Claudia Martin, Susan Hart, etc.) can be found at the Silver Palms Club, a campus hangout where Woodbury, Lynde and Tina Louise perform. "I really didn't get to know any of those people very well except for Nancy Sinatra," says Pamela. "Her then-husband Tommy Sands was away on tour. We were both young wives alone missing our husbands. Leslie Martinson knew this and he would take me back to his house for dinner with him and his wife. I remember he had a little sports car and we would drive through Beverly Hills. He is a very sweet man."

Though the mainstream press didn't appreciate the beach films (one critic commented, "*For Those Who Think Young* is for those who think stupid!") the film is lightweight yet charming. The major complaint is that there weren't enough scenes on the beach. Even still, the film was a box office hit. "We shot the beach scenes all in one day," recalls Pamela. "We were there from very early in the morning to late at night." Darren and Tiffin look great in swimsuits and make a fetching couple while Tina Louise is a knockout as a math-tutoring ex-stripper. ("Tina Louise was one of the most beautiful females I've ever seen in my life. Her beauty was unearthly and just a miracle of nature.") But it is Bob Denver as Darren's beatnik buddy who steals the film with his performance of the tribal surf stomp "Ho Daddy," with a crowd of beach boys and girls dancing around him.

The Lively Set (with songs by Bobby Darin) features Pamela as a persistent coed who pursues James Darren even though he prefers his hot rods to babes. "James Darren was very jazzy and flirty," recalls Pamela. "He was married at the time. I didn't know anything about his singing career. Another actress warned me about singers and that made me jumpy. I was very circumspect around him." Considering that she made films with Darren and Pat Boone and was

Pamela Tiffin (*center*) with Carol Lynley and Ann-Margret in *The Pleasure Seekers* (20th Century–Fox, 1964). "I didn't want to do *The Pleasure Seekers*. 20th Century–Fox suspended me and no other studio could hire me until I gave in."

under contract to Hal Wallis, it is surprising that Tiffin rejected working with Elvis Presley. She turned down *Blue Hawaii* (1961), *Girls! Girls! Girls!* (1962), and *Fun in Acapulco* (1963), because "*Everybody* told me not to do Elvis Presley movies. [Director] Peter Glenville and Dolores Hart in particular poisoned my mind against it. I felt obligated to do these films but Mr. Wallis said it was up to me. Here again I listened to other people. I even met Elvis. I thought he was adorable and an amazing gentleman. But I still didn't do the films. I regret it deeply."

Pamela's next film sent her back to Europe—this time Madrid. In *The Plea-*sure Seekers* (1964), Pamela, Ann-Margret and Carol Lynley go looking for fun and romance in Spain. This was a remake (with songs) of the studio's 1954 hit *Three Coins in the Fountain* updated to give it a "with it" 1964 feel. Ann-Margret flips her mane as a singer who falls for poor Spanish doctor Andre Lawrence while Lynley pouts over being ignored by her married boss Brian Keith. As the "naïve" one, Tiffin's character quips, "I know everything about Spain but Spanish," and nabs rich playboy Tony Franciosa in the process. "I didn't want to do *The Pleasure Seekers*," reveals Tiffin. "It was too frivolous and not honest enough for me. Fox suspended me and no other

In *The Pleasure Seekers* (20th Century–Fox), amorous playboy Tony Franciosa puts the moves on virginal Tiffin.

studio could hire me until I gave in. However, I was a good sport and went along. But I was embarrassed! When you're young, you have definite tastes and predilections. Now I find this and my other teenage movies adorable and innocent. We were *all* innocent back then.

"Making *The Pleasure Seekers* was strange. Nobody connected with anyone. When working people are very competitive or are only after money, it is agony to work with them because they bring their hang-ups to the set. I tried to make friends with Ann-Margret and Carol Lynley. But I think both of them at that time weren't interested in friendship with another woman. Carol was especially reserved and aloof. In retrospect, I recall that she just had a baby and therefore was entitled to be private. I don't know what Gardner McKay's problem was but he didn't talk to any of us. Tony Franciosa was very hostile—especially to Jean Negulesco [the director]. During a car scene, he got mad at Negulesco and drove off with me in the car. He drove for over two hours at breakneck speed out of Toledo, Spain. I thought he was going to kill us both! During another scene, Negulesco wanted Tony to change his tie. He took Negulesco, who had to be near 70, by the neck and threatened him. Brian Keith, though, was very nice. I never spoke with Gene Tierney because I was in such awe of her." The competitiveness between the actors continued well after the film was complete: A billing war erupted between the "stars." When Tiffin's husband learned that she was going to be billed fifth (after Ann-Margret, Franciosa, Lynley and McKay), he wanted to fight the studio, but Pamela talked him out of it. She just wanted to put this experience behind her. "I didn't understand that billing represented your current status. I didn't think it mattered where actors' names appeared because we were all in the movie anyway. Now I understand why it was such an issue."

Pamela began her next film *The Hallelujah Trail* (1965) one day after production wrapped on *The Pleasure Seekers*. Directed by John Sturges, *The Hallelujah Trail* (filmed in Cinerama) is a big-budget but disappointing Western satire about the temperance movement in the Old West starring Burt Lancaster, Lee Remick and Jim Hutton. "I really enjoyed making *The Hallelujah Trail* in Gallup, New Mexico, because of Burt Lancaster," Pamela says fondly. "There was something so charming and radiant about Burt. You get bored out there in the desert. One day we started eating watermelon and we ate it until we both got absolutely sick. It was one of those dumb things actors do. I couldn't get my corset on and he couldn't get his uniform on. We had to do this scene where we had to carry blankets. I couldn't breathe with all that liquid in me. I was fainting and Burt was vomiting. Finally John Sturges yelled, 'What the hell have you two been doing?!' He really didn't get mad. The atmosphere on this set was very relaxed."

After playing a number of ingenue roles, Pamela finally got a chance to act sexy and sophisticated in *Harper* (1966) starring Paul Newman. She portrayed Lauren Bacall's stepdaughter Miranda, whose father has disappeared. As a sex-starved heiress, Tiffin almost steals the film with her seductive dance in a bikini atop a diving board. Newman (whom Pamela describes as being "attractive, professional, and a car lover") played a private detective hired by icy paralyzed equestrienne Bacall to find her missing husband. As the hated daughter and stepmother, Tiffin and Bacall have a number of great catty moments, which were superbly acted. After hearing that Tiffin's Miranda has been rejected by her husband's bodyguard (Robert Wagner), Bacall's Elaine maliciously quips, "I should think you'd be accustomed to not being loved by now." Miranda responds, "I love your *wrinkles*. I revel in them." When an unmoved Elaine learns that her husband has been murdered, she calls out to Miranda in a singsong voice, "Miranda! *Mommy has something to tell you!*"

"I was very impressed with Lauren Bacall but she was very tense and stand offish," remarks Pamela. "Since Paul Newman likes to rehearse, we gathered around a long table and ran lines for a week, if not more. Everyone was there except Lauren Bacall because she wanted to be the *big* movie star. I couldn't be angry at her or feel slighted because I thought she was fascinating!"

After filming *Harper*, Tiffin went to Italy to star in the three-part *Oggi, domani e dopodomani* (1965). Each segment starred Marcello Mastroianni with a different leading lady—Tiffin, Virna Lisi and Catherine Spaak. Pamela played the flighty wife of Marcello Mastroianni, who tries to sell her into a harem in the segment titled "La moglie bionda." She was Mastroianni's first American co-star. To prepare for her role, Pamela took a crash course in Italian at Berlitz. "This was my second film where I was sexy so (being young and foolish) I was *thrilled* with all the attention I was getting," says Pamela. "When Carlo Ponti offered me this film, it was with the stipulation that I go blonde. In Hollywood, they always asked me to be blonde and I always said no because in the Midwest nice girls didn't dye their hair. So in Italy they bleached only the front of it because I said the back is mine—brunette. I was surprised that I enjoyed being a blonde so much that I promptly dyed all of my

Harper (Warner Bros., 1966) featured Tiffin as the sexually frustrated Miranda whose father disappears.

Tiffin emerged as a sexy blonde opposite Marcello Mastroianni in *Kiss the Other Sheik* (MGM, 1968).

hair." This film was never released as intended in the U.S. Instead, Tiffin's segment was released as *Kiss the Other Sheik* in 1968.

Tiffin's new sexy blonde persona included playing the Jean Harlow role in the 1966 Broadway revival of *Dinner at Eight* for which she won the Theatre World Award for "Most Promising Newcomer." However, she missed her opportunity for major stardom. Shortly after the play closed in 1967, Pamela relocated to Italy to escape an unhappy marriage. "To my great disillusionment, I found that my husband Clay liked that I worked, and that hurt me," whispers Pamela. "So that became a problem because the more he encouraged me, the more I felt unloved and rejected. I felt so alone and manipulated, I went to Italy to escape everybody. It was my running away from home. And of course, that was stupid on my part. I abandoned a career that deserved attention and nurturing. And regardless of agents and managers' presence in my life, their interest in me was not as devoted and supportive as they professed. None of them ever acted as long-term planners."

Pamela returned to the U.S. briefly in 1969 and resided at the Chateau Marmont in Hollywood. She returned to the stage in Harold Clurman's production of *Uncle Vanya*. It was backstage one night when she met actress Tisha Sterling, who Pamela describes as being "probably the most beautiful actress from my age group at that time. She was a simply stunning woman." While in Hollywood, Pamela also appeared in the first episode of the TV series *The Survivors* starring Lana Turner and George Hamilton ("He was delightful and fun!"). It was one of her few excursions into television. "I did this only because of producer Bill Goetz," Pamela says. "He was a very elegant, marvelous man. I liked him a lot. One day, he and Lana Turner were arguing and she slapped him. She was an old-time movie star—spoiled and very tough. A week later, I thought, 'Where's Bill?' I was the only one who didn't know that Lana wanted him fired. Gentleman that he was, Bill withdrew from the project."

After her 1969 divorce from Clay Felker, Pamela relocated permanently to Italy. But before she moved she made a stopover in Texas to film the comedy *Viva Max!* (1969), with Peter Ustinov and Jonathan Winters. She played a student activist who sides with Ustinov's inept Mexican general (Ustinov recaptures the Alamo, replete with a busload of tourists). "This is such an amusing film but it should have been funnier," comments Pamela. "It was based on Jim Lehrer's book, which was a political farce containing wonderful jokes, but they removed all the controversy. We shot most of it on location in Texas. The cast became friends and we'd all hang out together when we weren't filming. I enjoyed working with Jonathan Winters, who is a national treasure. And Peter Ustinov's courtliness, grace and wit made those months indelibly fixed in my memory."

While working in Rome, Tiffin co-starred with some of Italy's most popular leading men including Ugo Tognazzi,

Tiffin in her "hippie period" during the early seventies, while she was living in Italy.

Nino Manfredi, Vittorio Gassman, Lando Buzzanca and Franco Nero. Commenting on some of her co-stars, Pamela says, "I did a comedy called *L'Archangelo* [1969] with Vittorio Gassman. He was especially delightful and became a sort of big miracle brother to me. Lando Buzzanca in particular was not a decent man. We worked together on *Il vichingo venuto dal Sud* [1971]. He bet the crew that he could 'conquer' me within a week. I finally had to go to the producers to get him to leave me alone." Though Buzzanca was one of her least favorite co-stars, the light comedy *Il vichingo venuto dal Sud* is one of her favorite films. ("This was a farcical comedy contrasting Nordic and Mediterranean attitudes about men and women and life and love.") Pamela played a student who works as a porno actress to pay her tuition. She falls in love with shoe salesman Buzzanca but neglects to tell him how she earns a living. "This movie was filmed in Amsterdam during the winter but we were pretending it was summer. I would be wearing lightweight cotton dresses in 30-degree weather. I was always freezing. Between takes, the crew would wrap me in blankets. I remember filming a picnic scene with Lando where we were supposed to roll around on the soft ground. Except the ground was frozen and hard as a rock!"

Though Pamela played a porno actress, a body double was used for her nude scenes. Unlike many other young actresses at that time, Pamela was very reluctant about taking her clothes off in front of the camera. However, *Playboy* got hold of a few topless shots of her and ran them in a pictorial called "A Toast to Tiffin." "I was offered a film role that required nudity," recalls Pamela. "A supposed trusted woman friend of mine took semi-nude photos of me to see how I looked. I was very uncomfortable so I turned the film down. When the photos turned up in *Playboy*, I was furious. For years *Playboy* was after me to appear nude. They even offered me $100,000! But I always said no. I never filed a lawsuit because I didn't want to bring attention to it. I ignored the whole incident but even today it still makes me angry and sick! It wasn't me or my career."

In 1973, Tiffin appeared in her second Western, *Los Amigos*, which was retitled *Deaf Smith and Johnny Ears* for American audiences. Set during the time of upheaval in Texas, the film stars Anthony Quinn as a deaf mercenary and Franco Nero as his partner Johnny Ears. When an ex-general attempts to install himself as dictator, the Texas president Sam Houston calls on Deaf Smith for help. Tiffin played a whore with a heart of gold, who falls in love with Nero. "I so enjoyed making this movie," declares Pamela enthusiastically. "I love Westerns because I love nature and that kind of folklore. Anthony Quinn is larger than life and is attractive in a primordial kind of way. He was very easy to work with. Franco Nero is very tall, very handsome and very decent. He had the impact in Europe that Paul Newman had in America."

Pamela was especially fond of Nero because he helped her out during a love scene where she didn't have a top on. "I said to Franco, 'I don't want my bosom to show.' He understood and we thought how could we outsmart the director. We found a way to hold each other very tight or he'd have an elbow or an arm in the way. I can remember the frustrated director shouting in Italian, 'Do it again!' We'd respond, 'Well, we just did it!' Sometimes actors band together in a wonderful way. I'll always be grateful to him."

Tiffin's final movie *E se per Caso una Mattina* (1974) features one of her favorite roles. "I did this film for free as a favor to a friend of an Italian friend," says Pamela. "Harold Clurman said to me, 'Never work unpaid.' But I wanted to help this young director and spend the month of August working. The film wasn't very good but I enjoyed making it. I loved playing a hippie so much that I pretended to be one in real life. Sometimes roles hang on after filming whether you like them or not. I would braid my hair and wear shabby clothes. Finally it occurred to me that I have a PR man, an accountant, a manager and an agent. I'm not a hippie! I'm a businesswoman, though I don't go about anything in a businesslike way."

Regarding her Italian movies and why most of them were never released in the U.S., Pamela opines, "Most of them aren't geared for American audiences. *Straziami, ma di Baci Saziami* [1968] is considered to be very important in Italian commercial entertainment. It escapes me why people like it so much. I did it because I was playing an Italian caught in a love triangle with Ugo Tognazzi and Nino Manfredi. I love to do those character parts. I studied with Stella Adler for three years between films and my dream was to be a character actress." Another film of Tiffin's highly regarded in Italy is the giallo *Giornata nera per L'Ariete* (1971), which was originally released in the U.S. as *Evil Fingers*. Franco Nero played a reporter suspected of committing a series of murders. Tiffin portrayed his girlfriend, who he thinks is setting him up to protect her brother. Pamela says this film holds up to this day because of the "impressive cinematography by Vittorio Storaro, who captured the real Europe and not the Europe of tourists. During production, I noticed that Storaro lit our scenes the way Richard Avedon did during my modeling days. When I commented on this, he froze and then said, 'Tu sei molte intelligente!'"

In 1974, Pamela married Edmondo Danon (the son of film producer Marcello Danon of *La cage aux folles* fame). She retired shortly thereafter to raise a family. "I cared about my career when I was working and I didn't care about it the minute it stopped," remarks Pamela. "But looking back on it (from my Protestant work ethic), that was very wrong. I should have striven for more but I didn't." After her two daughters (Echo and Aurora) were born, Pamela was coaxed out of retirement twice. In 1981, she co-hosted (with Horst Buchholz) a segment of the Lincoln Center tribute to Billy Wilder. And in 1986 she appeared in the Italian made-for-TV movie *Rose* which, Pamela comments, "was pointless but I had a lot of fun making it. The director was a nostalgia buff and really wanted me. I was in Europe on vacation anyway so I did it. Valerie Perrine [rolls eyes] played this woman who falls in love with a much younger man. I played her old college friend who was very settled with her husband and son. My character was in contrast with Valerie's modern career woman."

Pamela still has long blond-white hair and that soft, sweet voice which enraptured moviegoers of the sixties and seventies. She is an elegant, charming woman who devotes most of her time to her gardening (she owns homes in New York and Illinois) and doing volunteer work "because so much has fallen into my lap. I'm also on the Board of Directors of the Daughters of Holland because my Dutch ancestors helped found New York." Her husband continues to hold the rights to *La cage aux folles* and *The Birdcage*. And to her surprise, her daughters have decided to follow her famous mother into an acting career. Echo Tiffin Danon is a SAG member and a student of Marcia Halfrecht. She can be seen in Abel Ferrara's film *New Rose Hotel* starring Willem DeFoe and Christopher Walken. And both daughters can be seen in James Toback's *Black and White*. "As far as acting goes for myself, I should be working now," says Pamela. "I love the series *Law and Order* and sometimes I get the urge to call someone. But I haven't worked in years and don't know where I would belong."

FILM APPEARANCES

1961 **Summer and Smoke** (Paramount) d. Peter Glenville.
One, Two, Three (United Artists) d. Billy Wilder.
1962 **State Fair** (20th Century–Fox) d. Jose Ferrer.
1963 **Come Fly with Me** (MGM) d. Henry Levin.
1964 **For Those Who Think Young** (United Artists) d. Leslie Martinson.
The Lively Set (Universal) d. Jack Arnold.
The Pleasure Seekers (20th Century–Fox) d. Jean Negulesco.
1965 **The Hallelujah Trail** (United Artists) d. John Sturges.
1966 **Harper** (Warner Bros.) d. Jack Smight.
Delitto quasi perfetto (Italy/France) d. Mario Camerini.
1968 **Kiss the Other Sheik** (Italy, MGM; expanded "Blonde Wife segment from **Oggi, domani, e dopodomani**) d. Luciano Salce.
I Protagonisti (Italy) d. Marcello Fondato.
Straziami, ma di Baci Saziami (Italy/France) d. Dino Risi.
1969 **Viva Max!** (Commonwealth United) d. Jerry Paris.
L'Archangelo (Italy) d. Giorgio Capitani.
1971 **Cose di "Cosa Nostra"** (Italy/France) d. Steno.
Giornata nera per l'Ariete/Evil Fingers/The Fifth Cord (Italy, Scotia American) d. Luigi Bazzoni.
Il vichingo venuto dal Sud (Italy) d. Steno.
1972 **I giorni del sole** (Italy) d. Franco Prosperi.
Prelude to Taurus (unreleased) d. unknown
1973 **Los Amigos/Deaf Smith and Johnny Ears** (Italy, MGM) d. Paolo Cavara.
1974 **La Signora e Stata Violentata!** (Italy) d. Vittorio Sindoni.
E se per Caso una Mattina (Italy) d. Vittorio Sindoni.
1986 **Rose** (Italy, TV-movie) d. Tomasso Sherman.

TELEVISION APPEARANCES

Here's Hollywood 10/5/62 NBC.
The Fugitive "The Girl from Little Egypt" 12/24/63 ABC.
To Tell the Truth [celebrity panelist] 10/26/64 CBS.
Three on an Island (pilot) 8/27/65 CBS.
This Proud Land (special) ["The Sun Country" segment host] 1/26/66 ABC.
The Mike Douglas Show [talk show guest] 4/5/66 Synd.
Girl Talk [talk show guest] 4/21/66 Synd.
The Merv Griffin Show [talk show guest] 7/25/66 Synd.
Password [celebrity panelist] 1/8/67 NBC.
The Survivors [recurring as Rosemary Price] 9/29/69 to 1/12/70 ABC.
The Tonight Show Starring Johnny Carson [talk show guest] 10/8/69 NBC.
The David Frost Show [talk show guest] 1/8/70 Synd.
Live from Lincoln Center: A Tribute to Billy Wilder (special) [co-host] 5/3/82 PBS.

Francine York

After her appearance on *Land of the Giants* in 1970, Francine York told an interviewer, "I can't escape playing the big parts. Why can't I play the girl next door? It seems I'm always blowing up the world or something." Standing five-foot-eight and measuring 38-23-35, it is no wonder the beautiful, statuesque, dark-haired Francine was usually cast in the Amazonian roles. Francine made her film debut in the cult low-budget *Secret File: Hollywood*. She then progressed from featured roles in the early sixties opposite Jerry Lewis, Marlon Brando and Elvis Presley to starring roles in such cult movies as *Curse of the Swamp Creature*, *Space Monster* and *The Doll Squad*. On TV, York held the Robinson family captive on *Lost in Space*, vamped the Dynamic Duo on *Batman*, beguiled Robert Conrad on *The Wild Wild West* and became the living goddess Venus de Milo on *Bewitched*. Francine became so adept at playing these types of roles that years later, when the casting director of the seventies Saturday morning series *Jason of Star Command* asked her if she could play the evil queen, she replied jokingly, "I *am* the queen!" Always a pro, York had the ability to command and dominate the screen with her poise and confidence. She has energetically played so many different roles wearing a variety of wigs and using an assortment of dialects (Italian, French, British, Southern, etc.) that she became somewhat of a chameleon in Hollywood. No one ever criticized her for giving a lazy performance. And in a business that can be cruel, especially to older actresses, the self-determined Francine continues to act today.

Francine York was born Francine Yerich on August 26 in Aurora, Minnesota, to Frank and Sophie Yerich. From the age of three, Francine knew she wanted to perform because "every time we had company, I would get up and sing or do a hula. I'm Slovenian so my father taught me how to Polka. I'd get up and dance at weddings for ten cents or some chewing gum. Now I'm a lot more expensive!" During high school, Francine was a majorette, wrote for the school newspaper and acted in all the class plays. From the beginning she always interested in health and exercise. She was a 4-H member who won a number of blue ribbons for her cooking skills and was a

On the ABC-TV sitcom *Bewitched*, the voluptuous Francine York brought Venus de Milo to life in 1972 (courtesy of Francine York).

big fan of health guru Gayelord Hauser. At age 14, she ordered his book *Look Younger, Live Longer*. "Can you imagine being worried about living longer at age 14?" asks Francine incredulously. As an adult, Francine would combine her love for cooking with her healthy regimen and throw lavish dinner parties which became legendary in Hollywood. Francine counts Clint Eastwood, Glenn Ford and Peter Ustinov as fans of her culinary skills. She also was featured on the covers of such health magazines as *Let's Live*, *Fitness Plus* and others.

Francine arrived in Hollywood via beauty pageants (with the Miss San Francisco title) and modeling after an unsuccessful stint as a secretary for Northwest Airlines. ("My boss suggested to me that I'd be happier without this job. He was right. I was cut out for the more aesthetic things.") Her first feature film role was a conniving magazine editor who pays a sleazy ex-detective (Robert Clarke) to set up show business people in compromising situations to help sell her scandal sheet (*à la Confidential Magazine*) in *Secret File: Hollywood* (1962). The film is a camp classic and is infamous for its shots of microphones dipping into the frames. Nevertheless, Francine is very proud of her work in it. "We shot this in 1960 and it was my first chance to play a character on the big screen," says York. "I had never been in front of a camera, really. And nobody knew! They had no idea because I hit my marks and knew my lines. When you look at this picture, I look like a seasoned actress! I guess I was good right from the beginning.

"I also have very sentimental feelings regarding *Secret File: Hollywood*," continues Francine. "I think every actor does when it comes to their first movie. For me it was even more so because it premiered in the Tacora Theatre in my hometown of Aurora, Minnesota. The whole town came to meet me at the airport. They had posters in the windows with "Welcome Home Francine." Thinking about it brings tears to my eyes. It was the most magnificent time of my life. I got a tour of my high school and everyone was so nice. When I was a student there, I would get in trouble a lot. In fact, my sixth grade teacher wanted to flunk me. After the premiere she invited my mother and me over for tea. My teacher said to me, 'My dear, you were always one of my best students.' My mom and I laughed our heads off. I whispered to my mother, 'This is the high point—having her kiss my fanny!'"

Francine gave another good account of herself in her second film *The Sergeant Was a Lady* (1961). *Variety* raved, "Francine York comes on strong as a sex-starved WAC." Casting director Eddie Morse took note of York and thought she would be a perfect foil for Jerry Lewis. Francine was late to her appointment to meet Lewis because she lost her wristwatch. Afraid that he would berate her, Francine was pleasantly surprised by Jerry's reaction. "I told Jerry that I lost the watch and that it was a graduation present," recalls Francine. "He said, 'Just a minute!' He called his secretary and told her to order me a new watch to be delivered to my home. I said to him, 'Gee, I never had anyone do something that nice for me here in Hollywood.' I then confessed to him that I was scared to death to meet him. Up to that point he was probably the biggest star I ever met. He tried to alleviate my fears and said, 'Just remember that the person behind the desk is probably insecure too. And my giving you that watch is really selfish.' I replied, 'What do you mean?' He said, 'By doing it, it makes *me* feel good.' I've always remembered that. I thought that was quite a statement. A lot of people don't really know Jerry. He likes to *do* for people. He thought I was perfect for this part in *It's Only Money* [1962]."

York went on to appear in five other Lewis films, including *The Nutty Professor* (1963), *The Disorderly Orderly* (1964) and *Cracking Up* (1982). As for working with Lewis, Francine comments, "Jerry could be a little bit of a maniac sometimes. When he had someone like Frank Tashlin directing him, he'd fool around a lot. But when he was directing himself using Paramount's money, he'd be more careful and serious. Watching him direct himself in *The Nutty Professor* was really something! When he called, 'Action!' he'd go from being Jerry the serious director to Jerry the actor playing the suave Buddy Love or the nerdy Prof. Kelp. It was amazing to watch. On *The Disorderly Orderly*, he missed one of his pratfalls and hurt his back. We filmed this up in the Doheny Estates for about eight weeks. When I did *Cracking Up* with him in 1982 he was really nervous. It was right before he had his heart attack and he was a basket case throughout the shoot. This was a funny movie but Orion went bankrupt and it didn't get released in the U.S. But it was a huge hit in Europe because they just revere Jerry. They thought my part was so funny because I was speaking fractured French and it was subtitled. But the average American didn't know I wasn't speaking real French."

Francine continued in the comedic vein with *Bedtime Story* (1964) and *Tickle Me* (1965). The former starred Marlon Brando and David Niven as fortune hunters out to fleece rich widows on the French Riviera. Francine plays an Italian used as a decoy by David Niven to distract Brando from honing in on his territory. Francine has a hilarious scene with Brando on a train. "Marlon Brando was adorable," says York. "But he was so dreadfully insecure and needed the producer there all of the time—sort of like Linus with his blanket. He had never done comedy before. We had a scene

A beguiling York as an Italian with Marlon Brando as a gigolo in *Bedtime Story* (Universal, 1964) (courtesy of Francine York).

before we boarded the train. He couldn't remember his lines and we did about 20 takes. On my last day of shooting, I went over to Brando to shake his hand goodbye and he was drunk—absolutely schnockered. He said, slurring his speech, 'Well, Francine, you're not really shaking my hand. You're shaking vodka and makeup.' I said, 'But Marlon, the most important thing is that it's your hand.' He mumbled, 'You're right.' I thought to myself that I would never feel insecure again when working with a legend. David Niven was an angel. After watching me do all those takes with Brando, he said to me, 'Francine, you're like the Rock of Gibraltar. You go on and on and on.' Physically, [Niven] was a beautiful man with sparkling blue eyes. He told me once that no one is indispensable—in Hollywood or in life. He had humility and a beautiful soul. I can't praise him enough. I thought he was wonderful!"

Tickle Me starred Elvis Presley as a singing rodeo star who gets a job at an exclusive dude ranch–spa and Jocelyn Lane (who Francine says "was a little snit, my dear") as the icy health instructor searching for her grandfather's hidden treasure. Francine is featured along with B-movie veterans Merry Anders and Allison Hayes as patrons of the spa who go gaga for Elvis, who Francine says "was just marvelous to work with. There was no ego with him and he wasn't snobbish at all! When Norman Taurog would give a direction, Elvis would talk under his breath and kind of kid around. I spent a lot of time with Elvis during the photo shoot for the film's poster ad. I liked him so much. I felt very sad when he died."

Francine next worked with an esteemed cast including Richard Crenna and Ed Asner on the critically acclaimed series *Slattery's People*. Crenna played a heroic state legislator always involved in some noble cause. York joined the cast during the second season as his secretary Wendy Wendowski. She won the role by giving an excellent performance at her screen test, which was at 10 A.M. "The

Publicity shot from *Tickle Me* (Allied Artists, 1965) with York (*second from left*), Jocelyn Lane and Elvis Presley.

script called for me to tell Richard Crenna's character that I was there strictly to be a secretary—I don't work any overtime and don't date any of my co-workers, and so on. I went on and on. By one o'clock that afternoon, they called me back to tell me the part was mine. The producer just adored me." Though the critics respected the show, it failed to find an audience against The Man from U.N.C.L.E. and was canceled. But Francine got a little compensation when casting director Lynn Stalmaster chose her to play Lillie Langtry in "Portrait of a Lady" on *Death Valley Days*. "This was the most fabulous role of my life," exclaims Francine proudly. "Peter Whitney played Texan Judge Roy Bean who renames the town of Vinegroon to Langtry in honor of Lillie. Our characters had been corresponding and my first scene is where Lillie's manager reads the letter from Judge Roy Bean saying he is going to name this town after me. No one expected me to play the character with a British accent but I did. Everyone was floored, particularly Dale Robertson who was the star of the series. Every time I see this episode I cry because even though Judge Roy Bean was so enamored of Lillie, he never met her. When she finally came to the town of Langtry to meet him, he had already died. I have a scene where I'm crying and said, 'I wanted so much to meet your Judge Roy Bean.' I became an aficionado of Lillie Langtry after this—collecting all of her memorabilia and all of her books. I was quite taken aback when they did a film about her in England because I felt Lillie belonged to me. They also did a movie in the U.S. called *The Life and Times of Judge Roy Bean* [1972], which was horribly miscast with Paul Newman. I was up for the movie but they gave it to Ava Gardner."

Though she gave an endearing performance as Lillie Langtry, Francine was more often cast in the science fiction and horror genres because of her physical stature and commanding presence. Like Raquel Welch and Julie Newmar, York had an authoritative quality that worked best in these bigger-than-life roles. In Larry Buchanan's ultra-cheap 1966 *Curse of the Swamp Creature* ("We shot this in Uncertain, Texas, and it certainly was!"), York played the wife of a mad scientist (Jeff Alexander) who is experimenting on the local natives and turning them into fish creatures (or, as he refers to one, "my beautiful indestructible fish-man"). John Agar plays a geologist who stumbles upon his laboratory deep in swampland. "Larry Buchanan was really wonderful," recalls Francine. "He wined and dined us while shooting the film. Jeff Alexander played my husband and he thought he was another Vincent Price. But he was the world's worst actor! I loved working with John Agar, though. He's a very special man and we've been friends ever since. My favorite scene is where my husband turns a girl into this monster and I go running out screaming, 'You were a beautiful woman. Look at yourself!' And she goes, 'Aagh!' She then picks up my husband and throws him into the alligator pond. In another scene, Larry forgot to dub in my scream and there is no sound. I never thought anybody was going to see this movie. Much to my surprise, it has become my number one cult film."

Mutiny in Outer Space (1965) was another low-budget sci-fi flick for AIP. A lunar fungus attacks a spaceship whose crew includes York, William Leslie, and Pamela Curran. During filming screenwriter Arthur Pierce fell madly in love with Francine but when he took her to meet producer Burt Topper who was readying the film *Space Monster*, "I fell in love with Burt and that was the end of

The low-budget *Space Monster* (AIP, 1965) starred York as the first woman in space. She is pictured along with James B. Brown and Russ Bender as fellow astronauts.

my relationship with Arthur. Burt and I dated for three years." In *Space Monster* (1965), York (as the world's first female astronaut) accompanies Russ Bender, James B. Brown and Baynes Barron on a mission to another planet. Francine screams a lot, especially during the film's climactic underwater crash. "The spaceship was actually a little model spaceship in a fish bowl filled with live crabs. That was the idea of Burt Topper. He had to electrocute them for some scenes where our spaceship was supposed to be shooting laser beams at them. He was up to four o'clock in the morning killing those poor things." As for the film's novice director Leonard Katzman, Francine states,

"I was just shocked that Leonard Katzman went on to do big things because he was scared to death when he directed this movie. He couldn't handle it so Burt Topper took over for him. I went on to work with Leonard on *The Wild Wild West* and *Dirty Sally* with Jeanette Nolan but he never hired me for *Dallas*. Oh, well."

With the advent of color television, the mid-sixties saw an influx of mod science fiction and fantasy programs on the small screen. These shows were perfect vehicles for Francine to display her talents. On *Batman*, she was the evil Lydia Limpet, henchgirl of the Bookworm (Roddy McDowall), an arch-villain who has a voracious appetite for books and uses them to try to outfox the Caped Crusaders. As Lydia, York is taken into the Batcave by Batman and Robin and, as they try to get her to reveal Bookworm's plans, Robin exclaims, "Let's give her some more Bat Gas." "We had to do this scene over and over," recalls Francine, chuckling. "Every time Burt Ward said that line, we all burst out laughing. They were both fun to work with. In the episode I got to ride in the Batmobile when Bookworm and I steal it. Everybody wanted to work on *Batman* and ride in that car. I also adored working with Roddy McDowall. He was wonderful and told an interviewer that *Batman* was one of his most favorite work experiences. I was saddened to hear of his passing. He will be truly missed." To this day, Francine gets the most requests for autographed photos from this episode.

Roddy McDowall as the Bookworm and York as his evil girlfriend Lydia Limpet on the ABC-TV series *Batman* (courtesy of Francine York).

With her appearance on "The Colonists" episode of *Lost in Space*, Francine began her long association with Irwin Allen. According to Francine, he was "the last of the Mike Todd showman producers. He did everything on a grand scale. I did six shows with Irwin, who could be wonderful or he could be a tyrant. Sometimes he would just come on the set and get hysterical over things." On *Lost in Space*, Francine has one of her best roles as the noble Niolani, an Amazon warrior (from a planet where men are second-class citizens) who imprisons the Robinson men to build a landing pad for her fellow colonists. This was Francine's first lead guest appearance. "I gave a powerful reading," recalls Francine. "It was a part I was born to play. Within minutes, director Ezra Stone and Irwin Allen offered me the role. Stone said later that I was marvelous and had such poise as Niolani! Paul Zastupnevich designed that wonderful costume with the scepter specifically for me. He told me it was one of his favorite creations."

Though she had trouble working with the *Lost in Space* cast at first ("Irwin Allen called them the goons because they were always cutting up"), she became friendly with Jonathan Harris and June Lockhart. "I love Jonathan," says Francine with a smile. "To this day he calls me 'that dear girl.' He was very helpful and we had such fun during the filming. Our rapport really made this episode extra-special. Before we started shooting, June Lockhart saw them putting this kind of armored chest plate on me. So she came over to me and drew nipples on it with a red marker. Later when she saw me, she thought I had the chest plate on underneath and poked me in the breasts. She was startled and said, 'Oh my God! It's you!' Junie didn't know that they decided not to use the chest plate. She was so embarrassed that she later invited me into her dressing room to have cookies. We've been good friends ever since."

In the episode's finish, Will Robinson (Billy Mumy) convinces the dastardly Dr. Smith (Harris) to sabotage the landing pad for Niolani's fellow warriors with an explosive sculpture. "I was almost seriously injured during this scene," recalls York with a shudder. "If you watch the episode, the explosion sends Niolani's couch up into the air and it just nearly missed my head because I was standing right near it. Everybody came running over to me asking if I was all right. When they told me what happened, I started to shake because I got nervous. The next day's newspapers had headlines like 'Actress Escapes Death' and 'Headdress Saves Actress' Life.' Until I saw the episode I didn't know how close I came."

Back on the big screen, Francine received notoriety for her brief nude scene in the western *Cannon for Cordoba* (1970), beautifully shot in Madrid, Spain. George Peppard leads a band of soldiers against Mexican bandits in Texas circa 1912. York got the role of beguiling Spanish belly dancer Sophia (who has a fling with Peppard's character) by "stretching the truth a bit. I knew basically how to belly dance but I had to take lessons to learn how to do the stomach rolls and a few other moves. There used to be a belly dance place on Sunset Boulevard. My press agent arranged for me to perform there one night with the regular belly dancers. Some of the patrons thought I was a real belly dancer. We got a lot of press on this and my picture was in all the papers." Though not happy with the way the film turned out ("This was such a male chauvinist picture and I was very upset the way they edited it"), Francine had a ball filming in Spain and, of course, turned more than a few heads. "When I arrived at the hotel in Spain, all these reporters were waiting for me," recalls York. "I thought, 'Wow! They really arranged a big publicity build-up.' They asked me questions about the film and took photos of me. The next day's newspaper headline said, '*Susannah* York arrives at Hilton.' After this, I became paranoid when fans would come up to me saying, 'It's you!' I'd think, 'Who? Barbara Eden? Julie Newmar?' But I loved working in Spain. When we did this, George Peppard was dating Judy Geeson and they'd invite me to go to dinner with them. The people treated me so beautifully. I stopped traffic wherever I went. I loved working in Spain. Those were the days, my friend! When I arrived, I couldn't speak a word of Spanish. I've been studying it ever since."

Doing the nude scene in *Cannon for Cordoba* was not a big deal for Francine, who later spoke about the issue of screen nudity in a number of forums. "This was the first and only time I appeared nude," says Francine. "I decided to do it because it was going to be shot in good taste. Besides, I have beautiful breasts, so I thought, 'What the hell!' They shot my nude scene with George Peppard two ways. The one where you see my breasts was to be for the European version only. There were supposed to be no still photographers on the set that day. But there were and my picture found its way into *Playboy*. My mother found out about it and she was furious with me. Soon after, I was asked to speak at a seminar on screen nudity. Shelley Winters was on the panel and she ranted, 'I would never do

Francine York belly dances up a storm in *Cannon for Cordoba* (United Artists, 1970).

a nude scene. I think it is terrible what's happening in movies. I think it's just disgusting that women are showing their breasts!' She then turned to me and whispered, 'My dear, if I looked like you I'd do it.'" [*Laughs*]

During this period, York played guest leads on a number of TV shows including *The Wild Wild West* with the height-conscious Robert Conrad ("To compensate for Conrad's height, I walked in the holes and he walked on the hills!"),

Bewitched as a seductive Venus de Milo ["Agnes Moorehead liked to hold my hand. I never could quite understand it until years later!"] and *The Odd Couple* as a bake-off contestant ("Jack Klugman was darling but Tony Randall was terrible to work with—he was very insulting and mean"). Francine also made three appearances on the ultimate TV show about relationships in the sixties, *Love, American Style*. One episode (titled "Love and the Wild Party") features York and Robert Reed ["Who was also mean and hateful to work with"] as married swingers whose newspaper ad is answered by yokels Peter Palmer and Jeannine Riley, thinking it is a notice for square dancing. "Wife-swapping was a touchy subject back then and we couldn't veer from the script at all," recalls Francine. "We had to say the lines as written. I wore this sexy red dress and was shaking my fanny. At one point I grab Peter and pull him into the bedroom. He runs out and says to Robert [*with Southern drawl*], 'I don't know what's wrong with your wife but she started breathing hard and I started to give her mouth-to-mouth resuscitation. She's in there hyperventilatin'!' It was a funny episode and even my grandfather Joseph Milanovich back in Gilbert, Minnesota, who I doubt knew what this was about, told my mom [*mimics with Yugoslavian accent*], 'Dis vas best show I ever see Francine do.'" [*Laughs*]

In the early seventies, York was featured in two drive-in classics. *Welcome Home, Soldier Boys* (1972) focuses on the cross-country exploits of four Vietnam veterans. When they run out of money, they rob a small town gas station, setting up a violent confrontation with the townspeople. This was just another exploitation film portraying Vietnam veterans as loose cannons waiting to pop. Francine played an unhappy wife of a rich Texan who sneaks off to have an encounter with vet Joe Don Baker. "This was not a happy experience," says Francine disgustedly. "Most of the cast and crew were doing drugs so I would lock my door and stay in my room at the hotel. In one of the scenes, I nearly got killed when Baker and I had to plop backward into the motel's pool after making love. We should have had stand-ins. I had a great part as originally written. But the way they edited the film, I looked like just one of the hookers because they cut out all my scenes with my husband. I was so furious that I walked out of the screening. A while after that, the producer ended up becoming a Jesus freak up in the mountains."

Ted V. Mikels took note of York's talent and cast her as the female lead in his way-out feature film *The Doll Squad* (1973), which he claims was ripped off by *Charlie's Angels*. "I agree with Ted," states Francine emphatically. "Ted went to the producers with the premise. The titles are exactly like our titles and the lead characters have the same names!" Francine plays Sabrina, the leader of an elite band of female commandos (including Tura Santana of 1965's *Faster Pussycat! Kill! Kill!*) who try to stop a madman played by Michael Ansara (whom Francine describes as being "a real professional and a sweet, wonderful man") from overthrowing the world's governments with the bubonic plague. "I like Ted as a director and although subsequently we became very good friends, we fought tooth and nail over many things in the script. One of the major things was that he was dating actress Sherri Vernon before the film and he put her in the picture. All of a sudden I was getting the feeling that she was taking over everything. He even wanted her character to kill Michael Ansara's. But I thought

Sabrina should kill him. Ted said to me, 'How are you going to kill Michael Ansara's character?' We were shooting at a little house in the Valley and I looked up and saw a sword on the wall. I said to him, 'Look, I'll weaken him with my mace ring (which I set up in a previous scene *à la* James Bond) and then I'll stab him with a sword.' That whole scene was my idea—choking me with the cord around my neck, spilling the martinis on him, *everything*." *The Doll Squad* has turned out to be another extremely popular cult film with Francine's fans.

The careers of most of Francine's contemporaries cooled in the late seventies and eighties, but York continued acting almost non-stop. Her TV appearances included *The Streets of San Francisco*, *The Love Boat*, *Riptide*, *Brothers* and *Mama's Family*. York also became one of the most hated women on daytime television as blackmailing ex-hooker Lorraine Temple on the hit soap *Days of Our Lives* in 1978. "This was the role of roles," exclaims Francine. "Lorraine Temple was a hard part to play. I had some very powerful scenes. Wes Kenney was the producer of *Days of Our Lives* but he would come down from the booth with some direction. He would give me three or four words and he would change my whole performance. I will never forget that. He had such a gift." Though York toiled on the show for less than a year, she began getting recognized on airplanes, at the supermarket—anywhere she went. And to this day, when fans ask her if she has plans to return to the soaps, Francine replies, "No. It is very hard work for me at this point in my life. One underestimates actors who toil on soaps. You have to learn pages of dialogue in a day and just before you go to shoot it they hand you all these changes."

The nineties Francine is blonde and as voluptuous as ever. So it is surprising to hear that she had never married though she admits to love affairs with actors James Arness and Clint Walker and John B. Kelly, the very handsome brother of Princess Grace of Monaco. "When I did *The Tonight Show*, Johnny Carson asked me the same question. I said to him, 'I suffer from the Cinderella syndrome—waiting for my prince to arrive on a white horse. But there is always a shortage of white horses and the shoe never fits.' I guess an actress needs a certain kind of a husband—someone supportive. The best husband would be someone not in the business. I'm still searching for my Prince Charming. And if he is reading this, I wear a size ten shoe!"

Francine has recently appeared in episodes of *Lois and Clark: The New Adventures of Superman* and *Beverly Hills 90210*. She also played Marilyn Monroe in the yet-to-be released *Marilyn Is Alive;* "I was *so* Marilyn, people would flip if they saw it. I even get to sing a song called 'I Never Had the Chance to Say Good-bye.'" In Fred Olen Ray's *Counter Measures* (1998) starring Michael Dudikoff, she played the wife of the American ambassador to Russia (Scott Marlowe). Regarding this movie, Francine comments, "Fred Olen Ray is fast. I would have preferred a little more time to work on the scenes. But we were under a heavy schedule and Fred had to get it done on time. Scott Marlowe played my husband and I shudder when I hear his name. He was just dreadful and couldn't remember his lines. Fred was going to cut our scenes. I said, 'No, no, no! I'll make this guy look magnificent.' Marlowe was all psyched out. But it all worked out and my scenes were left in the movie. I even get to kill the enemy and save my husband. Fred said to me, 'Francine, you've still got it!' He was a big fan of *The Doll Squad*."

Francine York (playing his wacky mother-in-law) poses with Nicolas Cage on the set of *Family Man* (Universal, 2000).

As for the new millennium, it seems to hold only wonderful things for Francine. She has supporting roles in the films *The Big Tease* ("I played Fifi Kingbridge, a wacky editor of *En Vague* magazine") and *Family Man* ("Nicolas Cage was very nice and always concentrating. I told him that I thought doing a comedy was a nice change of pace for him"). She is in the planning stages of helping to write and produce a few films and has appeared in a number of commercials. And with her vivacious personality, she is always a fan favorite at autograph shows and conventions. When asked why she thinks she outlasted most of her sixties contemporaries, the ever-confident Francine replies, with a laugh and a wink, "Because I'm really a bundle of talent!"

FILM APPEARANCES

1961　**The Right Approach** (20th Century–Fox) d. David Butler.
The Sergeant Was a Lady (Universal) d. Bernard Glasser.

1962　**Wild Ones on Wheels** (Emerson) d. Rudolph Cusumano.
Secret File: Hollywood (Crown International) [completed in 1960] d. Rudolph Cusumano.
It's Only Money (Paramount) d. Frank Tashlin.

1963　**The Nutty Professor** (Paramount) d. Jerry Lewis.
A New Kind of Love (Paramount) d. Melville Shavelson.

1964　**Bedtime Story** (Universal) d. Ralph Levy.
The Patsy (Paramount) d. Jerry Lewis. [Scenes deleted from final print.]
The Disorderly Orderly (Paramount) d. Frank Tashlin.

1965　**Mutiny in Outer Space** (Allied Artists) d. Hugo Grimaldi.

	Tickle Me (Allied Artists) d. Norman Taurog.
	The Greatest Story Ever Told (United Artists) d. George Stevens [Scenes deleted from final print.]
	The Family Jewels (Paramount) d. Jerry Lewis.
	Space Monster/Space Probe Taurus (AIP) d. Leonard Katzman.
1966	**Curse of the Swamp Creature** (AIP) d. Larry Buchanan.
1967	**Ride to Hangman's Tree** (Universal) [uncredited] d. Alan Rafkin.
1969	**Any Second Now** (TV-movie) d. Gene Levitt.
1970	**Cannon for Cordoba** (United Artists) d. Paul Wendkos.
1972	**Welcome Home, Soldier Boys** (20th Century–Fox) d. Richard Compton.
1973	**The Doll Squad** (Geneni) d. Ted V. Mikels.
	I Love a Mystery (TV-movie) [completed in 1967] d. Leslie Stevens.
1974	**The Centerfold Girls** (General Films) d. John Peyser.
1975	**Adventures of the Queen** (TV-movie) d. David Lowell Rich.
	They Only Come Out at Night (TV-movie) d. Daryl Duke.
1976	**Flood** (TV-movie) d. Earl Bellamy.
1977	**Time Travelers** (TV-movie) d. Alexander Singer.
1978	**Zero to Sixty/Repo** (Canada, First Artists) d. Don Weis.
1979	**Half a House** (First American Films) d. Brice Mack.
1983	**Cracking Up/Smorgasbord** (Orion) d. Jerry Lewis.
	The Night the Bridge Fell Down (TV-movie) [completed in 1979] d. George Fenady.
1985	**Between the Darkness and the Dawn** (TV-movie) d. Peter Levin. [Scenes deleted from final print.]
1987	**The Underachievers** (Lightning Pictures/PMS Filmworks) d. Jackie Kong.
1992	**Marilyn Is Alive** (Movie Media) [unreleased] d. John Carr.
	Private Obsession (Triboro Entertainment) d. Lee Frost.
1996	**Elvis: The Complete Story** (Direct-to-video) [documentary]
1998	**Counter Measures** (American Independent) d. Fred Olen Ray.
1999	**Dumped** (Tite-Belt Productions, LLC) d. Oliver Robins.
	The Big Tease (Warner Bros.) d. Kevin Allen.
2000	**Family Man** (Universal) d. Brett Ratner.

TELEVISION APPEARANCES

The Roaring Twenties "Big Town Blues" 1/21/61 ABC.
Bringing Up Buddy "The Education of Nicky Marlo" 2/12/61 CBS.
Shirley Temple Theatre "The Little Mermaid" 3/5/61 NBC.
SurfSide 6 "Portrait of Nicole" 3/26/62 ABC.
77 Sunset Strip "Falling Stars" 1/4/63 ABC.
I'm Dickens ... He's Fenster "Get Off My Back" 1/21/63 ABC.
Dick Powell Theatre "Luxury Liner" 2/12/63 NBC.
The Untouchables "The Butcher's Boy" 3/12/63 ABC.
The Gallant Men "Tommy" 3/30/63 ABC.
Burke's Law "Who Killed Jason Shaw?" 1/3/64 ABC.
Burke's Law "Who Killed April?" 1/31/64 ABC.
The Greatest Show on Earth "A Place to Belong" 2/11/64 ABC.
Bob Hope Comedy Special "School for Bachelors" NBC 3/20/64.
My Favorite Martian "Uncle Martin's Wisdom Tooth" 6/28/64 CBS.
Slattery's People "Question: What Became of the White Tortilla?" 10/26/64 CBS.
Hazel "Mind Your Own Business" 10/29/64 NBC.
Burke's Law "Who Killed Supersleuth?" 12/16/64 ABC.
Burke's Law "Who Killed Rosie Sunset?" 1/27/65 ABC.
Burke's Law "Who Killed the Rabbit's Husband?" 4/14/65 ABC.
Perry Mason "The Case of the Wrongful Writ" 5/6/65 CBS.
Cap'n Ahab (pilot) 9/3/65 CBS.
Slattery's People [series regular as Wendy Wendkowski] 9/17 to 11/26/65 CBS.
The Smothers Brothers Show "Pay the Man the $27.95" 10/15/65 CBS.
Death Valley Days "A Picture of a Lady" 12/30/65 Synd.
Perry Mason "The Case of the Sausalito Sunrise" 2/13/66 CBS.
The Double Life of Henry Phyfe "The Old Flame" 3/10/66 ABC.

Batman "The Bookworm Turns" 4/20/66 ABC.
Batman "While Gotham City Burns" 4/21/66 ABC.
Gomer Pyle, USMC "Marry Me, Marry Me" 11/16/66 CBS.
Lost in Space "The Colonists" 3/15/67 CBS.
Ironside "Memory of an Ice Cream Stick" 1/11/68 NBC.
It Takes a Thief "It Takes One to Know One" 1/16/68 ABC.
It Takes a Thief "One Illegal Angel" 2/13/68 ABC.
It Takes a Thief "Totally by Design" 2/20/68 ABC.
The Outsider "For Members Only…" 9/18/68 NBC.
The Name of the Game "Collector's Edition" 10/11/68 NBC.
Green Acres "The Agricultural Student" 11/27/68 CBS.
The Wild Wild West "The Night of the Pelican" 12/27/68 CBS.
Divorce Court (episode title unknown) 3/7/69 Synd.
Ironside "Not with a Whimper, but a Bang" 4/10/69 NBC.
Pioneer Spirit (pilot) 7/21/69 NBC.
I Dream of Jeannie "Jeannie and the Bachelor Party" 10/21/69 NBC.
Love, American Style "Love and the Wild Party" 11/17/69 ABC.
The Courtship of Eddie's Father "Who Pulled the Blues Right Out of the Horn?" 12/24/69 CBS.
Land of the Giants "Doomsday" 2/15/70 ABC.
Family Affair "The Boys Against the Girls" 2/26/70 CBS.
To Rome with Love "Spring Vacation" 4/26/70 CBS.
The Tim Conway Show (episode title unknown) 6/5/70 CBS.
The Odd Couple "They Use Horseradish, Don't They?" 1/7/71 ABC.
Mannix "What Happened to Sunday?" 1/9/71 CBS.
Adam-12 "Log 88: Reason to Run" 4/1/71 NBC.
Bewitched "Bewitched, Bothered and Baldoni" 10/3/71 ABC.
Love, American Style "Love and the Lovely Evening" 10/23/71 ABC.
Longstreet "I See, Said the Blind Man" 11/18/71 ABC.
The Chicago Teddy Bears "Annie Get Your Cue" 12/3/71 CBS.
O'Hara, U.S. Treasury "Operation: Lady Luck" 1/14/72 CBS.
Adam-12 "Sub-Station" 2/16/72 NBC.
Emergency! "Crash" 4/15/72 NBC.
Mission: Impossible "Break!" 9/16/72 CBS.
Love, American Style "Love and the Super Lover" 12/1/72 ABC.
Hec Ramsey "The Mystery of the Yellow Rose" 1/28/73 NBC.
Dirty Sally "The Old Soldier" 1/25/74 CBS.
Police Story "Dangerous Games" 4/16/74 NBC.
Kojak "Slay Ride" 10/13/74 CBS.
The Streets of San Francisco "Bird of Prey" 11/21/74 ABC.
Petrocelli "The Sleep of Reason" 1/15/75 NBC.
Columbo "The Forgotten Lady" 9/14/75 NBC.
The Barbary Coast "Irish Luck" 10/13/75 ABC.
The Barbary Coast "An Iron Clad Plan" 10/31/75 ABC.
Petrocelli "Falling Star" 1/21/76 NBC.
The Streets of San Francisco "Underground" 1/29/76 ABC.
Bert D'Angelo/Superstar "Murder in Velvet" 2/21/76 ABC.
Monsanto Night Presents Walt Disney's America on Parade (special) 4/3/76 Synd.
The Quest "Prairie Woman" 11/10/76 NBC.
The Streets of San Francisco "Monkey Is Back" 1/13/77 ABC.
Future Cop "Girl on the Ledge" 4/7/77 ABC.
Days of Our Lives [series regular as Lorraine Temple] 1978 NBC.
General Hospital [short-term role as Madame Thelma] 1979 ABC.
Jason of Star Command "Web of the Star Witch" 9/29/79 CBS.
Jason of Star Command "Little Girl Lost" 11/17/79 CBS.
Jason of Star Command "Mimi's Secret" 11/24/79 CBS.
General Hospital [short-term role as Madame Thelma] 1981 ABC.
Masquerade "The French Connection" 3/10/84 ABC.
Berrenger's "Overture" 1/5/85 NBC.
The Love Boat "There'll Be Some Changes Made" 2/2/85 ABC.
Riptide "Harmony and Grits" 5/14/85 NBC.
Mama's Family "Grandma USA" 12/86 Synd.
Mr. Belvedere "Truckin'" 10/7/89 ABC.
Matlock "The Dame" 11/15/91 NBC.
Lois and Clark: The New Adventures of Superman "I'm Seeing Through You" 10/10/93 ABC.

Beverly Hills 90210 "And Did It ... My Way" 11/10/93 FOX.
Burke's Law "Who Killed the Highest Bidder? 4/28/95 CBS.

Also:
Rescue 8, Manhunt, Hawaiian Eye, Route 66, The Tonight Show Starring Johnny Carson, Rituals, Brothers (3), and *Mr. Belvedere*.

Joy Harmon

With her big blue eyes, wild blonde mane, ample bosom and little-girl voice, actress Joy Harmon giggled her way through numerous films and TV shows during the sixties. For a short period she was everyone's favorite fair-haired ding-a-ling. While some actresses might have been dismayed at being typecast, Harmon adored playing these roles, which she described as "the fun parts." Even when she played juvenile delinquents and gun molls, Joy brought to her characters an endearing child-like quality that made them lovable despite their bad deeds. In *Let's Rock*, she vamps good guy singer Julius La Rosa; in *Village of the Giants* she grows to gigantic proportions and terrorizes a town; and in *One Way Wahine* she plays a beach bunny involved with felons. Joy alternated between film leads in these teen exploitation films with zany supporting roles in bigger-budgeted films such as *Under the Yum Yum Tree*, *The Loved One* and *A Guide for the Married Man*. Her most memorable role was as "the girl" in *Cool Hand Luke* starring Paul Newman. Though sexy Joy was on screen for all of five minutes, she left an indelible impression on the young men in the audience with her seductive car wash scene. Never has such a simple act been so provocative.

Joy Harmon was born on May 1 in St. Louis, Missouri. She is the daughter of Bernice and Homer Harmon and has a sister named Gay. Her father was connected with theater circuits throughout the Midwest and moved the family to Wilton, Connecticut, after getting a job in publicity for the famed Roxy Theatre in New York City. At the age of three, Joy was modeling fashions for 20th Century–Fox newsreels and two-reelers. Her love for performing continued and as a teenager she would emulate her idol Marilyn Monroe. "I would imitate the way she walked with that wiggle and copy her voice," says Joy with a laugh. "I even entered an amateur contest impersonating her while we were on a family vacation in Miami. My mom was so embarrassed. Later when I got roles, I had to be careful not to do Marilyn." Joy got her first taste of Hollywood when she was picked to be an extra in *The Man in the Gray Flannel Suit* (1956) starring Gregory Peck, which was filming in her hometown. Desperate to leave high school to pursue acting, Harmon began entering beauty contests as her ticket out of Wilton and was named "Miss Compo Beach." This led to the Miss Connecticut pageant, where she placed first runner-up.

Joy's dream to become an actress came to fruition when she landed a role as a blonde ding-a-ling in a tight sweater in the hit Broadway comedy *Make a Million* with Sam Levene. Joy's voluptuous figure (41-22-36) was used to get the play's biggest laugh when a man carrying two basketballs chest-high tries to squeeze by her in a narrow doorway. Joy's shapely body also got her the attention of all the popular men's magazines at that time and she posed (clothed) for a number of them, including *Rex*, *Show* and *Nugget*. "My measurements were always being touted in newspapers and magazines," remembers Joy. "During the heyday of Jayne Mansfield, there was always a competition to see who had the biggest chest. I did a lot of layouts for men's magazines but I never did nudity. They all wanted me to pose topless and I was always fighting it. The photographers would say, 'Now let's lose the top.' I'd reply, 'No!' Later I was asked to pose for *Playboy* as a Playmate but I turned Hugh Hefner down." At this time, buxom Joy also began entertaining TV viewers acting the dumb blonde with talk show hosts Steve Allen, Gary Moore, Earl Wilson and Dave Garroway, among others.

After catching a performance of *Make a Million*, Groucho Marx was so impressed with the blonde newcomer that he brought her out to Hollywood to appear on his show *You Bet Your Life*. All this publicity paid off for Joy, who landed a contract at Columbia/Screen Gems in 1958. She made her film debut as a tough-talking, cigarette-smoking juvenile delinquent in the rock 'n' roll mu-

A seductive Joy Harmon as "the girl" in *Cool Hand Luke* (Warner Bros., 1967).

sical *Let's Rock* (1958). After touring in *Make a Million* and replacing Arlene Golonka in the Broadway comedy *Come Blow Your Horn*, Joy relocated to California in 1962 to work with Marx on his new TV show *Tell It to Groucho*, replacing his long-time sidekick George Fenneman. However, due to Joy Soap sponsoring a rival program, Joy was billed as Patty Harmon. She later used Patty Joy Harmon before going back to just plain Joy. Regarding Groucho Marx, Joy fondly recalls, "He was like a dad to me. But when actors would stop by and say hi to him while we were doing the show at CBS, he would act like such a wolf. He treated me like I was his girlfriend but it was all for show. Though he put on an act in front of his friends, we just sort of played off each other until they left. He had a wife and daughter but neither of them was home very much. He was sad about that so he would invite me to his house for dinner and I would stay there and watch TV. My coming over became a family thing for him. He'd call me a lot because he knew I came out to California without my family. When I didn't see him at night, he'd have me come right into his dressing room to tell him what I did the night before."

Though *Tell It to Groucho* lasted only five months, Joy remained in Hollywood. Columbia kept her busy, casting her as a gun moll in *Mad Dog Coll* (1961) and as college coed Carol Lynley's friend in the hit comedy *Under the Yum Yum Tree* (1963) starring Jack Lemmon. On television, Harmon began popping up regularly as the ditzy blonde on such shows as *The Beverly Hillbillies*, *My Three Sons*, *Burke's Law*, *Batman*, *Gidget*, *That Girl* and *Bewitched*, among others. Recalling some of her TV appearances, Joy remarks, "*Batman* was a fun show to work on. I worked with Frank Gorshin, who played the Riddler. Adam West was very nice but I didn't get to know Burt Ward very well. Marlo Thomas of *That Girl* was very quiet. And when I did *Gidget*, Sally Field would shoot a scene with me and then go right to her dressing room. I knew the stars had a lot on their minds and lots of lines to memorize so they didn't have the time to say, 'Hi, how are you doing?' I got to know a lot of the crews who worked on these series, so I would joke and have fun with them instead."

Nineteen sixty-five turned out to be Joy's busiest year. She had a recurring role as Tony (*Leave It to Beaver*) Dow's girlfriend on the daytime soap *Never Too Young*. On the big screen, she could be seen in four movies. She played small roles in *The Loved One* as a ditzy blonde starlet and in *Young Dillinger* as a gun moll. The latter starred Nick Adams as infamous gangster John Dillinger and former Miss America Mary Ann Mobley as his girl. Supporting them was a crew of talented young actors including Robert Conrad (as Pretty Boy Floyd), John Ashley (as Baby Face Nelson) and Dan Terranova (as Homer Van Meter). "We shot this over in Burbank," remembers Joy. "The guys in this film were the hot up-and-coming young actors of that time. I was very impressed by them so it was like—wow!"

Joy starred in her next two films, *Village of the Giants* (1965), and *One Way Wahine* (1965) both aimed squarely at the youth market. *Village of the Giants* was loosely based on the H.G. Wells novel *Food of the Gods* and was produced and directed by Bert I. Gordon. Here science fiction meets teen exploitation head-on as boy genius Ronny Howard develops a magic goop, which is eaten by a cat and two ducks that grow to giant proportions. When a group of troublemaking teenagers (including Beau Bridges, Joy Harmon, Tisha Sterling, Tim Rooney, Gail Gilmore and Bob Random) hear of this at the local discotheque, they steal the goop, sprout to "new heights" and terrorize the small town. The local teens (led by Tommy Kirk and Johnny Crawford) join forces with the police to thwart the marauding giants, who have an axe to grind with the adult establishment. When the good teens fail to stop the overgrown delinquents, Howard develops a smoke gas that counteracts the growth formula. The "giant" teens shrink to normal size and are then run out of town.

The opening scene of *Village of the Giants* features a group of delinquents piling out of their wrecked auto after crashing on a mountain road during a rainstorm. They then begin dancing in the mud to the film's rockin' music score, which is heard throughout the movie. "This scene was awful," exclaims Joy. "I

Joy Harmon (*left*) and cast get down and dirty to Jack Nitzsche's groovy theme in the opening scene from *Village of the Giants* (Embassy, 1965).

had mud in my eyes and face—I was covered in mud all over my body! That scene was so true and authentic. They really made us get down in the mud. We just went for it and did the scene. The mud wasn't thick but slimy—very slippery. We couldn't stand up and were falling all the time. It was cold and I only had a little crop top on. The guys had a ball with it but the girls were freezing and dirty. I felt so ugly—there was nothing glamorous about it!" Regarding the music, the film's awesome theme was composed by Jack Nitzsche and is called *The Last Race*. Writing in *Hollywood Rock*, Marshall Crenshaw called it "the most dramatic soundtrack I've encountered in a rock 'n' roll film."

Bert I. Gordon, who made *Village of the Giants*, was known for his previous gimmick films involving giants or huge animals (*King Dinosaur* [1955], *The Amazing Colossal Man* [1957], *Attack of the Puppet People* [1958], and *Earth vs. the Spider* [1958]). He not only produced and directed *Village of the Giants* but was responsible for the special effects as well. Though the effects are cheesy and amateurish, they do have an endearing quality about them—none more so when giant-size ducks are seen doing the Jerk and the Watusi at the Whiskey a-Go-Go. Another interesting effects scene is when the giant teenagers are sitting on the stage of the town's movie theater and Tommy Kirk brings them food, which is supposed to be chicken. Gordon filmed the teens separately from Kirk and used rear projection to edit the scene together. According to Joy, "The prop guys gave us some really small bird that they fried to make it look like a tiny chicken. It came from a famous chicken place and it was horrible. I hated eating whatever it was and had to keep eating it over and over. They even duplicated the chicken box and the Coke bottles as small props. I thought Bert did a good job with the effects."

"Bert I. Gordon was a super nice man," continues Joy. "I could talk to him very easily. He wasn't a typical director who told you to stand here or there but more of a creative person. And I think the cast responded to that." Though Joy respected Gordon, she did have a bit of a problem with Bert regarding one of her scenes. "The only thing that irritated me while doing this film was the scene when my sweater pops open as I grow to a giant. You didn't see anything, but I hated that scene. I objected to wearing that sweater and asked Bert Gordon if I could wear something else to pop out of. Nobody else had that problem. They wore clothes that got smaller but mine had to open. I also felt very uncomfortable because I couldn't wear a bra and I don't like going without one."

To promote *Village of the Giants*, Gordon didn't leave any stone unturned. He cast popular teen actors Tommy Kirk and Johnny Crawford and hired the offspring (Beau Bridges, Tisha Sterling and Tim Rooney) of famous actors to play delinquents. "Everybody was just so nice to work with—we were just a bunch of kids having a really good time," Joy says. "I didn't have much to do with Tommy Kirk because he wasn't part of our group who becomes giants. Neither was Johnny Crawford, but he was sweet and would hang around to watch us do our scenes. Tisha is *so* beautiful in this film. I remember that she has such a gorgeous face. And Beau is a very nice guy and liked to joke around. He got married just before filming began."

Gordon also hired popular rock artists (the Beau Brummels, Freddy Cannon and Mike Clifford) to perform in a party scene and at the local discotheque. "We filmed the discotheque scene at the Whiskey a-Go-Go," says Joy exuberantly. "I used to have the best time at that club. I just loved dancing and used to go there or some of the other Sunset Strip clubs all the time. Dancing was my thing so it was great to dance to the Beau Brummels in the film. It was my favorite scene." A great ad campaign featured Johnny Crawford scaling Harmon's bountiful giant-size breasts. Though her sexy dancing and provocative poster art didn't offend Joy ("None of that stuff focusing on my bosom ever bothered me"), it did irk the MPAA Production Code, who requested scene cuts. According to *Variety*, Gordon was asked to snip portions of Joy doing a sensuous dance in a bikini-like garment and of Johnny Crawford stealing a piece of Joy's clothing. Gordon not only obliged but also played up the cuts in all the newspapers to attract an even bigger audience. It worked and *Village of the Giants* made money. As for Joy, she proved she was more than just a body and gave an amusing performance as a giant thrill-seeker with a conscience.

Harmon journeyed from the *Village of the Giants* to the land of bikinis in *One Way Wahine*, her final film released in 1965. This beach flick's great tag line read, "She's the Swingin'est Thing on Waikiki ... That Way-Out Gal the Smart Guys Call One Way Wahine—It Rhymes with Bikini!" And that pretty much sums

Village of the Giants (Embassy, 1965) featured Joy Harmon, Tisha Sterling, Beau Bridges and Bob Random as delinquents who grow to enormous proportions.

up Joy's role in this quickie that was filmed on location in Oahu. David Whorf plays a surfer who convinces beach babe Joy (who, *Box Office Magazine* commented, "is very adept at playing comedy") and two friends (Anthony Eisley and Adele Claire) to steal some stolen loot from two bank robbers hiding out in a beach house. When their plans go awry, beach bum Edgar Bergen (*sans* Charlie McCarthy) comes to their rescue. "My sister Gay went with me to Hawaii and she was in the movie too," recalls Joy with a smile. "I was the lead and worked everyday all the way through the shoot. I had a really good part—it was a very emotional role. At one point my character almost gets raped. It wasn't like any of my previous roles. The actors in *One Way Wahine* were all fun to work with—especially Edgar Bergen. He reminded me of Groucho Marx but he was warmer—more of a family-type of man. Groucho was always thinking and quick with the jokes. Edgar was more laid-back and relaxed. He just had a peace of mind about him."

One Way Wahine received only limited release. "It never was released in Los Angeles. Once in awhile I would think, 'When is it coming out?' Still today, I think 'When is it coming out?'" Joy's next film *Cool Hand Luke* (1967) was a huge hit and brought her national notoriety. Joy was basically a shy, old-fashioned girl and was not prepared for the fleeting fame this role brought her. "I never wanted to be a big star," Joy says

Beach denizens (*left to right*) Anthony Eisley, Adele Claire, David Whorf and Harmon look on as surf daddy Edgar Bergen is questioned by the police in *One Way Wahine* (United Screen Arts, 1965).

sincerely. "Whatever roles I got, I did my best because I loved acting. If I didn't work, I loved being home. I didn't have the drive to be on top. I had this agent named Leon Lance who was around forever in Hollywood. He got me the interview for *Cool Hand Luke* and told me that I had to wear a bikini for it. Paul Newman, [director] Stuart Rosenberg and somebody else were there. I remember Paul Newman said to me, 'Gosh, you have the bluest eyes!' They just talked to me and that was it. It was a small part with no lines but I wanted to work with Newman, so when they offered it to me I accepted."

Cool Hand Luke was an unsentimental prison drama starring Paul Newman as a disturbed loner who is sent to a correctional camp after decapitating a number of parking meters. Newman goes from outsider to camp hero after eating more than 50 hardboiled eggs in a contest, one of the film's many high points. He wins over his fellow cons, including tough George Kennedy, who won an Oscar for his performance. Though Joy has no dialogue, her scene is another standout as she comes out of her house attired in a skimpy low-cut ratty house dress and suggestively washes her car in front of the frustrated prisoners of a chain gang. This bit is truly one of the sixties' most provocative movie moments. "I never had any inclination that this would be such a memorable role,"

In *Cool Hand Luke* (Warner Bros., 1967), Harmon teases the chain gang (including George Kennedy and Paul Newman in background) as she seductively washes her car.

says Joy. "Except for being in a movie with Paul Newman, I never expected this part to be so notable and get the reaction it did. Of *all* the things I've done, people know me most from this film." *Cool Hand Luke* is an immensely entertaining relevant social drama examining life for men in a prison camp and should not be missed.

Cool Hand Luke was filmed in Stockton, California ("It was so country-like with acres and acres of land"). None of the actors was allowed to bring their wives because director Stuart Rosenberg wouldn't allow women on the set. He wanted his actors to have the feel of what it would be like to work on a chain gang without female contact so when they finally saw one their reactions would be believable. When Joy arrived to do her scene, she stayed in the hotel for two days and never saw anyone. They kept her away from all the actors until filming began. Joy's scene is very suggestive, especially for 1967. With Newman, Kennedy and the rest of the chain gang entranced, Harmon washes her car like she's making love to a man. While Kennedy dubs her his innocent "Lucille," Newman realizes she is just a tease and knows exactly what she is doing by getting the prisoners excited. Joy, however, had no clue what the scene would be like since it was shot out of sequence. "Stuart Rosenberg was very specific and knew exactly what he wanted," remembers Joy.

"I guess you can tell that by the way the scene comes off—but I didn't realize it. And I don't think I even realized it right after I did it. There were a lot of things he made me do a certain way—soaping the windows, holding the hose—that had a two-way meaning. He would tell me to look different ways and we kept shooting it over and over again. I just figured I was washing the car. I've always been naïve and innocent. I was acting and not trying to be sexy. Maybe that's why the scene played so well. After seeing it at the premiere, I was a bit embarrassed.

"Stuart Rosenberg was so sensitive and took time to work with me," Joy says fondly. "I didn't even have a line but he just wanted everything motivated with a thought behind it. He was an actor's director—more concerned with the actors than the lighting or anything else. He kept talking with me and it was like a bonding kind of thing, which is why I was able to release all that energy in that scene. Stuart Rosenberg was my favorite director."

Cool Hand Luke was one of the year's biggest critical and commercial hits. Newman, Kennedy, the Donn Pearce–Frank R. Pierson screenplay and Lalo Schifrin's rousing score all received Academy Award nominations with only Kennedy scoring a win. Despite the film's success, Joy didn't capitalize on the notoriety the movie brought her. In 1968, she met her future husband, TV and movie producer Jeff Gourson, while horseback riding. Soon after they were married, American International Pictures offered Joy a contract and a lead in *Born Wild* (1968), which was shooting in Arizona, but she turned it down. "Jeff didn't want me to do it," Joy says. "Instead we moved up north to a ranch that had about 25 horses. I was so into riding and caring for them that I didn't want to work. If a role came up I would take the part, but I never was a pusher. If I was someone more aggressive—and if I had the right person handling me—I think that I could have gotten bigger roles."

Joy continued playing the dumb blonde on such TV series as *Run for Your Life*; *I Dream of Jeannie*; *Love, American Style* ("It was like a party and they used some great directors") and *The Odd Couple*. Her favorite show to work on was *The Monkees*. Joy made two appearances playing—what else—a ditz. "I loved doing this show," Joy says happily. "I was able to go my fullest and they wouldn't say, 'Wait a minute. Tone it down.' I had the tendency to overplay a bit—my eyes would get huge and I would just feel it and go! They never held me back and let me play the scene however I wanted. I loved working with their directors because I could tell that they liked me. And that's what counts because if you feel that you're liked, you can come out and give them what they want. On some of the other shows I worked on, you didn't know what the directors wanted acting-wise. If you didn't have something to offer them, you'd be lost. You had to improvise and most TV shows were done very fast. I was on the daytime drama *Never Too Young* for about a year so that helped me a lot when I did primetime shows. It was good training because on soap operas you work quickly and have to deliver.

"The Monkees themselves were great to work with," continues Joy. "They were very talented and full of energy. I knew Michael Nesmith because his wife and I went to the same church and he would sometimes accompany her. But I had the best rapport with Mickey Dolenz. He was fantastic. I played his Las Vegas showgirl girlfriend in one episode and we had so much fun working

Behind-the-scenes shot from *Cool Hand Luke* (Warner Bros., 1967) with Harmon and director Stuart Rosenberg.

together. This show was even zanier to work on than *Batman* was because they could never find the guys. They built them a place where they could go and fool around. The studio knew about it but didn't care." That place was nicknamed "the Black Box" and the Monkees could be found there playing music, smoking grass or just goofing off.

Joy's last feature film was the Andy Griffith comedy *Angel in My Pocket* (1969). Griffith (whom Joy found to be "a very nice man") plays a minister trying to win the confidence of his new parishioners. Joy portrayed Miss Holland, a beauty contestant who had to go on stage in Griffith's church and dance in a windmill costume. "We had so much trouble because the windmill's arms wouldn't go 'round," remembers Joy with a laugh. "The batteries were taped to my bikini top and the crew had a lot of fun trying to get them to revolve!" Once they did, she was able to continue with the scene by sticking out her bosom and saying to an embarrassed Griffith, 'See, it works!'"

Joy retired from acting in 1973 to raise a family. She has a son, Jason, and two daughters, Julie and Jaime. "It was my husband's wish that I stop acting. I think I would have kept going if he wasn't against it because I always liked working, but I love being a mom even more." Joy didn't completely leave show business. She did looping and voiceovers on such series as *Columbo*, *B.L. Stryker* and *Quantum Leap*, which was produced by her husband. Looking back on a career where her body overshadowed her acting talent, Joy reflects, "Being blonde and busty were the things that got me the fun parts. I think it helped me. That's why I probably played the dumb sexpot role a lot. But I have an ability to act too. On the other hand, I probably lost a lot of roles because of my body [because] they thought of me as just that—a body. That's okay, though. Maybe I never would have worked in my whole life if I didn't look the way I did."

Today Joy has her own business, Aunt Joy's Cakes. "I've always loved baking," exclaims Joy. "While I was still acting, I would stay up late and bring all sorts of baked goods to the set. I started first just supplying local coffeehouses. Now I cater for Disney and a few other studios." She is also trying to restart her acting career and has signed with a commercial agent. Despite the years, Joy retains the same bubbly personality and look that she had during the sixties and hopefully will be gracing the screen once again. But for Joy the most important things in her life are her children. "I've had a fun acting career, a great family and now a successful business. I feel truly blessed."

Film Appearances

1958   Let's Rock (Columbia) d. Harry Foster.
1961   Mad Dog Coll (Columbia) d. Burt Balaban.
1963   Under the Yum Yum Tree (Columbia) d. David Swift.
1965   Young Dillinger (Allied Artists) d. Terry O. Morse.
       One Way Wahine (United Screen Arts) d. William O. Brown.
       Village of the Giants (Embassy) d. Bert I. Gordon.
       The Loved One (MGM) d. Tony Richardson.
1967   A Guide for the Married Man (20th Century–Fox) d. Gene Kelly.
       Cool Hand Luke (Warner Bros.) d. Stuart Rosenberg.
1969   Angel in My Pocket (Universal) d. Alan Rafkin.

Television Appearances

Tell It to Groucho [series regular] 1/11/62 to 5/31/62 CBS.
The Beverly Hillbillies "Elly Becomes a Secretary" 5/22/63 CBS.
My Three Sons "Tramp Goes Hollywood" 5/7/64 ABC.
Burke's Law "Who Killed the Richest Man in the World?" 11/11/64 ABC.
Burke's Law "Who Killed the Strangler?" 1/6/65 ABC.
Never Too Young [series regular as Marilyn] 9/27/65 to 6/24/66 ABC.
Mr. Roberts "Carry Me Back to Cocoa Island" 12/31/65 NBC.
Batman "A Riddle a Day, Keeps the Riddler Away" 2/16/66 ABC.
Batman "When the Rats Away, the Mice Will Play" 2/17/66 ABC.
Gomer Pyle, USMC "Gomer, the Would-Be Hero" 4/15/66 CBS.
Bewitched "Divided He Falls" 5/5/66 ABC.
The Rounders "The Scavenger Hunt" 10/1/66 ABC.
Occasional Wife "The Marriage Counselor" 11/22/66 NBC.
From Here to Eternity (unaired pilot) 1967 ABC.
That Girl "Pass the Potatoes, Ethel Merman" 9/7/67 ABC.
The Monkees "The Picture Frame" 9/18/67 NBC.
Run for Your Life "The Frozen Image" 10/4/67 NBC.
The Monkees "Monkees on the Wheel" 12/11/67 NBC.
Kraft Music Hall (w/ guest host Alan King) 9/17/69 NBC.
20th Century Follies (pilot) 2/16/72.
Love, American Style "Love and the Secret Habit" 12/8/72 ABC.
The Odd Couple "Don't Believe in Roomers" 12/22/72 ABC.
Thicker Than Water (episode title unknown) 8/4/73 ABC.

Also:
The Man from U.N.C.L.E., *Gidget*, *I Dream of Jeannie*, *McHale's Navy* and *That's Life*.

Eileen O'Neill

During the mid-sixties, television viewers could not change the channel without catching a glimpse of Eileen O'Neill. This beautiful brunette (sometimes blonde) Irish lass was a regular on *Burke's Law* starring Gene Barry for two years. She then made appearances on practically all of the era's top sitcoms including *The Beverly Hillbillies, I Dream of Jeannie, Bewitched, My Favorite Martian, The Munsters, Get Smart* and *Batman*. "Television in those days was kind of peeking out from the shelf," comments Eileen. "Up until that time, TV shows were more traditional. Then all of a sudden, shows like *Batman* were trying to be more bizarre and zany and different. I think that it was the sign of the times. The mid-sixties were mod with hippies and flower children who were breaking away from tradition. It was an expression and a breakthrough. Good or bad, it had to happen." Eileen's career was not limited to the small screen, though. She made her film debut in *A Majority of One* and then played a haughty rich girl in the teen exploitation film *Teenage Millionaire*. After taking small roles in *4 for Texas; Kiss Me, Stupid;* and *The Third Day*, Eileen played the heroine in the James Bond spoof *A Man Called Dagger* starring Paul Mantee. In 1973, she retired from acting to concentrate on her marriage.

Eileen O'Neill was born on July 3 in Philadelphia, Pennsylvania. Her parents Harry and Mary O'Neill are deceased and her sister Dolores ("She is absolutely the best!") recently relocated to Los Angeles. "My mother was a huge movie fan and took me to practically every movie that was ever made," recalls Eileen. "I would sit there from the time when I couldn't even see over the seats and I started to project myself up there on the screen. Some of the names that I ultimately worked with I had seen in those early days of going to the movies. I grew up quite a movie fan due to my mother. As a result, I wanted to act myself. There was one film in particular where Mitzi Gaynor was singing and dancing on the deck of a ship. She was having so much fun, I decided that is what I wanted to do."

In pursuit of her dream, Eileen decided to follow in the footsteps of her mother, who had been a fashion and

Eileen O'Neill (courtesy of Eileen O'Neill).

product endorsement model. While in high school, Eileen enrolled in the Philadelphia Modeling School. They began entering her in beauty contests and she landed a regular gig on *The Joe Pyne Show*, a locally televised talk show. "I went over there for an interview because they wanted a girl on camera," recalls Eileen. "While Pyne would be interviewing his guests, the home audience would call in questions to me. At a certain point in the show, the camera focused on me and I would select questions I thought were pertinent. [*Laughs*] It was kind of funny if you think of the scope of sophisticated issues addressed on the show and how I was just a teenager. Nonetheless, I would ask the guests three or four questions. I did this for about a year, then stopped because I was ready to come to California to further my acting desires. I didn't tell my parents that it was a permanent move because they wouldn't have permitted it. I told them I was going to California for a trip." Within her first week in California she got a Pepsi commercial. She began taking acting lessons and made her film debut in a small role in *A Majority of One* (1961) starring Rosalind Russell.

Eileen's second film was the rock 'n' roll musical *Teenage Millionaire* (1961). Young Jimmy Clanton is Bobby Chalmers, an aspiring singer and songwriter plagued by the title "Teenage Millionaire" when his parents are killed in a plane crash. His stuffy aunt (ZaSu Pitts) hires a bodyguard (Rocky Graziano) to keep her nephew out of trouble. Since he has an interest in the recording industry, his aunt arranges for him to work at one of the family-owned radio stations. There he falls for a record filer named Bambi (Diane Jergens) but his aunt pushes him to the more proper haughty Desidieria (Eileen O'Neill). Bobby secretly composes and records a song called "Green Light." After a series of mishaps, the song becomes a hit, Bobby is drafted and he is reunited with Bambi. As with most films of this ilk, *Teenage Millionaire* received tepid reviews. Though *Variety* said it "has teen appeal but lacks the quality to sustain itself," they commented that Eileen O'Neill "improves the scenery." Rock aficionados were more vehemently hard on it. Alan Betrock called it a "a pretty bad film" and Marshall Crenshaw commented, "The producers of this film are probably on the run because there's no statute of limitations on crimes like this." What makes *Teenage Millionaire* watchable is the 11 rock 'n' roll numbers interspersed throughout the movie. The music sequences featuring Jackie Wilson, Chubby Checker and Dion (among others) were filmed in a process called Musicolor, a duotone process that tinted the black-and-white film a different color—from chartreuse to orange to lavender. And as a last ditch effort to get the kids into the theatres, the producers offered "a free record of Jimmy Clanton singing the title song to every teenager who buys a ticket."

Eileen went to New York when she was chosen as one of the six finalists for the Miss Rheingold contest in 1963. ("We toured throughout New York and New England doing television, radio and public appearances. Everywhere we went, we were driven in cars adorned with banners featuring our names. It was a fun and exciting experience.") Though Eileen did not win, she began a close relationship with another finalist, actress Chris Noel—a friendship which continues to this day. "Chris is like family to me," says Eileen fondly. "She is so honest and genuine. When Chris moved out to LA we rented a house together on Coldwater Canyon in Beverly Hills. That was when she started to make her trips to Vietnam with her show for Armed Forces Radio. At that time, the anti-war protests were very strong and Chris began getting a lot of flack for her work. I remember one time I was shopping in the supermarket and somebody said to me, 'Why don't you tell Chris "enough is enough" and to stop with this Vietnam business?' What Chris was doing was very controversial at that time. But, bottom line, look what Chris went on to achieve—running all these homeless shelters for Vietnam vets. She has a heart of gold. She always had that tendency to help people and that was her only motivation in doing what she did."

Returning to Hollywood, Eileen focused solidly on her acting career. She landed small roles as one of Anita Ekberg's French maids in *4 for Texas* (1963) with Frank Sinatra and as a Las Vegas showgirl opposite Dean Martin in *Kiss Me, Stupid* (1964), directed by the legendary Billy Wilder. Describing Wilder's directorial style, Eileen comments, "Wilder knew what he wanted and was firm in that regard. But he also possessed this adorable, wry little smile. To me he carried a big stick but was very, very likable. I don't mind that kind of firmness and dedication as long as it is beneficial. His attentions were always for the good of the film as opposed to ego gratification." When asked to compare working with Martin and Sinatra, Eileen says, "Dean Martin was very funny. A lot of people think of him just as a singer and an actor but he had a tremendous sense of humor. Dean was a lot softer around the edges than Frank Sinatra. In those days, Frank would work only in the afternoon. He would come into the studio by helicopter, drop in to do his scene and then leave. If you were in the same scenes with Frank, he wouldn't feed you your lines when the camera was not on him. Dean wasn't quite like that. He was good-natured and easy to work with."

When asked if Sinatra's prima donna behavior bothered her, being a novice actress, Eileen replies, "Yes, it did. When it was time to shoot your closeups, the real giving actors would take the time to act with you even if they weren't on camera. It makes for a better working environment and a better movie. An actor finds his truth in the eyes of another actor. Acting is reacting. You lock in and have to have a connection with the person you are doing the scene with. If you are reading your lines to a script person standing beside the camera who really isn't skilled in the techniques of acting, your job is doubled. You don't have the feedback of another person playing their acting instrument. From that point of view, it makes your job harder."

Eileen's most memorable film role was playing Erica opposite Paul Mantee as *A Man Called Dagger* (1967), which was one of many James Bond imitations. "I was sent out on an interview for this role," remembers Eileen. "I read for Richard Rush, the director, who later received an Academy Award nomination for *The Stunt Man* in 1980. I was a brunette but he envisioned the character as a blonde so he asked me to come back wearing a wig, which I did. I read for him again and he said I read differently as a blonde, which is an interesting comment. I got the role and I didn't mind wearing the blonde wig. Since I am Irish, I have fair skin and blue eyes but I am naturally a brunette. But with my coloring, they were always putting blonde wigs on me. I was a blonde in this and on *Get Smart*. On *Amos Burke—Secret Agent* I was a blonde *and* a brunette. Chris Noel and I used to laugh over this because she was blonde and there were occasions where she would be cast to wear a brunette wig and I would be cast to wear a blonde wig. We'd say, 'They have this backwards.' Nowadays, it is very common to change hair colors—look at Madonna. But in those days it was unusual. I remember I was getting so many roles as a blonde, I took out an ad in the trades with my credits as a blonde and as a brunette."

In *A Man Called Dagger*, Eileen's character Erica is a beautiful, fair-haired Canadian newly arrived in California to work at a beauty farm run by the pampered Ingrid (Sue Ane Langdon). But Ingrid's evil paramour Rudolph Koffman (Jan Murray) kidnaps her. Koffman is a former SS colonel who operates a meat packing plant which is a front for his neo–Nazi group to take over the world. Erica is part of his plan and is brainwashed to follow Koffman's orders (transmitted via a small radio receiver drilled in her tooth). Tipped off by her friend Joy (Maureen Arthur), secret agent Dirk Dagger rescues Erica only to have her try to kill him. He returns Erica to Koffman in exchange for his kidnapped partner Harper Davis (Terry Moore). After Dagger forcefully persuades Ingrid to reveal the secret entrance to Koffman's hideout, he arrives just in time to rescue a tied-up Erica from a swinging scimitar.

Dean Martin and O'Neill almost share a kiss in Billy Wilder's comedy *Kiss Me, Stupid* (Lopert, 1964) (courtesy of Eileen O'Neill).

The climactic fight between Dagger and Koffman takes place in a meat locker with hundreds of hanging carcasses.

A Man Called Dagger is a passable entry in the spy spoof genre. Paul Mantee makes for a very sexy, masculine hero and Eileen is the perfect damsel in distress. One of their scenes takes place in a hotel room and is particularly well acted. "Paul is a very dedicated and a very giving actor—what I call an actor's actor," remarks Eileen fondly. Though a low-budget production, the film also features some elaborate sets and action sequences. "Fortunately, we didn't have any mishaps on the set in regards to the action scenes. I wore a one-piece knee-length white dress in the film but when I was tied up, it pulled it way up. It made it look quite short but no one seemed to mind that. [*Laughs*] There was one thing that we were all kidding about regarding one of the backers. He smoked these stinky, smelly cigars and inadvertently put one of them in someone's personal satchel. Terry Moore and I were giggling and laughing about it. I think that was the worse mishap that happened on that set."

The success of the film must be credited to the directorial skills of Richard Rush. Eileen wholeheartedly agrees. "Richard Rush was very focused. There are directors who are strictly technical directors but there also are directors who have the skill of knowing the actor's training and the actor's chores (things you have to do as an actor to be believable). Richard was in touch with that. To me, he was not just doing this film from a technical point of view—he was there in the characters. It was always refreshing to find a director like that because so many times you are left to your own devices. When you are doing a scene, you sometimes need that third eye because there are so many choices an actor can make in any role. Perhaps the choice the actor makes is not the best for the piece. You need that third eye to really guide you and say, 'Wait a minute. Maybe another choice will be a little better for the concept of the picture.' To have a director, like Richard Rush, who knows acting (from the inside out) deal with you is manna from heaven! [*Laughs*] He talks to you on a different level than a more technical director."

A Man Called Dagger was one of Eileen's few forays onto the big screen. She became almost typecast as a TV actress due to her regular role as Sgt. Gloria Ames (beginning in 1963) on *Burke's Law*, starring Gene Barry. While this may have bothered some actresses, Eileen relished the chance to do television and to develop a steady character week after week. "About the third week of the show, I replaced the original girl who was cast in *Burke's Law*," says Eileen. "My character was the only regular female on the show. I had to audition and audition to get this role. I was so excited when I got this part because it was an identity—*Burke's Law* was something Eileen O'Neill could be identified with. I think that is what started the television aspect of my career as opposed to working in films."

Produced and created by Aaron Spelling, *Burke's Law* ran for two seasons on ABC. Barry played the debonair Amos Burke, head of the metropolitan Homicide Squad Division for the Los Angeles Police Department. Burke was also a wealthy playboy who traveled by chauffeured Rolls-Royce. Partnered with eager, equally dashing Detective Tim Tilson (Gary Conway), they would solve each week's bizarre murder case. Aaron made sure to populate each episode with at least six major guest stars and to flank Barry with some of the sexiest starlets of

Secret agent Dagger (Paul Mantee) arrives in the nick of time to save Erica (O'Neill) from being sliced in half in *A Man Called Dagger* (MGM, 1967).

the day (two of whom, Joan Staley and Sharon Hillyer, appeared with O'Neill and Barry on the cover of *TV Guide*). "I felt very privileged to have worked on *Burke's Law* at that stage of my career," Eileen proudly remarks. "I could learn from so many seasoned actors who had years and years of experience. I felt I was having additional acting schooling in my environment of work. It was Aaron Spelling's idea to bring in big-name guest stars. He is the biggest fan of them all. And I have to respect him for being able to act out his fantasies."

Though the guest stars had the opportunity to play some outrageous characters, Eileen's character was more down-to-earth and most of her scenes took place at the police station. Recalling her working experience with Gene Barry, Eileen says, "Though my character was a police sergeant, she wore sexy clothes rather than a uniform and there was always an underlying sexual tension between her and Gene Barry's Amos Burke. While working on a regular basis with Gene, I never sensed any overt ego from him. Maybe because I wasn't a threat. His wife Betty and I became friends at the beauty shop, of all places. She would tell me all these sweet stories about Gene. That obviously had me look at Gene in a different light. Their marriage remains one of the major success stories in Hollywood. In that regard, there was a kind of generation gap between Gene and Gary Conway. Gary was younger and rather flirtatious. Though Gary was very professional with me, he had a way with the gals. He flirted with every pretty girl who walked in on the set with, 'Oh, hi. How are you?' Gary was married at the time and his wife was a former beauty pageant winner. I guess he just enjoyed pretty women."

Eileen's work on *Burke's Law* got her noticed and she became a very sought-after TV actress. She was able to play both comedy and drama to good effect. Her professionalism and talent got her voted "Most Promising Personalities of 1966" by casting directors from five major studios. She and seven other lovelies (including Chris Noel, Susan St. James, Melodie Johnson and Marianne Gordon) were introduced on *The Bob Hope Show*. Each girl came out and bantered with Hope and his guest Bing Crosby. When Eileen mentioned that she enjoyed playing a police sergeant on *Burke's Law*, Hope quipped, "You were a cop?! Where does a fellow go to turn himself in?" Eileen recalls, "When I came for rehearsal, I drove up to the guard gate. I announced my name and said that I was there for *The Bob Hope Show*. The guard looked on the list and found my name. He pointed to a lot that was a far distance from the building where the rehearsal was going to be and said to me, 'You park over there.' I looked at where he was sending me and then looked at the empty parking spaces around the building. I figured I better correct this error and told him that I was a Star of Tomorrow. He replied, '*Tomorrow* you park here by the building, *today* you park down there!'" [*Laughs*]

Because she was so adept at playing comedy, O'Neill seemed to have swung through every major comedy series during the mid-sixties including *The Beverly Hillbillies*, *I Dream of Jeannie*, *Bewitched*, *My Favorite Martian*, *Get Smart*, *The Munsters* and *Batman*. For his twenty-fifth anniversary TV special, Steve Allen chose a scene he performed with Eileen as one of his all-time favorites. And on *The Tonight Show*, O'Neill demonstrated to Johnny Carson the various techniques of kissing different leading men. "We discussed how I kissed Bill Bixby, George Peppard and Red Buttons and how it was awkward kissing an actor you may not know very well in front of the camera and a sound stage full of people. Johnny and I then demonstrated the various styles of kissing through the evolution of filmmaking—how they kissed in movies of the thirties and forties. It was a very funny segment."

Regarding her sitcom appearances, *Bewitched* was the most memorable. A scene from this episode ("…And Then I Wrote") was included in *Reader's Digest*'s videocassette compilation of TV's funniest scenes (*Laugh? … I Thought I'd Die*, produced in 1998). In this episode, Samantha (Elizabeth Montgomery) is tapped to write the town's pageant on the centennial of the end of the War Between the States. When Darrin (Dick York) finds her characters too pat, she takes

O'Neill and Bob Hope during rehearsals for the NBC-TV special *The Bob Hope Show* (courtesy of Eileen O'Neill).

Endora's (Agnes Moorehead) advice and brings them to life to help get the feel for them. Soon a Confederate Captain (Olan Soule), an Indian (Tom Nardini) and a beautiful Yankee (O'Neill) are walking around the Stevens' living room. Trouble brews when nosy neighbor Gladys Kravitz (Sandra Gould) spies the shenanigans. As Sam tries to deal with Gladys, the characters re-write Sam's ending for the pageant. "I had so much fun doing *Bewitched*," says Eileen. "I got to wear this long, beautiful Civil War–era gown. And Elizabeth Montgomery was such a doll to me. Months later when I was doing another show at Columbia, Elizabeth was there visiting the set. She made a point to come over and say hello to me." When asked to compare Montgomery to Barbara Eden of *I Dream of Jeannie*, Eileen opines, "If I had to choose, I'd say Elizabeth Montgomery was warmer."

Both *Bewitched* and *I Dream of Jeannie* featured complicated special effects for the day. Each show had people popping in and out of the frames. "In those days, they used what they called a plastic wall," recalls Eileen. "When I had to disappear on *I Dream of Jeannie*, it was hard because we stopped the scene right before lunch and we had to come back afterwards to pick it up in exactly that same spot. So I had to stand on one side of the plastic wall and they drew my body on it so when we returned I could match to the nth degree. Every part of my body had to be in the exact same position. Back then we were in the primitive stages of special effects so you had to do it in a very laborious manner. Today everything would be computer generated."

Things got even sillier for Eileen on *Batman*. She played the cleverly named character Millie Second, "henchgirl" to the devious Clock King (played by esteemed European actor Walter Slezak). "Walter Slezak was another kind man," comments Eileen. "We spent so much time talking. I sensed an effort on his part to share his richness of experience in the theater with me. We had extensive conversations on acting. Again, I appreciated the knowledge you can [soak up] like a sponge when you have an opportunity to talk to people who are so good at what they do."

During the course of Eileen's two-part *Batman* episode (co-authored by Bill Finger, an early writer of the *Batman* comic books), Clock King, along with Millie Second and his gang the Second Hands, rob a string of jewelry stores and are pursued by Batman and Robin. Among the crazy contraptions used in these episodes were giant clock-springs used to slow down the Dynamic Duo and a huge hourglass with sand pouring down on the captured Caped Crusaders to suffocate them. When asked if she had any problems working with Adam West and Burt Ward (especially since they have both admitted to their penchant for their female co-stars), Eileen replies with a laugh, "No, I didn't. But if I had had any problems with Burt Ward, he would have been in big trouble because he ultimately married my friend Kathy Kersh. Burt and Adam were professional and so much fun to work with. They both jumped into the zany spirit of their roles. They played their parts to the hilt and that is why *Batman* was so successful in its day."

Before the Smothers Brothers hit it big with their variety series, they starred in a sitcom called *The Smothers Brothers Show* during the 1965-66 season. Eileen guest-starred on four episodes as Wanda and was slated to become a regular during the second season if the show was picked up by CBS. Alas, it was not. In this offbeat comedy series, Tom Smothers played an inept, novice angel assigned to Earth to help people, while Dick was a brash publishing executive forced to share his bachelor pad with his late sibling and to help him with his deeds. The character of Wanda was brought in during the second half of the season to be a friend to Tom's angel. "There was one episode where I developed a crush on Dick and he went out with another girl," recalls Eileen. "Our romance never came to fruition but there was a little byplay between our characters. The Smothers Brothers were adorable to work with. They are exactly like what you saw when they did their variety show. They liked playing pranks on each other and they were professional and not prima donnas. I was disappointed when the network didn't pick the show up for a second season because I liked the working atmosphere."

Working steadily in television, Eileen had a lot of experience working with directors of that medium. When told a number of actresses bemoaned the fact that TV directors for the most part didn't give them guidance with their performances, Eileen agrees and opines why. "Working on TV, you had to come with your own wares. A couple of things caused that to happen. There was a time limit of approximately a week to ten days

O'Neill as Clock King's henchgirl Millie Second with thugs from the ABC-TV series *Batman* in 1966.

to shoot a half-hour sitcom or an hour drama versus months and months to put 90 minutes on a big screen. In movies, you had days to shoot a page of dialogue but in television you had to complete a show in one week. The time constraint was such that if you didn't come to the set knowing your lines and your acting, you couldn't make it through TV—it was much harder than film. Doing a film was a luxury in comparison to TV. It was almost like going on vacation because you had so much time and so much money to achieve those 90 minutes. But in television you were limited. It was in and out sort of like a production line. You had to know your craft and be skilled enough to be able to change on a dime. In television, you received the script in advance of shooting; then, after learning your lines, you could get rewrites immediately before you walked on the set to do the scene. If you were lucky, you'd receive the rewrites the night before. Doing television challenged your ability at all ends. However, dealing with those challenges aids in sharpening your acting skills."

In 1968, Eileen was cast as a regular performer on ABC's *Operation: Entertainment*, which was similar to Bob Hope's Christmas specials in that it was performed live in front of GIs. "One show was performed aboard the USS *Constellation*," remembers Eileen. "That audience was particularly enthusiastic as they had just returned from Vietnam." After the series ended, Eileen moved to New York. Though she relocated, that didn't stop the offers from coming in. She appeared in over 80 TV commercials and because she wore so many wigs in her acting roles, Adolpho, Halston and Clairol contracted Eileen to promote their wigs on national TV and radio talk shows. The William Morris Agency was still representing her and she accepted a small role in the comedy *Loving* (1970) starring George Segal. Esteemed director Joseph L. Mankiewicz saw some of O'Neill's work and offered her a role as a jailhouse missionary in the Western-comedy prison film *There Was a Crooked Man...* (1971) starring Kirk Douglas and Henry Fonda. But Eileen turned it down (Barbara Rhoades took the part). "When I read the script, my character is ravaged by the revolting prisoners and they tear her clothes off. She then had to run nude from the prison to an outside area lit with floodlights. I did not advocate doing nude scenes on film."

In 1973, Eileen moved back to Beverly Hills where she met and married attorney–real estate developer Richard Barich. Like a number of her contemporaries, she chose domesticity over acting. "Sixties actresses were raised in a period of time where a woman's place was really in the home. That was instilled in us as children. When I was growing up, you never saw a female anchorperson on the news. It was all men. If a female wanted to do anything in the news field, she became a weather girl. That was it. Having been raised with that kind of a mindset, it was always difficult for me to differentiate when I fell in love with a man and the love I had for acting. Both require your full attention."

Though Eileen gave up acting to become involved with her husband's real estate developments and investments, she kept her acting instrument in shape by studying with Jose Quintero, Daniel Mann, Stella Adler and Lee Strasberg. "Thinking about it today, perhaps it was an ill-thought-out decision to stop acting at the time that I made it. Today I see you can do both—it is possible to 'have it all.' But in those days it was new to do both to that extent—usually one or the other suffered. I would love to restart my acting

Eileen O'Neill, ca. 2000. (Courtesy of Eileen O'Neill).

career. I still have the same figure I had when I was acting full-time and the stamina. In March of 1999, I completed the 26.2 miles of the Los Angeles Marathon. But the reality of it is for an older female it is hard to get work today unless you are a real character actress. The statistics from the Screen Actors Guild are that acting is a younger person's profession and older females are definitely discriminated against. It is sad because today people are living longer and there is some audience interest in older women. There are gals out there like Cher who look wonderful. It is not something that is totally impossible but the odds are really not there." Here's hoping Eileen takes the gamble and we will see her on the small screen once again.

Film Appearances

1961   *A Majority of One* (Warner Bros.) d. Mervyn LeRoy.
       Teenage Millionaire (United Artists) d. Lawrence F. Doheny.
1963   *4 for Texas* (Warner Bros.) d. Robert Aldrich.
1964   *Kiss Me, Stupid* (Lopert) d. Billy Wilder.
1965   *The Third Day* (Warner Bros.) d. Jack Smight.
       The Loved One (MGM) d. Tony Richardson.
1967   *A Man Called Dagger* (MGM) d. Richard Rush.
1970   *Loving* (Columbia) d. Irvin Kershner.

Television Appearances

The Roaring Twenties "Two a Day" 2/4/61 ABC.
77 Sunset Strip "Once Upon a Caper" 2/10/61 ABC.
Guestward Ho! "Hawkeye's Stadium" 3/23/61 ABC.
Story of... "The Story of a Tiger Hunter" 2/4/63 Synd.
The Alfred Hitchcock Hour "I'll Be Judge, I'll Be Jury" 2/15/63 CBS.
Burke's Law [series regular as Sgt. Gloria Ames] 10/18/63 to 9/8/65 ABC.
Valentine's Day "How to Live Without Dying" 10/2/64 ABC.
The Rogues "Bless You, G. Carter Huntington" 1/17/65 NBC.
No Time for Sergeants "It Shouldn't Happen to a Sergeant" 2/22/65 ABC.
Tycoon (episode title unknown) 2/23/65 ABC.
Wendy and Me "Wendy's Private Eye" 3/15/65 ABC.
A Man Named McGhee (unaired pilot) 1965.
The Beverly Hillbillies "The Private Eye" 10/6/65 CBS.
I Dream of Jeannie "G. I. Jeannie" 10/16/65 NBC.
Bewitched "...And Then I Wrote" 11/11/65 ABC.
Amos Burke—Secret Agent "Or No Tomorrow" 12/15/65 ABC.
The Smothers Brothers Show "Never Trust a Naked Rembrandt" 1/21/66 CBS.
The Smothers Brothers Show "The Big Newsboy War" 2/4/66 CBS.

My Favorite Martian "Butterball" 2/13/66 CBS.

Get Smart "Smart, the Assassin" 2/19/66 NBC.

The Munsters "Cyrano de Munster" 2/24/66 CBS.

The Double Life of Henry Phyfe "Visit to Washington" 3/24/66 ABC.

The Smothers Brothers Show "How to Succeed in Business and Be Really Trying" 4/1/66 CBS.

The Smothers Brothers Show "A Wolf in Sheik's Clothing" 4/15/66 CBS.

Hey, Landlord! "Pursuit of a Dream" 9/11/66 NBC.

Batman "The Clock King's Crazy Crimes" 10/12/66 ABC.

Batman "The Clock King Gets Crowned" 10/13/66 ABC.

The Bob Hope Comedy Special 11/16/66 NBC.

I Dream of Jeannie "A Secretary Is Not a Toy" 3/20/67 NBC.

The Phyllis Diller Show "Krump, the Playboy" 3/24/67 ABC.

Rhubarb (unaired pilot) 1967 ABC.

The Second Hundred Years "San Juan Hill" 11/29/67 ABC.

Operation: Entertainment [series regular] 1/5/68 to 1/31/69 ABC.

Run, Jack, Run (pilot—produced in 1966) 7/20/70 NBC.

ABC's Wide World of Entertainment: Hi-Ho, Steverino! (Steve Allen's 25th Anniversary Special) 1/16/74 ABC.

Also:

I'm Dickens ... He's Fenster, Mister Roberts, Mona McCluskey, The Red Skelton Show, The Steve Allen Show, The Tonight Show Starring Johnny Carson, Somerset and *Trapper John, M.D.*

Julie Parrish

Dark-haired Julie Parrish arrived in Hollywood via a beauty pageant and immediately became popular with the teenage audience. With her wholesome beauty and fresh face, she had a special quality that she was able to get across on screen. In Jerry Lewis' classic comedy *The Nutty Professor,* she played coed Stella Stevens' naïve best friend. Parrish then appeared in a number of successful drive-in films opposite some of the sixties' most popular teen idols including James Stacy in *Winter a-Go-Go*, Elvis Presley in *Paradise, Hawaiian Style* and Frankie Avalon and Fabian in *Fireball 500*. On TV, Julie appeared in all the top programs of the sixties including *Gunsmoke*, *Burke's Law*, *Bonanza*, *Mannix* and *Star Trek*. She also starred in the sitcom *Good Morning, World* and went on to appear in two hit daytime dramas, *Return to Peyton Place* and *Capitol*. A true Hollywood survivor—a survivor of an abusive relationship and ovarian cancer—Julie persevered and landed a recurring role on the hit drama series *Beverly Hills 90210* during the nineties.

Julie Parrish was born Ruby Joyce Wilbar on October 21 in Middlesboro, Kentucky. When she was a toddler, her parents Gladys M. and William R. Wilbar uprooted Julie and her sister Janice and moved to Lake City, Tennessee. Julie's interest in acting began at the early age of six. "I was doing a school play and it felt really fun to be up there in front of an audience," says Julie. "And I remember my mother complimented me and said I did a good job. My mother didn't give compliments and that felt so good. I thought that if I just kept acting, I'd get lots more!" When Julie was 11 years old, the Wilbar family relocated to Tecumseh, Michigan, where Julie graduated from high school. Soon after, she enrolled in the Patricia Stevens Modeling School. "I was trying to save money to go to art school so I thought that modeling would be a fun way to make money," she says. Her school then began entering her in a number of beauty contests. She won every pageant she entered and placed first runner-up in a preliminary to the Miss America contest.

Julie was also one of three finalists for "Young Model of the Year," which was sponsored by the Patricia Stevens Modeling School and Paramount Pictures.

Julie won a trip to Hollywood and was chosen to play a bit role in Paramount's *It's Only Money* (1962) with Jerry Lewis. But when Julie arrived on the set, no one connected with the film knew anything about it. "Luckily, Frank Tashlin was directing," says Julie fondly. "The publicity people wanted to just take some stills of me and send me home but Tashlin said, 'No, you can't do that to her.' So he wrote in a part for me. I played a Saks Fifth Avenue saleslady who dressed actress Mae Questel. I'm billed as Joyce Wilbar. Frank Tashlin was such a wonderful man and became a good friend. He was not one of those directors who would chase you around the desk."

As a young naïve actress in Hollywood, Julie unfortunately ran into a number of directors and producers who didn't respect women. "I couldn't understand why an old guy with white hair would be after me. I was revolted by it. From the beginning, my agent taught me to make excuses to get out of these situations. The main thing was to not hurt their feelings because they might fix it so you didn't work again. I would look at my watch and say, 'I would love to stay and talk but I have another audition I've got to go to.' I really had nobody in Hollywood to guide me. Anne Helm and I talk about this a lot. We got ourselves into situations that were pretty insulting—just because we believed *everybody*. In those days, a lot of us were very naïve—much more than the young actresses of today."

Jerry Lewis as Prof. Kelp instructs his students (including a seated Julie Parrish) in *The Nutty Professor* (Paramount, 1963) (courtesy of Julie Parrish).

Julie made such an impression on Frank Tashlin that he introduced her to his friend Jack Cummings, Louis B. Mayer's nephew. Together they helped her get an agent. And although the studio contract system was ending, Julie was accepted into MGM's talent school. "My acting coach name was Zina Provendie," remembers Julie. "She was a real tough old bird and a fine actress. But I found her to be very intimidating and she scared me. I don't like that kind of teacher. She would say to us in her booming voice, '*You will never do anything right on my stage! I will always find something wrong with it.*' It was almost as if she had a stick in her hand. She also told me that I would have to change my name. I took Julie from the play *Make a Million*, which I did in Toledo. Being called Julie felt very comfortable. Parrish came from a former boyfriend. That was his adopted last name and I liked it."

Her stay at MGM was short, and she soon began working steadily at rival studio Paramount. There she landed a small role as one of Jerry Lewis' students in *The Nutty Professor* (1963). Some critics consider this to be Lewis' masterpiece. A hilarious takeoff on the Jekyll/Hyde formula, Lewis plays the nerdy Prof. Kelp and his alter ego, the suave Buddy Love, who romances coed Stella Stevens. "Overall I had fun doing this movie," remarks Julie. "Watching Jerry Lewis play this outrageous character was a great experience. He was always making the cast laugh. However, one moment he'd be a really nice person and the next minute he'd be crazy. He scared me. I had a scene with a few lines. I drank a lot of coffee that morning because we sat around a lot. Those were the days when you could be on a movie for three months and not do much. I don't even drink coffee but because I was bored I drank it. I got very nervous from drinking the coffee and I was also nervous about doing the scene. Since I didn't do it correctly, he yelled at me. I tried to do it right a second time and he yelled again. I started shaking all over. So he cut the scene entirely."

After concentrating on television with appearances on *Temple Houston*, *Gunsmoke*, *Burke's Law*, *Ben Casey* and *The F.B.I.*, Julie returned to the big screen in a small role as Michael Connors' bride in *Harlow* (1965) starring Carroll Baker. This film was rushed into production after an independent movie company, Electronovision, announced their plans for a film called *Harlow*, which starred Carol Lynley. Both films were flops. "I only met Carroll Baker briefly but she seemed sweet," recalls Julie. "Mike Connors was okay *then*. But not when I did an episode of *Mannix*. I think actors who are stars of shows get used to women coming after them. Well, *that* generation of actors anyway. So if you were friendly, they just *assumed* you wanted more."

That same year, Julie landed a co-starring role in *Winter a-Go-Go*, Columbia's answer to AIP's beach films. Julie (who *Variety* said "projects animation") played a ski bunny who helps pals James Stacy and William Wellman, Jr., turn their Lake Tahoe lodge into a rock 'n' roll haven. Also starring were Beverly Adams, Jill Donahue and Tom Nardini. As with a number of these films, the rock acts (Nooney Rickett Four, the Reflections and Joni Lyman) greatly add to its enjoyment. "This was a fun picture to work on," recalls Julie. "Beverly Adams and James Stacy were the stars and they were very nice to work with. But Jim was a bit insecure and could be difficult now and then. The only thing I didn't like about making this movie was that it was filmed during the winter in Lake Tahoe and we had outdoor bikini

Parrish, James Stacy and Linda Rogers hit the slopes in *Winter a-Go-Go* (Columbia, 1965).

scenes. We would be shaking and turning blue with blankets draped on us, waiting for the shot to be set up. But when the director yelled action, I'd forget I was freezing and really pretend it was warm. It was amazing!"

Julie next auditioned for a role in *Paradise, Hawaiian Style* (1966) starring Elvis Presley. But producer Hal Wallis was unimpressed. Julie was desperate to work with Elvis and asked for a second try. Wallis agreed and she got a part. "I *really* wanted to work with Elvis," exclaims Julie. "I was in every Elvis fan club around when I was a teenager. I would even do Elvis imitations with the long sideburns and guitar when I was in high school. So I convinced Hal Wallis to give me another shot and did the test over. Then I got the part. Mr. Wallis, who was married, was an old *lech*. I think he felt there was an unspoken promise that I would sleep with him since he allowed me to re-test for the part. On the day before filming began, he called me into his office, led me over to the sofa and briefly kissed me on the mouth. He said, 'Little girl, we're going to have a long talk about your future.' I made up any excuse to get out of there. While on location he was constantly calling me and asking me out. It was quite annoying and insulting. He called me one last time in Hawaii and said, 'Little girl, you'd better think again.' I knew I would probably never work for him again, but that was fine with me. This whole incident highly offended me. I'm not claiming to have been an innocent, but when I make mistakes, I like them to be due to choices of my own."

Paradise, Hawaiian Style features Parrish as one of a bevy of beauties (along with Marianna Hill, Irene Tsu and Linda Wong) who are romanced by Elvis. He uses them to help drum up clients for his and James Shigeta's fledging helicopter charter service by promising, "If you scratch my back, I'll scratch yours." "I was a bit awed working with Elvis," Julie admits. "It probably hampered me a little bit because I really was a huge fan of his." Julie's elation at getting the chance to work with Elvis was quickly eclipsed by her illness during production. "I began to have pain in my right leg while we were doing the scene where all the girls converge on Elvis to confront him about dating us all at the same time," recalls Julie. "We had to do the scene over many times and I was standing in high-heeled shoes. Suddenly there was pain in the whole right side of my body and I had to sit down. Elvis carried me to his dressing room and laid me down on his sofa. He was very spiritual and into healing with his hands. He'd hold them over parts of my body but I was too nervous. I was scared that people outside would be talking about what I was doing in there. [*Laughs*] *How stupid of me!* I told Elvis we ought to go back to the set and thanked him for his efforts. When we returned to the mainland, I went into the hospital for tests. It was thought that I had a slight stroke but my intuition told me that it was from taking Librium and diet pills with alcohol—we didn't know the dangers then. And in those days, taking those pills was not something we thought was wrong. After that experience, I never took another diet pill again. I had also been taking tranquilizers since age 14. I never took another of those either. It was a voice inside me that told me not to and not a doctor. The whole experience scared me."

Julie had the dubious distinction of being serenaded by the King with the infamous song "It's a Dog's Life" in *Paradise, Hawaiian Style*. "Elvis hated this song," says Julie, chuckling. "I have the outtakes on a rare bootleg album. He couldn't stop laughing while he was recording it. But we had a good time filming the scene. The dogs were great and I think the director, Michael Moore, did a good job with this scene. Luckily, I just had to sit there while Elvis sang that song for hours while they filmed from different angles because I had just gotten out of the hospital."

Paradise, Hawaiian Style tried to repeat the success of *Blue Hawaii*. And though the Hawaiian locations were

Elvis Presley warbles "It's a Dog's Life" to Parrish in *Paradise, Hawaiian Style* (Paramount, 1966) (courtesy of Julie Parrish).

stunning, the songs more than passable, and the girls gorgeous to look at, Elvis fans have been vehemently divided on this film. Despite the mixed reviews for *Paradise, Hawaiian Style* and her personal problems with producer Hal Wallis, Parrish has fond memories of this lush, tropical shoot. "It was customary that after a day's filming the crew and some of the actors would go to dinner at the club in the hotel," says Julie. "But never Elvis. His entourage and Colonel Tom Parker always surrounded him and kept him isolated. I had a great time hanging out with the crew and with Irene Tsu, Marianna Hill, and Linda Wong who played my rivals for Elvis. There was definitely no rivalry amongst us off the set. I never had that with anyone I worked with up until that time."

In Julie's last teenage film, *Fireball 500* (1966), Frankie and Annette abandon surfing the Malibu shores for racing stock cars in South Carolina. A blonde Julie portrays a vixen who is partners with race car sponsor Harvey Lembeck in an illegal still operation and vamps rival drivers Frankie and Fabian to run her moonshine over state lines. Julie played the part well, prompting *Boxoffice Magazine* to comment, "Julie Parrish, beautiful as a blonde, shows promise of acting capabilities far beyond the rest of the cast." Regarding her flaxen hair, Julie remarks (laughing), "I was a blonde because Annette Funicello did not want to work with another brunette. Maybe she thought the picture would look better with two contrasting women, I don't know. But they told us that at the last minute. They tried to bleach my hair but the hairdresser said, 'It's not going to work because her hair is going to fall out of her head.' They then dyed it red. So I reported to the set the next day and they went crazy—'No! No! No! We said make it blonde!' So they had to get a wig at the last minute—not a great wig. I hated how I looked in this film.

"But I had a good time doing *Fireball 500*," Julie continues. "I really liked Frankie Avalon. Fabian was nice but Frankie was fun to be with. I was still pretty new to the business when I did this film. But when William Asher [the director] told me that he thought my character wouldn't wear a bra beneath her clothes, I thought, 'Yeah, right!' [*Laughs*] By this time I was getting a little smarter about these guys. Of course, I had gone in there to read for the part with all these falsies on so he thought I had a better figure than I did. I took out the falsies so suddenly I had no chest. He may have been sorry he told me to do that! [*Laughs*] But the wardrobe woman and I tried to work it out so I could still have something on and not look like it."

While appearing on the big screen, Julie was also honing her craft on stage and on TV. She won the female lead in the Broadway-bound play *Memo* co-starring Macdonald Carey, Fred Clark and Alan Alda. Unfortunately, it closed in Boston due to a newspaper strike and one of the worst blizzards to hit the East Coast. Her other stage work includes the road company of *Absence of a Cello* and a local Beverly Hills production of Arthur Miller's *After the Fall*. "I was never

Fireball 500 (AIP, 1966) featured Parrish as a blonde vixen and Frankie Avalon as the race-car driver she tries to dupe (courtesy of Julie Parrish).

happy with the film and TV roles that were offered to me," remarks Julie. "It was very frustrating. My most beautiful moment was in the theater doing *After the Fall* around 1966 in a small theater in Hollywood. It was wonderful and I got fabulous reviews for it."

On TV, her most memorable appearance was as an ensign in the Hugo award–winning two-part episode "The Menagerie" on *Star Trek*. This episode is one of the series' best and used footage from *Star Trek*'s original pilot (titled "The Cage"). In Part 1, Spock mutinies, kidnaps his former officer Capt. Pike (Jeffrey Hunter) and sets a course for forbidden planet Talos IV. The second part revolves around Spock's trial and what happened to Pike on that planet. Julie was later told that this episode was made because "they were kind of running low on money so they decided to use the original pilot to make a two-part episode. I never expected this show would be the phenomenon it became." Most of Julie's scenes were with William Shatner. "I really didn't get along with Shatner," remarks Julie. "I'm not blaming him because he was of that generation of actors and really didn't think that women had feelings—we were just something to use. Even though it was early on, he really played up being the *star* of the series. There was one particular day when I was broke and decided not to go out to lunch. So I went to my dressing room to lay down and rest. Shatner knocked on my trailer and said, 'The electricity is out in my trailer. Do you mind if I use yours?' I said, 'Sure, come in.' But I didn't bother to get up. He entered and suddenly he was on me! I remember saying to him something like I would like to have a choice about this. [*Laughs*] He stopped but then he treated me badly for the rest of the week. It was so unprofessional. Majel Barrett [Nurse Chappel] told me that he used that excuse about the electricity with everybody."

During this time, Julie began honing her comedy timing as a member of Harvey Lembeck's Improv troupe and by working on such comedy series as *My Three Sons*, *Gidget*, *Captain Nice* and *Family Affair*. Julie's hard work and talent ultimately led to her starring role on the CBS sitcom *Good Morning, World* during the 1967-68 season. Carl Reiner and Sheldon Leonard (who produced the classic *The Dick Van Dyke Show*) created this series as well. "It was *wonderful* being the star of a series!" says Parrish, who played the wife of disc jockey Joby Baker. Ronnie Schell played his on-air partner, Billy DeWolfe the gruff station manager and a newcomer named Goldie Hawn played Parrish's kooky neighbor. Despite the talented cast and creators, the series resembled *The Dick Van Dyle Show* a bit too much and never found an audience opposite ABC's movies-of-the-week and NBC's *N.Y.P.D.* "*Good Morning, World* was a very well-written and -produced show done before a studio audience," comments Julie. "Carl Reiner was a dream to work with. He was patient, kind and fun to be around. And he is a very talented man. I was fortunate indeed to have had the pleasure. Sheldon Leonard was more reserved. I was not as comfortable around him, but he really knew his business. He was very quick with recognizing any problem with the script and knew how it could be fixed. I don't know why they never moved our time slot to save our show. At the time, I heard they were planning to replace Joby Baker because he was having personal problems. So even if the series did continue another year, I don't know if they would have just recast his part or they would have replaced both of us with new characters.

"I became very friendly with Goldie Hawn," continues Julie. "Goldie had actually read for my part. They told me about her audition later. They said they had this great actress who had come in to read for the role holding a teapot. She wasn't right for the wife but she was going to play my friend instead. Goldie got *Laugh-In* right after this and the rest is history. There was a part of me that thought, here *I* was the star of the show and suddenly *she's* a major star. I'm sure my heart really yearned for that recognition. Our friendship ended not because anything happened between us—we tried to remain friends and make appointments to see each other. But something would happen or come up, so we drifted. She had a lot of people pulling at her from every direction."

After the series ended, Julie wasn't

Cast shot from the CBS-TV sitcom *Good Morning, World*: (*clockwise from upper left*) Ronnie Schell, Billy DeWolfe, Goldie Hawn, Joby Baker and Julie Parrish (courtesy of Julie Parrish).

able to follow it up with anything substantial. "When I did *Good Morning, World*, I was represented by the William Morris Agency who packaged that show. They romanced me away from my old agent to sign with them. After the series went off the air, I didn't work for about a year and got cold." Julie began the seventies abandoning her demure image to play a couple of bad girls. On the daytime soap *Return to Peyton Place*, Julie starred as the villainous Betty Anderson Harrington. In the hit film *The Doberman Gang* (1972), she was part of a back-stabbing team of thieves who use trained Doberman Pinschers to rob banks. The crooks double-cross each other to get their hands on the loot but they are all outsmarted by the dogs, who wind up with all the money at the end. "Those dogs were great and well-trained," remembers Julie. "I took this role because I was broke. I wasn't very good with money. Nudity became an issue at this time and I'd only consent to do a back scene for this film. That's the farthest I would go. The funniest thing about this movie is this review by Norman Dresser in *The Toledo Blade*, which I keep on my wall. He called the film 'a dog' and said, 'Miss Parrish, a former Toledo model and actress who has many movie and TV credits and now plays a key role in the NBC-TV soap opera *Return to Peyton Place*, must have been suffering a protracted 'at liberty' period when she accepted this role. She has nothing to work with and she fails to make the character come alive. Of course, the character was dead to start with.' [*Laughs*] Isn't that great?" Regardless of Mr. Dresser's opinion, *The Doberman Gang* was a box office hit and spawned two sequels.

Julie didn't work from 1973 to 1977 but it wasn't by choice. "I was in a relationship where I lost *everything*, including my career," Julie says. "I got very depressed but knew I wasn't going to commit suicide. So I decided to do everything that felt good to me." One of those things was singing. Julie was singing all her life but was not confident enough to do it in public. She had a chance to sing a duet with Frankie Avalon in *Fireball 500* but was too scared. Julie persevered and pulled her life together. She took voice lessons and sang the National Anthem at a Dodgers game. Later, she recorded a country album titled *When We Dance*. She slowly returned to acting in 1978 with small roles in *The Rockford Files*, *Dallas* and *Dynasty*.

By the early eighties, her acting career was in full swing again and she enjoyed a successful five-year run as wacky secretary Maggie Brady on the popular CBS soap *Capitol*. The character began as a recurring role but Julie played the part comically and received a lot of attention. She was eventually put under contract and given her own storylines. But there was a downside to this. "Once they brought me out and made me glamorous—there were a lot of glamorous people on that show already—the character lost its edge," recalls Julie. "She should have stayed as she was."

"I had a lot of fun doing this series and became friendly with most of my costars. At one point my storyline was getting a real boost and a lot of money was being spent to glamorize my character. They took some fantastic photos of me to promote the new look for my character. But I learned how vicious Hollywood could be. There was someone on the show who I think went to the producers and told them that I was sick or something. Suddenly the producers were calling me into the office and asking me about my health and being real concerned. I

In the mid-eighties, sexy Parrish posed for a publicity shot to promote the CBS-TV soap opera *Capitol* (courtesy of Julie Parrish).

said, 'What? My health is fine.' I don't know what happened but my storyline then stopped and theirs went forward with a real boost."

The nineties saw Julie playing Joan Diamond, the wife of Peach Pit owner Nate, on the hit series *Beverly Hills 90210* beginning in 1996. "Joan Diamond is *me*," says Julie. "It's the closest character I've played that has the same traits as myself. I had to audition for the part but Joey Tata, who plays Nate, had asked for me. I knew him back from my days at the Improv. I really hadn't had much contact with him since then, only occasionally running into him. He called me and said, 'I told them to call you and don't know if they will but would you be interested in playing my love interest?' I said, 'Are you kidding?' [*Laughs*] So I went in and read for it. Joey keeps telling me I did it on my own—that I went in and knocked them dead. But I know he had some influence. They probably would never have seen me otherwise. Right after my first episode aired, I was in the drug store buying something. There was a lady in front of me leaning over writing a check and I was talking to the clerk. The woman said, 'I know that voice.' She looked up and said, 'I saw you last night on *90210!*' I thought that was really cool because I hadn't been on a TV show in years except for reruns."

Julie worked with a number of teen idols during the sixties and was one herself. When asked what is the difference between the young actors of today versus the sixties, she replies, "They are smarter, have better representation, and make more money! [*Laughs*] And they certainly aren't as naïve. Take Jason Priestley. He went from acting in *Beverly Hills 90210* to acting and directing some episodes, to producing. That would never have happened during the sixties. Today's kids have really high-powered representation who push them into doing films and TV movies. After I did *Good Morning, World*, all the William Morris Agency had me do was sit on my butt for a year."

Today, Julie has a new role as counselor for battered women at the Havens Hill Shelter. Her tortured experience and mental abuse dealing with a batterer has given her the courage and strength to help other women. "I have been on staff at Haven Hills Shelter for close to nine years," states Julie. "I got involved because it was close to my heart. My mom was mentally abused by my alcoholic father and my sister was physically abused by her husband. At the shelter, I run the group sessions, I answer the hotline and I bring women and children to live there for 30 days. My main thrust is to get women to recognize the red flags—if he starts controlling right from the start by telling you how to dress, not liking your friends and family, and trying to separate you from them—run like hell! It will only get worse. My batterer once accused me of making a pass at a motorist on the freeway. Often women think that his being so very jealous means that he loves her that much. It becomes very confusing for her and she's kept totally isolated. The insane jealousy is a control tool. I try to make these women see that and say to them, 'You didn't do it to him, and *you* can't fix it.' Like I was, these women are usually amazed when they realize that the batterer's profile is universal."

Regarding her longevity in a business that is cruel (especially to older actresses), Julie says, "I love acting but I didn't have a plan to become an actress. I just keep staying in there and keep an agent who sends me out for different things. Or maybe it is just luck. I think what happens to you is what's supposed to happen to you. And hopefully you learn from it."

FILM APPEARANCES

1962   It's Only Money (Paramount) d. Frank Tashlin.
1963   The Nutty Professor (Paramount) d. Jerry Lewis.
1965   Harlow (Paramount) d. Gordon Douglas.
       Winter a Go-Go (Columbia) d. Richard Benedict.
1966   Paradise, Hawaiian Style (Paramount) d. Michael Moore.
       Fireball 500 (AIP) d. William Asher.
1972   The Doberman Gang (Dimension) d. Byron Chudnow.
1978   The Time Machine (TV-movie) d. Henning Schellerup.

1979	When She Was Bad... (TV-movie) d. Peter H. Hunt.
1981	The Devil and Max Devlin (Buena Vista) d. Steven Hilliard.
1987	The Last Fling (TV-movie) d. Corey Allen.
1988	Baby M (TV-movie) d. James Sadwith.
	Two Soldiers Down (unreleased) d. Bruce Riesman.
1996	Elvis: The Complete Story (Direct-to-Video) [documentary]

Television Appearances

The Untouchables "The Lilly Dallas Story" 3/16/61 ABC.
The Many Loves of Dobie Gillis "Strictly for the Birds" 11/28/62 CBS.
Dick Powell Theatre "Charlie's Duet" 3/19/63 NBC.
Day in Court (episode title unknown) 9/63 Synd.
My Three Sons "How Do You Know?" 10/24/63 ABC.
Temple Houston "The Guardian" 1/2/64 NBC.
Temple Houston "Thy Name Is Woman" 1/9/64 NBC.
Gunsmoke "The Warden" 5/16/64 CBS.
Burke's Law "Who Killed the Toy Soldier?" 1/20/65 ABC.
My Three Sons "Steve and the Computer" 4/8/65 ABC.
Ben Casey "Journeys End in Lovers Meeting" 4/19/65 ABC.
The F.B.I. "The Monster" 9/19/65 ABC.
Gidget "The Great Kahuna" 9/29/65 ABC.
The Smothers Brothers Show (unaired pilot) 1965.
The F.B.I. "Flight to Harbin" 2/27/66 ABC.
Hank "McKillup's Best Seller" 4/8/66 NBC.
Bonanza "Horse of a Different Hue" 9/18/66 NBC.
Pistols 'n' Petticoats "Bitter Blossom O'Brian" 10/1/66 CBS.
Star Trek "The Menagerie" 11/17 & 11/24/66 NBC.
Captain Nice "Whatever Lola Wants" 3/20/67 NBC.
Family Affair "The Way It Was" 3/20/67 CBS.
My Three Sons "Ernie's Crowd" 4/6/67 CBS.
Death Valley Days "Along Came Mariana" 5/27/67 Synd.
Good Morning, World [series regular as Linda Lewis] 9/5/67 to 9/17/68 CBS.
The Dating Game [celebrity contestant] 2/10/68 ABC.
Lucky Pair [celebrity panelist] 1/69 Synd.
Family Affair "Speak for Yourself Mr. French" 1970 CBS.
This Is the Life (episode title unknown) 1/3/70 Synd.
This Is the Life (episode title unknown) 1/10/70 Synd.
Mannix "The Lost Art of Dying" 10/24/70 CBS.
Family Affair "Feat of Clay" 12/17/70 CBS.
This Is the Life (episode title unknown) 3/13/71 Synd.
The Smith Family "The Anniversary" 9/15/71 ABC.
The Man and the City "Reprisal" 10/13/71 ABC.
The Dating Game [celebrity contestant] 11/71 ABC.
Mannix "To Draw the Lightning" 2/23/72 CBS.
Return to Peyton Place [series regular as Betty Harrington] 4/3/72 to 12/73 NBC.
Return to Peyton Place (special primetime episode) 1/21/73 NBC.
This Is the Life (episode title unknown) 7/28/73 Synd.
W.E.B. "Good Night and Good Luck" 9/28/78 NBC.
Dallas "Act of Love" 11/19/78 CBS.
Next Step Beyond "Cry Baby" 12/31/78 Synd.
The Rockford Files "The Man Who Saw Alligators" 2/10/79 NBC.
Greatest Heroes of the Bible "Sodom and Gomorrah" 5/22/79.
The Runaways "The Breaking Point" 7/31/79 NBC.
Laverne and Shirley "What Do You Do with a Drunken Sailor?" 10/18/79 ABC.
The Rockford Files "Lions, Tigers, Monkeys and Dogs" 10/12/79 NBC.
The Young and the Restless 11/79 CBS.
Shirley "Three Dates of Shirley Miller" 1980 NBC.
Days of Our Lives [short-term role as Sister Theresa] 4/80 NBC.
Hagen "More Deadly Poison" 4/20/80 CBS.
Dynasty "The Oil Company" 1/12/81 ABC.
The Fall Guy "No Way Out" 1/6/82 ABC.
Capitol [series regular as Maggie Brady] 3/29/82 to 3/20/87 CBS.
Dynasty "The Mirror" 2/16/83 ABC.
Fantasy 10/19/83 NBC.
You and Me Kid "Famous and ½" 11/3/83.
Alive and Well [talk show guest] 12/21/83 Synd.

Jessie "The Psychic Connection" (unaired episode) 1984 ABC.
AM LA [talk show guest] 9/26/84.
The Pat Boone Show [talk show guest] 10/16/84 Synd.
The Merv Griffin Show [talk show guest] 2/15/85 Synd.
This Is the Life "False Witness" 3/85 Synd.
This Is the Life "While Love Lasts" 12/85 Synd.
Hour Magazine [talk show guest] 12/23/85 Synd.
Hotel "Child's Play" 2/5/86 ABC.
Divorce Court "Pettrie vs. Pettrie" 6/86 Synd.
This Is the Life "Wednesday's Child" 8/86 Synd.
This Is the Life "Dreams Die" 12/86 Synd.
Nothing in Common (episode title unknown) 4/87 NBC.
The Judge "Cruising for Love" 8/87 Synd.
General Hospital 12/87 ABC.
Superior Court "Post vs. Campbell" 3/88 Synd.
Superior Court "State vs. Korsky" 8/88 Synd.
Divorce Court "Withers vs. Withers" 10/88 Synd.
Murder, She Wrote "A Little Night Work" 10/30/88 CBS.
The ABC Afterschool Special "Just Tipsy Honey" 3/16/89 ABC.
Soup to Nuts (unaired pilot) 1989.
Hunter "The Legion" Part II 11/18/89 NBC.
F.B.I.: The Untold Stories "The Berg Case" 1/13/91 ABC.
Beverly Hills 90210 "Fade In Fade Out" 1/10/96 FOX.
Beverly Hills 90210 "Coming Out, Getting Out, Going Out" 3/13/96 FOX.
Beverly Hills 90210 "You Say It's Your Birthday" 5/22/96 FOX.
Beverly Hills 90210 "Remember the Alamo" 8/21/96 FOX.
Beverly Hills 90210 "A Mate for Life" 9/4/96 FOX.
Beverly Hills 90210 "Gift Wrapped" 12/18/96 FOX.
Beverly Hills 90210 "The Wedding" 5/20/98 FOX.

Also:
Family Medical Center.

Jean Hale

Beautiful, blonde Jean Hale was a theatrically trained actress in New York before making her film debut as a coed stalked by a madman in *Psychomania*. Arriving in Hollywood in 1963, Hale played a variety of roles including WAVEs, movie stars and gun molls on television and in such films as *McHale's Navy Joins the Air Force*, *The Oscar* and *The St. Valentine's Day Massacre*. But her convincing performance as the icy blonde manipulator Lisa in *In Like Flint* is the high point of her career. During the mid-sixties, the spy boom was in high gear due to the success of the James Bond films with Sean Connery. It seemed every studio was releasing spoofs featuring an assortment of secret agents. There were the cool Napoleon Solo and Ilya Kuryachin in the *Man from U.N.C.L.E.* series, the wisecracking Matt Helm in *The Silencers* and its three sequels, and the suave, high-living Derek Flint in *Our Man Flint* and *In Like Flint*. All featured debonair leading men, futuristic gadgets, exotic locales and some of the world's most beautiful actresses. Few were as lovely and talented as *In Like Flint*'s femme fatale, Jean Hale. Unfortunately for her fans, Jean retired from acting shortly after *In Like Flint* was released to concentrate on her children and her marriage to actor Dabney Coleman. Today, Jean Hale Coleman is back in show business but on the production side as co-head with Gino Tanasescu of Coleman/Tanasescu Entertainment.

Born in Salt Lake City, Utah, Jean Hale was raised in Darien, Connecticut. From the age of eight, Hale desired to become an actress but "my dad insisted I get at least two years of college in first." After attending the University of Utah and Skidmore College for Women, she was accepted at the Neighborhood Playhouse in New York. There she studied with Sydney Pollack and met Dabney Coleman. She was a model for the Conover Agency and the Huntington Hartford Agency. Upon graduation from the Neighborhood Playhouse, Jean was hired as a dancer on the TV series *Sing Along with Mitch* and she did some theater, including *The Male Animal* with Tom Poston and *Everybody Loves Opal* with Nancy Walker.

Jean's first chance at stardom came while strolling down fashionable Fifth

Jean Hale as a vile sex goddess in *The Oscar* (Embassy, 1966).

Avenue in New York in 1960. "This man gave me his card and told me he was an agent," recalls Jean. "Of course I was skeptical. But he turned out to be this wonderful man named Len Luskin who was Sandra Dee's agent." Working quickly, Luskin arranged a screen test for Jean with MGM. She so impressed the powers-that-be with her beauty and talent, a special scene for her as a young call girl was arranged to be written into Daniel Mann's *Butterfield 8* starring Elizabeth Taylor. Jean was to be listed in the credits as "and introducing Jean Hale." But Jean turned the part down, choosing to remain in New York. "This offer was almost every undiscovered actress' dream. But Dabney and I had previously broken up and had just gotten back together. I didn't want to leave him. I also just didn't want to go to Hollywood yet. I wanted to go with more stage experience and a good reputation as a New York actress." Soon after, Jean married Dabney and then journeyed to Puerto Rico for her first film, *Felicia* (1963) with Louise Allbritton. Though it received much ballyhoo as the first of many films to be shot on this tropical paradise, it was never released.

Hale's second feature, the low-budget programmer *Psychomania* (1963), co-starring Lee Philips, James Farentino and Sylvia Miles, *was* released—to her dismay. "Producer Del Tenney was a very bright man," recalls Jean. "He had financing and hoped his film was going to be this edgy art film *à la La Notté* [1961]. The film just didn't quite cut it so it was turned into a horror flick with gruesome murders and bloody knives. It played drive-ins and 42nd Street at four o'clock in the morning. I then realized with movies, you do them but you don't know what's going to happen afterwards." In the film, Hale played a college coed stalked by a knife-wielding maniac. Philips, as a brooding artist subject to blackouts, is police officer James Farentino's number one suspect. Though Jean was disappointed with *Psychomania*, *Variety* called the film "a well-done shocker with a tightly knit plot and a believable surprise ending" and described Jean as "an attractive near-victim." James O'Neill, writing in *Terror on Tape*, thought the film had "some stylish moments and an upscale cast."

Despite her inauspicious film debut, Hale snapped up a contract with Universal soon after arriving in Hollywood in 1963. She appeared in the Louis L'Amour Western *Taggart* (1964) and the comedy *McHale's Navy Joins the Air Force* (1964) as well as episodes of TV's *Bob Hope Chrysler Theatre*, *Kraft Suspense Theatre*, *The Virginian* and *The Alfred Hitchcock Hour*. "I love doing comedy," remarks Jean. "I remember I did two episodes of *McHale's Navy* almost back-to-back. The first time I played the blonde girlfriend of Carl Ballentine, and the next I played an over-the-top movie star. They had me wear a brunette wig so that I wouldn't be recognized from the first episode. Tim Conway is as funny in person as he is on screen. Ernest Borgnine, however, was a very serious actor and a bit intimidating. I believe he didn't do the movie with us because he was in a contract dispute with Universal."

Hale's big break didn't come until she "grabbed" the role of the spoiled movie star in *The Oscar* (1966). This is the story of an unscrupulous actor (Stephen Boyd) who uses everyone to get ahead in Hollywood. He meets his match when the studio arranges a date for him with Hale's self-absorbed actress. Hale remembers, "I originally auditioned for the role of the stripper because the movie star part was already cast. I went in and read for it but told the producers that I wanted the other role. They said, 'Sorry, but it has already been cast.' I pleaded with them to let me read for it and they finally relented. Before I got home, they had called my agent to say the movie star role was mine." Jill St. John was then cast as the stripper.

Most film buffs consider *The Oscar* one of the best "worst" movies of all

Publicity photograph of Jean Hale from *In Like Flint* (20th Century-Fox, 1967).

time. *Bad Movies We Love* included it in their Hall of Shame and commented, "Bad Movie nirvana beckons in this foot-stompingly funny movie about a louse who stomps all over other louses to reach the top of the Hollywood dung heap." However, this film was a boost for Hale. She received probably the only good reviews this movie ever got. "I had a ball playing such a nasty character. Before

Publicity shot of Tim Conway and Jean Hale in *McHale's Navy Joins the Air Force* (Universal, 1964).

this, I always got parts where I had to cry and kiss the guy. It was so nice not to have to do that for this role." Though the film received a drubbing from the critics, it went on to receive Academy Award nominations for art direction and for the costumes designed by the legendary Edith Head who, Hale says, "was an absolutely amazing woman and a creative genius. She had an office about 60 to 70 feet long. At the entrance to it there was a light panel with a great number of switches. At the other end of the room, she'd have you stand on this pedestal with mirrors three-quarters of the way around it. Three or four of her assistants would then take a piece of fabric and with their hands create all different looks for the evening gowns she was designing for me—from various necklines to all types of skirt styles. They would literally create the dress on you while you were standing there. Edith could see you from every angle in every type of light and would decide your finest look. I remember her telling me that my best look was a scoop neck. She designed three gowns for me and all of them had a variation on that type of neckline."

While pursuing other film roles, Hale continued guesting on various TV shows. She donned Western garb for the short-lived TV series *The Legend of Jesse James* starring Christopher Jones. ("Chris was an untamed actor who resembled James Dean. He had so much talent but you could see he had a lot of problems.") Hale also turned up on *Batman* playing Polly the Hat Check Girl, the devious accomplice to David Wayne's Mad Hatter. In this cleverly written two-part episode (based on an original story that appeared in the *Batman* comics in 1956), the Mad Hatter and his crew hide out at the abandoned Green Derby Restaurant and crash rich matron Hattie Hatfield's Headdress Ball to steal her prized ruby. The first episode ends with the Dynamic Duo trapped inside a giant X-Ray Accelerator Tube and Fluoroscopic Cabinet. They survive the deadly rays due to their Bat X-Ray Deflectors. "The atmosphere on the set was as zany as the show itself," remarks Jean. "When you get good actors to play cartoon characters, it's a terrific experience. David Wayne is wonderful as the Mad Hatter. And Adam West is such a nice man. I loved doing this show."

Though it has been reported that a number of actresses (including Natalie Wood, Tuesday Weld and Sue Lyon) were offered or tested for the role of Bonnie Parker in *Bonnie and Clyde* (1967), most researchers omit Jean Hale from this list. According to her William Morris agent, Hale was one of the final contenders for the part, which eventually went to Faye Dunaway. "I wanted this role intensely, not only because it was such a wonderful script, but I also wanted the chance to play something other than the shallow glamour girl," remarks Jean. "At first, Warren Beatty and Arthur Penn dismissed me for being too soft. However, I sent another tape of myself and they agreed to a reading, which led to more meetings. There was a moment when I thought I had the role. I was told it was down to Faye Dunaway and myself. Whether this was true or not, it's a nice thought nonetheless.

"Another role I lost out on was the female lead in *The Trouble with Girls* [1969] with Elvis Presley," continues Hale. "I was a very big Elvis fan, hence my disappointment. When I auditioned for the film, I told the producers I could dance but not sing. They had no problem with that because they said my singing part could be dubbed. Just as we were ready to close the deal, Marlyn Mason was brought to the attention of director Peter Tewksbury. She could sing *and* dance and was right for the role as well. So to save money paying a singer to dub me, they gave the part to her." Tough choice on the part of the cost-conscious producers.

Though she lost out on *Bonnie and Clyde*, Jean beat out a number of actresses to play opposite James Coburn in *In Like Flint* (1967), which ranks among the best of the James Bond spoofs. (*Variety* describes it as "Girls, gimmicks, girls, gags, and more girls." Reporting to Lloyd

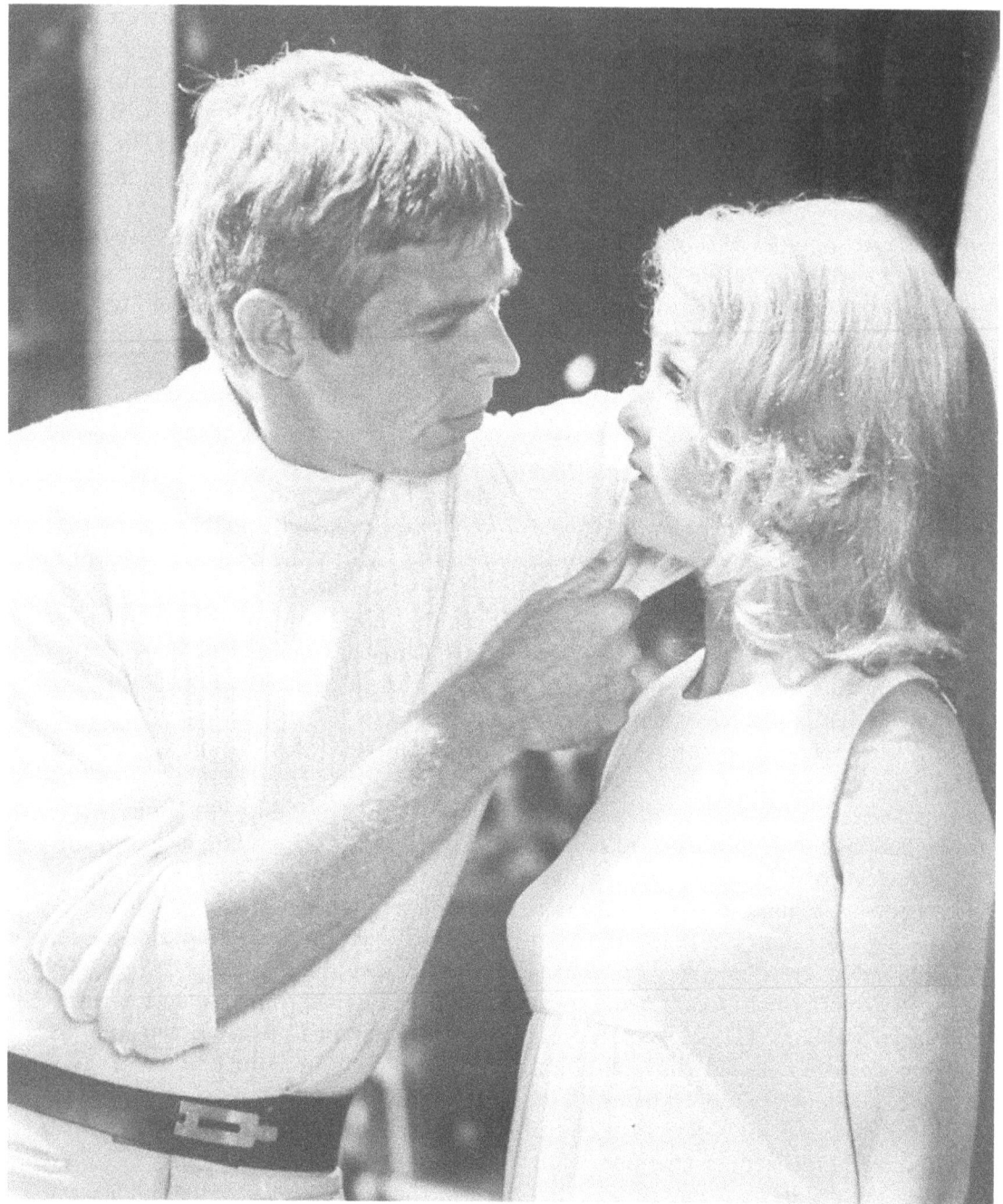

In Like Flint (20th Century–Fox, 1967) starred James Coburn as high-living secret agent Derek Flint and Hale as the femme fatale.

Cramden (Lee J. Cobb), the head of ZOWIE, Flint (James Coburn) must thwart a secret society of women who are plotting to take over the world. Led by Lisa (Hale) and the three top female fashion leaders, they operate from a lavish Virgin Islands spa called Fabulous Faces. Their plan is to take over a space station that controls nuclear weapons. To reach their goal, they disguise two of their women as golf caddies and kidnap the president of the U.S. and replace him with an impostor (who eventually turns on them). To get the rest of the female population to support them, their clientele get "brain- and hair-washing at the same time."

"I can't tell you what I had to go through to get this role," says Jean. "It was a very sought-after role because *Our Man Flint* was such a big success. From what I heard, Fox head Dick Zanuck wanted Catherine Deneuve. But producer Saul David thought I was just right for the part. Since Zanuck wanted a Grace Kelly–type, I had to screen test doing a scene from one of her movies. It apparently went very well but Zanuck still didn't want me. Finally Saul was able to convince him. I got the part and a contract with Fox—one picture a year for seven years! After Zanuck saw the dailies, he made me feel very welcome at 20th Century-Fox."

Of course, Jean credits a great deal of *In Like Flint*'s success to James Coburn. But she also has the highest regard for Hal Fimberg's screenplay. "His script foreshadows a lot of things that really happened. For instance, when Flint learns of the impostor posing as president, he says incredulously, 'An actor—*as president*?' It was supposed to be a joke. Who would ever have thought years later it would come true? *Flint* was brilliantly written in a satirical, farcical way but played straight. For a mid-sixties spy spoof, the film was pretty aggressive in the way it tackled the issue of oppression. We were women who loved men but were tired of being oppressed by them. We were trying to exert our dominance over men while staying feminine at the same time. But I think the studio got scared that the film went too far and pulled in the reins. They cut Flint's speech to the women about the nature of the oppressed."

Though Hale enjoyed working on location in Jamaica, the studio-lensed restaurant scene with Lee J. Cobb is her favorite. Her character disguises herself as a straight-laced schoolteacher from Roanoke, Virginia, to set up Cobb's character on an indiscretion charge. "It was my idea for the disguise," states Hale proudly. "They originally wanted me to play the scene glamorously. Gordon Douglas would only agree to the disguise if I looked a certain way. So I had the hair stylist put my hair in a bun and I wore those thick horn-rimmed glasses. Lee and I then changed the scene around a bit. Everyone seemed very pleased with it. I was so happy. My other scenes are pretty lightweight. This scene had a little substance to it."

Hale did the scene so well, in fact, that Saul David wanted her to don another disguise. She explains, "Since I had studied ballet, Saul wanted me to be Natasha, the Russian ballerina-cum-spy, who dances with Flint. But they decided it wouldn't work because of the timing of my character being in Russia and the Virgin Islands simultaneously. So he got another ballerina turned actress, Yvonne Craig, to play the part. She was terrific."

As for Coburn, Hale has nothing but praise for him. "James is adorable and easy, yet challenging to work with," says Hale happily. "He is a very sweet, gentle man. When I went on tour to promote the film, the big question was always, 'What was it like to kiss James Coburn?' I'd respond, 'It was lovely but all in a day's work.' I was overjoyed when he won an Oscar recently for *Affliction* [1998]."

One of Hale's last theatrical film appearances was in *The St. Valentine Day's Massacre* (1967), directed by Roger

Corman. If Hale thought *In Like Flint* gave her a workout, she was in for a shocker when she agreed to play George Segal's feisty gun moll. "Roger Corman is a wonderful, no-holds-barred talent," says Hale, laughing. "He asked George and me if we'd do our fight scene without stunt doubles. We both said yes and we literally massacred each other. Each part of our fight had its own set-up. In one portion, I had to hit George over the head with a breakaway radio. I didn't think I could do it without hurting him. They told me, 'Just don't hit him with the edge—the rest is breakaway.' George told me not to worry about him and just act. And so of course I hit him with the edge and he developed a lump the size of a goose egg. During the part where I jumped on his back, I pulled his hair and caught my fingernail on something. I tore the whole nail off right down to the root. Then when he was supposed to throw me on the couch, Corman told him to throw me up so I wouldn't hit this brass lamp. Of course, my ankle hits the lamp, causing a pretty bad injury. It was pretty scary. My legs were covered for days with these huge bruises and poor George could hardly stand up."

During production, Hale caused a little disturbance for studio head Dick Zanuck when she refused to wear the skimpy costume for her scene with Segal. She recalls, "Zanuck came down to the set and tried to convince me to wear this

George Segal as a mobster and Hale as his moll massacre each other in *The St. Valentine's Day Massacre* (20th Century–Fox, 1967).

very revealing piece of lingerie. I said, 'Please let them put some lace around the bottom and I guarantee it will still be sexy.' He reluctantly gave in. When we watched the dailies, everyone agreed it accomplished its purpose." At that time, a lot of actresses were beginning to do nude scenes. But Hale wouldn't. She passed on *Valley of the Dolls* (1967) because of the semi-nudity and turned down an offer to do a layout *sans* nudity in *Playboy* modeling men's pajama tops to promote *In Like Flint*.

Despite her glowing notices for both *In Like Flint* and *The St. Valentine Day's Massacre*, Hale disappeared from the limelight. "Soon after *Flint*, I had my third child. Then Dabney and I separated. All of a sudden I had three children and a difficult marriage to contend with. I couldn't focus on my career. My priority was always my family. Twentieth Century–Fox was not happy when I turned down *Valley of the Dolls*. Also, the studio was not pleased when I became pregnant with my second child and was out of commission for about a year. There was also some publicity assignments they wanted me to do that I was unable to accommodate for personal reasons. Fox's goal was to make their talent well-known and famous. I wasn't always comfortable with that side of being an actress. I knew publicity was important, especially when you were under contract. For instance, they wanted to send me to Europe for a few months to promote *In Like Flint* and arranged for me to be interviewed by many of the top European magazines. I didn't want to be away from my family for that long a period of time, so I didn't go. During those contract days, your career was completely run by the studio and it was difficult to have a personal life. The two just didn't go together. So we parted company."

During the late sixties and early seventies, Jean made sporadic appearances on such TV series as *Bonanza, Hawaii Five-O, The Mod Squad* and *Cannon*. She even traveled to Durango, Mexico, for the feature *something big* (1971), starring Dean Martin. But don't look for Jean in it—all her scenes were cut out. "It seemed to be a very problematic production," recollects Jean. "I never knew why my scenes were deleted."

Jean's troubled marriage to Coleman finally ended in the early eighties. She briefly returned to acting later in the decade. Today, she runs her own production company (Coleman/Tanasescu Entertainment) with partner Gino Tanasescu. "I love working with screenwriters and participating in the creative process of packaging and producing movies," says Hale. Currently her company has in development *Altered Ego*, a bizarre true story that is stranger than any science-fiction tale. In 1965, a woman who impersonated Jean Hale stole more than $10,000 worth of merchandise from some LA boutiques. It was learned that she had even sneaked onto the Universal lot to study Hale's mannerisms and look. Years later, after serving prison time, the same woman pretending to be Hale married about ten men across Texas and Oklahoma. She was even mounting Hale's comeback with a nightclub act. One of the men duped by her contacted the real Hale, which ultimately led to the woman's arrest. "This is such an unbelievable story it should make a great film," remarks Jean. "We need a very talented actress to play both myself and the impostor."

Though Jean Hale stopped pursuing her acting career, she has few regrets. "I'm very happy with my work now," says Jean with a smile. "I have two glorious grandsons and my three wonderful children, Quincy, Randy and Kelly, are all talented artists pursuing careers in the music and acting fields." Although Jean Hale will unquestionably find great success in her new role as producer, to movie fans she'll always be remembered as James Coburn's beautiful antagonist in *In Like Flint*.

Jean Hale, ca. 1990.

FILM APPEARANCES

1963 Felicia (unreleased) d. David Durston.
      Psychomania (Emerson) d. Richard L. Hilliard.
1964 Taggart (Universal) d. R.G. Springsteen.
      McHale's Navy Joins the Air Force (Universal) d. Edward J. Montagne.
1966 The Oscar (Embassy) d. Russell Rouse.
1967 In Like Flint (20th Century–Fox) d. Gordon Douglas.
      The St. Valentine's Day Massacre (20th Century–Fox) d. Roger Corman.
1971 something big (National General) d. Andrew V. McLaglen. (Scenes deleted.]
1987 Pals (TV-movie) d. Lou Antonio.
1990 Thanksgiving Day (TV-movie) d. Gino Tanasescu.
1991 Lies Before Kisses (TV-movie) d. Lou Antonio.

TELEVISION APPEARANCES

The Original Amateur Hour 2/13/54 NBC.
Sing Along with Mitch (series regular as dancer) 1961 NBC.
The Twelfth Annual New York "Local" Emmy Awards (special) [model] 5/13/61 NBC.
Dick Powell Theatre "A Rage to Silence" 1/29/63 NBC.
The Alfred Hitchcock Hour "Starring the Defense" 11/15/63 CBS.
My Favorite Martian "The Atom Misers" 12/15/63 CBS.
The Bill Dana Show "The Beauty and the Baby" 12/29/63 NBC.
The Alfred Hitchcock Hour "Three Wives Too Many" 1/3/64 CBS.
The Virginian "A Matter of Destiny" 2/19/64 NBC.
McHale's Navy "Stars Over Taratupa" 3/10/64 ABC.
Wagon Train "The Stark Bluff Story" 4/6/64 ABC.
McHale's Navy "Lester the Skipper" 9/22/64 ABC.
90 Bristol Court: Tom, Dick and Mary "Mary Gentry, Girl Cupid" 10/12/64 NBC.
Bob Hope Chrysler Theatre "Double Jeopardy" 1/8/65 NBC.
The Rogues "Gambit by the Golden Gate" 1/10/65 NBC.
Bob Hope Chrysler Theatre "In Any Language" 3/12/65 NBC.
Perry Mason "The Case of the Murderous Mermaid" 3/18/65 CBS.
The Tycoon "Dragster Andrews" 3/23/65 ABC.
The Fugitive "The Old Man Picked a Lemon" 4/13/65 ABC.
McHale's Navy "A Star Falls on Taratupa" 5/18/65 ABC.
Kraft Suspense Theatre "Twixt the Cup and the Lip" 6/3/65 NBC.
Perry Mason "The Case of the Laughing Lady" 9/12/65 CBS.
The Wild Wild West "The Night the Terror Stalked the Town" 11/19/65 CBS.

The John Forsythe Show "The Daring Escape" 12/13/65 NBC.
The Smothers Brothers Show "The Rise and Fall of the Wedding Cake" 12/31/65 CBS.
The Loner "A Question of Guilt" 1/29/66 CBS.
The Legend of Jesse James "Return to Lawrence" 1/31/66 ABC.
Bob Hope Chrysler Theatre "Brilliant Benjamin Boggs" 3/30/66 NBC.
Hogan's Heroes "I Look Better in Basic Black" 4/1/66 CBS.
Hollywood Backstage "The Oscar Premiere" 12/6/66 Synd.
Batman "The Contaminated Cowl" 1/4/67 ABC.
Batman "The Mad Hatter Runs Afoul" 1/5/67 ABC.
Art Linkletter's House Party [talk show guest] 7/25/67 CBS.
Tarzan "Hotel Hurricane" 11/10/67 NBC.
Bonanza "The Real People of Muddy Creek" 10/6/68 NBC.
Hawaii Five-O "Golden Boy in Black Trunks" 2/12/69 CBS.
The Silent Force "A Deadly Game of Love" 10/5/70 ABC.
The Men from Shiloh "The Politician" 1/13/71 NBC.
Men at Law "The Truth, the Whole Truth, and Anything Else That Works" 3/3/71 CBS.
The Mod Squad "Kristie" 12/14/72 ABC.
Cannon "Lady on the Run" 3/5/75 CBS.
Tattletales [celebrity contestant] 5/3 to 5/6, 5/9/77 CBS.

Also:
Burke's Law, Naked City and *The Eleventh Hour.*

Irene Tsu

During the 1960s, beautiful Chinese actress Irene Tsu played a variety of "native" girls in a number of popular drive-in films including *Sword of Ali Baba*, the beach movie *How to Stuff a Wild Bikini* and *Paradise, Hawaiian Style* with Elvis. Tsu had poise and talent which was noticed by producer-writer Arthur C. Pierce, who wrote the part of a space traveler in *Women of the Prehistoric Planet* with her in mind. It was her first starring role. She then played a South Vietnamese spy in *The Green Berets*, John Wayne's homage to our boys in Vietnam, before becoming part of the spy boom. She portrayed a geisha on *The Man from U.N.C.L.E.* and a fashion model in the secret agent spoof *Caprice* starring Doris Day. The 1970s saw Irene mature into a fine actress as she progressed from exotic parts to playing doctors, lawyers, and scientists in both film and television. But she was at her most fun when she abandoned her sweet, docile image to play a karate-chopping terrorist in *Paper Tiger* and a police detective in the martial arts film *Hot Potato* with Jim Kelly. "I really don't consider myself a sixties performer," reveals Irene.

"It wasn't until the seventies [that] I became more aware of my standing as an actress." Irene still acts today (*The Single Guy, Star Trek: Voyager*, etc.) and is a successful real estate agent.

Irene Tsu was born in Shanghai on November 4 to Z. M. and Dulcie Lynn Tsu. When the Communists took over in 1949 she and her family fled first to Formosa and then to Hong Kong, where they remained for six years before immigrating to New York. Her father, an economics adviser to the Nationalist Chinese government, remained in Hong Kong. Once in the U.S., Tsu began ballet training, which was her stepping stone into the performing arts. At age 14, she borrowed her aunt's cheongsam and got the role of Gwenny in the road company of *The World of Susie Wong*. Her friendship with the play's star Nancy Kwan led to a small part as one of the teenage dancers in the 1961 film version of the Rodgers and Hammerstein musical *Flower Drum Song* starring Kwan and James Shigeta. "Nancy got me an audition with choreographer Hermes Pan," remembers Irene with a laugh. "I was terrified because I thought he was Fred Astaire—they looked

Irene Tsu

so much alike! He hired me as a dancer and later cast me as one of Elizabeth Taylor's handmaidens in *Cleopatra*. This was a very wild time for me. I was a crazy teenager who looked mature for my age. I was 14 passing for 21 and I was off to Rome by myself. My mom was an artist so she just let me do whatever I wanted—or maybe she had no clue to what was going on. Neither did I."

Back in Hollywood, Irene appeared as a French-speaking actress in the James Stewart comedy *Take Her, She's Mine* (1963), directed by Henry Koster, whom

Irene has nothing but praise for. "He gave me my first chance in acting," says Irene. "He thought I was a natural and offered me parts in two other films. He was my first mentor and gave me the confidence and inspiration to set foot in an acting career. I remained close to him and his family for many, many years."

Tsu continued playing exotic supporting roles in *John Goldfarb, Please Come Home* (1964) and *Sword of Ali Baba* (1965). ("None of these parts required much acting. All I had to do was pose and look decorative.") In 1965's *How to Stuff a Wild Bikini* (the last official AIP beach movie), Irene hit the beach as a native girl who romances Frankie Avalon while he is on reserve duty away from Annette Funicello. "Hit the beach," says Irene with a chuckle. "This film was so low-budget that we shot our supposedly tropical beach scenes in the studio with about six inches of sand. In fact, the director, William Asher, told Frankie and me not to play with the sand with our hands because you'd see the floor. Frankie was a sweetheart and Asher was very nice also. But on my first morning of shooting, he gave me a tape of a song he wanted me to sing later that day as a duet with Frankie. I said, 'You must be kidding! I have to learn this now?' Asher said, 'Oh, but you have about an hour and a half.' That's how every scene in this film was shot—wham bam bam."

Irene's first starring role was in the sci-fi cheapie *Women of the Prehistoric Planet* (1966), whose title is a misnomer because there aren't any prehistoric women to be found anywhere! "Producer-screenwriter Arthur Pierce really wanted to hire me," Tsu says. "He told me he wrote the part with me in mind. I did it because it was my first lead. We shot it in 11 days on this soundstage. The sets were so cheap and phony-looking. The cast was constantly worried that we would knock them down." Tsu portrays a space explorer who is part of Admiral Wendell Corey's crew (which also included John Agar, Merry Anders and Stuart Margolin) from the planet Centaurus. While returning home from a mission in space, they receive a distress call from another ship that has crashed on an uninhabited planet. While it takes Corey's ship only three months to reach the site, 18 years has gone by on the jungle planet. A search party discovers that all the ship's crew members are dead except for one boy (Robert Ito, later of *Quincy* fame) who was born after the crash and is now 18 years old. He falls in love with the lovely Tsu, who discovers that Corey is her natural father. A volcanic eruption forces the Centaurians to abandon the planet, leaving Tsu behind with Ito. While in space, Corey dubs the planet Earth—hence Ito and Tsu are Adam and Eve. Though the twist ending can't save this turkey, *Variety* took notice of Irene and commented, "Probably the most interesting figure is Irene Tsu as a native of another planet."

Irene was next cast in the big budget epic *Seven Women* (1966), directed by John Ford (whom Irene describes as being "so famous and so frightening"). *Seven Women* features Anne Bancroft, Sue Lyon, Mildred Dunnock and others as a disparate group of missionaries in China circa 1935 who put aside their differences when faced with an attack from a Mongolian war lord (Mike Mazurki). Tsu had the small role as his reluctant concubine. The film was a dull soaper and was not a hit. And despite being filmed on a soundstage the size of a football field, the sets looked phony and distracted from the drama. "They recreated a whole Chinese village with all kinds of animals on the backlot of MGM,"

Bobbi Shaw (*left*) and Tsu (*right*) assist witch doctor Buster Keaton in *How to Stuff a Wild Bikini* (AIP, 1965).

recalls Irene. "I had one scene where I entered sitting atop a galloping horse, which wasn't to my liking because I'm not too keen about horses. I'm afraid of them."

The film also had a very troubled production. Patricia Neal was set to star and filmed a number of scenes but she then had a stroke. The film was shut down for weeks and Anne Bancroft was hired to replace her. Ford had to re-shoot all of her scenes. Ford was also ailing and *Seven Women* turned out to be his final film. "John Ford wore an eye patch over one eye and was scary as hell," remarks Irene. "All the actors were terrified of him. Every day he would break for tea and have the whole cast sit around him. I was very new and nervous. One day we were rehearsing a scene and I missed a cue because I couldn't understand what Ford was saying. He'd always be chewing tobacco and talking at the same time. He screamed, 'I'm talking to you, Irene!' I then lost my place in the script. Anne Bancroft who was sitting next to me reached under the table and squeezed my hand. Then she whispered, 'You're not the only one terrified. Feel how clammy my hands are.' She was so sweet. I loved her for that."

Irene graduated to more substantial parts after receiving good notices for her dramatic performance in *Seven Women*. In *Paradise, Hawaiian Style* (1966), Tsu plays one of several island cuties romanced by Elvis Presley. "I wanted to work with Elvis so badly that I even went to an acting coach for help," reveals Irene. "I was very nervous during my audition but Hal Wallis [the producer] loved my test so much that he offered me my choice of roles. I picked the part of Pua because she was featured in one of the film's most lavish production numbers. Elvis and I come down a river in a canoe as he's singing 'Drums of the Islands.' But this turned out to be difficult because we never rehearsed it. All they told me was where to get on the boat and that it would float down river. As the scene started, they blasted the song from these huge boom boxes hidden along the banks of the river. As we sailed along, Elvis just lip-synched to himself. Nobody told me what to do so I decided to just sit there and look pretty. Our heads kept going back and forth. Elvis was looking one way and I was looking another. It looks pretty silly. Michael Moore never gave us any direction. He was kind of a novice. Hal Wallis let him direct this because he was the assistant director on a couple of Wallis' other films. The guy was terrified of everybody, most of all Elvis. He never directed Elvis at all and let him do whatever he wanted.

"I didn't meet Elvis until my first day of shooting in Hawaii. It was a very hot day and the air conditioner in my trailer was broken. I went to Elvis' dressing room, which was in this huge hut to escape the heat. One of Elvis' bodyguards let me rest in an extra bedroom. I dozed off and was woken by Elvis himself. We became very good friends after that. Elvis was such a nice guy. At that time, he also was very spiritual. A number of times I was invited back to have dinner with him. But it was very uncomfortable. He would be sitting there with Col. Parker and his entourage. Nobody really had a conversation—it was more like trying to say something to entertain Elvis. It was horrible and I felt sorry for Elvis so I stopped going."

Irene's career was progressing nicely by 1966 but she had an experience that almost made her quit the business. She was director Robert Wise's choice for the role of Maily in his epic film *The Sand Pebbles*, starring Steve McQueen. But studio machinations kept her from getting the role. "I interviewed with Wise a few times and he set up an expensive screen test for me on a massive set with other actors. I thought I did very well but then weeks went by with no word. I went to see Wise and he told me he wanted me for the part but the producers overruled him. They gave the part to Marayat Andriane, who was rumored to be Fox head Darryl Zanuck's current mistress. When I found out, I burst into tears and hoped never to have to go through something like that again." Though Irene was devastated, she wound up with a contract with 20th Century–Fox because "I had to sign with them before they allowed the screen test. For a short time I was treated like a star of the Golden Age. They gave me my own dressing room that was as big as a house. I even had my own parking space. Unfortunately, after only one film the studio went bankrupt. My contract was dropped along with all other such commitments Fox had."

That one Fox film was the zany spy spoof *Caprice* (1967), starring Doris Day as "the spy who came in from the cold cream." Richard Harris co-stars as an agent who may or may not be working for Interpol and Tsu (in her sexiest role) as a hair model who holds the key to a secret formula wanted by rival cosmetics company owners Edward Mulhare and Jack Kruschen. Irene acquits herself admirably and holds her own opposite the esteemed cast. The film is at its best spoofing the mod settings and styles of the cosmetics industry but fails with its confusing plot line involving the companies

Paradise, Hawaiian Style (Paramount, 1966) features Tsu as just one of several lovelies romanced by Elvis Presley.

being fronts for a narcotics ring. (Not to mention the fact that Day was a bit too long in the tooth for her role as a sexy spy.) "Doris Day is very talented with a sparkling, animated personality," comments Irene. "When we did *Caprice*, she was in her mid-forties trying to look younger. And I was trying to look older. They kept telling me that I couldn't be in the same scene with her. They were always cutting away from her to me. I didn't understand it and thought I did something wrong. Leon Shamroy was the cinematographer and he finally explained why—they were filming her through filters and I would be a blur.

"Frank Tashlin was the first director after Henry Koster to give me any sort of guidance into what film acting is all about," continues Irene. "Su Ling was my first really interesting part and I needed to be able to manifest some kind of personality. Mr. Tashlin was very talented and taught me how to create this screen energy. He was the only one to explain to me what the hell to do out there in front of the camera. He also educated me a lot as a person. Since I was beginning to earn money, he helped me open a checking account and apply for credit cards. I was on my own from the age of 14 so I never had anyone to assist me with these matters. He taught me how to paint and took me to different museums to learn about art and furnishings. But unfortunately, he was a very unhappy man.

In *Caprice* (20th Century–Fox, 1967) Tsu is a hair model who holds the key to the secret formula developed by scientist Ray Walston.

With all his wealth, he was very frugal and lonely."

Paradise, Hawaiian Style and *Caprice* were both box office hits, but Tsu's next film, *The Green Berets*, was a blockbuster and one of the ten biggest grossing (and, in some quarters, most hated) movies of 1968. John Wayne's simplistic view of the war depicted the Americans as heroes and the Vietcong as savages. The film is chock-full of absurd situations, unfunny comedy relief and inaccuracies, most notably the film's end as the sun sets in the east. Critics (mostly the anti–Vietnam ones) savaged the film for being a blatant piece of propaganda. (One reviewer commented, "We've dropped so many bombs on Vietnam, one more couldn't hurt.") David Janssen co-stars as a liberal reporter who changes his mind about the American presence in Vietnam after tagging along with Wayne and his Special Forces. Jim Hutton, Aldo Ray, Raymond St. Jacques, Jack Soo, Luke Askew and George Takei played various soldiers and officers. Tsu does a good job as a sultry South Vietnamese spy who seduces and betrays a Vietcong general. "I was the only female in the cast," recalls Tsu. "Though I had a lot of admiration for John Wayne, he didn't like me. I heard that he described me to a friend as 'that little hippie chick.' We would take Jeeps from the hotel out to the location where we were filming. I always tried to get out there early so I wouldn't have to ride with Wayne. I had a lot of friends in Hollywood who were very upset with me for doing this film. Some of the guys I knew were dodging the draft and they would say, 'How could you do this movie?' I told them that I'm an actress and have to take all kinds of roles."

The Green Berets was filmed on location in Georgia substituting for the jungles of Vietnam. It was the second film directed by Wayne. "Wayne wasn't very communicative and didn't have the patience for a director," remarks Irene. "I think he knew what he wanted to do in terms of the big picture but he was not very good working with actors. He was from John Ford's school of using intimidation and absolutely terrified some of us. During one scene, he berated poor Luke Askew for not saying his lines the way Wayne wanted. Instead of taking the guy aside, he humiliated him in front of the cast and crew. Wayne screamed at him, 'Walk over here! Say your line! Then walk over there!'"

During the sixties, Tsu was active on television and appeared in many series including *Voyage to the Bottom of the Sea*, with guest star John Cassavetes. ("He was very temperamental. He caused a fight in wardrobe because he refused to wear his costume.") West Coast audiences remembered Irene most from a TV commercial, of all things. For two years, beginning in 1968, she was the perky "Chevron Island Girl," spokesperson for Standard Oil. Not only was Irene seen on television but her face was plastered across the western states on billboards, newspaper ads and on the back of taxicabs. Her face was even on hula dollar game cards, the company's promotion at that time. Standard Oil's ad agency, Batten, Burton, Durstine and Osborne, produced eight spots shot on location in Florida and the Bahamas, which all featured a bouncy Tsu on an island with a different car. "Serious actors in those days were not supposed to do commercials," remarks Irene. "In hindsight, it was a great thing for me both financially and emotionally. It helped me create a screen persona and I experimented with different acting tools. I also had the best time!"

In 1969, Irene began work on *The Yin and Yang of Mr. Go*, directed by Burgess Meredith on location in Hong Kong. A spoof of Asian spy movies, the film stars James Mason, Broderick Crawford and a young Jeff Bridges as a writer–CIA agent assigned to retrieve a set of stolen plans for a weapon of destruction. The lovely Tsu was cast as Bridges' romantic interest. The film, however, was shelved and never completed. "This was a very problem-laden production," states Irene. "First there was tremendous discord between Burgess Meredith and James Mason. It got so bad that at one point they weren't even speaking to each other. They tried to involve the rest of us in their dispute but Jeff and I wouldn't take sides. Then the Canadian investors who were backing the movie ran out of money and skipped town. The film was never completed and most of us never received all the money owed us." (*The Yin and Yang of Mr. Go* turned up on video years later with additional scenes narrated by Broderick Crawford and animated sequences to bridge the gaps.)

The seventies found Irene married to Hungarian director Ivan Nagy. To please her husband, she abandoned her glamorous sixties look for something more down-to-earth. ("Ivan liked his women boyish and thin, so I lost weight and cut my hair very short. Ivan had a great deal of influence on me in art and cinema.") On the big screen, she could be found supporting well-known stars in a number of films including *Three the Hard Way* (1974) with Jim Brown, *Airport*

1975 (1974) with Charlton Heston and *Damien's Island* (1976) with Don Murray. She also journeyed to the Far East to appear in *Paper Tiger* (1975) and *Hot Potato* (1976). "These two shoots in particular were difficult because you were shooting on location every day in extreme heat. They would have to hire boys to bring us water all day long. Our clothes would be drenched from perspiration. Also I was afraid to eat anything, so I lived on hard-boiled eggs, oranges and vodka."

Paper Tiger features one of Irene's most enjoyable roles. Cast against type, she plays a vicious revolutionary whose terrorist group kidnaps an ambassador's son (Ando) and his English tutor (David Niven). The film flopped because of its indecision. The creators couldn't decide if it was going to be a cutesy Disney-style adventure or a hard-hitting tale of political terrorism. Tsu, however, seemed to be having fun in her role and even got to rough up Niven. "I did my own stunts," says Irene with a chuckle. "I am trained in karate. I'm a blue belt. That's like being a high school dropout.

"I so enjoyed working with David Niven. He was a classy oldtime movie star who never ate lunch but would go for walks instead. He lived in the south of France and was always offering me wine. To avoid hangovers, he said with his proper British accent, 'Irene, drink a lot of water before you go to sleep. You'll pee a lot but you won't wake up with a hangover.' He was such a wonderful rogue." In 1975, Tsu told columnist Earl Wilson, "One night David Niven came to my room at two in the morning gloriously smashed. I happened to be making out with his son. He was so smooth about it. He just said, 'Oh, just carry on.'"

Hot Potato featured Tsu as a police detective in Thailand who assists martial-arts fighter Jim Kelly rescue the U.S. ambassador's daughter, who has been kidnapped by a warlord. The film was originally intended for Bruce Lee, who passed away before filming began. According to Irene, "They then botched it up and re-wrote it for Jim Kelly, who wasn't very good. We shot it in Thailand, which was hard, because it was a Buddhist country. One day we were shooting in a Buddhist temple. It was over 100 degrees so I was wearing only a bikini so my costume would be dry for the next shot. The director called me out for a rehearsal so I threw a shirt on over my bikini. Well, the temple went crazy. The monks punished the producer and the director by making them carry this Ping-Pong table back and forth about 100 times. And they did it! I felt so bad."

After a brief hiatus from acting in the early eighties to concentrate on her second career as a fashion designer, Irene returned to the big screen as one of Bette Midler's friends in the hit comedy *Down and Out in Beverly Hills* (1986). Nick Nolte plays a bum who attempts to drown himself in the pool of *nouveau riche* couple Midler and Richard Dreyfuss. Dreyfuss saves him and he becomes their houseguest, turning their lives upside down. Irene was cast as the wife of a Jewish dentist. "I went in to audition for the small part of a plain Chinese interpreter," remembers Irene. "I impressed the casting director and he informed me that Paul Mazursky was changing one of the friends' wives into an ethnic part and to come back tomorrow to meet with him. I was so nervous. I had to read a scene with Mr. Mazursky. He liked me and instantly dubbed me Sheila Waltzberg.

"Bette Midler and Richard Dreyfuss were wonderful to work with. Bette is just so funny and is as wild in person as

In *Hot Potato* (Warner Bros., 1976), Tsu played a police detective in Thailand who takes on a warlord's goons in this fight scene.

she is on the big screen. Nick Nolte is a strange guy. Though he is a movie star, he doesn't look like much in person but on screen he lights up. During a big party scene, I was hot and dying of thirst and Nick offered me a sip of his drink. It was straight vodka with a touch of orange juice!"

Irene has been working steadily ever since in such films as *Steele Justice* (1987), *Snapdragon* (1993) and *Mr. Jones* (1993) and on television in episodes of *The Single Guy* and *Star Trek: Voyager*. Though she lost out on doing 1993's *The Joy Luck Club* ("They said I was too young looking to play one of the mothers. If you are going to lose a role that is a better reason than any"), Irene was cast in *Comrades: Almost a Love Story* (1997).

"This was my first Chinese-language film," states Irene proudly. "It was directed by the gifted Peter Chan, who next directed *The Love Letter* [1999] with Kate Capshaw. I played Leon Lai's aunt. It's my first real character role. I play a person, not a Chinese or some sort of foreigner, just a person. Hopefully I will get to play more of character-type roles in the future. My motto has always been, 'Do whatever keeps you humble and be happy.' For the very near future that means adopting my three-year-old niece from China and rehearsing a Frank Chin play called *The Year of the Dragon*, which I hope will open in the near future."

FILM APPEARANCES

1961 Flower Drum Song (Universal) [uncredited dancer] d. Henry Koster.
1963 Cleopatra (20th Century–Fox) [uncredited] d. Joseph L. Mankiewicz.
Take Her, She's Mine (20th Century–Fox) d. Henry Koster.
1964 **John Goldfarb, Please Come Home** (20th Century–Fox) d. J. Lee Thompson.
The Pleasure Seekers (20th Century–Fox) [uncredited] d. Jean Negulesco.
1965 Sword of Ali Baba (Universal) d. Arthur Lubin/Virgil Vogel.
How to Stuff a Wild Bikini (AIP) d. William Asher.
1966 Seven Women (MGM) d. John Ford.
Paradise, Hawaiian Style (Paramount) d. Michael Moore.
Women of the Prehistoric Planet (Realart) d. Arthur C. Pierce.
1967 Caprice (20th Century–Fox) d. Frank Tashlin.
The Karate Killers (MGM; edited two-part episode of The Man from U.N.C.L.E.) d. Barry Shear.
1968 The Green Berets (Warner Bros.) d. John Wayne/Ray Kellogg.
Island of the Lost (TV-movie) d. John Florea/Ricou Browning.
1970 The Yin and Yang of Mr. Go (unreleased) d. Burgess Meredith.
1974 Three the Hard Way (Allied Artists) d. Gordon Parks, Jr.
Airport 1975 (Universal) d. Jack Smight.
Judge Dee and the Monastery Murders (TV-movie) d. Jeremy Kagan.
1975 Paper Tiger (Great Britain, MacLean) d. Ken Annakin.
1976 Hot Potato (Warner Bros.) d. Oscar Williams.
Damien's Island d. Don Murray.
1980 **Damien ... The Leper Priest** (TV-movie) d. Steven Gethers.
1986 **Down and Out in Beverly Hills** (Touchstone) d. Paul Mazursky.
1987 Steele Justice (Atlantic) d. Robert Boris.
1990 A Girl to Kill For (Columbia) d. Richard Oliver.
1992 Unbecoming Age (Direct-to-video) d. Alfredo Ringel/Deborah Ringel.
1993 Snapdragon (Direct-to-video) d. Worth Keeter.

Irene Tsu, ca. 2000—no wonder the producers of *The Joy Luck Club* felt she was too young-looking to play one of the mothers (courtesy of Irene Tsu).

Mr. Jones (Tri-Star) d. Mike Figgis.
1994 Widow's Kiss (HBO/Rysher Entertainment) d. Peter Foldy.
1997 **Comrades: Almost a Love Story/Tianmimi** (Golden Harvest) d. Peter Chan.
Tell Me No Secrets (TV-movie) d. Bobby Roth.

TELEVISION APPEARANCES

Perry Mason "The Case of the Floating Stones" 11/21/63 CBS.
Breaking Point "And If Thy Hand Offend Thee" 1/13/64 ABC.
The New Phil Silvers Show "Trombones" 4/11/64 CBS.
My Favorite Martian "Double Trouble" 11/22/64 CBS.
The Man from U.N.C.L.E. "The Hong Kong Shilling Affair" 3/15/65 NBC.
I Spy "A Cup of Kindness" 9/22/65 NBC.
The Wackiest Ship in the Army "The Sisters" 9/26/65 NBC.
The John Forsythe Show "The Nightingale of Koorbahu" 10/25/65 NBC.
Voyage to the Bottom of the Sea "The Peacemaker" 11/14/65 ABC.
My Three Sons "Robbie and the Slave Girl" 1/20/66 CBS.
Laredo "The Bitter Yen of General Ti" 2/3/67 NBC.

The Man from U.N.C.L.E. "The Five Daughters Affair" Part II 4/7/67 NBC.
The Wild Wild West "The Night of the Samurai" 10/13/67 CBS.
The Dating Game [celebrity contestant] 3/15/69 ABC.
Insight "The Day God Died" 11/17/68 Synd.
The Name of the Game "Island of Gold and Precious Stones" 1/16/70 NBC.
Family Affair "Eastward Ho" 10/1/70 CBS.
Sarge "Ring Out, Ring In" 9/28/71 NBC.
Cade's County "Delegate at Large" 11/21/71 CBS.
Mission: Impossible "Double Dead" 2/12/72 CBS.
The Smith Family "San Francisco Cop" 4/26/72 ABC.
Cannon "Bitter Legion" 9/27/72 CBS.
Owen Marshall, Counselor at Law "An Often and Familiar Ghost" 1/3/73 ABC.
Hawaii Five-O "Engaged to Be Buried" 2/27/73 CBS.
The New Perry Mason "The Case of the Spurious Spouse" 12/9/73 CBS.
Ironside "Terror on Grant Avenue" 1/31/74 NBC.
Future Cop [series regular as Dr. Tingley] 3/5/77 to 4/22/77 NBC.
The New Adventures of Wonder Woman "The Man Who Made Volcanoes" 11/18/77 CBS.
The Rockford Files "Irving the Explorer" 11/18/77 NBC.
Airwolf "The Deadly Circle" 11/30/85 CBS.
Trapper John, M.D. "Heart and Seoul" 1/28/86 CBS.
Noble House (mini-series) 2/21 to 2/24/88 NBC.
Baywatch Nights "Code of Silence" 3/16/96 Synd.
The Single Guy "Double Date" 11/14/96 NBC.
Star Trek: Voyager "Favorite Son" 3/24/97 UPN.

Also:

Ryan's Four, Murder in Paradise, MacGyver, E.R. and *First Love.*

Chris Noel

Pretty, perky Chris Noel was once described as "devastation in a bikini." A former model, this green-eyed blonde was discovered while doing summer stock. With her fresh-faced, innocent look, Noel was perfectly cast as the wholesome girl-next-door looking for fun or romance on the beach, on campus, or on vacation. Wearing the skimpiest of bikinis, she wiggled and danced her way through a gaggle of teenage and beach films—*Get Yourself a College Girl* ("The swingin'-est blast ever filmed"), *Beach Ball* ("Nothing bounces like *Beach Ball*!"), *Girl Happy* ("Elvis jumps with the campus crowd to make the beach 'ball' bounce!!!"), *Wild Wild Winter* ("A surfin' snow ball!") and *For Singles Only* ("See how the single half lives ... in co-ed pads where the unmarrieds swing 24 hours a day!"). When the beach films became passé in the late sixties, Noel segued to the biker genre with roles in *The Glory Stompers* and *The Tormentors*. Unlike other actresses who didn't want to be known just for their bodies, Chris loved all the attention. "I was proud of my body and never had any aspirations to become an Academy Award–winning actress," comments Chris. "I wanted to be a celebrity! I loved dating actors and going to parties." No wonder this bikini-clad cutie stunned Hollywood when she became the first female disc jockey on Armed Forces Radio in 1966 and began visiting Vietnam on her own to help boost the morale of the GIs.

Chris Noel was born Sandra Louise Noel in West Palm Beach, Florida. By age ten she had become fascinated with Hollywood and would buy every movie magazine on the stand. Her favorite film star was Marilyn Monroe. As a teenager, Chris began modeling using the name Sandee Noel. Though she was very shy, she began getting lots of work and by age 16 she was featured on the cover of *Good Housekeeping* magazine. Two years later, this timid young girl had turned entrepreneur and had her own modeling school. "I took modeling lessons at the Palm Beach Modeling School and then began teaching classes for them," recalls Chris. "So I thought, if I could teach for them I could have my own agency. I went to a dance studio and made a deal to use the studio certain times of the week. I then had business cards made up. I remember they were lavender and white. I taught children and adults. After about a year, I got real bored and decided I didn't want to do it any more."

Noel then entered and won the Miss Palm Beach Beauty Pageant. First prize was a drama scholarship to a local college. But Chris quickly dropped out because "I was put in with a bunch of wealthy kids who all had been in school plays. When I went to do my first scene on stage, they all started yelling at me that I wasn't speaking loud enough. I felt so awful that I quit and moved to New York." To earn a living in the Big Apple, Chris began working as a model again and was chosen to be a cheerleader for the New York Giants football team. She turned down an offer to be a *Playboy* playmate ("I thought I looked better with my clothes on") and became a finalist in the Miss Rheingold contest. This led to a chance meeting with actor Hugh O'Brian, who became her boyfriend. "Hugh was doing *Mister Roberts* in summer stock and asked me to try out for the part of a nurse," remembers Chris. "I got the part and did it well, which surprised me considering my prior stage experience. During the run, some talent scouts from MGM saw me. They contacted my agent and offered me a contract. So I left the production to go to Hollywood."

However, before Noel even walked onto the MGM lot, she won a role opposite Steve McQueen in Allied Artists' underrated comedy-drama *Soldier in the Rain* (1963), directed by Ralph Nelson. Chris, however, immediately got the taste of how difficult it could be for young actresses in Hollywood. On her first day of shooting, she was called into producer Martin Jurow's bungalow. "The wardrobe woman escorted me into his office," says Chris. "The next thing I know, he starts pulling down all the shades and asks her to leave. Then he reached over and kissed me on the lips! I stared at him aghast. He said, 'Okay, you can leave now.' That was it! It had to be one of the strangest things that ever happened to me in Hollywood." Compared to other actresses' horror stories of lecherous old producers, lucky Chris got off relatively unscathed.

Soldier in the Rain stars Steve McQueen as Pvt. Eustis Clay, a good-natured but not-so-bright soldier who hatches one harebrained get-rich-quick scheme after another before he leaves the service. Jackie Gleason played the exasperated Sgt. Slaughter, who Eustis is always trying to interest in his plots, and Tuesday Weld co-starred as Bobbie Jo Pepperdine, a callous high school beauty who is set up on a date with Gleason. Noel was featured in a small role as McQueen's nymphomaniac girlfriend. Though her commendable performance got her voted a Hollywood Deb Star of 1963, this role gave Chris problems because she was so naïve that she didn't know what a nymphomaniac was. "Ralph Nelson felt I wasn't relaxed enough in the role," says Chris. "When we were filming this scene on a golf course, Nelson began chasing me for no reason. He chased me right into this pond! I guess he thought this would help loosen me up. All it did was make me soaking wet and delay the shoot. There was also a photographer on the set who took pictures of me and the next day they were in all the newspapers. It was so embarrassing. I was new to making movies and the only one who helped me was Steve McQueen.

"Steve was incredible," continues Chris, excitedly. "He was a fascinating and sexy actor. I had a major crush on Steve but I wouldn't go to bed with him because he was married. One time he invited me into his bungalow and began

Chris Noel and Steve McQueen take a break from golfing in *Soldier in the Rain* (Allied Artists, 1963).

kissing me. I told him, 'No!' He responded, 'But I've been to bed with every one of my leading ladies!' I very politely left and we became friends." Though Chris adored working with McQueen, she got the cold shoulder from her other co-stars. "Tuesday Weld was bitchy and didn't like me. I even had to darken my hair because of her! And Jackie Gleason liked only who he chose to like. He wasn't friendly. I'd say hello to him and he'd grunt something back. He didn't like rehearsing either. But I got used to it. I liked working with Steve McQueen so much that it didn't bother me how everybody else was."

Back at MGM, Chris co-starred with Gary Lockwood and Robert Vaughn in *The Lieutenant* during the 1963-64 television season. This series (produced by Gene Roddenberry) depicted the adventures of a young career officer in the Marines during peacetime. Chris played a different role in each episode, ranging from guest leads to bit roles. "I had so much fun doing *The Lieutenant*," recalls Chris fondly. "It was so exciting to have the opportunity to work with Gene Roddenberry. He only wanted one girl on the show. How many actresses do you know appearing in a series that got to play a different role week after week? Not many. That was such an original idea. It goes to show you how creative Roddenberry was. He was a genius! I was very proud that I got to work with him."

Recalling her co-stars, Chris remarks, "Gary Lockwood was very cute and we flirted. That made it interesting. He was likable but he could be moody,

moody, moody. For instance, one day he commented to me, 'Why do you do all these pictures for the studio? Why do you go to all the parties? It's never going to make you a star!' Robert Vaughn is a very good actor but he wasn't nice to me. He was very cold and distant."

Returning to the big screen, Chris had small decorative roles in her first two MGM films, *Looking for Love* (1964) with Connie Francis and Jim Hutton and *Honeymoon Hotel* (1964) with Robert Morse and Robert Goulet. A bigger part followed in *Get Yourself a College Girl* (1964) with Mary Ann Mobley, Joan O'Brien, Chad Everett and Nancy Sinatra. Produced by Sam Katzman, the weirdly titled *Get Yourself a College Girl* was originally to be called *Watusi a-Go-Go* to cash in on the dance craze. But when the film was ready to be released, the Watusi had become passé. Like a number of Noel's subsequent films, it is best remembered for the varied rock acts used including the Dave Clark Five, the Animals and Astrud Gilberto. "This was a fun picture to do," comments Chris. "Mary Ann Mobley and Joan O'Brien were very nice. Chad Everett was *so* handsome and down-to-earth. And Nancy Sinatra was fabulous! She was one of the kindest women I knew in Hollywood. They were all great to work with."

Chris had a banner 1965 working with three of the biggest teen idols of the late fifties–early sixties—Elvis Presley, Richard Chamberlain and Edd "Kookie" Byrnes. First up for Chris was *Girl Happy*,

Noel (*left*) as a vacationing coed whoops it up in *Get Yourself a College Girl* (MGM, 1964) as Mary Ann Mobley and Joan O'Brien peer on.

one of Elvis' best and highest-grossing films of the mid-sixties. The King returns to the beach after appearing in *Blue Hawaii* (1961), the precursor to the sixties beach films. Here he plays the leader of a musical combo which consists of Gary Crosby, Joby Baker, and Jimmy Hawkins. He and his pals are sent to Fort Lauderdale during spring break by a Chicago club owner (Harold J. Stone) who wants them to keep an eye on his vacationing daughter (Shelley Fabares) and her friends (Noel and Lyn Edgington). Elvis finds Fabares to be a square but every time he and the guys are about to score with some beach cuties they have to race off and rescue the trouble-prone Fabares. *Girl Happy* is one of the better mid-sixties Elvis films, helped immensely by better-than-average musical numbers including the song "Spring Break." Using a split-screen, director Boris Sagal had Elvis and the guys juxtaposed with Fabares and the girls singing as they all were driving south to Florida. "I remember I was so excited because I got the opportunity to sing with Elvis,' exclaims Chris. "The song 'Spring Break' was pre-recorded. When we filmed the scene of us heading down to Fort Lauderdale, we lip-synched the song to a tape.

"Elvis was fabulous to work with," continues Noel. "He was a wonderful man! I remember meeting him the first day on the set. I walked in and noticed that Shelley Fabares and Mary Ann Mobley had received flowers from him. But Lyn Edgington and I hadn't. I said to

In *Girl Happy* (MGM, 1965), guests (*left to right*) Lyn Edgington, Chris Noel, Shelley Fabares and Elvis Presley get a lecture from hotel manager John Fiedler.

Elvis, 'How come we don't have any flowers? Don't you like us?' The next day we had flowers in our trailer. He would frequently sing to me 'Leon, Leon' [Noel spelled backwards] to the Christmas carol 'Noel, Noel.'"

Chris was cast in a small role as a college coed in *Joy in the Morning* (1965) starring Richard Chamberlain as a struggling law student newly married to poor-but-proud Yvette Mimieux during the Depression. As with *Soldier in the Rain*, Noel had to darken her hair to become a brunette contrast to the fair-haired Mimieux. "Unlike Tuesday Weld, Yvette was nice to me," says Chris. 'But one day I saw her just sobbing. We couldn't shoot because she wouldn't come out of her dressing room. Alex Segal, the director, went in to talk to her. She still wouldn't come out and we were all sent home." During production of this film, there was reportedly a lot of tension between Mimieux and Chamberlain. Hollywood columnists noted that the two stars did not get along. Noel couldn't verify that but she also found Chamberlain to be "sweet to work with. I even went out with Richard on a studio-arranged date."

Chris had her first starring role in her next film, *Beach Ball* (1965) co-starring Edd Byrnes. But she had to leave MGM to get it. "What was greater than being under contract to Metro-Goldwyn-Mayer," asserts Chris. "I was a fool for leaving them but I felt they were holding me back and that I could get bigger parts elsewhere. I did—but the quality of films couldn't compare to MGM's." *Beach Ball* was a blatant rip-off of *Beach Party*, throwing in everything from surfing, skydiving and hot rodding to a battle-of-the-bands contest to match the zaniness of AIP's beach films. But what really distinguishes *Beach Ball* is a great lineup of rock acts including the Four Seasons, the Hondells, the Righteous Brothers and the Supremes (who sing the title tune "Come to the Beach Ball with Me"). The plot features Byrnes as the leader of a combo whose instruments are repossessed. He then tries to convince the college credit union manager (Noel) to give him a student loan to continue school to study African tribal rhythms. In actuality, Byrnes and his friends (Aron Kincaid, Robert Logan and Don Edmonds) are all college dropouts living among the denizens of Malibu Beach. When Noel and her finance committee (Brenda Benet, Gail Gilmore and Mikki Jamison) realize they've been duped, they rip up the check. Feeling guilty, the nerdy girls tease up their hair, don bikinis, head for the beach, and try to convince the guys to return to school. The film climaxes at a Hot Rod and Musical Show with the guys performing in drag.

Beach Ball, as directed by Lennie Weinrib, is good, clean, goofy fun. The beach and surf scenes are plentiful, as are the bikini-clad girls. Byrnes and Noel are attractive and charming in the leads. ("I think we made a good beach couple and kind of held our own with Frankie and Annette," remarks Chris.) Among the supporting players, blonde hunk Aron Kincaid stands out and was grabbed by AIP shortly thereafter. "I liked doing *Beach Ball* very much," says Chris. "Aron Kincaid is a great guy. He is a fabulous artist and one of the most fun people I met in Hollywood. But I did not like Edd Byrnes. He was so egotistical! We had a kissing scene and he would slip his tongue practically down my throat. I felt that was uncalled for. I didn't like it. It was invading my privacy. I told him he was a jerk. He still wouldn't stop! So I went to Lennie Weinrib and said to him, 'Get Byrnes to stop or I'm walking off the set.' I had no problem with Lennie. I

Beach Ball (Paramount, 1965) with Chris Noel and Edd Byrnes.

thought he was a good director and worked with him again on *Wild Wild Winter* [1966]. That was hysterical because it was a beach movie done in the snow. It was very innocent and fun."

As with her previous films, *Wild Wild Winter* (in which, *Variety* commented, "Chris Noel is prettily effective in the hands-off department") also featured a great array of rock acts including Jay & the Americans, the Beau Brummels and the Astronauts. But according to Chris, the actors very rarely mingled with the rock stars. "They had to do take after take like we did and it wasn't much fun to sit around and watch," remembers Chris. "I guess the only group that stands out for me was the Supremes. I remember Diana Ross was so gorgeous. She, Florence Ballard and Mary Wilson always looked so spectacular. We never met. I only saw them when they were working."

By 1966, Chris' career was in full swing. Not only was she getting movie leads but she was also appearing regularly on television in episodes of such popular sixties series as *Dr. Kildare*, *Burke's Law*, *Perry Mason*, *My Three Sons*, *My Mother, the Car* and *Bewitched*. ("Elizabeth Montgomery was a *real* witch," says Chris vehemently. "She never spoke with me and walked by me haughtily like she hated me.") On the debut episode of *Occasional Wife*, Noel played a sexy girl in pursuit of star Michael Callan, who is pretending to be married to the girl (Patricia Harty) in the apartment above him to get ahead at work. *Variety* took notice of Chris and commented,

"Noel handles her guest stint with comic zest." She made such an impression that she was invited back for two additional episodes.

It was at this point that Chris became more keenly aware of the war that was raging in Vietnam. A visit to a veteran's hospital in San Francisco would change Noel's life forever. "I was invited to go with a group of stars [including Dan Rowan & Dick Martin, Beverly Adams, and Eileen O'Neill] to entertain the wounded soldiers," remembers Chris. "I saw first hand the devastation of war. It was something you just didn't see. It really hit me. I decided then I wanted to go to Vietnam but I didn't think there ever would be a chance for me." Noel tried to become a part of Bob Hope's entourage to Vietnam but she was rejected because she wasn't a big enough star. Seeing how dejected she felt, her then-boyfriend, singer Jack Jones, told Chris that they were auditioning female disc jockeys for Armed Forces Radio. Chris auditioned and got the job.

Chris became the first female disc jockey for Armed Forces Radio since World War II. Her program, *A Date with Chris*, was broadcast to the servicemen in Vietnam and around the world from 1966 through 1971. "I taped the show in Los Angeles," Chris says. "It was then transferred to LP and played wherever our troops were located around the world. I had a signature way to begin each show. For example, I'd might say [*with breathy voice*], 'Hi, luv! This is Chris Noel. Welcome to *A Date with Chris*. I've got all kinds of really *groovy* songs to play for you from the United States of America. And this first one is by the Beatles. I think you'll like it. I'd like to dedicate it to all you guys with the 199th infantry brigade in Vietnam.' I also would have guests on the program—Nancy Sinatra, Ray Charles, Marvin Gaye and most of the top rock acts. I hosted one of the few entertainment programs for those guys in Vietnam."

After she began doing the show, Chris received a letter from the Department of Defense that asked her if she would volunteer to go to Vietnam to help build the morale of the troops. She jumped at the chance without even considering the danger. But unlike Joey Heatherton, Raquel Welch, Jill St. John and others who were part of Bob Hope's entourage, Chris traveled on her own to hospitals, firebases and remote outposts. Clad in the shortest of mini-skirts ("my fatigues"), Noel would sing, dance, comfort and bring joy to many servicemen. It is no wonder she became the favorite pin-up of GIs in Vietnam. "It was the most courageous thing I ever did," remarks Chris. "All I had with me was a tape recorder and a portable record player. I would play all the latest music for the guys and I would dance with them. I also would tape messages from them to their families. I eventually traveled the entire scope of South Vietnam many times and was shot at on more than one occasion. I probably had one of the most unusual experiences of the Vietnam War." The Vietcong, however, did not take too kindly to Chris. "They put a bounty on my head," says Chris, laughing. "Bob Hope's head was worth $25,000. Mine was only worth $10,000."

While Noel's personal life was being fulfilled aiding the servicemen in Vietnam, her acting career was suffering. Hollywood in the late sixties was anti–Vietnam and Noel received a backlash from the acting community for doing her radio show and for visiting Vietnam. "My family and friends thought what I was doing was neat," says Chris. "People I knew casually just started to hate me for going to Vietnam. I never expected the backlash I received. And, I'll tell you, it's bothered me ever since. But at the time I was so absorbed in it that I just threw my hands in the air and said, 'What will be, will be.' I believed in supporting my country. Since I was asked to visit Vietnam, I felt it was my duty to go. Reporters would always question me if I were a hawk or a dove. And I would refuse to answer. I wouldn't discuss the war. I would only speak about my work and the needs of the GIs. I would not take sides. Now, however, I believe we were all told a lot of lies in the beginning and most of us bought it."

Acting-wise, Noel appeared in the TV pilot *Pistols 'n' Petticoats* starring Ann Sheridan as a newly elected sheriff of a small town. Noel played her snobbish daughter who returns to the family ranch after graduating from a finishing school in the East. When the pilot was picked up my CBS, Noel threw a party in celebration. However, her agent had to give her the disheartening news that the network was going to recast her role with someone else. "CBS conducted a focus group to preview the pilot," states Chris. "Then the audience was asked to evaluate the show. My role came off as unsympathetic since I am always putting down my family. The audience didn't like my character. Even so, Universal still wanted me but CBS didn't. I was shocked when the network dropped me from the series at the last second. They replaced me with another actress [Carole Wells]. I was so disappointed!"

Despite this setback, Noel was back on the big screen in the biker film *The Glory Stompers* (1967). Chris played the girlfriend of Stompers leader Jody McCrea. She's kidnapped by his rival Dennis Hopper, leader of the Black Souls, and dragged off to be sold into white slavery.

"Dennis Hopper was stoned throughout the entire shoot," snickers Noel. "So were practically the rest of the cast and crew. Hopper was a friend of Jane Fonda's so he gave me a lot of grief about my work in Vietnam. But I liked making this film because I love riding on motorcycles. It is a great feeling. I also did another biker film called *The Tormentors* [1971] with Anthony Eisley. It was about a bunch of Nazi-loving bikers who brutalize anyone who gets in their way. I have never seen it but heard it's available on video."

Chris returned to the bikini roles with a supporting role in *For Singles Only* (1968). Two girls (Mary Ann Mobley and Lana Wood) move into a swinging singles complex and get involved with their new neighbors. "I don't remember too much about this film," says Chris. "It was a very hectic time in my life. John Saxon was a nice guy. He is very handsome and very bright. And I liked Lana Wood. I never liked her sister Natalie but Lana was neat. Natalie was stuck-up. I recall one scene where I had body paint all over me. They put flowers on my legs. I had to get up on this stage and do this wild, crazy dance."

That same year, Chris journeyed back to Vietnam and finally hooked up with Bob Hope. Hope too received a backlash from Hollywood, but since he and John Wayne were such big stars, the White House always recognized their achievements in Vietnam. Chris enjoyed working with Hope immensely but "when I walked in I heard all these other stars complaining about *everything*. Yet they were sitting in an air-conditioned room and they had makeup artists, hair stylists and costume designers. They were treated like royalty. And they were still griping. I was ashamed of them because I knew what it was like being out in the

Psychotic gang leader Dennis Hopper threatens biker chick Noel in *The Glory Stompers* (AIP, 1967).

boonies without any of that stuff. I'd fly by helicopter all over Vietnam to entertain the troops. And to hear them bellyache disgusted me. I thought they were so fortunate to be even on this trip. They were never in danger. Most of them would fly to Thailand to spend the night and fly back to Vietnam the next day. And they were all paid for rehearsals and their trips. I was asked to volunteer and I did!"

Noel's last trip to Vietnam was in 1969. "I stopped going after my first husband committed suicide. He was a Vietnam vet and killed himself that Christmas. It was too hard for me to ever go back." Though her involvement in Vietnam seriously hurt her career, Chris persevered. "Acting was my world. I had to go through some transitions first before I could return to it. I went back to Hollywood in 1978 and did a few TV movies. I remember I ran into Farrah Fawcett's manager Jay Bernstein once. He asked me, 'What ever happened to you? I thought you were going to be the next Marilyn Monroe.' I told him, 'I went to Vietnam instead.'"

One of those TV movies was *Detour to Terror* (1980) starring O.J. Simpson as a heroic bus driver trying to protect his wealthy passengers from three thugs (one of whom is a young Lorenzo Lamas) who are terrorizing them on their way from Los Angeles to Las Vegas. Among the travelers are Anne Francis, Arte Johnson

Noel leads a band of psychedelic body-painted beauties in a dance number from *For Singles Only* (Columbia, 1968).

as the tour guide, Chris Noel as a high-class hooker and the future Mrs. O.J. Simpson, Nicole Brown. "We filmed this in the desert," remembers Chris. "One day O.J. finished his scenes early and went back to the hotel. Nicole had to stay there in the hot sun and she told me that she was never going to do a movie again. I asked why. She replied, 'I only did this film to be with O.J. Now he gets to go back to the air-conditioned hotel and I'm stuck out here in the blazing sun!' Both

O.J. and Nicole were very nice and they even posed for a picture with me, which I still have."

In the early eighties, Noel cut a number of singles including "I'm an American" and "Time for Healing." It was around this time that she discovered that she was suffering from Post-Traumatic Stress Disorder. "While I was in California, I became completely stressed out and anxiety ridden," says Chris. 'I thought I had the Marilyn Monroe complex. It would take me forever to get ready to go out on an audition. I would be so nervous I'd barely be able to hold the script without shaking. I got help and learned that not only soldiers could have PTSD. I still have PTSD but I've learned how to manage it."

Noel's last theatrical film was the powerful *Cease Fire* (1985). Don Johnson stars as a Vietnam veteran who struggles with readjusting to life at home and the effect of Post-Traumatic Stress Syndrome. Chris received the best reviews of her career playing the wife of a Vietnam vet who commits suicide. *Variety* raved, "Former 1960s starlet Chris Noel shines in a heartfelt monologue delivered at a group session for veterans." "This role was hard for me to do because it hit so close to home," remarks Chris. "I cried when the camera turned on. Then I decided that it was right, and I did my scene in only one take. It's a true compliment when the cast and crew applaud your work. I'm very glad I did this movie because it is such a meaningful film. It has a very strong message to it regarding the effects of Post-Traumatic Stress Syndrome. The film has helped a lot of people who have been around vets to understand them a little bit better.

"I also have to praise Don Johnson," continues Chris. "He gets a bad rap from the press because of his addictions. He had a real feel for his role as a vet and did a lot of research. Don spoke with a lot of guys and saw that many were deeply wounded both physically and emotionally from the war. He had real compassion for them. He was also so nice to me and signed a picture to me as 'a friend forever.'"

In 1987, Noel's book *Matter of Survival: The "War" Jane Never Saw* was published detailing her experiences in Vietnam. "Regarding the title, people always ask me, 'Jane who? Jane Fonda?' I respond, it could be or it could just be Jane Doe." Noel and other women Vietnam veterans were then asked to share their experiences on a special episode of *China Beach*. Though she had a lot of problems with *China Beach* because she felt it degraded the women who went to Vietnam by having a prostitute as a lead character, Noel agreed to appear because "I definitely want to be part of things that have to do with Vietnam. It's amazing how many times I am overlooked." Commenting in the episode in regards to seeing young men dying, Noel said, daubing her eyes, "See, the whole thing was that you had to be brave all the time and pretend nothing affected you no matter if it did or it didn't." She also remarked later on in the program, "The primary thing I tried to do was to stay upbeat, have energy and just keep in the back of my mind that my sole purpose for doing this was to keep the morale up."

Noel's last TV gig was playing Neil Patrick Harris' daffy Palm Beach mother who doesn't understand her son in an episode of *B.L. Stryker*, starring Burt Reynolds. Her performance earned her a Crystal Reel Award from the Florida Motion Picture & Television Association for Best Comedic Actress. "I dated Burt during the sixties," recalls Chris. "As a boyfriend, I wasn't too impressed with him.

Chris Noel, ca. 2000 (courtesy of Chris Noel).

[*Laughs*] But as an actor and a director, I think he is fabulous! He is very kind and quiet on the set. If an actor has a problem, he is very approachable. He has a lot of compassion towards the actors and their work. I enjoyed working with him very much."

Today Chris still finds time to act (mostly in commercials) while managing Vetsville Cease Fire House, Inc., which she founded in 1993. Her organization consists of four halfway houses in three Florida cities that provide shelter, food, clothing and counseling for homeless Vietnam vets. "I had a desire of doing this about five years before I did it. As a leader in the national Veteran's community, I've always been on top of the needs of the vets. As I traveled around, people would tell me of vets who killed themselves. I had a real feeling for that because my husband had killed himself. And I started to see that many vets were suffering from PTSD or the effects of Agent Orange. Many were living on the streets because they couldn't afford to even rent an apartment. So one day I just decided to go out and rent a house for homeless vets. I began this using my own money until we started fundraising. Vetsville now has an apartment building and four houses in three cities." Though the Vietnam War is long over, Chris Noel's commitment to the men who served there is unwavering.

Film Appearances

1963	**Soldier in the Rain** (Allied Artists) d. Ralph Nelson.
1964	**Honeymoon Hotel** (MGM) d. Henry Levin.
	Diary of a Bachelor (AIP) d. Sandy Howard.
	Looking for Love (MGM) [uncredited bit] d. Don Weis.
	Get Yourself a College Girl (MGM) d. Sidney Miller.
1965	**Girl Happy** (MGM) d. Boris Sagal.
	Joy in the Morning (MGM) d. Alex Segal.
	Beach Ball (Paramount) d. Lennie Weinrib.
1966	**Wild Wild Winter** (Universal) d. Lennie Weinrib.
1967	**The Glory Stompers** (AIP) d. Anthony M. Lanza.
1968	**For Singles Only** (Columbia) d. Arthur Dreifuss.
1971	**The Tormentors/The Terminators** d. David B. Eagle (a.k.a. David L. Hewitt).
1980	**Wild Times** (TV-movie) d. Richard Compton.
	Detour to Terror (TV-movie) d. Michael O'Herlihy.
1981	**Fly Away Home** (TV-movie) d. Paul Krasny.
1985	**Cease Fire** (Cineworld) d. David Nutter.
1986	**Sin of Innocence** (TV-movie) d. Arthur Allan Seidelman.
1987	**Back to the Beach** (Paramount) [cameo] d. Lyndall Hobbs.

TELEVISION APPEARANCES

The Eleventh Hour "Try to Keep Alive Until Next Tuesday" 4/17/63 NBC.
The Lieutenant (series regular in various roles) 9/14/63 to 9/25/64 NBC.
The Steve Allen Show 11/28/63 [Deb Star] Synd.
The Hollywood Deb Star Ball (special) [Deb Star] 12/28/63.
Hollywood and the Stars "Teenage Idols, Part 2" (w/ host Fabian) 1/20/64 NBC.
The Lawyer (unaired pilot) 1965.
American Bandstand 2/27/65 ABC.
Burke's Law "Who Killed Mr. Colby in Ladies' Lingerie?" 3/3/65 ABC.
Burke's Law "Who Killed the Grand Piano?" 4/28//65 ABC.
My Mother, the Car "Many Happy No Returns" 9/21/65 NBC.
The Smothers Brothers Show "I Wouldn't Miss My Own Funeral for Anything" 11/5/65 CBS.
Perry Mason "The Case of the Silent Six" 11/21/65 CBS.
O.K. Crackerby "Crackerby and the Cuckoo Game" 12/9/65 ABC.
Bewitched "Love Is Blind" 12/10/65 ABC.
My Three Sons "Marriage and Stuff" 12/16/65 CBS.
Pistols 'n' Petticoats (unaired pilot) 1966 CBS.
The Good Old Days (pilot) 7/11/66 CBS.
Occasional Wife (pilot) 9/13/66 NBC.
Occasional Wife "Danger: Woman at Work" 11/1/66 NBC.
The Bob Hope Comedy Special 11/16/66 NBC.
Occasional Wife "Peter by Moonlight" 12/27/66 NBC.
The Bob Hope Show (special) 1/18/67 NBC.
The Pat Boone Show [talk show guest] 2/14 & 2/15/67 NBC.
Dream Girl [celebrity panelist] 2/20 to 2/24/67 ABC.
The Hollywood Palace (w/ guest host Van Johnson) 2/25/67 ABC.
The Mini-Skirt Rebellion (special) 2/28/67 ABC.
The Dating Game [celebrity contestant] 3/25/67 ABC.
Password [celebrity contestant] 3/27 to 3/31/67 CBS.
Pat Boone in Hollywood [talk show guest] 1/25/68 Synd.
The Mike Douglas Show [talk show guest] 8/20/68 Synd.
The Donald O'Connor Show [talk show guest] 1/10/69 Synd.
The Skitch Henderson Show [talk show guest] 1/28/69 Synd.
Going Platinum (special) 5/2/80 Showtime.
CHiPs "11-99: Officer Needs Help" 1/18/81 NBC.
China Beach "Vets" 3/15/89 ABC.
B.L. Stryker "Blues for Buder" 5/15/89 ABC.
Vietnam: The Soldier's Story "Women at War" 2/7/00 TLC.
The CBS Evening News with Dan Rather [segment profile] 5/3/00 CBS.

Also:
Dr. Kildare, The Red Skelton Hour, Love on a Rooftop, The Tonight Show Starring Johnny Carson, The Merv Griffin Show, The Joey Bishop Show, What's My Line, The Edge of Night and *Welcome Home Special.*

Lana Wood

"Hi, I'm Plenty," said Lana Wood to Sean Connery's James Bond at the gaming tables of Las Vegas in *Diamonds Are Forever*. "Plenty O'Toole." Glancing at her cleavage, Bond wittily deadpanned, "But of course you are." With this small exchange, audiences were introduced to one of the most popular Bond girls to ever hit the screen. As Plenty, Lana Wood was finally able to step out of the shadow of her sister Natalie Wood. "Throughout the years, people have always asked me if being Natalie's sister helped or hindered my career," comments Lana. "I still cannot answer that. It's up to you to make that decision." Sixties genre fans have known all along that Lana was sexier and just as talented as her more famous sibling. And though her films weren't as prestigious as Natalie's, they were definitely more fun. Lana made a splash, literally, in *The Girls on the Beach* and *For Singles Only* before playing a hippie chick in the hard-to-find biker-drug film *Free Grass* ("If you ever locate this movie, I'll have to kill you," quips Lana, chuckling). She posed semi-nude for *Playboy*, which indirectly led to her being chosen to play Plenty O'Toole. Her post *Diamonds Are Forever* films include such noted exploitation fare as *A Place Called Today* with Cheri Cafaro, *Nightmare in Badham County* with Tina Louise, *Speedtrap* and the infamous *Dark Eyes*.

Lana Wood was born Svetlana Gurdin on March 1 in Santa Rosa, California. Her parents were Soviet immigrants. Being the younger sister of child star Natasha Gurdin (a.k.a. Natalie Wood), it was just presumed that Svetlana (renamed Lana Wood for the movies) would follow her sister into show business. "Nobody ever asked me if I wanted to act," says Lana. "I don't think anyone asks a seven-year-old what they want or not want to do—well, back then, anyway. Even if my mother asked me, I don't think I would have had an answer. She didn't think acting was such a terrible thing."

In 1955, Lana's mother brought her to meet legendary director John Ford for a role in *The Searchers* (1956). The audition was for the Natalie Wood role as a young child. Though she was only a kid, Lana remembers everything about this film. "I went in on an interview with John

Ford and John Wayne," recalls Lana. "All Ford did was puff on his cigar and tell Wayne to pick me up. They determined I was the correct size and the next thing I knew, we were on our way to Monument Valley. John Ford really didn't have much to do with me during the shoot. I don't know if he was uncomfortable around kids or just assumed that there wasn't much to be said or done. He basically gave me my standing directions. I understood *action* and *cut* so he really didn't talk to me. I remember Jeffrey Hunter a lot more. He was a very dear, sweet man. John Wayne was also very nice and was kind enough to always chat with me. He used to bring me a little box of Allenberry pastilles [black currant candy]. He was very considerate."

After completing *The Searchers*, Lana appeared in a number of live television shows playing the daughters of Jack Lemmon, Charlton Heston and Walter Matthau. When Lana hit her early teens, she decided show business was not for her. "I stopped acting because I just didn't want to do it any more," Lana says. "After school, I was supposed to go on this interview. And I just didn't want to go. I had finally formed some friendships—I had girl friends and boy friends. My mom was going to pull me out of school to go to work again but I was just beginning to enjoy junior high school. So in tears I called my sister Natalie and R.J. [Robert Wagner]. Natalie told me to stay put and that I didn't have to act if I had no desire to. She sent R.J. to pick me up and I stayed with them for a couple of weeks. We discussed putting me into a private school so that I could be away from any kind of influence having to do with working. Natalie had also spoken with my mom a great deal. My mom finally relented and said that if I didn't want to act she wouldn't set up interviews until I was ready to go back."

Lana Wood

Lana finished high school and began working in a trendy Beverly Hills boutique called Jax. A chance meeting with Steve McQueen's wife Neile would change her life forever. Neile told Lana of a part on the TV series *Dr. Kildare* that they were having trouble casting. Neile thought Lana would be perfect and that she should go for it. Lana took Neile's advice, interviewed and won the role. ("During the audition, I decided that acting was important to me.") A part in the beach movie *The Girls on the Beach* (1965) soon followed. In the film, a group of coeds (including Noreen Corcoran, Linda Marshall, Ahna Capri, Linda Saunders and Wood) are trying to raise money to save their sorority beach house

Lana Wood in a publicity shot from *The Girls on the Beach* (Paramount, 1965).

"*The Girls on the Beach* was a lot of fun to do," says Lana. "What I especially remember is having to wear the Beatles wigs and that dreadful gold lamé bikini. It was a really *ugly* bathing suit. We shot the sorority house and club scenes on this little bitsy stage but most of the film was shot at the beach. For a low budget independent film, it went very smoothly. I made some friendships on the film that I have to this day—Aron Kincaid, in particular, is still a good friend of mine." Tuneful songs, a humorous script and great-looking boys and girls in bathing suits all add up to a film that is as pleasant as spending the day at the beach.

In 1965, Lana was cast in the TV series *The Long Hot Summer*, based on a story by William Faulkner. The series was set in the Southern town of Frenchman's Bend and centered on the conflict between middle-aged Will "Boss" Varner (originally Edmond O'Brien) and young, ambitious Ben Quick (Roy Thinnes). Wood beat out dozens of actresses to play Varner's vixenish daughter Eula. The show was not a hit with the critics or the audience and was cancelled after only one season but Fox was so impressed with Lana that they moved her into their hit soap *Peyton Place*. For close to two years, Wood portrayed waitress Sandy Webber, a sexy tease from the wrong side of the tracks who was married to a bullying garage

after discovering that their house mother has donated all their funds to charity. They put all their faith in some surfer dudes (Martin West, Aron Kincaid and Peter Brooks) who falsely claim to know the Beatles. The girls fall for the ruse and arrange a musical show. The boys have a change of heart but don't know how to reveal the truth without losing the girls. When the coeds realize that they have been duped, they impersonate the Beatles themselves and it all works out in the end. Of course, the Beatles do not appear in the film but the Beach Boys, Lesley Gore and the Crickets all perform.

mechanic (Stephen Oliver) while always running after rich Rodney Harrington (Ryan O'Neal). The large cast also included Mia Farrow as Allison McKenzie, Dorothy Malone as Constance McKenzie Rossi and Barbara Parkins as Betty Anderson Harrington. "Barbara Parkins and I did not get along at all," remarks Lana with a laugh. "I have lots of memories about her and *none* of them are all that terrific. I don't know what her problem was but she was *so* rude and petty all of the time. I just found her behavior to be so silly that I would goad her. Mia Farrow was friendlier. We would go to lunch a lot together. She lived on cottage cheese and spinach! That's all she ate. I couldn't understand how she could do it. She was very sweet but a bit unusual and off the wall. One day she went to lunch and had her long hair all cut off. The producers panicked but they wrote it into the script and it worked out just fine. We were all young and constantly playing pranks on that show. The finicky Ruth Warrick was always an easy target for us. We were very naughty." Naughty indeed. Lana admits to love affairs with co-stars O'Neal and Oliver. In fact, she married Oliver but their marriage lasted all of two weeks.

Sandy Webber was written off *Peyton Place* in 1968 ("They ran out of ideas for my character"). Wood then returned to the big screen in two youth-oriented films, *For Singles Only* (1968) and *Free Grass* (1969). The former starred Mary Ann Mobley and Wood as friends who move into a swinging Southern California singles complex run by Milton Berle. The hip residents included John Saxon, Peter Mark Richman, Chris Noel and Ann Elder. Though advertised as a lighthearted view of the singles set, Wood's character falls in love with a married man, contemplates suicide and then gets gang-raped on the beach. "There's a funny story pertaining to the rape scene," says Lana. "I had to have a double to do all the rough stuff. This casting company sent out a bunch of girls and they were all lined up. The director asked them to walk up and down. This one girl named Ginger had a build very similar to mine and she had my walk down perfectly. But I didn't realize that I walked like that. I was in stitches because her walk was so funny. I thought, 'My God, I have a strange walk!'" Wood enjoyed working with the cast, especially Noel whom she describes as being "just so sweet. I remember being absolutely intimidated by Chris because she was so gorgeous. I thought, 'Why do I have this part and she has a small role that isn't that interesting?' Chris was very uncomfortable when she had to do this dance in a bikini with flowers drawn on her body. She really hated that a lot. I felt for her." Though *For Singles Only* was not a hit, Lana garnered some decent reviews. *Variety* commented, "Miss Wood ... delivers the most convincing emotions upon learning her lover is really married."

Free Grass was a motorcycle-drug film reuniting former *West Side Story* gang members Richard Beymer and Russ Tamblyn. Beymer plays a cash-strapped biker who is tempted by sadistic drug dealer Tamblyn to make a lot of money smuggling marijuana from Mexico. With his hippie girlfriend (Wood) along for the ride, Beymer makes a few successful runs but things turn sour when two federal agents are killed by Tamblyn's gang. Beymer tries to break his arrangement with Tamblyn, who kidnaps Wood in retaliation. Beymer eventually comes to her rescue. "I had to wear a very long blonde wig with bangs straight across and a little tiny slip of a dress that they had designed for me," recalls Lana. "It was ridiculous! After they had cast me, they

For Singles Only (Columbia, 1968) co-starred Wood as a naïve young woman and Peter Mark Richman as the married guy she falls in love with.

decided that they wanted me to be a blonde. I wouldn't dye my hair so they bought a wig." Though the low-budget *Free Grass* was a far cry from the Oscar-winning *West Side Story*, Lana found that both actors had no bitterness towards this film. "Richard was very nice and I enjoyed working with him. Russ was very odd and didn't have much to do with me at all. He wasn't on the film long anyway.

"I vividly remember there was a

scene in *Free Grass* where I'm tied up with rope and I'm drugged," continues Lana. "I'm supposed to be tripping out and as I look down the ropes have turned into snakes. They used Coral Snakes because they are a very pretty color. The handlers brought them in and they had the snakes' mouths Scotch taped. I thought, 'Oh, geez! I wonder if their jaws are powerful enough to break the tape?' In another scene I was pushed through this beaded curtain and it kept snatching the wig off my head. We had to do this over and over. It was hysterical."

Lana also appeared on a number of TV shows during this period including *Bonanza*, *Felony Squad* and, most memorably, two comedic turns on *The Wild Wild West*. Defending her forays on the small screen, Lana states emphatically, "I did a lot of television and didn't differentiate between films and TV. To me, work was work. I loved just to be acting. I remember running into Ryan O'Neal and I told him I was leaving to go to San Francisco to work on this new TV show with Harry Guardino. Ryan very rudely said to me, 'Television show! Aren't you embarrassed to tell people?' I thought, 'What a jerk!' I was delighted to be acting. To me there wasn't any difference. I also didn't have a burning desire to be on top of the world and starring in films. I was very happy and pleased doing the actual acting. I never enjoyed posing for pictures or going to Hollywood parties that I didn't want to go to just to be seen. Or dressing a certain way because that was what people expected. Natalie picked up on this and told me once that she wished she could be like me. I thought, 'Why?' It was for that sort of quality. I wasn't concerned what was the right or wrong thing to act in. I *was* concerned with doing the work and just being myself. People either accepted me for who I was or not. It didn't really trouble me. That's what Natalie meant."

In 1970, a photographer friend of Lana's asked her if she would be willing to pose for shots he wanted to sell to *Playboy*. He was having a difficult time making a living so Lana agreed to help him out. She felt comfortable enough with her body to do it. A photo shoot was arranged at Aron Kincaid's house. *Playboy* bought the photos but contacted Lana soon after. "They wanted to shoot more photos of me with a photographer of their choice," says Lana. "I told them as long as my friend Eric was paid for *his* that I would be happy to do some more. They set me up with Mario Casselli, who is absolutely amazing! He made me feel very comfortable. Nudity has never been a worry for me.

"After I posed for the pictures, I began getting grief from a lot of people—particularly Natalie and my mother," continues Lana. "I thought, 'Oh, God, is everybody in the world going to come down on me for this?' The layout didn't mean anything to me so I decided to cancel it. I literally got Hugh Hefner on the phone and told him not to use the photos. He said okay but then he called me back and said, 'I understand you are also a writer. What if we published some of your poetry with the photos? Would that make you feel better?' I responded, 'Actually, it would.' I thought the layout was absolutely beautiful but the reason I changed my mind was because I didn't want to build a career or even a persona on 'Gee, aren't I pretty.' I don't think that's what's important. By publishing some of my poetry, it gave me more depth, which I think I deserved. That's how I felt at the time anyway. I was a bit naïve and thought that would remedy everything."

The *Playboy* pictorial indirectly led

to *Diamonds Are Forever* (1971) but Lana first worked on the independent feature *A Place Called Today* (1972). She played a radical reporter. Lana got two things from this movie: husband number four, co-star Richard Smedley ("He was very relaxed and natural in this film but the director seemed to use his worst takes. Hence he never acted again!") and a memory of Cheri Cafaro she will never forget. "Cheri Cafaro was having her hair bleached as I walked into the dressing room early in the morning," remembers Lana with a laugh. "Cheri was preparing for a [full frontal] nude scene later on and was making sure her 'collars and cuffs' matched, if you get my drift. It was more than I ever wanted to see. I will never be able to shake that image for the rest of my life!" [*Laughs*]

Though Lana has appeared in numerous films and TV shows, her small but significant role opposite Sean Connery's comeback in *Diamonds* is the most notable. After passing on *On Her Majesty's Secret Service* (1969), Connery was persuaded to return to his role of suave secret agent 007 in *Diamonds*. With a salary of one million dollars, he became the highest-paid actor up to that point. To make sure *Diamonds* was a success, producers Cubby Broccoli and Harry Saltzman reassembled the behind-the-scenes crew responsible for *Goldfinger*. Guy Hamilton (whom Lana describes as being "wonderful and just terrific to work with") directed *Diamonds Are Forever* from a screenplay by Richard Maibum and Tom Mankiewicz. John Barry composed the exciting score with Shirley Bassey singing the brassy theme song over the title credits. Giving support to Connery's James Bond were Jill St. John as duplicitous Tiffany Case, Jimmy Dean as missing millionaire Willard Whyte, Charles Gray as the evil Ernst Blofeld, Norman Burton as CIA operative Felix Leiter and Lana Wood as golddigger Plenty O'Toole. "I didn't have to audition *per se* for this role," recalls Lana. "My dear friend Tom Mankiewicz told me that Cubby Broccoli was looking for an actress to play this character named Plenty O'Toole. Tom thought I would be perfect for it. He asked me if I would meet with Cubby. I said, 'Absolutely!' I was en route to do *A Place Called Today* in New York. Before leaving for that, I went in to chat with Cubby, who was adorable! I tried to look as tall as humanly possible because Tom had told me that they were thinking of Plenty O'Toole as this giant of a woman in *every way*. For me that wasn't easy—I'm only five feet, four inches—but those were the days of hot pants and really high heels. I didn't hear anything until I started filming the other picture. I was thrilled to get the part!"

Lana was excited to be part of a Bond film as she arrived in Las Vegas to begin shooting. Not into the nightclub or gambling scene, Lana brought her cat with her for company. As she stepped out of the taxi at the hotel, her finger got stuck in the cat carrier. Then she was told by the desk clerk that her suite was not ready but she could use Sean Connery's suite until hers was prepared because he was supposedly not in. As Lana recounted in her book *Natalie: A Memoir by Her Sister*, "I was handed a key and off I went, assured my luggage would be placed in my suite. It didn't occur to me to knock or to otherwise announce myself. I simply unlocked the door and walked right in. 'Well, hello there!' Sean Connery boomed at me. He was stark naked and sitting on the toilet. I let out a shriek. He stood up, smiled and said, 'Don't be frightened. I'll be right out. Put your animal carrier down anywhere

In *Diamonds Are Forever* (United Artists, 1971) Wood as Plenty O'Toole meets Sean Connery's James Bond at the craps table.

you'd like.'" When Lana told Connery her predicament, he just laughed and closed the door. After finishing his business, he was able to extract her finger from the cage. Sean and Lana became fast friends and spent a lot of time together off the set. They eventually had an affair or as Lana describes it "an interlude."

"Sean Connery is very charming and attentive," comments Lana. "He was very

relaxed on *Diamonds Are Forever* and was very easy to work with. As long as we did things in a rapid pace so he could get out to play golf, then he was fine. But I had no problems working with Sean at all. Later on we heard that he was battling with the producers during the shoot. If that was true it wasn't in front of the cast or crew."

When Lana arrived on the set for her first scene, director Guy Hamilton realized how short she was. He then made her do all her scenes standing on an apple box. ("If you notice, you never see me full length standing next to Sean Connery.") The other problem Lana had was in the scene where her character—topless in a skimpy pair of bikini underwear—is thrown out the hotel window and plummets into the swimming pool. The nudity bothered Lana but the fall itself terrified her. In the story, Bond meets Plenty O'Toole at the craps table in Vegas. He takes her up to his hotel room where she seductively slips out of her evening gown. But before Bond can make love to her, four thugs burst in. While two scuffle with Bond, the others fling Plenty out the fifteenth floor window. "This actually was a little first floor window and I landed on a mattress," remembers Lana. "Then the second unit shot a dummy falling outside of the hotel. Finally they had me on a platform with a stuntman [Dick Butler] to help me fall straight into the pool. It ended up being a longer drop than I ever really wanted to do. I was also concerned because I was topless and they said for me not to worry because we were going to shoot it in the middle of the night. But it never occurred to me until I was on Dick's shoulders, 'We are in Las Vegas. People are up all night!' The crowd got a nice view of me in nothing but pale blue underpants. And we had to do the scene twice! We picked up and started all over again after they dried my hair." Ironically, it is for this sequence that Bond fans remember Plenty O'Toole most.

Lana next appeared as Ben Gazzara's mistress in the prestigious mini-series *QB VII* (1974) but she was dropped by her talent agency over her decision to accept the small role. "After appearing in *Playboy* and doing *Diamonds Are Forever*, my agents put me up for sexpot roles. They arranged an interview with Sergio Leone and were trying to get me a contract in Italy to do spaghetti westerns. But I just didn't want to go that route so I turned it down. Since I was only going to be in three scenes in *QB VII*, they thought that it would be a horrible mistake. They told me that if I accepted the part, they didn't want to represent me any more. So I said, 'Okay, bye!' I really wanted to be a part of this film. I didn't care what the size of the part was or who the character was." Lana's performance so impressed director Tom Gries that he put her name on the Emmy ballot.

Returning to exploitation fare, Lana appeared in *Little Ladies of the Night* (1977), *Speedtrap* (1978) and *Grayeagle* (1978). She also played a vicious lesbian prison guard in the women-in-prison flick *Nightmare in Badham County*. ("I didn't want to do this film because it would be the first time that I was separated from my daughter Evan. I relented because it was an Aaron Spelling production. My agent told me that since they specifically requested me that it would be a mistake to turn it down since they could use me in more of their shows.") Originally made for television, the film was expanded and released theatrically overseas

Opposite: Poster art from *Diamonds Are Forever* (United Artists, 1971).

where it became a huge hit (especially in China, of all places). Deborah Raffin and Lynne Moody play college students who are pulled over by the creepy sheriff (Chuck Connors) of a small Southern town as they are driving through. They are sent to a work farm where they experience all sorts of atrocities, including bigotry, rape, murder and white slavery. The film has a great feel because it was shot on location in Mississippi in the middle of summer. "That particular area in Mississippi wasn't the most pleasant place to be in," remarks Lana. "Bad enough that it was *so* hot but quite honestly Della Reese wasn't welcomed in some restaurants and stores because she was black. I find bigotry very unsettling. And it was just always at the back of your mind when we went out."

The eclectic B-movie cast includes Robert Reed as the warden, Tina Louise as the sadistic head prison guard and Reese as a hardened prisoner. Lana's character acted as flunky to Louise's. When they weren't in uniform terrorizing the prisoners, they could be found lounging in their underwear, drinking beer and watching women's wrestling. The lesbianism wasn't overt but implied. Lana had a problem with director John Llewellyn Moxey and the producers after it was decided to add an explicit lesbian scene between Wood and Louise. After finishing shooting her scenes on a Friday, she was handed revised script pages, which included this new scene. "I just didn't feel comfortable about doing it and they got really mad at me. Della and Fionnula Flanagan helped me get the courage to say no. I wasn't used to saying no when it came to work. If it was originally in the script, I could have made that decision before I accepted the part. But because it was added later, it just didn't sit well with me. I know Tina Louise wasn't

A wide-eyed Wood during the seventies.

thrilled about doing it. Tina is nice but just a little off-center. We never really made a connection. She was always either under an umbrella trying to protect her skin from the sun or she was off meditating."

With the acting roles being offered to her dwindling, Lana worked in production in the late seventies. As vice-president of development for Jay Bernstein, she was associate producer on the made-for-TV movie *Mickey Spillane's Mike Hammer* (1983). But she returned to the screen in *Dark Eyes* (1982). This film has become notorious for its multiple titles (*Satan's Mistress*, *Demon Rage*, *Bride of Satan* and *Fury of the Succubus*) and Lana's many nude love scenes with a ghost. ("Doing those scenes didn't bother me. I'm comfortable with my body. It's just acting to me.") Lana plays a bored housewife living with her husband (Tom Hallick) and daughter (Sherry Scott) in a beach house in San Juan Capistrano. She begins having visions of a tall, dark stranger (Kabir Bedi). They begin having sex and the spirit turns out to be Satan himself. Lana then descends into madness. Her husband brings in a psychic (Britt Ekland) to help but she turns up dead. It all climaxes in the house's basement complete with guillotine, devil worshippers and a pyre. "I was sent out on an interview for this and it seemed interesting," recalls Lana. "The producers and the director [James Polakof] seemed nice and pulled together. I didn't realize that they were going to have two cents for special effects and costumes. It wasn't until I saw the monster costume that I realized I was in trouble. It was hard after that to keep a straight face during the rest of the film. Nobody thinks they are making a silly film. To everybody, the film they're making is a good movie."

Though Lana has the lead role, co-star Britt Ekland for some unknown reason received top billing. This didn't bother Lana as much as Ekland's lousy attitude did. "Britt is another incredible person that drove me crazy," laughs Lana. "She is way up there on my Barbara Parkins list. Britt is just an *adorable, sweet* person. Phooey! She is useless and just difficult to be around! It's not important that I get along with everybody so I'm entitled to say that, aren't I?"

On an episode of *The Fall Guy* starring Lee Majors, Lana had the misfortune to work with Ekland again. ("I'm a glutton for punishment, what can I tell you?") Majors and crew are hired as stuntmen for a fictitious James Bond movie called *Always Say Always*. While shooting in Hong Kong, they become involved in searching for a stolen art collection. Wood, Ekland and Joanna Pettet (all former Bond girls) play themselves, hired to act in the film. "It was the weirdest thing in the world playing myself," comments Lana. "It was the only time I have ever gone to a set and was so puzzled as to what the heck I should do. I didn't know how to play Lana Wood. I just played myself in the loosest mood that was humanly possible." Though Lana disliked Ekland, she found Joanna Pettet to be wonderful because "she is a *real* person. I love to be around people who just present themselves the way they are. I don't have time for airs and false pride."

Lana had a year-long role on the daytime soap *Capitol* as Fran Burke and appeared in an episode of *Mickey Spillane's Mike Hammer* before she returned to production full-time. "I didn't make the conscious effort to stop acting," says Lana. "I think acting sort of decided it wasn't interested in me anymore. Production makes me feel good at the end of the day when I go home. I don't want to feel like a piece of meat and like I'm only somebody because I look good. I'm not always going to look good. The worldwide tour of *Diamonds Are Forever* left a bad taste in my mouth. I was run around without any regard whatsoever. That tour is a book in itself. The experiences I had are absolutely amazing. I felt like that if they were able to move the film's moon buggy around as easily as they moved me from country to country and city to city, they would have. My feelings weren't important to them."

After a long stint as a casting director, Lana Wood is returning to the big screen playing a villain in *Dead Wrong*. Co-starring Olivia Hussey, the film is to be released in 2001. And to this day, she is flabbergasted at the amount of fan mail she receives from around the world regarding *Diamonds Are Forever*. Although on-screen for only a few scenes, she is one of the most popular Bond girls in the history of this series.

Film Appearances

1956	**The Searchers** (Warner Bros.) d. John Ford.
1962	**Five Finger Exercise** (Columbia) d. Daniel Mann.
1965	**Girls on the Beach** (Paramount) d. William Witney.
1968	**For Singles Only** (MGM) d. Arthur Dreifuss.
1969	**Free Grass** (Hollywood Star Pictures) d. Bill Brame.
1970	**Black Water Gold** (TV-movie) d. Alan Landsburg. **The Over-the-Hill Gang Rides Again** (TV-movie) d. George McCowan.
1971	**O'Hara, U.S. Treasury: Operation Cobra** (TV-movie) d. Jack Webb. **Diamonds Are Forever** (United Artists) d. Guy Hamilton.
1972	**A Place Called Today** (Avco-Embassy) d. Don Schain.
1975	**Who Is the Black Dahlia?** (TV-movie) d. Joseph Pevney.
1976	**Nightmare in Badham County** (TV-movie) d. John Llewellyn Moxey.
1977	**Little Ladies of the Night** (TV-movie) d. Marvin J. Chomsky. **Corey: For the People** (TV-movie) d. Buzz Kulik.
1978	**A Question of Guilt** (TV-movie) d. Robert Butler. **Speedtrap** (First Artists) d. Earl Bellamy. **Grayeagle** (AIP) d. Charles B. Pierce.
1982	**Satan's Mistress/Dark Eyes** (MPM) d. James Polakof.
2001	**Dead Wrong**

Television Appearances

Playhouse 90 "Winter Dreams" 5/23/57 CBS.
The Bob Hope Special [Hollywood Deb Star] 3/13/63 NBC.
Dr. Kildare "Man Is a Rock" 9/24/64 NBC.
Wendy and Me "George Burns While Rome Fiddles" 9/28/64 ABC.
The Fugitive "Detour on a Road Going Nowhere" 12/8/64 ABC.
The Hollywood Deb Stars of 1965 (special) [presenter] 1/2/65 ABC.
The Long Hot Summer [series regular as Eula Varner] 9/16/65 to 7/3/66 CBS.
Peyton Place [series regular as Sandy Webber] 4/21/66 to 11/67 ABC.
The Wild Wild West "The Night of the Firebrand" 9/15/67 CBS.
Bonanza "The Gentle Ones" 10/29/67 NBC.
Peyton Place "Episode #404" 1/22/68 ABC.
The Felony Squad "The Last Man in the World" 1/3/69 ABC.
My Friend Tony "The Lost Hours" 2/2/69 NBC.
The Wild Wild West "The Night of the Plague" 4/4/69 CBS.
Marcus Welby, M.D. "Don't Kid a Kidder" 3/2/71 ABC.
The Mike Douglas Show [talk show guest] 4/13/71 CBS.
Monty Nash (episode title unknown) 10/22/71 NBC.
The Wonderful World of Disney "Justin Morgan Had a Horse" 2/6 & 2/13/72 ABC.
Night Gallery "You Can't Get Help Like That Anymore" 2/23/72 NBC.
Mission: Impossible "The Deal" 9/30/72 CBS.
Joanne Carson's VIPs [talk show guest] 12/15/72 Synd.
Celebrity Bowling [celebrity contestant] 11/21/73 Synd.
Police Story "Countdown" 1/15 & 1/22/74 NBC.
QB VII (mini-series) 4/29 & 4/30/74 ABC.
Starsky and Hutch "Running" 2/25/76 ABC.
Baretta "Shoes" 10/27/76 ABC.
Police Story "A Dream of Conquest" 3/8/77 NBC.
Police Story "Ice Time" 5/10/77 NBC.
Fantasy Island "Fool for a Client" 5/15/78 ABC.
The Next Step Beyond "Ghost of Cellblock Two" 12/2/78 Synd.
Starsky and Hutch "90 Pounds of Trouble" 2/6/79 ABC.
David Cassidy—Man Undercover "Nightwork" 7/5/79 NBC.
Captain America (pilot) 11/23 & 11/24/79 CBS.
Nero Wolfe "Might as Well Be Dead" 2/13/81 NBC.
Capitol [series regular as Fran Burke] 6/83 to 2/84 CBS.
The Fall Guy "Always Say Always" 2/22/84 ABC.
Mickey Spillane's Mike Hammer "Deadly Reunion" 1/12/85 CBS.
The Martin Short Show [talk show guest] 11/9/99 Synd.

Celeste Yarnall

In 1967, former model Celeste Yarnall risked her life savings to travel to the Cannes Film Festival in hopes of being "discovered" even though she had begun acting in 1963 on television and in films such as *The Nutty Professor* and *Around the World Under the Sea*. Discouraged that her career hadn't taken off, she and her husband Sheldon Silverstein headed to that international city hoping Celeste would wow some producers. And wow them she did! Producer Harry Alan Towers, who was looking for a girl to play a female Tarzan in *Eve*, spotted her strolling down the street. According to Yarnall, "He yelled and pointed, 'Stop that girl! That's my Eve!'" Yarnall made a breathtaking jungle goddess in *Eve* but the film wasn't a success. But Yarnall's talent was appreciated and she went on to act in such drive-in fare as *Live a Little, Love a Little* with Elvis Presley, *Beast of Blood* and her most notorious film, *The Velvet Vampire*. After a very successful stint as a real estate agent during the seventies and eighties, Celeste has returned to acting and is a prominent author and expert on holistic health care for pets.

Celeste Yarnall was born in Long Beach, California, on July 26. ("I'm an ageless Leo," she quips.) The daughter of navy man Forest Yarnall and his wife Helene, Celeste grew up in Los Angeles in the Silver Lake area and graduated from John Marshall High School. As a child, acting was the only thing that ever interested Celeste. "I was born a ham and danced in my pajamas," says Yarnall with a laugh. "I joined the drama club in high school and I just loved it." Also around this time, Celeste began modeling for Max Factor and auditioning for professional acting roles. With her mother signing notes to excuse her from school early, Celeste would take the bus to auditions at MGM in Culver City or Warner Bros. in Burbank. Her first acting job occurred when Ricky Nelson spotted her as she was cutting through the studio for a commercial audition. His catcalling brought Ozzie Nelson out from his trailer to see what the commotion was about. "Ozzie said to me, 'You just stopped traffic on this lot. How would you like to be on our show?' I said, 'I'd love to but I'm not a member of the Screen Actors Guild.' He said, 'Don't worry, we'll get

Celeste Yarnall

you signed up.' So I got that part and the TV commercial. I became a member of SAG and AFTRA on the same day!"

Celeste's first cattle call audition was for a tiny role as a college coed in *The Nutty Professor* (1963) starring Jerry Lewis. Though she was only 17, with her high cheekbones and dark hair she looked older and more sophisticated than other girls did her age. Celeste was a stunner and Jerry Lewis himself chose her for the film. "It was supposed to be for a day's work only," recalls Celeste. "I wore a black suit and a kind of a Greta Garbo black hat for this very tricky scene—Jerry's famous entrance as Buddy Love into the nightclub. They did freeze frames of people walking in. Being the director also, Jerry was having a very difficult time with it. They had stand-ins for us and he told me that I could sit down to take a break. But I said I'd stay even though I was in very high heels and my feet were killing me. I didn't move off my mark and knew that impressed him. He saw that I was trying to help him get his shot. At the end of the day, they told me I had a run-of-the-picture contract because I had pleased Jerry. He worked me in as a student. I had one line at the conference table.

"I was so in awe of Jerry Lewis and thought he was amazing," continues Celeste. "Frenetic is a good word to describe him on the set but he could be charming as well. He wore Alfred Dunhill cologne, which smelled wonderful. One day when he walked by I said, 'Jerry you smell so good.' The next day he handed me a bottle of it. He also gave me a very good talk about being a young girl in Hollywood and what I should expect. I think he could see that I was a very straight-laced young person. I was very pristine and was lucky to have gone out in a car on a date at this point."

Celeste's acting career was put on hold for a bit when she was voted Miss Rheingold of 1964. Rheingold Beer sponsored a yearly contest where they would audition girls across the country. Six finalists were chosen from a board of celebrities. The public voted for the winner through ballots placed in stores that sold the beer ("I got close to 20 million votes, which meant I would have beaten Richard Nixon for president!"). As Miss Rheingold, Celeste was their spokesmodel in TV and radio commercials, print ads and billboards. She also made public appearances, rode in parades and even threw a football to Joe Namath ("He was *very* cute!") at the New York Jets opener. Returning to Hollywood, Celeste met and married Sheldon Silverstein after a three-month courtship. For a few years he tried to manage her career. "Misman-age it is more the case," quips Celeste with a laugh. "He turned down a contract for me with Universal Pictures, which I think really would have made me a star. It was the most lucrative term contract that they had ever offered a contract player. My wonderful husband and agent maneuvered me right out of it. They were too greedy. That would have been the best thing that could have happened to me."

Despite the setback, Celeste's acting career progressed as she appeared as a lab assistant in the Ivan Tors film *Around the World Under the Sea* (1966) and in a number of television series, including playing a French girl in *The Man from U.N.C.L.E.* with Robert Vaughn ("He is a very elegant, intelligent man"). One of Celeste's first lead guest roles was in "The Apple," an episode of *Star Trek* which Celeste found to be "some silly show." At that time, most guest stars on this series concurred with Celeste. During its original three year run, *Star Trek* was not the phenomenon it is now. To make matters worse for Celeste, she broke a fingernail during shooting and developed a terrible allergic reaction to the stick-on-nail she used to replace her real one. She had to keep her hand hidden during her kissing scenes with Walter Koenig. In this episode, Celeste played Yeoman Martha Landon, the only female crewmember to beam down to a jungle planet run by Vaal, an ancient computer who controls the planet's environment and its peaceful inhabitants. Vaal provides for his people in return for offerings of appeasement. However, Vaal kills four *Enterprise* crew members ("expendable red shirts") and imprisons the others (Kirk, Spock, McCoy, Chekov and Landon) in a cave. When it threatens to obliterate the *Enterprise*, Spock destroys Vaal, leaving the child-like inhabitants to develop their own way of life and to experience physical intimacy. Regarding their ways of reproduction, Celeste's character inquires, "How do they do it?" This results in an amusing scene with Kirk, Spock and McCoy, who begin speculating on this matter. "It took us many takes to get this scene because they all fell on the floor laughing," recalls Yarnall. "It really was hysterical. The censors were present during this scene. There is another scene in the cave where I'm not there because the censors had them cut me out of that scene. I was the only woman from the *Enterprise* on the planet so the audience would have made the assumption that I slept in the cave with all those men if they kept me in it."

Unlike some of his other female co-stars, Celeste enjoyed working with William Shatner immensely. It was Leonard Nimoy who disturbed her. "The cast had a way of teasing the guest stars and playing little tricks on them," says Celeste. "Leonard Nimoy scared me to death. I'd see him coming and start to shake. He and Bill Shatner were playing good guy/bad guy. Shatner was kind of taking care of me and we had quite an attraction to one another. He is a very handsome man and I was quite taken with him. I was married at the time and, though I was flattered, I had to say no to his romantic interest. I believe he respected that and never felt abused by him as a guest star. He never crossed the line. A few years later, after my divorce, I dated Shatner for awhile."

It was during this time that Celeste decided to risk it all and go to Cannes. During the mid-sixties, actress Raquel Welch propelled herself to the number one international sex symbol of that time. Guided by her husband Patrick Curtis, Welch was perhaps the most publicity-driven actress to hit Hollywood since Jayne Mansfield. Wanting film success for herself, Yarnall and her husband decided to try for it à la Raquel and Patrick ("We even pretended not to be married like they did"). After renting out her home in Bel-Air and selling her beautiful white Jaguar 3.8 Mark II, Yarnall and her husband headed off to the Cannes Film Festival. After stops in London and Rome, Yarnall was now a sexy blonde with a new wardrobe and tons of publicity. However, she was out of money and had no place to stay in Cannes. As luck would have it, she and her husband ran into a man named Eddie Chapman who said he was a good friend of film director Terence Young and that they could stay at his villa. They reluctantly agreed. "This couple who were the caretakers met us and they treated us like royalty," recalls Celeste. "Then other people started arriving and we began feeling uncomfortable when I received a phone call from Terence Young. I said, 'Hello, this is Mrs. Silverstein.' And he said in his British accent, 'Who the hell are you bloody people and what are you doing in my villa?' I said, 'Mr. Chapman invited us.' He said, 'I haven't seen Eddie since we did the film *Triple Cross* [1966]. I was just told Sean Connery couldn't stay in his room at my villa because the Silversteins are there! You get the hell out of my house, you interloper!'" Another guest named Helen Parnell was aghast at Young's behavior and offered them the use of her condo. Soon after, Yarnall was signed by Towers to do *Eve*.

The jungle adventure *Eve* (1968) was in the tradition of *One Million Years B.C.* (1966) with Raquel Welch and *She* (1966) with Ursula Andress. From a screenplay by Harry Alan Towers, *Eve* ("The original flower child" as the ad proclaimed) was the story of an alluring half-savage jungle woman living in the wilds of Brazil where the natives worship her as a goddess. Trouble begins for Eve when she rescues a downed pilot (Robert Walker, Jr.) who brings back news of this female Tarzan to civilization. A smalltime showman (Fred Clark) wants to capture her to put her on display while villainous Diego (Herbert Lom) wants her dead because he has been passing off his mistress (Rosenda Monteros) as the long-lost Eve, heir to her grandfather's (Christopher Lee) fortune. To make matters worse, the natives want to kill Eve for helping a white man and there is Incan treasure wanted by all. In the end, the villains get their due and Eve is reunited with her grandfather on his deathbed. However, she rejects the noise and confusion of the civilized world in order to return to the jungle, despite her love for Walker who vows to find her again. The ending left it open for an intended sequel which was never made (to the relief of Yarnall, who calls *Eve* "one of the worst movies of all time").

"I don't know why Towers thought I was right for this part," speculates Celeste. "I was never a tomboy and hadn't climbed a tree in my life. I was more the sedate type. I even had to take some Judo classes to train for the role." When the start date of the film was postponed, Celeste returned to Los Angeles and was signed by Columbia Pictures to play a showgirl in *Funny Girl* (1968) starring Barbra Streisand. Yarnall had to back out of that film because "the start date for *Eve* was at the same time. I then got a threat on my life that if I didn't show up to do *Eve*, I wouldn't live to do *Funny Girl*. So I had to walk out on Columbia." This was just the first of many problems Yarnall would encounter during the production of *Eve*.

Eve began filming in Spain, where

Celeste Yarnall as the jungle goddess *Eve* (Commonwealth United, 1968).

Yarnall developed food poisoning from the rancid oil used on their vegetables. Then Towers stopped paying his actors' salaries. While the rest of the cast kept working, Yarnall walked off the picture. "Towers was a notorious schemer," remarks Celeste. "He was absolutely wild! He had a little German girlfriend named Schnitzel and he worked in a small part for her. My husband didn't take kindly to me not getting paid and showed up at Towers' office with a water pistol pretending it was a gun. Shelley said, 'If you don't pay Celeste, she's not going to show up.' I'm missing from the film for a long stretch when Rosenda is pretending to be me. They re-wrote the whole middle of the script so that they could keep shooting. The movie's called *Eve* and you're wondering, 'Where in God's earth is Eve?'"

When filming shifted from Madrid to Brazil, things got even worse. According to Celeste, she took one look at the jungle and exclaimed, "I'm never going to get out of here alive!" A supposedly tame monkey bit her. She suffered multiple scratches and abrasions when a cable holding a vine she was swinging from snapped. She developed dysentery from the accumulation of mosquito bites. Celeste was also almost killed while filming the fight scene with Spanish actress Rosenda Monteros on a bluff 200 feet above ground. "A stuntman had taught me some moves for my fight scene with Rosenda," recalls Celeste. "It was carefully choreographed because we were high up on a bluff. Rosenda was supposed to put the sole of her right boot into my stomach and I would fall into the stuntman's arms.

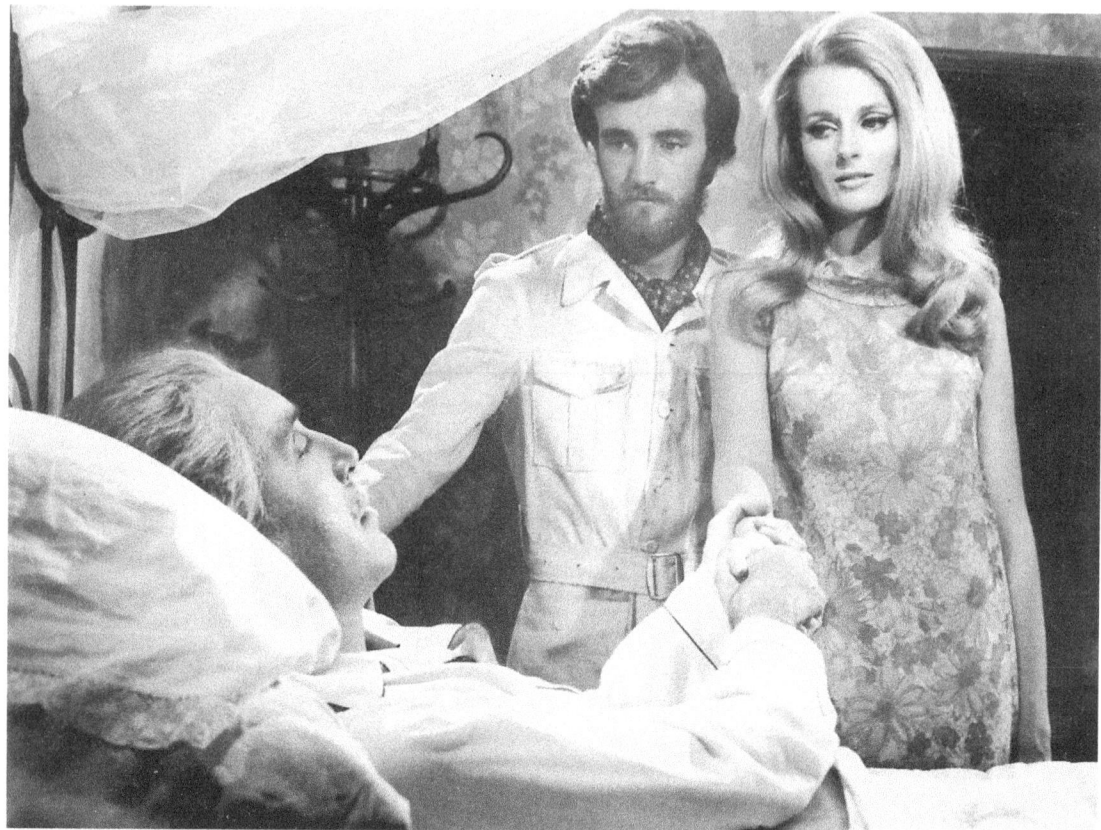

In *Eve*, a dying millionaire played by Christopher Lee is reunited with his missing granddaughter Eve (Yarnall) due to an adventurer (Robert Walker).

But she used her left foot and pushed me the wrong way. And I almost went over the cliff. The stuntman did one of those flying leaps and caught the back of my head in the palm of his hand. We both fell into this bush—I was all cut up—but he saved me from a huge drop." After all the trouble Celeste went through during the production of *Eve*, she was incensed after seeing the final print because "I think they dubbed my voice—it doesn't sound like me. I remember that Harry Alan Towers was too cheap to fly me back to do the looping."

Despite Yarnall's dislike for *Eve*, it is actually a decent adventure movie helped greatly by the stunning Celeste in a lemur-skin bikini, the beautiful locations and an above-average cast. Producer Towers had a knack for getting high caliber actors to appear in his foreign productions, which were rarely given a wide distribution in the U.S. Recalling her co-stars, Yarnall says, "Herbert Lom was an amazing gentlemen—just a very elegant, intelligent man. Robert Walker was very much a sixties movie star—very far-out. He was into psychedelia and meditation. I know for awhile that he and his family lived off of nature somewhere in the canyons of Santa Monica. They bathed in a creek! He is very interesting and I liked him but at that time he was too way out there for me. He now owns a beautiful store in Malibu that sells books and artwork. Christopher Lee was totally bent out of shape that he was playing my grandfather because he felt he would

Celeste Yarnall in costume on tour promoting *Eve*.

have been a much better leading man for me than Robert Walker was. And he just hated being made up to look old!"

After *Eve*, Celeste was featured as a fashion model in *Live a Little, Love a Little* (1968) starring Elvis Presley as a photographer juggling two jobs at two different magazines while being pursued by a free-spirited girl (Michele Carey). Though Elvis looked great and seemed to be having fun with his role as a hip cameraman (he even has a pill-induced psychedelic dream), the film is severely hampered by the miscast Carey, who is more annoying than alluring. "I thought so too," agrees Celeste. "Michele spent years trying to get rid of a Texas accent. I think I was a better height for Elvis and had more electricity with him than he had with Michele. I actually auditioned for Michele's part. But I had a model's figure and wasn't really voluptuous looking. I was very slender and if they wanted me to look sexy I would have needed a lot of padding. So they cast me instead as the model that meets Elvis Presley at the party."

Recalling her first scene with Elvis, Celeste says, "I was introduced to Elvis right on the soundstage. The director [Norman Taurog] said, 'Elvis, this is Celeste Yarnall. Celeste, this is Elvis.' I thought I was dreaming. He was exquisitely handsome and looked fabulous. I don't think people knew how incredibly beautiful and absolutely electrifying he was—the epitome of the word 'charismatic.' Our very first shot was our kissing scene. It was filmed right before lunch. They had cameras up on a crane and at a couple of different angles. So we did the kiss and the director yelled *cut* but Elvis wouldn't let me go. All the lights were being turned off and Norman Taurog is yelling, 'Lunch everybody! Cast one hour! Crew 30 minutes! *Elvis, you can let her go now!*' He wouldn't let me out of his embrace and I'm cracking up. It was clear that Elvis was flirting with me. Actually, flirting is an understatement. Elvis had the ability to make you feel like you were the most special person in the world. We became dear friends and that will be the subject of *my* book."

Due to her performances in *Eve* and *Live a Little, Love a Little*, Celeste was voted the Most Promising New Star of 1968 by the National Association of Theatre Owners; "I remember climbing up on a drive-in movie theater marquee where they were playing *Eve* and having my picture taken." She next appeared in a small role as a model who has a fling with Robert Culp in the groundbreaking comedy *Bob & Carol & Ted & Alice* (1969). Though Celeste received co-star billing, most of her scenes were cut because they were with Bill Cosby, who was totally excised from the film. "Paul Mazursky really liked me and wanted me in the movie," says Celeste. "He thought I was too young for the role of Alice so he offered me the choice of two other parts. One of them required nudity so I chose the other role. I had a number of scenes revolving around a fashion show with Cosby, who was just extraordinary. I think all that is left of me is me saying, 'Hi, Bob.' Though most of my scenes were cut, I was still happy I was in it. I had the honor of meeting Natalie Wood, who was one of the sweetest people I had ever met. I didn't think quite so highly of

Elvis Presley and Yarnall in a publicty photo from *Live a Little, Love a Little* (MGM, 1968).

Dyan Cannon, who was rather cold to me."

Celeste appeared in the memorable "The Golden Cage" episode on *Land of the Giants* and gave a poignant performance as a Lorelei-type girl used by the giants to capture the little people. "After I finished the scene, some of the crew members said, 'You made us cry. We hardly have any actors on this show that make us cry.'" She returned to the jungle (three months pregnant) for the horror film *Beast of Blood* (1970), the sequel to the previous year's *Mad Doctor of Blood Island*. In Eddie Romero's Philippine-lensed quickie, Yarnall plays a reporter who accompanies adventurer John Ashley back to Blood Island to investigate a mad doctor who is turning the natives into zombies. According to *The Psychotronic Encyclopedia of Film*, "At original showings, 'survival kits' containing airplane barf bags were thoughtfully handed out." But some of the film's more gruesome moments never made it into the final print. "There was a scene where the bad guys are chasing me through the jungle and I fall into what is supposed to be quicksand," remembers Celeste. "When one of the guys—they were played by stuntmen—reached me, his rifle accidentally slipped off his shoulder and the sight on the rifle cracked open my cheekbone. It missed my eye by about an inch. Even though there was blood coming down my face, I kept going with the scene. They ended up not using this shot because it was so bloody horrific! The nearest hospital was four hours away so all I could do was tape my face back together with Band-Aids and put makeup over it. This was a very rough shoot and I almost lost my baby when I began hemorrhaging."

Celeste's most notorious role came next—that of vampire Diana Le Fanu in *The Velvet Vampire* (1971), whose great tag line proclaimed, "She's waiting to love you ... to death!" After meeting married couple Susan and Lee Ritter (Sherry Miles and Michael Blodgett) at an art gallery, Diana entices them to stay the weekend at her Mojave Desert home. Soon both husband and wife find themselves sexually drawn to their mysterious host, who suffers from a rare blood disease. Unlike vampires of lore, Diana was able to journey out into the sunlight as long as she is covered up. In the course of 24 hours, Diana feasts on a mechanic, his girlfriend and a servant. After making love with Diana, Lee wants to depart but Susan is fascinated with the charming Diana and wants to stay. Their delay in leaving costs Lee his life while Diana meets her gruesome end at the hands of a cult hippie gang. "I dyed my hair black for this role," says Celeste. "Though the part was a bit corny, I got into playing a vampire. The film had an interesting script by Charles S. Swartz, which explained Diana's condition very well. This was one of the first films released by Roger Corman's new production company [New World] and was more original than some of Roger's other films, which were ripoffs of other movies. I became good friends with Roger and have a lot of respect for his talent."

Celeste accepted the role of Diana despite the nude scenes ("I had my daughter Cami to support") after turning down previous parts that required nudity, including a role in *Winning* (1969) with Paul Newman. "Though I was only semi-nude, it still bothered me," remarks Celeste. "Charles Swartz also produced the film and his wife Stephanie Rothman directed it. They both were very nice and one of the ways that they persuaded me into doing the nude scene with Michael Blodgett was by making it an absolutely

Yarnall as *The Velvet Vampire* (New World Pictures, 1971) doffs her clothes for a love scene with Michael Blodgett.

closed set. After it was lit, everyone left except the cinematographer, Stephanie and her husband. The cinematographer's name was Daniel Lacambre and he was brilliant. He lit and shot the film beautifully.

"I worked well with Sherry Miles but this was a very dark period for Michael Blodgett," continues Celeste. "He was drinking heavily throughout the shoot. I was not at all pleased with him as my leading man. In the scene where I have to stab him and he dies, he's laying on top of me. Michael had his hand behind me and he didn't realize that as he was acting he was closing his hand around my spine. He really hurt me—my whole back was bruised. But he had no clue what he was doing. He had been drinking the night before. Consequently, it was difficult for me to work with him and retain my air of professionalism. I tried to just put up with it. The producers finally got his girlfriend to come on location so he sobered up a bit when she arrived. It was murder until she got there. Michael ultimately cleaned up his act and is now a successful writer."

Despite the film's less than stellar reviews, *The Velvet Vampire* was a hit and has reached cult status due to the fact that it was directed by the talented and under-appreciated Rothman. Also, Celeste created a fascinating and mysterious vampire figure who had the ability to intoxicate her guests. Roger Corman was so impressed with Celeste that she was set to star in his next New World feature *Sweet Sugar,* but she backed out of it at the last minute. "I was offered a small part in Michael Winner's *The Mechanic* [1972]," says Celeste. "I chose this instead because Michael had promised me a better part in his next movie, called *Scorpio* [1973]. However, that role was taken away from me and given to Gayle Hunnicutt. I never knew why I lost this role—Gayle didn't have a bigger name than I had. I think studio politics were involved. Passing on Corman's film turned out to be a bad career move."

Recounting her experiences doing these films, Celeste remembers, "The great pleasure of doing *The Mechanic* was meeting Jill Ireland. Charles Bronson was a very unusual character but Jill was just amazing. We became very good friends. I also got to see some beautiful parts of the world—we shot on the Amalfi coast. While there, Michael Winner arranged a dinner party and Terence Young of all people was there. Michael thought it was very funny to introduce him to the notorious Mrs. Silverstein. Not only did he remember me but also he was *still* angry! While filming *Scorpio*, we were staying at the Watergate Hotel during the Watergate break-in. There were some very scandalous stories about the film's star Alain Delon, who had been suspected of murdering his chauffeur in Paris but he was never charged. His date one night for dinner with Michael and me was 13 years old. We had a giggle over that."

By the early seventies, acting roles began drying up for Celeste. Though she was only in her late twenties, that is unfortunately considered old in Hollywood, which is always on the lookout for younger nubile actresses. Celeste also accounts her lack of work due to just plain bad luck. "I had some missed opportunities and doors slammed in my face," remarks Celeste. "The Universal contract mishap was probably the most detrimental to my career. In 1969, I was chosen by Jon Hall to star in his film called *Arielle*. Jon was a wonderful director and cinematographer. However, they ran out of money and the film was never completed. I also lost a number of high-profile roles. I was cast as one of the three female leads in *Bracken's World* but David Gerber maneuvered his then girlfriend (and later his wife) Laraine Stephens into the role. And Irwin Allen wanted me for the role of Nonnie in *The Poseidon Adventure* [1972] but the studio vetoed it because my name wasn't big enough." Carol Lynley got the part.

While a number of her contemporaries became residential real estate brokers to pay their bills, Celeste entered the commercial real estate business in 1973 to supplement her income. In 1979, she founded Celeste Yarnall and Associates, which specialized in the leasing and selling of high rise office buildings. Her clientele included such entertainment giants as Paramount Studios, Dino DeLaurentiis and Chuck Fries. Though she never needed to earn her living from acting again, Celeste wanted to return to show business in some capacity. In 1987, she started a company called Artists Management Group representing young upcoming screenwriters and directors. Recently, Mike Ovitz used the same name for his talent management company so Celeste has changed the name of her company to Celeste Yarnall & Associates. "I took a lot of writing courses and worked with a lot of writers," says Celeste. "We just sold one screenplay I shared credit on called *Code: 99* to Overseas Film Group, who own it outright. We don't know if it is going to be made into a film or not. I also have begun acting again."

Some of Celeste's more recent film appearances include *Funny About Love* (1990), *Ambition* (1991), the direct-to-video horror film *Midnight Kiss* (1993)

Today's Celeste Yarnall—actress, agent, author, and champion of animal rights (courtesy of Celeste Yarnall).

and Luis Mandoki's remake *Born Yesterday* (1993) starring Melanie Griffith, John Goodman and Don Johnson. Celeste was cast as a senator's wife and though she received prominent billing, her role is nothing more than a glorified cameo. "I had been a fan of director Luis Mandoki since I saw his film *Gaby: A True Story* [1987]," states Celeste. "He's a brilliant director and when he offered me this part I said yes. But I think when you're a blonde and are in some of the same scenes with Melanie Griffith, you get pushed aside—I'm almost conspicuous by my absence. I had an odd experience doing this film—Don Johnson and John Goodman were wonderful to work with but Melanie Griffith seemed *only* interested in the other stars of the film. I guess my part was too small. She did, however, remember that I knew her mother Tippi Hedren."

Though Celeste loves acting and the world of show business, her first love is and always was animals. Juggling these businesses and an acting career became very stressful to Celeste, who decided to get a kitten about ten years ago. She began buying all the cat care books she could find and was chagrined to learn that the commercial pet food she was feeding her cat was made up from slaughterhouse waste and grains unfit for human consumption. Horrified, she amassed so much information on this subject that she authored her first book in 1995, *Cat Care Naturally: Celeste Yarnall's Complete Guide to Holistic Health Care for Cats*, combining nutrition and holistic health care with a bit of pet astrology. She has since bred six generations of Tonkinese cats on her natural regime and has released an updated version of her book entitled *Natural Cat Care* as well as a new book called *Natural Dog Care*. Celeste also had her own call-in radio show called *Celestial Pets* on this subject but was surprised that the television talk shows expressed no interest. "Here we are feeding our pets garbage and they're dying from cancer at a horrible rate and the Leezas, Oprahs and Rosies couldn't have cared less! And these are the people who are supposedly into animal rights. It amazed me about their and their producers' indifference. I've become the voice of what these animals should be eating. Humans have a choice of what to eat but since these animals took this enormous leap of faith to come in from the wild where they could catch their dinner to sleep on our pillows, their birthright shouldn't be cancer, now should it?"

Celeste has recently left the real estate business to devote herself full-time to consulting on the care of cats and dogs. Her company promotes her books and produces a line of pet supplements and instructional videos on making your own pet food. And amazingly, Celeste found time to return to school to get a Ph.D. in Nutrition from Pacific Western University. Will we ever see Celeste on the big or small screens again? "You bet," exclaims Celeste. "I started as an ingenue and progressed from the bride to leading lady to mother of the bride. Now my agents send me out on young grandmother roles. It's kind of an insult to me since I'm only 54! Then again, I actually *am* a grandmother so I guess I shouldn't be too insulted. Work is work."

Film Appearances

1963	**The Nutty Professor** (Paramount) d. Jerry Lewis.
	A New Kind of Love (Paramount) d. Melville Shavelson.
1966	**Around the World Under the Sea** (MGM) d. Andrew Marton.
1968	**Live a Little, Love a Little** (MGM) d. Norman Taurog.
	Eve (U.S./Great Britain/Spain, Feature Film Corp. of America) d. Jeremy Summers.
1969	**Bob & Carol & Ted & Alice** (Columbia) d. Paul Mazursky.
	Arielle (never completed) d. Jon Hall.
	In Name Only (TV-movie) d. E.W. Swackhamer.
1970	**Beast of Blood/Beast of the Dead** (U.S./Philippines, Hemisphere) d. Eddie Romero.
1971	**Ransom for a Dead Man** (TV-movie) d. Richard Irving.
	The Velvet Vampire (New World) d. Stephanie Rothman.
1972	**The Mechanic** (United Artists) d. Michael Winner.
	The Judge and Jake Wyler (TV-movie) d. David Lowell Rich.
1973	**Scorpio** (United Artists) d. Michael Winner.
1979	**The Jerk** (Universal) d. Carl Reiner [scenes deleted].
1987	**Fatal Beauty** (MGM) d. Tom Holland.
1990	**Funny About Love/New York Times** (Paramount) d. Leonard Nimoy.
1991	**Daughters of Privilege** (TV-movie) d. Michael Fresco.
	Ambition (Spirit Films) d. Scott Goldstein.
1992	**Driving Me Crazy/Trabbi Goes to Hollywood** (Motion Picture Corp. of America) d. Jon Turtletaub.
1993	**Midnight Kiss** (Overseas Film Group) d. Joel Bender.
	Born Yesterday (Hollywood Pictures) d. Luis Mandoki.

Television Appearances

Burke's Law "Who Killed Beau Sparrow?" 12/27/63 ABC.
Mona McCluskey "Into Every Life a Little Life Must Fall" 1965 NBC.
The Wild Wild West "The Night of a Thousand Eyes" 10/22/65 CBS.
The Smothers Brothers Show "Boys Will Be Playboys" 11/26/65 CBS.
Bewitched "And Then There Were Three" 1/13/66 ABC.
Gidget "Independence—Gidget Style" 3/17/66 ABC.
The Man from U.N.C.L.E. "The Monks of St. Thomas Affair" 10/14/66 NBC.
Captain Nice "May I Have the Last Dance?" 4/17/67 NBC.
Star Trek "The Apple" 10/13/67 NBC.

Hogan's Heroes "LeBeau and the Little Old Lady" 2/24/68 CBS.
It Takes a Thief "Locked in the Cradle of the Keep" 4/15/68 ABC.
The F.B.I. "The Mercenary" 4/28/68 ABC.
Bonanza "Queen High" 12/1/68 NBC.
Hogan's Heroes "Will the Blue Baron Strike Again?" 12/14/68 CBS.
Land of the Giants "The Golden Cage" 12/29/68 ABC.
Mannix "Eagles Sometimes Don't Fly 9/27/69 CBS.
The Survivors "Chapter One" 9/29/69 ABC.
The Survivors "Chapter Two" 10/6/69 ABC.
The Bold Ones: The Protectors "Draw a Straight Man" 12/14/69 NBC.
It's Your Bet [celebrity panelist] 11/8 to 11/12/71 NBC.
McMillan and Wife "Terror Times Two" 12/13/72 NBC.
Love, American Style "Love and the Postal Master" 3/9/73 ABC.
ABC Wide World of Mystery "Night Train to Terror" 5/23/73 ABC.
Knots Landing "My First Born" 1/18/90 CBS.
Melrose Place "Oy! To the World" 12/11/95 FOX.
Melrose Place "Amanda's Back" 11/11/97 FOX.

Also:

The Adventures of Ozzie and Harriet, The Defenders, The Double Life of Henry Phyfe and *Sisters*.

Judy Pace

Beautiful Judy Pace was a pioneer of African-American actresses during the sixties. "I was the first dark-skinned black actress to play female leads and glamorous roles," says Judy proudly. "Actresses before me with my skin tone were relegated to playing slaves and maids. It was only actresses like Dorothy Dandridge and Lena Horne, who were light honey brown, that got the leads. But during the Civil Rights Movement with 'black is beautiful,' I was able to break through." Judy surely did. Like the Caucasian actresses in this book, she was a contract player (at Columbia) and she went the publicity route. On TV, she began appearing in small roles on such series as *Bewitched*, *Tarzan*, *Batman* and *I Spy* before landing a regular role on *Peyton Place* as a blackmailing villainess. In 1971, she starred in her own series *The Young Lawyers* as an idealistic law student. On the big screen, Judy was known for playing hip college coeds in such films as *Three in the Attic* and *Up in the Cellar*. Her best performance was as the street-smart Iris in the groundbreaking comedy *Cotton Comes to Harlem* but most fans remember her for her role as the wife of football great Gale Sayers in *Brian's Song*. After appearing in the cult horror film *Frogs*, and starring opposite Thalmus Rasulala in *Cool Breeze* and Jim Brown in *The Slams*, Judy began focusing more of her time on her children during the seventies. She retired from acting in 1983.

Judy Pace was born on June 15 in Los Angeles, one of five children. (Only her sisters Betty Pace and Jean Pace, who is married to jazz vocalist-songwriter-playwright Oscar Brown, Jr., are still living today.) Her father was a jet plane mechanic and her mother owned a dress shop called Kitty's Boutique in Los Angeles where a young Judy worked and designed her own clothes. "My mother's shop was the largest owned African-American establishment west of the Mississippi during the late fifties and early sixties," states Judy proudly. "My mother was very forward and entrepreneurial. It was unique for an African-American person to own this type of establishment. She sold top-of-the-line ready-to-wear couture and designer clothes. That's the element I grew up in—the fashion industry. We had a design room and work

Portrait of Judy Pace as a college coed in *Up in the Cellar* (AIP, 1970).

persons. My sisters and I even designed originals for the shop. It was just part of our family. In America the women who did the sewing and did the designing were the African-American women, starting in plantation time. Abraham Lincoln's wife's fashion designer was a black woman who was also her best friend. That was very common. And that was part of my family heritage."

While attending Los Angeles City College, Judy had a recurrence of a childhood bone disease in her left leg, which threatened to have her confined to a wheelchair for the rest of her life. While recuperating in the hospital, she decided to pursue an acting career because "I just became very honest with myself and decided I was going to do what I really wanted to do. Growing up middle-class, I was expected to go off to school and become a teacher, a nurse or a social worker—a traditional, middle-class career. I was supposed to graduate college and start a family like all my girlfriends did."

After regaining the use of her legs, Judy entered the Miss Bronze beauty contest along with her friend Marilyn Mc-Coo, later of the 5th Dimension singing group. Though she did not win, she was selected by *Ebony* magazine to go on an international tour modeling the latest fashion designs for the *Ebony* Fashion Fair. ("I started at what was considered the very top for a black model. I was the first girl chosen from the West Coast to travel with the *Ebony* Fashion Fair.") When Judy returned to California, producer-director William Castle offered her a role in his film *13 Frightened Girls* (1963) after seeing her photo in *Ebony*. "The publisher and owner of *Ebony*, John Johnson, called me and told me Columbia Pictures was looking for me to co-star in this film," recalls Judy. "John was just as excited as I was. I interviewed with William Castle and he offered me the role. Young ladies from all over the world were selected to do this film." In this spy adventure aimed at teenagers, Judy, Kathy Dunn, Gina Trikonis and others played the daughters of international diplomats, attending boarding school in Switzerland. They then get involved with Chinese Communists, steal top-secret files and find a body in the school's freezer all due to Dunn's infatuation with CIA operative Murray Hamilton.

Deciding acting was what she wanted to do, Judy devised a five-year plan for her career—study for two years, work on the stage for one year and then spend the remaining two years doing films and television. Judy stuck to her plan and studied drama with Corey Allen, comedy with Harvey Lembeck and voice and drama with Lillian Randolph, the star of

Beulah. "Lillian Randolph was a beautiful dramatic actress and also my mentor," says Judy. "She gave me this advice that I followed throughout my career, which is why I think I never had a problem with the casting couch. She said, 'You have to think of all the men in positions of power in the industry as your brother or a family member. With those thoughts in mind, your conversations will be such, your mannerisms will be such and they will never approach you.' It worked. I never had a problem and I believe it was due to her guidance." After appearing in *13 Frightened Girls*, Pace showed her singing and dancing ability in the musical comedy *Cindy* at a West Hollywood supper club. She won raves and followed this with roles in *My Fairfax Lady*, *What the Country Needs*, *Goldfinkle* and *The Zulu and Zeda*.

It was at this time that Judy became a client of the William Morris Agency and signed a contract with Columbia Pictures. Her agents were Sy Marsh and Jimmy Hyde, the son of agent Johnny Hyde who discovered Marilyn Monroe. "Jimmy was a wonderful agent and he was going to make me the black Marilyn Monroe," says Judy, laughing. "But seriously, they schooled me very well in the fact that acting was a business for young women. They told me, 'Most young women who come to Hollywood will work for 15 years or so but if you are not winning Oscars or considered a Bette Davis, then you move on. You more than likely will marry someone in the business.' If you look at many directors and producers, most of their wives were actresses or vocalists. You live comfortably and happily ever after but *you get out of the business!* It's as if you are going to play major league baseball. You don't play pro ball until you're 50. It's a young man's game."

At Columbia, Judy immediately began working on a number of its Screen Gems sitcoms including *Bewitched*, *I Dream of Jeannie* and *The Flying Nun*. On the big screen, she had small roles in the Billy Wilder comedy *The Fortune Cookie* (1966) and in the mod thriller *The Thomas Crown Affair* (1968) starring Steve McQueen and Faye Dunaway. "I never worked with either of them," says Judy disappointedly. "But this was a nice role because I got a trip to Boston. I played one of the witnesses to the bank robbery. My scenes were with Yaphet Kotto, who played one of the detectives. Norman Jewison was just a wonderful director. He let me stay on the set and watch the great talents work. I would always do that if I had a small role. I'd get permission to sit and observe the pros working. That's how I learned—by being there on the set."

Pace's first lead role was in AIP's campus drama *Three in the Attic* (1968). This was Judy's first of three films for the independent film company. Commenting on AIP, which was criticized for being exploitative, Judy opines, "To me, AIP had taken the position the studios had when they were doing B-movies. No one ever called their movies exploitative. What were all those gangster, Tarzan and monster films that they were producing in the thirties and the forties? They looked like American International Pictures films to me. [*Laughs*] AIP took the place of the B-movies after the studios started changing that whole star system. There were no longer contract players and starlets and a whole staff of people to put out all those B-movies. During the late sixties, everyone went freelance. You had no choice once the studio system collapsed. There was also never mention of race in regards to my characters in their movies [*Three in the Attic*, *Up in the Cellar*, and *Frogs*].

Poster art for *Three in the Attic* (AIP, 1968).

It was the time of the Civil Rights Movement and my color was never an issue. It was a very forward move for AIP."

In *Three in the Attic*, Christopher Jones played college Casanova Paxton Quigley who, though in love with fellow student Tobey Clinton (Yvette Mimieux), beds art major Eulice (Pace) and Jewish hippie Jan (Maggie Thrett). When the girls learn of each other, they devise a plot to drain him of his virility until he tells why he cheated on Tobey. To reach this end, they keep him prisoner in the dormitory attic and have sex with him on a timed schedule. When he mounts a hunger strike, Eulice and Jan want to let him go but Tobey persists in keeping him a prisoner until he explains why he cheated on her. The dorm monitor discovers the weakened Paxton and Tobey flees the campus after being confronted by the school's dean. As she awaits the next bus out of town, Eulice drives Paxton to the depot to stop her. "We filmed this in Chapel Hill [North Carolina]," recounts Judy. "I enjoyed playing Eulice immensely. This was *the* first time a black female was being romanced by a white male and they were equals. My character was neither a slave nor a maid. *She* was a college student and *he* was a college student. Eulice was an artist and a volunteer schoolteacher. Those kinds of characters were not on the screen at that time. They didn't exist. Eulice was in cahoots with the other two women as equals in their plot against Chris Jones' character."

Three in the Attic was a huge box office hit for AIP as it broke the boundaries on a lot of issues. The women in the movie stand up to the Casanova and give him all the lovemaking he thinks he wants, making a statement on physical sex versus love. It was done with a feminist's viewpoint a few years before the women's movement took off. "I thought it was a very comedic twist on a woman scorned," remarks Judy. The film also featured one of the first nude scenes done by a famous actor: Christopher Jones' backside is exposed as he poses for Judy's character, who sketches him for her art class. "I never saw Chris naked," says Judy, laughing. "They had him wrapped in a blanket and when we shot the scene I was positioned behind an easel so I never saw him!

"Christopher Jones became sort of a buddy to me," continues Judy. "We'd be out playing Frisbee or just hanging out laughing and talking. He was just a good guy. My boyfriend at that time was Curt Flood—major league baseball player and World Series great. He was in spring training in Florida so one weekend he came to visit me on the set. However, it got really cold and rainy. Curt arrived from warm sunny Florida with only summer clothes. Christopher was about the same size as Curt so he loaned him some sweaters, pants and a jacket. They hit it off well. Both of them were artists."

Though Pace won good reviews for her role in *Three in the Attic* (she's called "an African-American charmer" by *Variety*), her film career was put on hold for

Pace and Christopher Jones get it on in *Three in the Attic* (AIP, 1968).

a bit while Judy concentrated on television. One TV role that Judy craved but did not get was *Julia*. "There was this woman named *Diahann Carroll* and they just wanted her," quips Judy, chuckling. "I'm saying this in a joking manner because Diahann was a woman I looked up to. She, Dorothy Dandridge, Lena Horne and Ruby Dee were my role models." Though Judy lost out on *Julia*, she was cast as duplicitous Vickie Fletcher on *Peyton Place* in 1969. ("I got to work with Ruby Dee and hang out with Diahann Carroll who filmed on the same lot. I was in heaven!") This was the soap's sixth season and with the ratings dropping, the producers brought in a black family to inject new vitality into the show. Vickie was a vile teenage schemer who comes to town to blackmail Harry and Alma Mile's (Percy Rodrigues and Ruby Dee) son Lew (Glynn Thurman) after she claims to be pregnant by him during an out-of-town tryst. She insinuates herself into his family, making their lives hell. "As with the role I played in *Three in the Attic* which had never been seen on the big screen before, this part on *Peyton Place* had never been done on television before. You would normally see a Caucasian girl play this type of role. Vickie was from the wrong side of the tracks, streetwise and a blackmailer. It was a fun part to play. I had women hating me all over the country. You never saw a black woman play such an evil, bitchy character on television like this on a regular basis. In fact, the Miles family was the first black family to be featured on a dramatic series. And we got wonderful feedback from the audience." Unfortunately, the series was cancelled, denying the audience the opportunity to watch Vickie's comeuppance.

During the sixties, Judy and her co-stars from *Peyton Place* along with Bill Cosby of *I Spy*, Nichelle Nichols of *Star Trek*, Diahann Carroll of *Julia*, Clarence Williams, III, of *The Mod Squad*, Don Mitchell of *Ironside* and Don Marshall of *Land of the Giants* were some of the first black actors to have leading roles on television, breaking the color barrier. They paved the way for later seventies TV shows such as *Sanford and Son*, *Barefoot in the Park*, *That's My Mama*, *Good Times*, *What's Happening*, *The Jeffersons* and *Roots*. However, as we approach the millennium the four major network offerings are once again featuring predominately white casts. "I find this situation disheartening and frightening," comments Judy. "The black shows have been segregated to the lesser networks like UPN and cable TV. There needs to be more diversity amongst the people in control. It is wonderful to see black actors in front and behind the camera like Spike Lee, Oprah Winfrey, Bill Cosby and Halle Berry form their own production companies to produce movies and TV shows. And with the cable networks producing original programming, there are more opportunities for black actors and producers, more so than in the sixties. But the problem still exists with the major networks. The people in control need to have more of a varied ethnic background."

After *Peyton Place* was cancelled, Judy returned to the big screen in the comedy *Up in the Cellar* (1970) set on a university campus rife with student unrest. Wes Stern plays Colin Slade, a student whose scholarship is revoked when a computer deems his poetry below the required "Aesthetic Quotient." He appeals to the school's arrogant, ambitious president Maurice Camber (Larry Hagman), but when he agrees with the computer, a devastated Colin climbs the school's radio tower to commit suicide

Larry Hagman as a university president manhandles a protestor while students Wes Stern and Judy Pace look on in *Up in the Cellar* (AIP, 1970).

during Camber's candidacy announcement for the Senate. Though he has no regard for his students, Camber rescues Colin and is hailed by the media as a hero. Colin plots revenge by seducing the women in Camber's life—his wife (Joan Collins), a secret astrology nut, and his beautiful daughter (Nira Barab) who thinks she's ugly. To seduce Camber's black mistress (Pace), who though emotionally involved with Camber can't sleep with him because she thinks whites expect too much of blacks in sexual relations, Colin convinces her he is black too and takes her to bed in a very funny scene. The film's running gag is that the campus protests heat up and the police and National Guard are called in, but no one seems to notice or care. After Colin helps all three women overcome their hang-ups, the film ends with a love-in. As expected, the film's reviews ran along the lines of "a tasteless, dull piece of idiocy" and "far-fetched and unconvincing." However, Judy did well in her role. *Variety* raved, "Judy Pace is obviously enjoying herself enormously, and hers is one of the more rewarding roles." Judy recalls that working with Larry Hagman was fun and she recently ran into him and Joan Collins at the Golden Camera Awards held in East Berlin. "I accompanied my very best friend Nichelle Nichols [of *Star Trek* fame] who was also a recipient. We were at this lavish cocktail party when Larry spotted me and yelled across the room, 'My mistress! There's my mistress!' His wife chimed in with him. It was hysterical. It was nice seeing them again."

Judy's next film was a huge box office hit and took Hollywood by surprise. Ossie Davis directed *Cotton Comes to Harlem* (1970) on location in Harlem during the summer of 1969. ("It might be one of the first films totally shot there," remarks Judy. "We even did the interior scenes at a studio in Harlem.") Rather than focusing on social issues *à la* a number of previous black films, *Cotton Comes to Harlem* is an entertaining cops and robbers comedy. Raymond St. Jacques and Godfrey Cambridge star as detectives Coffin Ed Johnson and Gravedigger Jones. They try to prevent Reverend Deke O'Malley (Calvin Lockhart) from swindling the good people of Harlem of $87,000 donated to O'Malley's bogus "Back to Africa" cause. O'Malley is in cahoots with white ex-con J.D. Cannon. And all are in pursuit of a lost bale of cotton where O'Malley's men have stashed the money after a bungled robbery. Judy played Iris, O'Malley's feisty girlfriend who goes on a rampage after finding O'Malley in the arms of another woman. The film's climax takes place at the Apollo Theatre where the bale of cotton turns up (*sans* the $87,000) as part of a singer's act.

Judy gives one of the film's best performances as the feisty, foul-mouthed Iris. *Newsweek* remarked, "Judy Pace is lovely and skillful," *New York Magazine* commented, "Judy Pace offers fine support" and the *Newark Evening News* raved, "Judy Pace is stunningly beautiful, and proves herself to be a very competent actress." Judy had come to the attention of director Ossie Davis the year before when she co-starred with Davis' wife Ruby Dee on *Peyton Place*. "Ossie had seen all of my work on that series so I was able to immediately get an audition," recalls Judy. "He asked me to come to New York to meet with him. I read for him and got the part. I love doing comedy so to me this was a comedic role. Iris was this crazy woman. [*Laughs*] And I loved the extreme that I had to go through—from being overdone and glamorous to getting beat up and being thrown in jail. Ossie Davis was the very first black director I worked for and he is just a genius. It was an amazing adventure doing *Cotton Comes to Harlem*. There were just so many talented people in this film—Raymond St. Jacques (we became best buddies and he taught me so much), Godfrey Cambridge, Redd Foxx and Calvin Lockhart, to name a few. It was a joy to work with them all. It is just my instinct, but I believe Ossie chose the actors he believed would do a wonderful job on screen but would also bring harmony to the set—he didn't have problems with any of the cast."

For the most part, *Cotton Comes to Harlem* won good reviews. But more importantly it proved to Hollywood that a film with a mostly black cast could make money. The film grossed $5.2 million and was the 22nd highest grossing film of 1970. "This was the first black film that was a major hit," says Judy proudly. "People were lining up to see this movie." And when money talks, Hollywood listens. Soon the blaxploitation craze began. When asked how she felt being a part of it, Judy replies, "I don't know what blaxploitation means. I think it is a phrase that came about from I-don't-know-where. It is a racist statement and it really annoys me. That term is a put-down of all the talented people who worked in films labeled blaxploitation. They didn't call the gangster films of the thirties white exploitation. The only black exploitation movie I saw was the Tarzan movie series of the thirties and forties. If you have black exploitation films, where are the movies that are called white exploitation films? When I've asked people in the business what blaxploitation means, they respond that *the studios made those films only to make money.* Well, hello. I thought the purpose of studios producing films was to make money! [*Laughs*] *Well, they exploited the actors!* That's what's called being a performer!"

Beginning in the fall of 1970, Judy reprised her role as an idealistic young lawyer from the TV-movie *The Young Lawyers* for the series with the same name. Around that time, the networks seemed to have discovered young people. The 18–49 demographic became the audience the networks wanted to reach—especially people from the big cities. Such popular series as *Green Acres*, *Petticoat Junction*, *The Red Skelton Show*, *Gomer Pyle*, etc., were cancelled to make way for more hip shows directed at a younger audience. *The Young Lawyers* starred Lee J. Cobb as the director of a Boston Legal Aid facility and Zalman King and Judy as law students who are permitted by Massachusetts statute to represent clients under the supervision of an experienced attorney. Instead of focusing on spectacular murder cases, the students represented runaways, an unmarried couple seeking to keep their child, a young man charged with drug possession, etc. It was reminiscent of ABC-TV's *The Mod Squad*. "Lee J. Cobb was such an incredible actor," exclaims Judy. "That was one set where I'd go to work just to watch him even if I didn't have to be there." Judy did well in her role and won the NAACP's Image Award for "Outstanding Black Television Actress" after previous nominations for her work in *Peyton Place* and *Cotton Comes to Harlem*. But the series was cancelled after only one season—a victim of the debut of ABC-TV's *Monday Night Football*. On the East Coast, *The Young Lawyers* preceded the game but in the West Coast it followed it, running at erratic times and failing to build an audience.

During this period, Judy also played the wife of football great Gayle Sayers in the classic Emmy-winning made-for-TV movie *Brian's Song* (1971) starring James Caan, Billy Dee Williams and Shelley Fabares. It was based on the true story of the friendship between Chicago Bears football players Brian Piccolo (Caan) and Gayle Sayers (Williams), the first white and black teammates who became roommates while on the road. Their friendship took a tragic turn after Piccolo developed cancer and died soon after. "This was such a good story," remarks Judy. "Some of the scenes were so emotional, especially the death scene. Who knew what kind of stars James Caan and Billy Dee Williams were going to be? James Caan is a comedian. One minute he is lying in bed doing his dying scenes and the next minute he is rattling off jokes. Jimmy had the same charisma as Bill Cosby where everyone just likes you—from the light guy to the cameraman to the gaffers, they all loved him. He just had that quality about him. While we were shooting this, Billy Dee was trying to get an interview with Berry Gordy for *Lady Sings the Blues* [1972]. He couldn't get one and he was so upset! He tried everything and of course as we all know he finally succeeded. [*Laughs*]

"Louis Gossett was originally signed to play Gayle Sayers," reveals Judy. "When I auditioned it was with Lou. It was his role. However, about three days after I signed to play his wife, the casting director called me and told me that Lou had been hurt playing basketball with some

Godfrey Cambridge as Det. Gravedigger Jones questions Pace as the hot-tempered Iris in *Cotton Comes to Harlem* (United Artists, 1970).

of his actor friends. He injured his knee and couldn't do the football scenes. They then asked me to come in and read with about six actors who were going to test for Lou's role. And they were all so good! Every one of them had us in tears. *I didn't know who they were going to pick!* After Billy Dee got the part, everyone commented that Lou ruined his career by missing out on this great role. But his career went on quite nicely."

Judy returned to the big screen in *Cool Breeze* (1972) with Thalmus Rasulala and the scary nature-on-a-rampage film *Frogs* (1972). The outrageous *Frogs* ("Millions of slimy bodies squirming everywhere—millions of gaping mouths!") is the more memorable. *Terror on Tape* commented, "A first-rate cast is done in by spiders, leeches, snakes, alligators and snapping turtles in scenes that are genuinely creepy. Much better than you'd think." Ray Milland played a wealthy reclusive industrialist who made his money from paper mills decimating the surrounding ecology in the process. He invites his relatives to his isolated island home to celebrate his birthday. Frogs, lizards and other reptiles crash the party, intent on wiping out Milland and his family for their careless polluting of the area. Sam Elliott portrayed an environmentalist and freelance photographer who is documenting the pollution when he is involved in a boating accident with Milland's reckless grandchildren (Adam Roarke and Joan Van Ark). Elliott accompanies them back to the estate where the terror begins. Nicholas Cortland, David Gilliam, Holly Irving and Lynn Borden (the second Mrs. B. of *Hazel* fame) played other ill-fated family members

(Gilliam is feasted on by spiders in their web; Borden is devoured by an alligator turtle, etc.). As a sassy fashion model and girlfriend of Cortland, Pace is the only one who backs Elliott against the tyrannical Milland. She convinces Milland's butler and maid to flee the island with her. Though it is left open if her character lives (you see a shot of her open suitcase at the end), Judy states assuredly that her character survived.

"Making *Frogs* was creepy," comments Judy. "The poor little frogs had wires on their feet and some were nailed to the ground. They were not treated well. And we filmed this out in the middle of nowhere. The house in the film was an old plantation, which was also used for costume changes and makeup. Physically, this was not a fun shoot. The bug situation was unreal. Some of us had to go the doctor because we were bitten by insects so badly, causing these skin irritations. My arm swelled up from the bites I got. But it was worth it to work with Ray Milland. He had incredible timing! He'd go from playing this gruff old man to his happy normal self once the director yelled, cut. And Adam Roarke was such a character. He'd always want to go out and party. But the thing that was so bizarre was that there was nowhere in that town to go party. [*Laughs*] There were a few bars and one little restaurant."

Pace's last theatrical film appearance was *The Slams* (1973) for Roger Corman's company. ("I thought Roger was brilliant and underrated. He was doing then what you see independent producers doing now—putting together these films with little money, a lot of creativity and a lot of promotion. He also gave a lot of people behind the camera an opportunity to prove themselves.") In 1972, Judy married actor Don Mitchell of *Ironside* fame and their first daughter was born in 1973. She continued doing television guest shots but her career began to taper off. Judy says, "I was just not concerned about it. If there was work, there was work, and if there wasn't work, there wasn't. I was in love with Don and we had a beautiful girl so that was my focus at that time. It was not a conscious decision on my part not to make any more films. It's just what happened. Then in 1977, I was able to do something I always wanted to do—a big Broadway show. They revived the musical *Guys and Dolls* on Broadway with an all-black cast. It was such a big hit that they brought it to Las Vegas. They re-cast all the leads and I won the role of Adelaide, which I consider the most wonderful comedic role ever written. I got to do everything I love to do—dance, sing and do comedy. I surprised a lot of people because I was not known as a vocalist because I had stopped singing professionally many years ago. It was like, '*they hired Judy Pace?! Can she sing?*' Yes, she sings quite nicely! [*Laughs*] The show was such a hit, our run was extended an additional six months. And then I was pregnant with my second daughter. There was just no way after that to juggle my two children, my husband and my house."

In 1971, Judy established the Kwanza Foundation. This was an organization made up of black actresses (including Nichelle Nichols, Pam Grier, Rosalind Cash, Jayne Kennedy, Esther Rolle, Debbie Allen, Beverly Todd, Marla Gibbs and Isabel Sanford) who organized fundraisers for scholarships for black students. "This is the only non-profit organization whose membership are actresses," says Judy. "Back then you would see only one black female face on a TV show or film. We never had the chance to work together like white actresses. This was a way for us to get to know one another and to give something back to the community."

Today Judy is still is stunningly beautiful. Her husband, baseball great Curt Flood, the father of free agency, passed away in 1997. "He saw me on the premiere primetime showing of *The Dating Game* in 1966 and pursued me for about a year, sending me baseball cards, magazines, flowers, anything to get me to go out with him," recalls Judy. "My dad was very impressed and convinced me to go out with him. I did and Curt was my boyfriend until 1970. I was with him during his battle with the baseball owners over free agency that reached the Supreme Court in 1970. When Curt lost, he exiled himself from the U.S. to live in Spain. I moved on with my life and I married actor Don Mitchell whom I dated first during 1964. After my divorce from Don in 1984, Curt and I were reunited when a writer wanted to interview me for a movie he was writing about Curt's life. Curt and I met for dinner and we were together until his death."

Judy is contemplating a return to the acting field now that she is single and her two daughters are beginning their careers. Shawn Mitchell Flood is an attorney and Julia Pace Mitchell is an actress. Both are graduates of Howard University where Julia was awarded the Debbie Allen and Phylicia Rashad Scholarship given to young women who can do comedy, sing and dance. Judy says in conclusion, "I think acting again might be a fun thing to do in the sense that it would not be '*I have to get a job!*' It would be almost a hobby. I think what is wonderful is the change in show business and our whole society with regards to the image of women. The image of a woman in her forties or fifties 30 years ago is not the same image today. Women in their fifties today do not look and act like women that [date] back in the 1960s. Look at Raquel Welch. Look at Lena Horne. Look at Tina Turner. This image of a fifty-year-old woman is brand new. Women are healthier today and they keep their bodies fitter. In the relationship to age, I think in the entertainment industry it's 'what age can you play?'—not 'how old are you?' And I truly did enjoy my acting career. I was very blessed in that regard."

Film Appearances

1963 **13 Frightened Girls** (Columbia) d. William Castle.
1966 **The Fortune Cookie** (United Artists) d. Billy Wilder.
1968 **The Thomas Crown Affair** (United Artists) d. Norman Jewison.
Three in the Attic (AIP) d. Richard Wilson.
1969 **The Young Lawyers** (TV-movie) d. Harvey Hart.
1970 **Up in the Cellar/Three in the Cellar** (AIP) d. Theodore J. Flicker.
Cotton Comes to Harlem (United Artists) d. Ossie Davis.
1971 **Brian's Song** (TV-movie) d. Buzz Kulik.
1972 **Cool Breeze** (MGM) d. Barry Pollack.
Frogs (AIP) d. George McCowan.
1973 **The Slams** (MGM) d. Jonathan Kaplan.
1999 **Looking for Oscar** (Lesser-Montague Prod.) [documentary] d. Eric Porvaznik.

Television Appearances

Profiles in Courage "The Mary S. McDowell Story" 11/15/64 NBC.
Bewitched "Follow That Witch" 4/14 & 4/21/66 ABC.
Batman "Death in Slow Motion" 4/27/66 ABC.
Batman "The Riddler's False Notion" 4/28/66 ABC.

I Spy "One of Our Bombs Is Missing" 11/16/66 NBC.
The Dating Game [celebrity contestant] 11/24/66 ABC.
I Dream of Jeannie "Fly Me to the Moon" 9/12/67 NBC.
The Flying Nun "A Fatal Hibiscus" 10/5/67 ABC.
Tarzan "King of the Dwsari" 1/26/68 NBC.
Soul-In (special) 10/17/68 NBC.
The Mod Squad "Deadly Circle of Violence" 11/12/68 ABC.
Peyton Place [series regular as Vickie Fletcher] 1/1/69 to 6/2/69 ABC.
My Friend Tony "Corey Doesn't Live Here Anymore" 1/5/69 CBS.
The Dating Game [celebrity contestant] 11/8/69 ABC.
It Takes Two [celebrity contestant] 12/1 to 12/4/69 NBC.
The New People "The Prisoner of Bomano" 12/29/69
The Young Lawyers [series regular as Pat Walters] 9/21/70 to 5/5/71 ABC.
Oh, Nurse (pilot) 3/17/72 CBS.
Shaft "Hit-Run" 11/20/73 CBS.
Medical Center "Trial by Knife" 1/14/74 CBS.
Kung Fu "In Certain Bondage" 2/7/74 ABC.
That's My Mama "Whose Child Is This?" 9/4/74 ABC.
Ironside "Fall of an Angel" 12/19/74 NBC.
Caribe "Lady Killer" 3/17/75 ABC.
Good Times "The Weekend" 10/14/75 CBS.
The Rowan and Martin Report (pilot) 11/5/75 ABC.
That's Enough [talk show hostess] 1976 KCOP-TV.
What's Happening "Shirley's Fired" 2/23/79 ABC.
Beyond West World "Take-Over" (unaired episode) 1980 CBS.
The New Odd Couple (episode title unknown) 11/26/82 ABC.
E! True Hollywood Story "Christopher Jones" 4/99 E!

Also:
Run for Your Life, The Danny Thomas Hour, Sanford and Son, Insight, Divorce Court, Harry O, Adam's Girls, What's Happening Now! and *Bryant Gumbel's Real Sports.*

Salli Sachse

Her name may not be familiar, but to fans of American International Pictures' series of beach movies her face is easily recognizable. With her waist-long honey brown hair and adorable smile, actress Salli Sachse appeared in every beach film (perhaps the most popular sixties drive-in movie) from *Muscle Beach Party* (1964) through *How to Stuff a Wild Bikini* (1966) and everything else in between including *Pajama Party* (1964) and *Dr. Goldfoot and the Bikini Machine* (1965). During the early sixties, the beach movies were extremely popular carefree fantasies epitomizing the clean wholesome fun of surfing and the Southern California lifestyle, aimed directly at the teen market. AIP varied the formula for each subsequent film by involving the surfer set in various situations (i.e. drag racing, skiing, sky diving, treasure hunting, etc.). Bickering lovebirds Frankie Avalon and Annette Funicello as Frankie and Dee Dee usually held center stage, surrounded by a zany cast of regulars including John Ashley, Jody McCrea, bungling motorcycle leader Harvey Lembeck, singer Donna Loren and Swedish bombshell Bobbi Shaw, plus a host of beach girls and surfer boys (Salli, Mary Hughes, Patti Chandler, Mike Nader, Ed Garner, etc.). When the beach films became passé during the turbulent mid-sixties, Salli graduated to biker films (*The Wild Angels, Devil's Angels*) and to her most famous role as the LSD freak-out girl in *The Trip* (1967).

Salli Sachse (pronounced Sox-see) was born Salli Rogers on June 25, in San Diego, California. She grew up in La Jolla frolicking on the shores of Windansea Beach ("I was a *real* beach girl!") and began modeling during high school. She had just married folk singer Pete Sachse and was working as a receptionist at the Bank of La Jolla when her friends Mike Dormer and Lee Teacher went to Hollywood to market their cartoon strip hero Hot Curl. With his shaggy hair, knobby knees and a can of beer in his hand, Hot Curl epitomized the thousands of young men who surfed the shores of Southern California. Dormer and Teacher eventually found their way to AIP, which was about to begin production on *Muscle Beach Party*, the follow-up to the 1963 hit *Beach Party*, starring Frankie Avalon and Annette Funicello. The film's pro-

A body-painted Salli Sachse as she appeared in Peter Fonda's LSD-induced fantasy in *The Trip* (AIP, 1967).

ducers Sam Arkoff and Jim Nicholson decided to use the cartoon character as a backdrop in a nightclub scene and asked the guys if they knew any beach girls or surfer boys. Did they ever! "About ten or fifteen of us piled into a couple of Woodies and drove up to Los Angeles," remembers Salli. "We met Arkoff and Nicholson at their offices. They asked us to line up in our bathing suits. They literally went right down the line pointing and saying, 'You. You. You.' When they were done choosing they told us, 'This is Jack Gilardi. He'll be your agent.' That's how it started."

Muscle Beach Party was Salli's first film and she wasn't cognizant of the ways of filmmaking: "I found it so confusing because we shot everything out of order. I thought, 'How is there going to be any continuity?'" *Muscle Beach Party* veered from the first film by having the surfers clash with Don Rickles' bodybuilders rather than Harvey Lembeck's motorcycle gang. The film opens as the surf gang heads for the shore singing Brian Wilson's boss song "Surfer's Holiday." Frankie and Annette are at their most appealing here and, along with Dale and his Del-Tones, Donna Loren and Little Stevie Wonder, perform some great Brian Wilson–penned tunes. During filming, director William Asher took a liking to Salli and her friend Linda Opie and dubbed them "the bookends." "Linda and I both had long brown hair," recalls Salli. "He liked us to wear our hair up in a kind of swirl or bun. While shooting he'd call, 'Bookends!' and frame the shot with us on each side." Asher, who helmed the five core beach films—*Beach Party, Muscle Beach Party, Bikini Beach, Beach Blanket Bingo* and *How to Stuff a Wild Bikini*—is described by Sachse as being "a lot of fun to work with because he had experience with actors and just loved directing. Always with a cigar in his mouth, he'd watch the scenes closely and loved having things happen between Frankie and Annette. He lived in Malibu and I think he was a surfer so he also was more enlightened to what was going on water-wise—he was beach smart, as we would say."

The success of *Beach Party* and *Muscle Beach Party* is no doubt helped by the great chemistry of Frankie and Annette, whose names became synonymous with beach movies. "Frankie and Annette were very easygoing and a pleasure to work with but they weren't real beach people," says Salli, chuckling. "Frankie was raised in Philadelphia so I don't think he ever saw a surfboard in his life! And Annette refused to wear a bikini. She would only wear a one-piece but I think that had something to do with her contract with Walt Disney. Annette was such a straight girl—a good Italian Catholic. Because we grew up on the beach, a lot of us thought we were so cool compared to Frankie and Annette. I remember that on one movie we were filming some beach scenes late in the afternoon. It was really chilly and we were fighting the light. Wrapped in terry cloth robes, a group of us huddled together to keep warm. Carl the prop man handed us a bottle of brandy. We were surprised when Annette took a couple of swigs. She got a bit tipsy and was clowning around. It was the only time I ever saw her let herself go wild."

Though the beach films were zany comedies, filming them was not all fun and games. The budgets for the films ranged from $500,000 to $1,000,000—not much for the major studios but a lot for an independent company like AIP. Shooting lasted for about three to four weeks so, because of the time constraints, life on the set wasn't always a beach. "There was a time to be very businesslike and there was a time to goof off," states Salli. "But we knew when the camera was running, you had to do your thing. There was a lot of pressure sometimes because we were working against the weather or the sun or the budget. A lot of us were squeezed into these tiny changing rooms. We'd have these long hours on the beach where we would be waiting and waiting for our shot and everybody had to be ready. John Ashley would sit with us girls and we'd joke and laugh. He paid great attention to details and would tell us if something—like our hair, for instance—was out of place. Yvonne Craig ate nothing but fudge and Coca-Cola between takes up in Sun Valley for *Ski Party*. I was amazed because she had the most beautiful white skin I had ever seen. And I remember that Donna Loren's father was always on the set. He was very over-protective of her and would even follow her to the bathroom! He was just so afraid that some guy was going to hit on her or something."

In late 1964, AIP released *Pajama Party*, which was a variation on the typical beach film shenanigans. Tommy Kirk stars as a Martian who crashes the beach party and falls for Annette. The film also stars Jody McCrea, Susan Hart (who went on to marry the boss, James Nicholson) and Frankie Avalon in a cameo. What stands out in *Pajama Party* are the elaborate production numbers choreographed by David Winters and Toni Basil. The scenes where the kids gyrate poolside to Annette's "It's That Kind of Day" and the girls go-go dancing at a fashion show are intense. However, not all the dance sequences in this or the other films were choreographed, according to Salli. "The scenes where we would be dancing on the beach or at a nightclub weren't choreographed. The music would go on and we'd just do our own thing. Sometimes if there was dialogue to record, there would be no music to dance to. The music was added back later in the editing process. It was hard because you had to pretend you were having a good time dancing but there was no beat to follow. I felt very silly. Those scenes also got to me after awhile because people would push or bump you out of the way to get their face in the camera. You really had to stand your ground."

(*Left to right*) Sachse, Mary Hughes, Annette Funicello, Marianne Gaba and Sue Hamilton in *How to Stuff a Wild Bikini* (AIP, 1965).

Pajama Party and *Bikini Beach* (1964) brought back bungling leather-clad motorcycle leader Harvey Lembeck as Erich Von Zipper from *Beach Party* to antagonize the beach crowd. His gang of Rats and Mice were always making trouble for those "surfer bums." "Harvey was a lot of fun with an incredible sense of humor," recalls Salli. "He did a lot of pratfalls in the films so they would work with him regarding the breakaway walls and doors. He was very professional in that respect." Though the actors who portrayed gang members and surfers were all on the set together, there was not much interaction because "a lot of Harvey's gang members were from his acting classes while the rest of us were from the beaches of California. His entourage loved him. They were very bonded and we were very bonded."

One of the reasons the AIP beach films were so popular for a time was because each film featured a crop of young actors as well as seasoned veterans. Among the "oldsters" to appear in these films were Bob Cummings, Dorothy Malone, Don Rickles, Buster Keaton, Paul Lynde, Morey Amsterdam and Buddy Hacket. AIP knew they had crossover appeal, which would help bring in an older audience as well as teenagers. Salli has fleeting memories of these actors and remembers that "Don Rickles kept the set

Sachse in a publicity photo from *Devil's Angels* (AIP, 1967).

in stitches. He was so funny. In *Muscle Beach Party* and *Beach Blanket Bingo*, Don had these nightclub set monologues which I believe weren't scripted. They just let him ad lib and do his own thing. Before filming, he'd warm up and he would be hysterical. He especially loved picking on Frankie and Annette. We would be in tears half the day listening to him. The makeup men kept coming around daubing our faces. Don comes across very gruff but he has a warm, big heart. I didn't work with Buster Keaton much but he was kind of grouchy. Bobbi Shaw became a friend to him because they had a lot of scenes together."

Around this time, Salli was signed to a contract with AIP and entered their *Starburst of Youth* Program. She took acting classes and went on tour to promote AIP's films by appearing on local talk shows, attending premieres and hosting luncheons. "Fans would meet us at the airfields with banners saying, 'Welcome *Beach Party* Stars.' They treated us like big movie stars. It made you feel like a million bucks!" Though she worked exclusively for AIP, Salli didn't have much contact with the company's founders. "Sam Arkoff and Jim Nicholson weren't very accessible," says Salli. "They would only come around occasionally to the set. Arkoff was the more aggressive one while Nicholson was more introspective. 'Deke' Heyward [an AIP writer-producer] was accessible. He would talk with us whereas Arkoff and Nicholson did not. It didn't really bother me because they had a lot of things to worry about but it was nice that Deke took the time to get to know us." As a contract player, Salli appeared in the remaining beach films as well as *Sergeant Deadhead*, *Ski Party*, *Dr. Goldfoot and the Bikini Machine*, *Fireball 500* and *The Ghost in the Invisible Bikini*, the last official beach movie.

In 1966, Salli turned in her bikini for leather pants in *The Wild Angels* starring Peter Fonda and Nancy Sinatra. ("I was one of the last people left under contract at AIP. Not many of us made the transition from beach films to biker flicks.") This Roger Corman–directed film about the fictitious exploits of the Hell's Angels motorcycle gang became such a hit that it began the biker flick genre that lasted into the early seventies. Sachse has a small role as a biker chick in *The Wild Angels* and recalls that "Nancy Sinatra was a lot of fun—very friendly and easy to talk with. And Peter was just great. We had several mutual friends so we had fun hanging out off-camera. Peter was really into music. He couldn't wait until the Beatles' *Revolver* album came out. We went to the music store and played it, trying to hear any hidden messages. He also introduced me to David Crosby when we were on tour promoting the film in New York. David and I became very close a couple of years later."

In 1967, Salli journeyed to Hong Kong along with Frankie Avalon and Patti Chandler to appear in *The Million Eyes of Su-Muru*. Shot at the Shaw Brothers Studio, the film features Avalon and George Nader as American agents trying to thwart Shirley Eaton (as the sadistic Su-Muru) and her army of women from taking over the world. Salli's time in Hong Kong was cut short when she received notice that her husband had been tragically killed in a plane crash. After only four days of shooting, she left to return to the States and never finished filming all her scenes. "This was a real marker in my life," says Salli. "I was struggling emotionally because I felt that my heart had been ripped out. After Pete's funeral, I moved back to Los Angeles and tried to keep busy. The studio was really great and kept me under contract. I did *Thunder Alley*, *Devil's Angels*, *The Trip* and *Wild in the Streets* after I was widowed. This was the beginning of a big change in my life—the fairy tale sort of ruptured and blew up. I felt very sad for a long, long time. I had to do a lot to keep my head above water and to make myself feel good."

Devil's Angels (1967) features Salli (along with Beverly Adams, Wally Campo, Nai Bonet and Marc Cavell) as part of a motorcycle gang led by John Cassavetes, whom Salli describes as being "a wild man. At night he just liked to go crazy—drinking, partying, and carrying on till all hours. But on the set he was always professional and acting with him was fun because he brought an artistic, manic energy to the role." While heading for a West Coast haven for renegade motorcycle gangs, the biker club stops in a small town and is joined by local girl Mimsy Farmer. When she suspects the gang plans to rape her, she flees—setting the stage for a biker versus townspeople showdown. Salli is a gas as a tough-talking, hog-straddling biker chick. As she stands with a beer in her hand and watches with amused detachment while the gang terrorizes Farmer, her wholesome beach persona is long forgotten. "The actors in *The Wild Angels* and *Devil's Angels* also made me feel a bit insecure," remarks Sachse. "They came from a more professional background and had appeared in some good movies. Mimsy Farmer was very talented and pleasant to work with. And Beverly Adams and I shared a trailer. This was soon after she met Vidal Sassoon and she was still living at home with her parents. She was in love and always talking about Sassoon. She met him in London while doing a movie. Vidal cut her hair really short and began a new fad. Soon lots of actresses in Hollywood [including Mia Farrow, Jane Fonda, Joey Heatherton, Carol Lynley, etc.] were getting the Sassoon cut."

The role that brought Salli international notoriety was as the LSD freak-out girl in *The Trip* (1967). Directed by Roger Corman, *The Trip* follows a TV commercial director (Peter Fonda) who takes an LSD trip to grasp something from his inner nature as a way to deal with his problematic personal life. Also appearing are Bruce Dern as Fonda's LSD guru, Dennis Hopper as a drug supplier and Susan Strasberg as Fonda's estranged wife. Sachse plays a sexy blonde named Glenn who meets Fonda a few hours before his trip. While under the influence of LSD, Fonda imagines Salli with a painted face and dressed in a wild bikini as she accompanies him on his psychedelic journey. He experiences visions of strobe lights, witches, hooded riders, a torture chamber, sex and death. "I never had any problems with Roger but Peter Fonda did," recalls Salli. "Peter was livid with Roger for making changes to the screenplay, which was written by Jack Nicholson. I don't actually know what was cut because I didn't see the original script. But I do know that Peter was very upset about it. He had agreed to do *The Trip* as it was originally written. He was always raving about all the incredible things that were in the first script. From what I remember, I don't think Corman got the points Nicholson was trying to make so he cut them."

The Trip received criticism from the mainstream press for not taking a stand against drug use. But Corman wanted to portray what he thought an LSD trip would be like. According to Salli, "Roger went into a clinical setting to take LSD so he would know what it was all about. That impressed me. Roger was a very linear director—everything went from A to B to C. He was very serious. You didn't goof off or kick back while working with him. You had to be very on-task. It was a stricter atmosphere than I was used to. Roger felt that there had to be a distinction between Susan Strasberg's character and mine so he wanted me to appear as a blonde. I didn't want to bleach my entire hair blonde because it was really long—just past my waist—and I didn't want to damage it. What I did was just streak the front. I'd go on the set and Roger Corman would look at it and say,

An intent Salli Sachse (*center*) as a biker chick in *Devil's Angels* (AIP, 1967).

'No, you need some more blonde!' The hairdresser would get some blonde spray out and spritz the back. I tried everything so as not to have to bleach all my hair because I had visions of it all falling out after the shoot."

Because of its subject matter, there were rumors swirling that real drug use was taking place during filming. According to Salli, "*The Trip* didn't deserve all the bad press it received. There was no drug use going on during filming—it was strictly professional. Maybe after hours, but I couldn't talk for anybody else. I wasn't into drugs so I know I didn't do any. I do believe though that a few people—Peter Fonda and Dennis Hopper—had experienced taking LSD." As for working with the cast, Salli says, laughing, "Dennis played the bad boy on camera and was a *real* bad boy off-camera. Bruce Dern used to literally run in from Malibu, do his scenes and then run home as part of his training for the Olympics. Peter was great to work with and always professional even though he was upset about the script changes. We had two nude lovemaking scenes together that were shot in this house on the beach in Malibu. Peter made it very comfortable for me because I was embarrassed. I had never been nude on-camera before. I grew up real fast! They gave me some pasties so I wouldn't be *quite* so nude. You just take off your robe, get into bed and do the scene. Thankfully it was a

Peter Fonda as a TV director talks about the wonders of LSD with hippie chick Sachse in *The Trip* (AIP, 1967).

closed set with a minimal crew and everybody was very understanding and professional." People wonder: When doing nude love scenes, do actors get aroused? Recalling his scenes with the curvaceous Salli in his autobiography *Don't Tell Dad*, Peter Fonda truthfully addressed this issue: "At one point, the camera was panning up and down our bodies, while Salli Sachse lay on top of me. The view was gorgeous and Mister Happy came to full attention just as that part of our bodies entered the frame. Salli went rigid, trapping Mister Happy."

Salli's last film appearance was as a hippie mother in *Wild in the Streets* (1968) starring Christopher Jones (whom she describes as being "a bit odd"). Needing a change, she continued modeling and became part of Crosby, Stills, Nash and Young's entourage, touring with the band for two years as their personal photographer. Her photos appeared in *Rolling Stone Magazine* and on the group's album covers. "I moved up to Marin County and became a sort of housemother to the guys," recalls Salli. "It was very communal living. The Grateful Dead lived around the block and they would come over and hang out a lot. I loved to cook so they would pass my food around along with some *other* things they were passing around. The one particular thing I remember was when I accompanied them to Altamont. We flew in by helicopter. The guys knew something was not quite right when they saw the Hell's Angels being used as bouncers in front of the stage. They performed their set and told me we were leaving right away. They had another gig down at UCLA anyway so we took right off and didn't stay to see the Rolling Stones. The next day we heard about all the violence and a guy being killed."

Salli spent the seventies living the life of an artist in Europe. Today Salli resides in La Jolla again and is getting reacquainted with the white sands of Windansea Beach. Armed with a Bachelor of Arts degree in fine arts and a Master's Degree in psychology, Salli is in the process of becoming a licensed psychotherapist but still finds time to act in television commercials. As you can see, she has left the beach party far behind.

But not too far behind. "We've had two beach party reunions," Salli says cheerily. "They've been so much fun. Patti Chandler is happily married and lives in Arizona; Mary Hughes is a fitness instructor in Malibu; Bobbi Shaw teaches acting to children in Hollywood; and Mike Nader stars on *All My Children*. A great part of doing the beach films was that everybody knew each other so it was like an exclusive club. There was a lot of warm feeling on the set and it shows on the screen. I think that's why these movies are so loved."

FILM APPEARANCES

1964   **Muscle Beach Party** (AIP) d. William Asher.
         Bikini Beach (AIP) d. William Asher.
1965   **Beach Blanket Bingo** (AIP) d. William Asher.
         Ski Party (AIP) d. Alan Rafkin.
         How to Stuff a Wild Bikini (AIP) d. William Asher.
         Sergeant Deadhead (AIP) d. Norman Taurog.
         Dr. Goldfoot and the Bikini Machine (AIP) d. Norman Taurog.
1966   **The Ghost in the Invisible Bikini** (AIP) d. Don Weis.
         Fireball 500 (AIP) d. William Asher.
         The Wild Angels (AIP) d. Roger Corman.
1967   **Thunder Alley** (AIP) d. Richard Rush.
         Devil's Angels (AIP) d. Daniel Haller.
         The Million Eyes of Su-Muru (AIP) d. Lindsay Shonteff.
         The Trip (AIP) d. Roger Corman.

Salli Sachse, ca. 2000 (courtesy of Salli Sachse).

1968   **Wild in the Streets** (AIP) d. Barry Shear.

TELEVISION APPEARANCES

The Wild Weird World of Dr. Goldfoot (special) 11/18/65 ABC.
Mannix "The Girl Who Came In from the Tide" 2/1/69 CBS.

Also:
The Steve Allen Show and *The Dating Game*.

Deanna Lund

In 1969, adolescent boys could be found sitting in front of the television on Sunday nights enthralled by the sci-fi series *Land of the Giants*. Created by Irwin Allen, the show focused on seven people stranded on a planet identical to Earth except everything is 12 times bigger. Though the special effects were impressive, most boys were captivated by the antics of red-haired, mini-skirted actress Deanna Lund as intergalactic castaway Valerie Scott. Lund was perhaps every young teenage boy's first crush at that time. During the course of the series, Deanna's character is menaced by cats, imprisoned in a dollhouse, cloned, prodded by scientists, carried off by an ape and even used as a human pawn on a giant's chessboard. Of all the actresses who toiled in sixties sci-fi television, Lund was arguably the only one who portrayed more than a one-dimensional character. She was able to bring real strength to her role, as Valerie evolved from selfish party gal to likable team player. Lund made the transition beautifully, giving skilled performances. By the time she landed *Land of the Giants* she had honed her craft on film in the spy spoofs *Dr. Goldfoot and the Bikini Machine* and *Dimension 5* and in the beach film *Out of Sight*. But her most memorable movie role was as a lesbian stripper in *Tony Rome* with Frank Sinatra.

Before being marooned on the *Land of the Giants*, Deanna Lund was a busy young actress. She was born on May 30 in Oak Park, Illinois. Soon after, her parents relocated Deanna and her two sisters to Daytona Beach, Florida. Being relatively shy, she spent most of her childhood competing in rodeos with her horse. When Lund entered college, her father suggested she take a drama class to overcome her bashfulness. "My dad created a monster," remarks Deanna, laughing. "I loved acting, especially on the stage." Deanna appeared in college and local theater productions of *Bus Stop*, *The Crucible* and *A Streetcar Named Desire*. ("I loved doing *Bus Stop* and *The Crucible* on stage. It was such a dichotomy because one was a bad girl and the other was sweet and innocent.") She was spotted by a talent scout and offered a contract from Columbia Pictures but turned it down because "my dad said no." A compliant Deanna did as she was told but

A sexy Deanna Lund in a publicity shot from the ABC-TV series *Batman*.

perhaps in rebellion she married a rider from the rodeo. Their four-year marriage produced two children, Randy and Kim. Forced to leave Daytona because of the machinations of her ex-husband, Deanna moved to Miami with her two children. She supported her family by modeling and as a weather girl (at $10 a show) on a local TV station.

Deanna made her film debut as a waitress disguised as a boy in the obscure comedy *Once Upon a Coffeehouse* (1965). While doing the weather one night, an Italian movie producer called the station because he wanted to use Lund in his new movie. Though she at first thought he was "a psycho," he was legit and cast her as a blonde thrill-seeker who hooks up with Ugo Tognazzi in the Italian comedy *Run for Your Wife* (1965) co-starring Juliet Prowse. "This was such an insane production," exclaims Deanna. "No one spoke English except Gray Frederickson (who went on to become the co-producer of the *Godfather* films). But somehow you know how to communicate. The movie was a sort of improv type of film because they were going to dub it into Italian or English anyway. Italians don't work the same as Americans. They do much more physical stuff and I remember thinking, 'Gee, I didn't know acting was so dangerous.' I was doing a car scene with Ugo Tognazzi roaring down the beach at a very high speed, fish-tailing all over the place. I don't even remember now why we were doing all that. In another scene he had me driving at reckless speeds and taking out my pretend contact lenses, which I don't wear but he had me faking it. And I had no idea why that was done."

Johnny Tiger (1966) starring Robert Taylor was Lund's third film lensed in Florida. She played the slutty girlfriend of half-breed Seminole Chad Everett ("We became very good friends and still are to this day") who is trying to figure out his place in the modern world. Taylor portrayed a doctor who tries to help Everett. Recalling Taylor, Lund recalls that "he was very cold and grouchy and wouldn't sign autographs for fans when they would approach him. I believe he also was very ill. His wife was very protective of him, as she should have been. He died shortly after completing the film." Overall, Lund was disappointed with this film because her big dramatic scenes were cut from the script. "I had a fight with the director Paul Wendkos before we ever started shooting," says Deanna. "The producer hired me in spite of Wendkos because he felt I should do the role. They needed to save time, so the director cut my scenes. Usually they cut it after you film them but I don't know if funds were short or if it was personal, which I suspected at that time. It was too bad because it was the reason I did the movie. That was disheartening but that happens."

Hollywood took notice of Deanna in these films and beckoned a second time.

Chad Everett pours his heart out to bar girl Deanna Lund in *Johnny Tiger* (Universal, 1966).

This time Deanna jumped at the chance. Unfortunately, the agent who promised her fame and fortune wanted something in return. He got a knuckle sandwich instead. Dismayed, Lund was about to return to Florida when she had a chance meeting with agent Max Arnow, the former talent scout who had wanted to sign her to a contract a few years before. Knowing Deanna had a family to support, he got her bit parts in a number of films (including two with Elvis Presley). "I would do an Elvis Presley movie in the morning and in the afternoon do another film," Deanna recalls. "This was called bicycling and not what you were supposed to do according to SAG. But I somehow got around it. I had met Elvis years earlier in Daytona before he was really famous. I was really young and he asked me out on a date. He came over to the house to talk with my dad. My father took one look at Elvis with his long sideburns and said, 'No way!' When I worked with Elvis on the films—*after* I had kids—there wasn't much interest left on his part." [*Laughs*]

Bigger roles followed for Deanna. In the sci-fi quickie *Dimension 5* (1966) starring Jeffrey Hunter and France Nuyen, Lund played a secretary and in the spy-beach spoof *Out of Sight* (1966) she was Tuff Bod, an assassin from F.L.U.S.H. sent to kill agent Jonathan Daly. ("This was fun and I didn't have to wear a bikini!") *Dr. Goldfoot and the Bikini Machine* (1965) featured Deanna as part of an army of bikini-clad robots. "Vincent Price, Frankie Avalon and Susan Hart were all very nice and fun to work with," Deanna says. "However, I wasn't very happy standing around in a gold bikini for six weeks. But I needed the money." Lund began getting steady work on television and could be seen in episodes of *The Loner* ("My favorite guest stint"), *Batman*, *Captain Nice* and *The Bob Hope Chrysler Theatre*.

By 1966, Deanna had become disenchanted with Hollywood and wanted to return East. Knowing that the new Frank Sinatra movie titled *Tony Rome* (1967) was to be lensed in Florida, she told her agent to get her an audition. Though she wanted the ingenue role (Sue Lyon got the part), she was cast in the role of lesbian stripper Georgia McKay. She begrudgingly took the part because "I needed the money to fly my kids back to Daytona." Sinatra plays a hard-boiled detective hired by a millionaire (Simon Oakland) to investigate the odd behavior of his daughter (Lyon), who keeps disappearing and turning up drunk. Sinatra's search leads him to the seedy side of Miami where he meets tough stripper (Lund) and her older, blowsy lover (Joan Shawlee). As Sinatra is questioning the curvaceous Lund in her trailer, she strips down to her bra and panties. "I was very intimidated about working with Sinatra," says Deanna. "The hair and makeup people told me he was one take. If you blew it, he'd leave. So that added even more pressure. But funnily enough, Sinatra blew the take. Off-screen, Sinatra was very friendly. When we finished the scene, he came over and put my robe around me and escorted me back to my chair. He was just terrific." After seeing the film in previews, Lund asked the producers to remove her name from the credits because she was embarrassed. Though they obliged, they used her image in the film's poster. And ironically enough, her good notices for this role led to her starring in *Land of the Giants*.

When ABC decided to use *Land of the Giants* as a fall series instead of a mid-season replacement, production of the show was halted. With time to kill before filming resumed, Deanna auditioned and

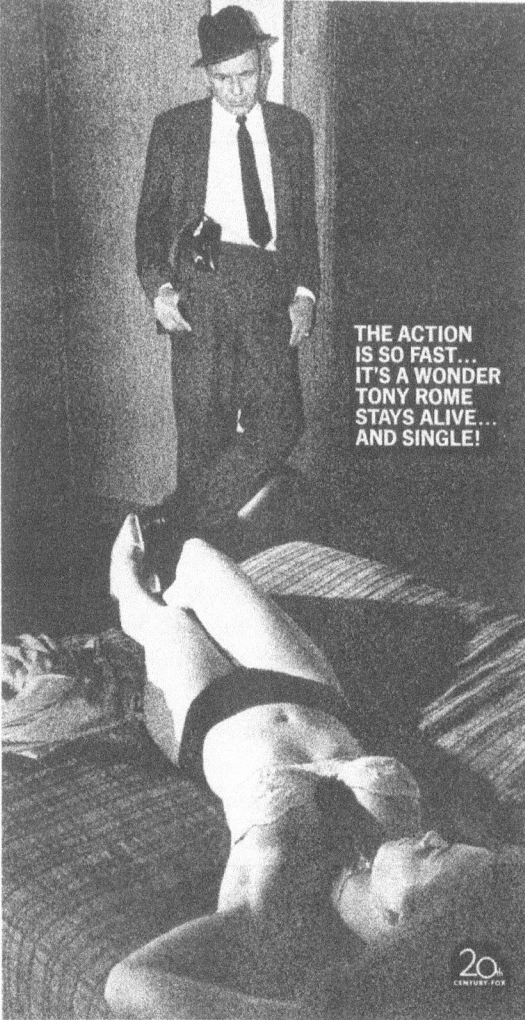

Poster art from *Tony Rome* (20th Century–Fox, 1967). Though the producers honored Lund's request to remove her name from the credits, it didn't stop them from using her image on the film's poster.

won the role of Mia Farrow's friend in *Rosemary's Baby* (1968) but turned it down to her regret. "I had read for Roman Polanski with John Cassavetes and Roman told me right on the spot that the part was mine," says Deanna. "Even though Roman promised he'd finish with me in time for *Giants*, Irwin didn't trust him and said no. My first obligation was with Irwin so I couldn't do it. I really didn't fight for it—I wimped out. Roman somehow got my home phone number and just read me the riot act. It was stupid on my part for passing on it. [Victoria Vetri took the part.] I should have fought harder but I didn't."

Land of the Giants was the fourth series from Irwin Allen, whose name became synonymous with TV fantasy and science fiction. After scoring on the big screen with such fantasy epics as *The Lost World* (1960) and *Voyage to the Bottom of the Sea* (1961), Allen turned his attention to the small screen. Twentieth Century–Fox asked him to create a weekly series based on *Voyage*. Starring Richard Basehart and David Hedison, it premiered to mixed reviews and high ratings. Allen then went on to create *Lost in Space* (sort of a Swiss Family Robinson in outer space) and *The Time Tunnel* (Allen's only misfire, about two men who travel through time) before *Land of the Giants*, whose story idea supposedly came to him in a dream. After seeing Lund in an episode of *Batman* and the rushes of *Tony Rome*, Allen offered the role of spoiled jet setter Valerie to a skeptical Deanna without even meeting her. "I just signed with a new agent named Maury Calder and didn't believe him when he told me I had this part," says Deanna. "Being in Hollywood for awhile, I knew you had to audition and screen test before you get a role. Maury said, 'Deanna, I swear it's true.' I replied, 'Don't jive me,

Maury!' I finally believed him but everybody told me not to do television—especially science fiction. When I was offered the series, I had to do it for financial reasons. I had two little children to raise."

Co-starring with Deanna Lund on *Land of the Giants* were Gary Conway (as Captain Steve Burton), Don Matheson (as tycoon Mark Wilson), Don Marshall (as co-pilot Dan Erickson), Heather Young (as stewardess Betty Hamilton), Stefan Arngrim (as orphan Barry Lockridge) and Kurt Kaszner (as resident schemer Col. Alexander Fitzhugh). Though the series premiered in the fall of 1969, the pilot was produced almost a year before. ABC was so impressed that instead of using it as a mid-season replacement, they decided to wait for the new fall season. The first episode, titled "The Crash" (9/22/68), set the story of how three crew members and four passengers on a suborbital flight from New York to London in 1983 pass through an electrical storm and crash on a planet of giants. Amid the gargantuan flora and fauna, the "little people" (as they were referred to) are menaced by a cat, a giant spider and a scientist who captures Steve and Valerie. The pilot received Emmy nominations for photography and special effects. It garnered huge ratings—especially among younger audiences. And at $250,000 per episode, *Land of the Giants* was the most costly series on the air. Giant props such as a slice of bread made from foam rubber, a six-foot pencil, gigantic leaves and a nine-foot revolver were expertly but expensively created. "*Land of the Giants* was not an actor's show," remarks Deanna. "We were always being upstaged by the visual effects. At the time I was embarrassed by the series because it wasn't Chekhov, it was *Land of the Giants*! I thought then, 'My God, is this what I studied acting for?'

Lund poses (reluctantly) in a bikini to promote her TV series *Land of the Giants*.

But I recently have seen some of them on the Sci-Fi Channel. Some episodes I haven't seen in 30 years. I'm impressed with how good they are. The effects are so well done. And, imagine, none of this is computer generated! It amazes me how fantastic the show is but I did wish that the character relationships were developed more fully." The critics agreed. *Variety* commented that "the series' strong suit is its special effects." *Newsday* said, "Visually, this science fiction series is a gas." And Cleveland Amory in *TV Guide* wrote, "If you're under 11, you're bound to enjoy this show." And did they ever! A young audience (mostly boys) propelled the series into the top 25. Soon there were *Land of the Giants* lunchboxes, board games, model kits and Colorforms.

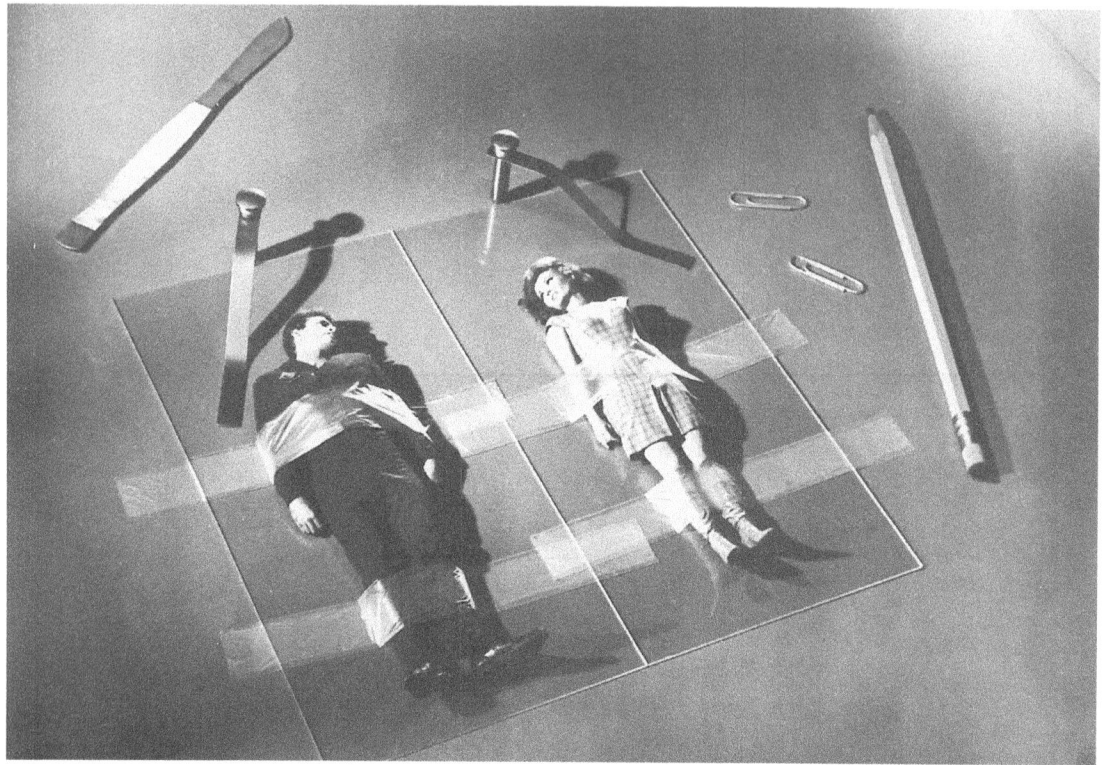

Lund and Gary Conway are taped onto a giant's examining table in the premiere episode of ABC-TV's *Land of the Giants* in 1968.

The premise of each episode of *Land of the Giants* had the Earthlings trying in some way to find a way to return home while being hunted by the giants. It was reminiscent of the old Saturday morning serials. "*Land of the Giants* was a sort of child-like fantasy—even working on it," says Lund. "Not that it wasn't hard work—it was long hours and it wasn't all fun and games. It was actually pretty intense with a lot of stunt work and a lot of repeating the same thing. We would shoot some scenes three times and everything had to be exactly the same for each. Not only did I have to worry about learning the dialogue but my costumes and hair had to match perfectly. Irwin Allen hated that we changed clothes. It was much more economical if we wore the same thing because he could intercut any of the shows if he was short screen time and not worry about matching up the wardrobe. Paul Zastupnevich was the costume designer and he was great! His costumes were a bit futuristic yet not too outlandish to be contemporary. He'd get these boots and paint them to match the plaid skirts we were wearing. Of course, Paul couldn't do just a few. He had to do tons of them because they were trashed so quickly."

As for Irwin Allen, who was known for being a taskmaster, Deanna says, "Irwin was a larger than life character. He directed the pilot and was very meticulous with details. Later he kept a very close tab on all the show's directors. I respected that. *Land of the Giants* was his baby. He created it. I think any kind of a good manager is going to see that the ship is running his way. I didn't find fault with it—I didn't *always* like it—but as an actress

Land of the Giants cast shot circa 1969: (*clockwise from top left*) Stefan Arngrim, Kurt Kaszner, Deanna Lund, Gary Conway and Don Matheson.

and a professional I had to respect his input and caring. I'd rather have someone who cares than didn't care but sometimes it was a pain in the butt. I'm a natural blonde and every time we had a hiatus I would add a little blonde streak to my hair. I would casually go back to work and Irwin would nail me every time. He'd yell, '*I bought Rita Hayworth red and Rita Hayworth red you're going to be!*'"

During the run of the show, the Earthlings found themselves in some bizarre situations. Deanna was featured prominently in a number of them. Unlike *Lost in Space*, which became "the Will and Dr. Smith show," Irwin wanted the cast of *Land of the Giants* to be featured evenly throughout. In "Deadly Pawn" Lund is a human pawn on a giant's chessboard. She is fancily dressed and placed in a giant music box in "Collector's Item" and is duplicated and sent back to the spaceship to capture the others in "The Clones." "I was exhausted doing this episode because I had to run around this drain so many times chasing the other Valerie," says Deanna with a laugh. "I lost so much weight doing this." In "Chamber of Fear," Deanna and co-star Don Matheson were almost seriously hurt when Deanna got stuck in the gears of a giant robot. When Matheson fell trying to free her, Lund wasn't able to reach the lever to stop the grinding gears. When the crew realized they weren't acting but in trouble, they came to their rescue.

As the series progressed, Deanna's haughty rich girl softened (much to her chagrin) "because it was more interesting if I stayed kind of witchy. But Irwin wanted me more likable. Heather Young's character of Betty was gone a lot because Heather was pregnant a lot." Despite Lund's disappointment, the writers were able to make the progression of her character believable, which was no doubt helped by the acting skills of Lund. And her character was constantly tempted by the rascal Fitzhugh to join him in his duplicitous schemes. "Kurt Kaszner and I had a great rapport, on screen and off," says Deanna. "We really liked each other. He was so hilarious. The funniest stuff was never on camera. We'd just be laughing hysterically. In the "Graveyard of Fools" episode our characters were trapped in quicksand and Kurt was goosing me under this guck we were in. I remember yelling, 'Who do you have to sleep with to get out of this show?!' The two of us would tease the rest of the cast unmercifully. They were good sports and fun to work with."

As for her other co-stars, Deanna comments, "Gary Conway was a perfectionist. He would always stand up to Irwin Allen if he felt something wasn't being done right. Don Marshall was very solemn and intense. He was one of the first black actors to be a regular on a primetime series and took his position seriously. Heather Young was wonderful and we are still in contact to this day. And Don Matheson was a good friend to me on the show. Everybody adored him. He was just so nice to everyone. We became romantically involved and were married after the series was cancelled." A number of well-known actors (Warren Oates, Jack Albertson, Yvonne Craig, Bruce Dern, Diane McBain, Francine York, etc.) guest-starred as giants, but the regular cast never got to work with them. Usually when the little people interacted with these actors' characters they would be talking up to the klieg lights while the actors portraying giants would be talking down to some object on a table or the floor. The scenes were then edited together. "The actors playing giants usually worked on different days and on a different sound stage," recalls Deanna.

After the end of the second season, Deanna and Don Matheson announced their engagement. Ever the publicity mongrel, Irwin wanted their characters to be married on the show as well. "He said if we agreed he'd pay for our honeymoon anywhere we wanted to go," remembers Deanna. "So we said, 'Hmmm!' But we were cancelled because the show was too expensive to mount. It was too bad because I think another season would have been really fun and interesting. If our characters had a relationship, it would have been a first for an Irwin Allen series. It might have taken it into a whole different direction and brought in more of an audience. I probably would have also fought to make my character go the other way some more and be witchier."

Though *Land of the Giants* was cancelled in the fall of 1970, the show's popularity made Deanna one of the most liked and sought-after actresses of the seventies. She remained very active on the big and small screens. Lund was a regular panelist and co-producer on the game show *Stump the Stars* for one season. She also did guest shots on such TV shows as *Love, American Style* ("I remember getting clobbered with a club as I played a cave girl who invented the first kiss"), *The Waltons*, *The Incredible Hulk* and *Remington Steele*. She also had a recurring role on the soap *General Hospital* (as bad girl Peggy Lowell). On the big screen she had a small role in *Hustle* (1975) and a bigger role in *Stick* (1984), from a story by Elmore Leonard, starring fellow Floridian Burt Reynolds. "I had a great part in *Stick* as the philandering wife of millionaire George Segal," remarks Deanna. "She sleeps with everyone including Reynolds' character. But most of my scenes were cut." This was due to studio pressure on director Reynolds to make his character of an ex-con avenging the death of his buddy in the drug underworld of Miami more likable. Lund's part was originally the second female lead (after Candice Bergen as Segal's financial advisor who become romantically involved with Reynolds) but after re-shoots and re-edits she doesn't have much screen time left. When asked what she thought of Reynolds, Lund replies, "No comment."

In 1981, Deanna, looking absolutely radiant, landed the role of Jerry Lewis' love interest in his comeback film, *Hardly Working*. Lewis marvelously captured all of Deanna's beauty and playfulness in his film. Lewis co-wrote, directed and starred as an unemployed circus clown who cannot hold a job. Lund plays a divorcée he first meets at a gas station, where he nearly destroys her car. "Jerry didn't tell me that he was really going to blow up the gas station," says Deanna. "And in the scene I absolutely lost it. I started giggling and then laughing and just couldn't stop. He just kept shooting. I don't remember how much of it he left in the film. He was always pulling pranks and I should have expected it. There was another scene—he never tells you what he's going to do—when we're sitting at a restaurant and he's holding up his menu. He peered around it and he has this big glass sticking out of his mouth.

"Jerry was just lovely to work with," continues Lund. "But to be honest, it was a little confusing. Because he wore so many hats on *Hardly Working*—actor, director and co-writer—it was hard for me to get my character in tune with the right person. First you're listening to Jerry the intellectual analyzing the scene and speaking with the cameraman and the rest of the crew. And then all of a sudden he's this lunatic. It was quite an experience. I think it is very difficult for an actor

A cover of the quarterly Deanna Lund fan newsletter *DeannaGram* (courtesy of Fred Eichelman).

to direct himself. I know it's done all the time and sometimes extremely successfully but it's hard. Jerry's health also wasn't very good at the time."

Today Deanna has expanded her interests beyond acting. Though she still appears in films, mostly of the direct-to-video kind (*Witch Story*, *Elves*, *Transylvania Twist* and *Roots of Evil*), Deanna now concentrates on conducting acting workshops in Los Angeles and at the Rising Star conventions. After being brutally attacked by two thugs outside her home in the late eighties ("One guy put his knife in my mouth and ripped my whole mouth open—it was very traumatizing for me and my daughter who found me all cut up"), Deanna founded Victims of Violence No More to help deal with her pain as well as to help other women victimized by abuse. And on a happier note, Deanna has her own homepage on the web and one of the most organized and vocal fan clubs (Friends of Deanna Lund) of any film or TV star. Started by Fred R. Eichelman, it produces the quarterly *DeannaGram* newsletter highlighting Deanna's appearances at conventions around the country. Actually, Friends of Deanna Lund is more of a support organization than fan club and helps promotes Lund's career as well as the charities she endorses. They also campaign regularly for a *Land of the Giants* reunion movie, which is long overdue. "I love meeting the fans at conventions," remarks Deanna. "*Land of the Giants* is probably more popular now than it was back then. Personally, doing *Land of the Giants* was wonderful for me. I got a husband and a beautiful daughter named Michelle out of it. Career-wise, it was not a good move for any of us. It wasn't an actor's show." Even so, Deanna has worked consistently to this day. When asked why, when a number of her contemporaries haven't, she replies with a chuckle, "I don't know. Maybe because I'm still alive?"

FILM APPEARANCES

1965 **Once Upon a Coffeehouse** (Fred Burney Prod.) d. Shepherd Traube.
Una Moglie Americana/Run for Your Wife (Italy/France, Allied Artists) d. Gian Luigi Polidoro.
Dr. Goldfoot and the Bikini Machine (AIP) d. Norman Taurog.
1966 **The Oscar** (Embassy) [uncredited bit] d. Russell Rouse.
Johnny Tiger (Universal) d. Paul Wendkos.
Out of Sight (Universal) d. Lennie Weinrib.
Paradise, Hawaiian Style (Paramount) [uncredited bit] d. Michael Moore.
Dimension 5 (Feature Film Corp. of America) d. Franklin Adreon.
Spinout (MGM) [uncredited bit] d. Norman Taurog.
Sting of Death (Thunderbird International) d. William Grefe.
The Swinger (Paramount) [uncredited bit] d. George Sidney.
1967 **Tony Rome** (20th Century–Fox) d. Gordon Douglas.
1968 **Panic in the City** (Commonwealth United) d. Eddie Davis.
1973 **I Love a Mystery** (TV-movie) [completed in 1967] d. Leslie Stevens.
1975 **Hustle** (Paramount) d. Robert Aldrich.
1976 **Revenge for a Rape** (TV-movie) d. Timothy Galfas.
1979 **Hanging By a Thread** (TV-movie) d. Georg Fenady.
1981 **Hardly Working** (20th Century–Fox) d. Jerry Lewis.
1985 **Stick** (Universal) d. Burt Reynolds.
1986 **Hammerhead** d. Enzo G. Castellari.
1989 **Witch Story** (Italy, United Entertainment) d. Alessandro Capone.
Elves (Direct-to-video) d. Jeffrey Mandel.
Girl Talk/If We Knew Then (Frameline) d. Frank Harris.
1990 **The Girl I Want** d. David DeCoteau.
Transylvania Twist (Concorde) d. Jim Wynorski.
1991 **Red Wind** (Cable TV-movie) d. Alan Metzger.

1992 Roots of Evil/Naked Force (Direct-to-video) d. Gary Graver.
Obsession (Cable TV-movie) d. Jonathan Sanger.

Television Appearances

Florida Weather News Show [weather girl] 1962–1964 Local Network.
Amos Burke—Secret Agent "Peace, It's a Gasser" 11/03/65 ABC.
The Loner "The Trial in Paradise" 1/22/66 CBS.
The Smothers Brothers Show "We'd Rather Fight Than Switch" 2/11/66 CBS.
The Road West "Ashes and Tallows and One True Love" 10/24/66 NBC.
Laredo "The Sweet Gang" 11/4/66 NBC.
Batman "Batman's Anniversary" 2/8/67 ABC.
Batman "A Riddling Controversy" 2/9/67 ABC.
T.H.E. Cat "Design for Death" 2/10/67 NBC.
Captain Nice "May I Have the Last Dance?" 4/11/67 NBC.
Bob Hope Chrysler Theater "Deadlock" 5/17/67 NBC.
Land of the Giants [series regular as Valerie Scott] 9/22/68 to 9/6/70 ABC.
The Donald O'Connor Show [talk show guest] 1/30/69 Synd.
Allen Ludden's Gallery [talk show guest] 8/15/69 Synd.
The Hollywood Squares [celebrity panelist] 8/18 to 8/22/69 NBC.
Stump the Stars [regular celebrity panelist/co-producer] 8/18/69 to 9/20/70 Synd.
Life with Linkletter [talk show guest] 1/16/70 NBC.
The Andy Williams Show 1/24/70 NBC.
Love, American Style "Love and the First Kiss" 12/1/72 ABC.
The ABC Afternoon Special "Secret Life of T. K. Dearing" 4/23/75 ABC.
The Waltons "The Prophecy" 10/2/75 CBS.
General Hospital [series regular as Peggy Lowell] 1975 to 1976 ABC.
The Incredible Hulk "Of Guilt, Models and Murder" 3/24/78 CBS.
The Bob Hope Christmas Special 12/13/79 NBC.
One Life to Live [as Virginia Keyser] 1980–81 ABC.
The Judge "Daddy's Little Girl" 1986 Synd.
Superior Court "Case 87-3814" 1987 Synd.
The Fantasy Worlds of Irwin Allen (special) 9/30/95 Sci-Fi Chanel.

Also:

The Danny Kaye Show, The Red Skelton Show, The Mike Douglas Show, Search (pilot), *Remington Steele, The Mary Tyler Moore Show, Good Morning, New York* (co-host) and *Divorce Court.*

Karen Jensen

Unlike *Beach Party* star Annette Funicello, Karen Jensen actually looked like she grew up on the shores of Malibu. With her short-cropped flaxen hair, blue eyes and shapely figure, Jensen was exquisite in the beach film *Out of Sight*, director Lennie Weinrib's follow-up to *Beach Ball* and *Wild Wild Winter*. Though she left an indelible impression on fans of the genre, Karen quickly progressed to more mainstream films (*The Ballad of Josie*, *Sullivan's Empire*, etc.) and TV shows (*The Wild Wild West*, *Run for Your Life*, *Bob Hope Chrysler Theatre*, etc.). In 1970 she was cast as one of a trio of starlets looking for fame in the series *Bracken's World*. As the ambitious one, Jensen had the breakout role and for a time captured the public's attention. "This was an actress' dream role," comments Karen. She received numerous invitations to appear on all the popular talk and game shows and graced the covers of such magazines as *TV Guide* and *Show*, who called her "television's first real sex symbol." After *Bracken's World* folded in 1971, Karen's most notable credit was the espionage thriller *The Salzburg Connection* (1972) co-starring Barry Newman. She retired from acting a few years later and today she is an accomplished writer and painter.

Karen was born on August 18 in San Francisco. Her parents Charles and Claire Jensen divorced when she was a child; she was raised in Sacramento and in a "cute little town called San Carlos." Though a timid young girl, she had a desire to be "up on the stage" after watching the Miss America contests on television. When she was older, her mother encouraged her to enter local beauty pageants to overcome her shyness. "I was the youngest contestant who ever won the Miss San Carlos pageant," Karen says. "I won the Miss San Mateo rung of the Miss America Pageant but I placed second runner-up in the Miss California finals. But the one that really stands out for me was the Fiesta Dream Girl contest. As the winner I was sent to Washington, D.C., to meet President Kennedy. I waited in the Oval Office but I never got to see him—though I did meet the speaker of the House and got to plant a rose bush in the White House garden."

Karen began modeling and her face graced the billboard for Granny Goose

Karen Jensen hits the beach in this publicity photo (courtesy of Karen Jensen).

Potato Chips across the country. "When I was doing photo layouts, I would have to portray all different kinds of emotions—sexy or cute or funny—depending what look they wanted for the photographs. I started learning to project different feelings. And I liked it." A talent scout named Jerry Zitman from William Morris spotted Karen on television in the Miss California pageant and launched her acting career. Jack Warner saw her screen test and signed her to a contract. One of Karen's first jobs was a role on the George Burns–Connie Stevens sitcom called *Wendy and Me*. "I remember walking into the office with my agent and not recognizing George Burns because he didn't have his toupee on," says Karen with a laugh. "He looked so different. And I didn't know who he was until I was introduced. He was a very sweet, kind man. I really liked him. His son Ronnie was also there and we started dating for awhile. Ronnie was very nice and he was my first Hollywood date."

Jensen left Warner Bros. to work at Universal because "they had more for me to do. There wasn't a whole lot of work at Warners. There were not many TV shows in production. Universal was just hustling and bustling. They had a ton of film and TV projects so there were more opportunities for me. They also had an acting school, which I wanted to enter but it was sort of complicated for me. I was chosen by a Universal executive to go under contract but didn't get into the acting program, which was run by a woman named Monique James. She'd only let in the actors she chose to put under contract. I was always aware that there were two camps at Universal—hers and the executives'."

Karen starred for Universal in her first feature film *Out of Sight* (1966), a spoof on spy and beach films. This was the third beach film directed by Lennie Weinrib, whom Karen describes as "always having a smile on his face." Jensen played a beach beauty who calls secret agent John Stamp for help when she overhears madman Mr. D of the crime syndicate F.L.U.S.H. plotting to sabotage an upcoming rock 'n' roll festival. However, unbeknownst to her, Stamp's butler (Jonathan Daly) answers and, wishing to be an agent himself, takes the case. Though the film's rock stars (Gary Lewis & the Playboys, the Turtles, the Knickerbockers, etc.) and the George Barris–designed hot rods received all the publicity, Karen got decent reviews—a rarity for actors in beach films. *Variety* commented, "Karen Jensen looks good in a bikini and is believable as the innocent sweet young thing."

"I remember that I had never worked harder nor gotten less sleep in my life while doing *Out of Sight*," says Karen. "We shot it on a two-week schedule. There was no time off. Lennie managed to get it all done without anyone getting angry with him. That's a pretty good feat in this business. Most of the exteriors were filmed on Zuma Beach. And we spent most of our time there. After doing a long day's work, the cast would sit around for awhile because we were so tired and then we'd all race home to get four hours' sleep before we had to show up again. It was most exhausting. But it was a nice experience working with other young actors and I made a lot of friends. My leading man was Jonathan Daly and I liked him a lot. He is very talented. Deanna Lund was very friendly and we worked together again on a film for television. Carole Shelyne and I became roommates and I became very close with an actress named Rena Horten. Even though it was a short shoot, the cast would hang out together and we became

The beach-spy film *Out of Sight* (Universal, 1966) featured (*left to right*) Vicki Fee, Robert Pine, Karen Jensen, Jonathan Daly and Carole Shelyne plus a number of George Barris–designed hot rods.

like a big family. I never got to socialize with any of the rock groups because their songs were filmed very quickly."

Decorative supporting roles in *Sullivan's Empire* (1967) and *The Ballad of Josie* (1967) with Doris Day followed for Jensen. The latter was an unsuccessful Western spoof directed by Andrew V. McLaglen, whom Karen describes as being "a very tall and strong man who was tough and no-nonsense on the set. This was a big picture with a lot of actors and a lot of stuff going on. McLaglen directed it like a general. He'd yell, 'You over here and you stand over there!' I felt his focus was more on the big picture rather than the acting and the individual actors." Set in turn-of-the-century Wyoming, *The Ballad of Josie* featured Doris Day (photographed through layers of camera gauze) as a widow who is acquitted in the death of her husband but loses custody of her eight-year-old son to her father-in-law. She decides to build up her rundown ranch to raise sheep. She becomes a sort of frontier feminist as she organizes the women into a woman's suffrage movement and feuds with cattle ranchers who want to run her out of business. Co-starring with Day are Peter Graves as her love interest, George Kennedy as a villainous cattleman and Jensen as a saloon girl who joins Day in the temperance cause.

Recounting working with Day, Karen says, "I could be wrong, but when we did

The Ballad of Josie it may have been after her husband died. But I do remember that she and her dogs would disappear into her trailer the minute a scene was over. She was very unreachable and kept herself separate from the rest of the cast. She was very nice working on the scenes together. But she might have been depressed or going through a bad stage in her life and didn't want to socialize."

Universal also kept Karen busy working in television. "On *Bob Hope Chrysler Theatre* Jean Simmons nicknamed me 'Legs' and commented that I was the Earth-mother type. I thought her remarks were unusual. On *Run for Your Life* I played the sweet innocent young girl held captive by a biker gang. I liked working with Ben Gazzara very much. But John Drew Barrymore, actress Drew Barrymore's father, was odd. He played the lead biker. One day, he came over to where I was sitting and started speaking with me. I couldn't understand what he was talking about. He was very incoherent. I couldn't tell if he was drinking or high on drugs but he wasn't making any sense. It was very strange. However, when we were shooting he was fine and gave a very good performance.

"I had no problems working with Robert Conrad on *The Wild Wild West*, unlike some other actresses. Conrad was very professional, businesslike and easy to work with. He was also a very good-looking man. I really liked doing this show and westerns in particular. I like the outdoors and I like horses. Westerns were easy to do. You don't work with a whole lot of props. I also liked wearing the costumes. It was nice to wear a dress with a cinched, tiny little waist. I think the clothes from that period are very flattering."

In 1967 Karen was one of the few actors who were not stars of a series to be featured on the cover of *TV Guide*. The article "Starlet 1967: A Revealing Study of a Unique Species" portrayed Jensen as a typical young ambitious actress whose life was ruled by wearing the latest styles and doing the right things to become a star. When asked if this was an accurate portrait, she replies, "No, not really. I was even a little embarrassed about it. Nothing in the cover photo was mine—not the silver mini-dress I'm wearing, not the man who was my supposed date and not the dog I'm holding. They were trying to go for a certain kind of a story and for me to be chosen to do it was a good thing. It got me a lot of publicity. But they made me fit into the story—the story did not fit me. I've always put people and relationships first before my career. That may have been one of my problems. But I don't look at it as a problem. I know I made the right choice."

Feeling that she was floundering at Universal, Karen made headlines when she took her new agent's advice and walked out on her contract. "At that time, not many actors broke studio contracts," remarks Karen. "Nobody could believe I was willing to leave all that steady money. Except for one bad experience of being chased around the desk by a producer—I was faster than he was and did not get the part—I enjoyed working there even though I had to do every part the studio wanted me to do whether I liked it or not. I was happy to be working so I did as I was told. I changed agents during my contract and my new agent, Bill Robinson, said, 'Universal is not really grooming you for stardom. They give you a good part and then make you do a tiny part. They are having you do things arbitrarily, not thinking of your future. I'd like to see if we could get you out of this contract and get you up for leads in motion pictures.' Being young and impressionable, I listened to him and said, 'Okay. If you think you can do it, let's go for it.' He was able to get me released from the studio and we took a stab at a couple of movie roles." Karen screen tested for a number of films including *I Love You, Alice B. Toklas* (1968) and *Skidoo!* (1968) directed by Otto Preminger (whom Karen describes as being "really tough and unpleasant to work for") but failed to get cast.

Karen came close to getting the role of the ill-fated Jennifer in *Valley of the Dolls* (1967) but lost out to Sharon Tate. Recalling the audition, she says, "When you go on interviews, sometimes you get the sense if they like you or don't. I really sensed that either producer David Weisbart or director Mark Robson—I can't remember which—took a real liking to me and was pulling for me to get the part. I went back a couple of times and I thought I had a real chance for it." When asked if she had a problem with the semi-nudity, a surprised Karen replies, "I didn't even know about that. They never discussed nudity with me. If I had known, I wouldn't have wanted to do it. I turned down another picture because I wouldn't do nude scenes. I felt that basically it wasn't necessary for that to be in a film."

Jensen's beauty and talent were better served in the Oscar-nominated short *Prelude* (1968). She played the beautiful mini-skirted dream girl of an average guy who tries to win her love while shopping in a grocery store. While some actresses might have felt doing a short film was a career risk, Karen jumped at the chance because the role was so well-written. "John Astin [of *The Addams Family*] produced, directed and acted in *Prelude*," Karen says. "He gave me a call and said, 'I heard about you from some people. I'm doing this short and I would like to meet with you to see if you are right for it. Would you be interested?' I said, 'Sure!' He came over to my house and we got along great. John was such a sweet man. He told me I was perfect for the part. John put a lot of time and effort into this film. I was not surprised it was nominated for an Academy Award. The story revolved around a man, played by John, who meets his fantasy girl, played by me. But he can't get anywhere with her and learns to appreciate who he's with—forget the fantasy and accept the reality."

Though she plugged away for movie roles, it was television that offered Jensen stardom as she snagged one of the lead roles in *Bracken's World*. This series (which premiered in September 1969) took a behind-the-scenes look at life at a fictitious Hollywood studio replete with the workaholic director (Peter Haskell), the dedicated assistant to the studio head (Eleanor Parker), the lonely talent school coordinator (Elizabeth Allen), the arrogant leading man (Dennis Cole), the naïve actress (Linda Harrison) with the domineering mother (Jeanne Cooper), the icy sophisticate (Laraine Stephens) and the ruthless glamour girl. As played by Karen, the latter was a conniving, publicity-driven actress who would do anything for a role but deep down was a lonely, vulnerable little girl craving the attention she never got as a youngster. Karen's audition went so well that she was offered her choice of roles. "I really hit it off with the producers and the writers," says Karen. "It was just one of those magical times in life when everything turns out well. I had just returned from Europe where I auditioned for an Italian film that required nudity so I turned it down. But I had been dieting and exercising and I felt really good about myself. The timing was perfect when I walked in

The cast of the NBC-TV series *Bracken's World* included (*left to right*) Jensen, Peter Haskell and Laraine Stephens.

for my audition and I hit it off with the entire production team. They asked me which part I wanted to play. I said, 'I would like to do the rich girl part rather than the bad girl.' So I read for it and they liked me. I had to come back to read again because they were sifting through a lot of actresses. When I read again for it, they felt I was good but too strong for that part. They then offered me the role of Rachel Holt. I didn't want to play that role. The character wasn't a very nice person. But I relented.

"Rachel Holt was every actress' dream role," continues Karen. "Rachel was very ambitious and would do anything to get a part. As the series progressed, the character stayed bitchy but they tried to show why she was like that—she had a terrible childhood living with foster parents and came from a very poor background. Her vulnerability began to surface, which I thought was interesting. I learned after doing the role that the bad girls are the best parts. I'm glad I got that part." Karen made the most of this role and her performances earned kudos. Kay Gardella in the *New York Daily News* raved, "The ambitious Rachel is played with great skill by the voluptuous Karen Jensen."

During the series' first season, Jensen's character was the focus of a number of episodes. In "Fallen, Fallen Is Babylon" Rachel is kidnapped by a religious fanatic; in "Day for Night" she finds her long-lost foster parents; and in "It's the Power Structure Baby" she dates Peter Haskell's black assistant. Karen reveals that all of the *Bracken's World* stories were based on real events. They would change things around a little so they weren't obvious to the public. "The rumor about 'It's the Power Structure Baby' was that it was a take-off—if I remember correctly—on how the studio tried to break up Sammy Davis, Jr., and Mai Britt," says Karen. "Each episode was a true story and as we'd film it, they let us in on who it really was about."

"In 'Fallen, Fallen Is Babylon,' Richard Thomas played the religious nut and I thought he was one of the best actors I have ever worked with. And he was a very nice guy. He was very young—this was before he did *The Waltons*. I was *so* impressed with his acting. He was absolutely brilliant in that part. He was so good I felt that he really was that character. This is my favorite episode. I was really focused working with Richard and got into the acting. I think we worked well together."

NBC invested a lot in *Bracken's World* so their publicity machine was in full gear. Karen and her two co-stars, Linda Harrison and Laraine Stephens, made the rounds of all the talk and game shows. They even did a photo shoot with Cary Grant, who was representing Faberge, one of the series' sponsors. *Show Magazine* did a cover story on Karen, calling her "television's first real sex symbol." And all three actresses were featured on the cover of *TV Guide*. But like her previous *TV Guide* cover story, Karen again had problems with the article, which was written by Richard Warren Lewis, who ridiculed her home. He wrote, "The aroma of chocolate-chip cookies baking in the kitchen of the dwelling high in the Hollywood Hills was wafted into an otherwise bleak living room adorned with plastic ferns, artificial roses and sunflowers." Karen says, "Looking back on it and re-reading his piece, I may have overreacted. I was very sensitive in those days. But back then I was upset, angry and hurt. I told myself I would never trust another publicity person and writer as long as I lived. The other girls were so smart. They had the interview conducted at the publicist's office or somewhere else—not at their homes. I was stupid enough to invite him into my house and make myself vulnerable. I just bought this home—I didn't have a whole lot of money—but I was really proud of it. I had plastic flowers just for a temporary decoration. He made fun of them in the article for the whole country to read. It was very embarrassing." After these unpleasant experiences, did she try to gain more control when talking to the media? Karen replies with a laugh, "I wish I could say yes but I still was very open and trusting. But I never had plastic flowers in my house again!"

Karen was receiving recognition for her role as Rachel, but the series itself received mixed reviews along the lines of the one in *Variety*, which described it as an "incredible but remarkable brew of suds and camp." The series did have problems. Each episode focused on a big name guest star, relegating the regular cast to the background. Also, the gimmick of having the head of the studio remain just a voice grew thin. With the ratings floundering, the second season saw the axing of a number of characters and the introduction of Leslie Nielsen as John Bracken, the previously unseen studio head. But the show still failed to find an audience up against ABC's popular *Love, American Style* and was cancelled midseason. "I was so disappointed when the series got cancelled," remarks Karen. "I wanted to see it go on forever. Working on *Bracken's World* was one of the best experiences of my life. I loved the producer Stanley Rubin and his wife, Kathleen

Hughes. They are one of the most wonderful couples in the whole world. One of my favorite directors on the series was Walter Doniger who helmed the pilot. He was very good and didn't put any pressure on me. I was relaxed with him and he helped me be the best I could in a scene.

"The cast and crew really liked each other and it felt like a family. Laraine, Linda and I got along nicely and had a good time working together. I loved Peter Haskell like a brother. He was wonderfully fun to be with. He was relaxed and always had a smile for you—just a great guy. I didn't work too much with Dennis Cole but I liked him. He is a nice guy. And Elizabeth Allen became a very good friend to me. She, Jeannie Cooper and I hung out together. Leslie Nielsen is a good actor and added a lot of personality to the show. What I remember most is that he was so much fun on the set. I knew he was a comedian right then and there before he had done any comedy. He was always laughing, teasing and making jokes. Leslie even had a flatulence cushion. [*Laughs*] Eleanor Parker was the only one who was very reserved. She reminded me in a way of Doris Day only in the fact that she kept herself very much removed from everybody else. After a scene, she would disappear into her trailer and didn't mix with the cast and crew. I finally got to know her a bit when one day she offered me a lift in her car from one set to another. I was absolutely shocked! And she turned out to be a very nice lady and I got to like her after getting to know her. I never knew why she left the show." (Parker left the series halfway through the first season.)

After *Bracken's World* ended, Karen found herself typecast as a sex symbol and appeared in a few decorative television roles. "I knew that sometimes when you play a TV role for a couple of years, you could get typecast. It is hard to break that perception because people see you only in that way. For a long time, I was only getting offered the sexy roles. I wanted to play other kinds of parts but I wasn't offered them."

Karen's last theatrical role was as a triple agent in the espionage thriller *The Salzburg Connection* (1973), based on a novel by Helen MacInnes. Beautifully filmed on location in Austria, the film stars Barry Newman (whom Karen describes as being "very nice and easy to work with") as a vacationing attorney drawn into a complicated web of intrigue as agents from various countries descend on Austria when a chest containing a list of Nazi collaborators is recovered from a lake. Newman meets Jensen at a hotel, where she is posing as a tourist and is

Karen Jensen as the grasping starlet Rachel Holt in NBC-TV's *Bracken's World* (courtesy of Karen Jensen).

secretly tailing him. Playing all sides against each other, Karen's duplicitous character meets her demise in a car explosion. "That blast was so loud and I was very close to it," says Karen with a shudder. "My ears were ringing for days. As a matter of fact, I've had an ear problem and have always wondered if it was from that. I was scared shooting this scene. We never did a run-through because they only wanted one explosion as the camera was running. But they felt I was standing far enough away and that I would be safe. I don't think they knew enough about safety precautions back then."

Critical reaction to *The Salzburg Connection* was mediocre at best. Most reviewers found the film to be confusing. Judith Crist's review was very much the norm as she commented, "This one is so dull you can't tell the CIA agents from the Neo-Nazis." Regarding the critical barbs, Karen says, "After reading the book, I knew that it was going to be a difficult movie to make. It wasn't an easy novel to adapt to the big screen. And I remember Barry Newman, myself and a couple of other people sitting around saying, 'What can we do to make this script better?' None of us had any solutions. We tried a little bit here and there and we talked to the film's producer Ingo Preminger. Some changes were made but we all kind of knew there was a bit of a problem with the script. That happens sometimes trying to translate a book into a motion picture. The director was Lee H. Katzin and I think it was his idea to use the stop-motion technique in the film but even that couldn't help."

In 1975, Karen copped one of her favorite roles as Red Buttons' wife in the made-for-TV movie *Louis Armstrong—Chicago Style* (1976). Red played Louis Armstrong's agent and Karen played his wife. ("This was a role I really wanted to do because it wasn't a sexy part but a *real* woman.") Shortly thereafter, Karen took a break from acting: She and her then-husband, actor John Neilson, abandoned Hollywood for the rustic comforts of their northern California ranch. "John wanted to be a writer and I wanted to get away from Hollywood for a bit and live a real life and have children. I needed some time to myself and had always wanted to have animals. I had a horse, a goat and chickens. I cooked and did all the wifely things. It was a totally different lifestyle for us. But we discovered we didn't like it after a year or two. We missed the activity, the creativeness and the people in Hollywood. We learned a hard lesson—once you leave Hollywood, it is very tough to re-establish yourself when you return. I signed with an agent and gave acting a little bit of a try again and got *Happy Days*. But my advice to other actors would be, *don't leave unless you've really made your mark*."

In 1982 Karen quit acting because "I didn't like going on auditions and all the rejection that comes with being an actor." After her divorce from Neilson in 1990, Jensen married actor Michael Stroka of *Dark Shadows* fame. Her first manuscript, titled *Primo Baby*, was picked up and made into a Canadian movie. The happiness this brought her was marred by the slow death of her husband from cancer in early 1997.

Today Karen Jensen's future holds many wonderful things. She recently wed prolific actor Brendon Boone of *Garrison's Gorillas* fame on January 30, 1999. When asked if she knew Boone from the sixties, Karen hesitates and replies with a laugh, "We're not sure. I don't remember meeting him and he doesn't remember meeting me back then. We recently met at the Golden Boot pre-awards party. A mutual friend of ours, Marvin Paige, introduced us." According to Boone, they seemed fated to be together because "our careers and lives—both personal and professional—follow close parallels through all the years. When she was making a film in Europe, I was making a film in Europe. When she was at Fox, I was at Fox right at the same time. My ex-wife had died within the last three or four years and Karen's husband died also within the last three or four years. When Marvin called me over at that party and said, 'Brendon, you remember Karen Jensen from *Bracken's World*,' I did remember her and that her name was in my personal phone book. I told her that and later on in the evening she suggested that I should have her new number. [*Laughs*] I raised my 21-year-old son Brendon and I had not dated in his lifetime, so it was really an awakening to recognize my soulmate standing there. We both certainly consider that God's hand was in this reunion because it is too much for happenstance." Brendon Boone is also the head of Beehive Films Ltd. and has a film in development called *Preacher & Co*. It is a heartwarming post–Civil War drama that will return Karen and him to the big screen. "Our relationship is so good because we have a close walk with God," says Karen in conclusion. "I've never been with a man who was religious and believed in God before. It has made such a difference in my life. I'm incredibly happy." As the title of her first movie implied, Karen Jensen really is "Out of Sight!"

Actor Brendon Boone and his radiant bride Karen Jensen-Boone on their wedding day in early 1999 (courtesy of Karen Jensen).

Film Appearances

1966	**Out of Sight** (Universal) d. Lennie Weinrib.
1967	**Sullivan's Empire** (Universal) d. Harvey Hart/Thomas Carr.
	The Ballad of Josie (Universal) d. Andrew McLaglen.
1968	**Prelude** (Excelsior) [short] d. John Astin.
1971	**Congratulations, It's a Boy!** (TV-movie) d. Bruce Kessler.
1972	**The Salzburg Connection** (20th Century–Fox) d. Lee H. Katzin.
	The Snoop Sisters (TV-movie) d. Leonard Stone.
1973	**I Love a Mystery** (TV-movie; completed in 1967) d. Leslie Stevens.
1976	**Louis Armstrong—Chicago Style** (TV-movie) d. Charles Fries.

Television Appearances

No Time for Sergeants "Case of the Revolving Witness" 3/8/65 ABC.
Wendy and Me "Wendy's Private Eye" 3/15/65 ABC.
Hank (episode title unknown) 9/4/65 NBC.
Run for Your Life "Hoodlums on Wheels" 2/21/66 NBC.
The Virginian "A Bald-Faced Boy" 4/13/66 NBC.
Bob Hope Chrysler Theatre "One Embezzlement, Two Margaritas" 5/18/66 NBC.
Bob Hope Chrysler Theatre "Crazier Than Cotton" 10/12/66 NBC.
Dragnet "The Big Masked Bandits" 2/16/67 NBC.
The Wild Wild West "The Night of the Legion of Death" 11/24/67 CBS.
The Dating Game [celebrity contestant] 9/13/69 ABC.
Bracken's World [series regular as Rachel Holt] 9/16/69 to 1/1/71 NBC.
The Hollywood Squares [celebrity panelist] 10/27 to 10/31/69 NBC.
The Tonight Show Starring Johnny Carson [talk show guest] 11/16/69 NBC.
His and Her of It [talk show guest] 2/9/70 ABC.
It Takes Two [celebrity contestant] 3/16 to 3/20/70 NBC.
Stump the Stars [celebrity contestant] 5/25 to 5/29/70 Synd.
The Virginia Graham Show [talk show guest] 11/30/70 Synd.
Love, American Style "Love and the Operation Model" 1/15/71 ABC.
Insight "Love Song of the Coo Coo Bird" 3/8/72 Synd.
Kid Talk [talk show guest] 4/10/72 synd.
The Ted Bessell Show (pilot) 5/8/73.
Bob & Carol & Ted & Alice (episode title unknown) 10/17/73 ABC.
Movin' On "The Time of His Life" 9/12/74 NBC.
Mannix "A Choice of Victims" 12/22/74 CBS.
Emergency! "The Bash" 12/28/74 NBC.
Happy Days "Fonzie vs. the She Devils" 11/26/79 ABC.

Also:
The Merv Griffin Show.

Linda Harrison

Though Linda Harrison never appeared in a beach, biker or Elvis movie, her most memorable role featured her wearing nothing more than a loincloth, which more than qualifies her to be included in this book. Linda left an indelible impression on sixties moviegoers as the mute Homo sapiens Nova in the classic sixties sci-fi film *Planet of the Apes* (1968) and its sequel *Beneath the Planet of the Apes* (1970) and she will always be remembered as the beauty among the beasts. With her long, dark hair and big brown eyes, Linda had the perfect look to bring Nova to life on the big screen. "Nova meant new," reminds Linda with a twinkle in her eye. "I felt very comfortable playing her. I didn't even have to audition. Dick told me I had the quality they wanted." Dick is Dick Zanuck, the then head of 20th Century–Fox. It was on the Fox lot that Linda met and began dating Zanuck, which culminated in marriage in 1969. Linda's romance with Zanuck made her witness to one of the studio's most turbulent decades involving him and his father, the legendary Darryl F. Zanuck.

Linda Harrison was born in Berlin, Maryland, the third of four sisters. Though she looks Latin, she is of English-Irish decent. As a child she began taking acrobatics, ballet and dancing. When she was 12 years old, she won the Miss Delmarva Talent Contest and at age 16 won her first beauty crown as Miss Berlin. After a brief career as a photography model in New York City ("I had to sell encyclopedias to make money. It wasn't for me!"), Linda returned home. She entered and won the Miss Maryland contest, which resulted in a trip out West for the finals in the Miss USA contest. "I was voted first runner-up," remembers Linda. "Mike Medavoy at that time was a young agent at William Morris and he came up to me and said I should me in movies. He took me over to 20th Century–Fox for a screen test. They liked me and signed me to a contract. Incidentally, that test is featured in Van Ness Films' documentary *Hollywood Screen Tests: Take 2* for American Movie Classics."

Linda began dating Richard Zanuck before she ever made a film. He was the head of Fox at that time and his father, the legendary Darryl F. Zanuck, was chairman of the board. They met at the

Linda Harrison as mute Homo sapiens Nova in *Planet of the Apes* (20th Century–Fox, 1968).

premiere of *The Agony and the Ecstasy* (1965) and became inseparable after that first meeting (Linda was the date of Zanuck's best friend attorney Harry Sokolov). Zanuck became so protective of Linda that when he discovered that she was taking acting classes outside the studio, he built an acting school on the Fox lot. "Dick allocated a great deal of money to this school," says Linda. "We had a voice coach, an acting coach and a dance instructor. We were completely taken care of from head to toe and inside and out. It was just like the old studio talent schools but probably even better.

"It was neat studying there," continues Linda. "The contract player roster grew to include Tom Selleck, Sam Elliot, Christina Ferrare and Jackie Bisset. We were all these unique kids that got picked to be in this talent school. So we knew we were special. We learned our craft doing scenes together. I remember how all of them were so honored to be there. I just kept thinking, 'Little do they know that the whole school was created because Dick wanted to know where I was at all times.'" [*Laughs*]

Between dating Zanuck and taking acting classes, Linda found the time to make her film debut in a small role as astronaut James Brolin's wife in the Jerry Lewis comedy *Way ... Way Out* (1966). On television, she played a biker chick ("My first line was 'Go, man, go!'") in a pilot called *Men Against Evil* which later became the series *Felony Squad* with Dennis Cole and Howard Duff. As a cheerleader in an episode of *Batman*, Linda got to work with Cesar Romero as the Joker. "They got us up around 6:00 A.M. and started working us out," remembers Linda. "Cheerleading is very strenuous. I said to the teacher that if you work us too hard, we won't have any energy left for the shot. By the time we did the scene at five o'clock in the afternoon I was so exhausted that I fell over. My legs gave out. But they kept the shot anyway! Then the teacher reported me to the head of the talent school and said I was being difficult. My body was so sore that Dick had to carry me up the steps to my apartment."

As Linda's relationship with Zanuck (who was separated from actress Lili Gentle) got serious, he brought her to New York to meet his father. Linda (all of 20 years old) was excited and nervous about meeting the esteemed Darryl Zanuck. However, both she and Dick took a nap after arriving at their hotel and overslept. They were running so late that Zanuck wouldn't let Linda put on any makeup. "Darryl Zanuck was about the same height as Dick—five feet, six inches," recalls Linda. "He was about 64 years old at that time—very friendly. He paid me a great deal of respect. But the whole evening I was preoccupied wondering how I looked without makeup. We dined at Peter Luger's in Brooklyn and we had a wonderful dinner. Darryl had a young French girlfriend with him—my age. She wasn't one of the *major* girlfriends—just an interim one [*Laughs*]. Anyway, I was wearing this polka dot dress and kept thinking, 'I must look awful.' The interesting thing was that later on, Darryl told Dick that I reminded him of Raquel Welch. So I guess I didn't make too bad of an impression.

"The relationship between Dick and Darryl was interesting," continues Linda. "I liked the dynamics of it. There was a very deep admiration for each other. He and his dad had an unspoken dialogue between each other by virtue of being father and son. Dick both respected and feared his father and theirs was a lively liaison. Most of their conversations were thoughts on upcoming projects. It wasn't that they were preoccupied with their films. Their relationship was two-pronged. One was the business and creative side of making movies. The other side was personal. At that time, Darryl was separated from Virginia, Dick's mom, for about 20 years. But she was still waiting for him to return to her. And, of course, Dick was sensitive to his mother's feelings as well as his dad's. Dick tried to take a very neutral position."

Linda returned to the big screen in the hit comedy *A Guide for the Married Man* (1967), directed by Gene Kelly. Walter Matthau played a happily married man who is taught the fine art of adultery by his lascivious friend (Robert Morse), with guest stars in amusing vignettes enacting his advice. But the joke of the film is that Matthau is married to the gorgeous Inger Stevens. Harrison abandoned her brunette tresses to play a blonde Hollywood starlet named Miss Stardust in a wonderfully amusing segment with Carl Reiner as a married movie star who wants to bed her. He devises this complicated plan to meet halfway around the world so his wife won't find out. ("The irony here was the wife was played by a very dear friend of Dick's wife Lili Gentle. He was not yet divorced and found this very amusing.") After traveling by plane, boat, rickshaw, etc., they meet in a Swiss chalet and before he can even get her into bed, his wife barges in with photographers. "Carl Reiner was great,"

Harrison with her future husband, 20th Century–Fox studio head Richard Zanuck, at a Hollywood film premiere, circa 1966 (courtesy of Linda Harrison).

remarks Linda fondly. "And Gene Kelly was very easy to work with, probably because he is an actor also. He liked to do a kind of give and take, which was really wonderful. A lot of directors did not want much input from their actors. But I remember Dick telling me from the beginning, 'Just do what your director tells you.' You don't hear that very often. But being 20 years old with not much experience, it was a very wise suggestion to follow."

Zanuck then handed Harrison the part for which she will always be remembered—Nova in *Planet of the Apes* (1968). The film became a huge box office hit that spawned four sequels and a TV series. It received two Academy Award nominations (for Scoring and Costume Design) and won a special Oscar for John Chambers makeup creations.

Planet of the Apes would never have been filmed if it weren't for the persistence of producer Arthur P. Jacobs. He had purchased the rights to Pierre Boulle's novel *Monkey Planet* while still unpublished. A few years later, while working at Fox, Jacobs persuaded studio head Dick Zanuck to let him produce a five-minute "test reel" to see if the concept would work on film. Charlton Heston played the Taylor character with Edward G. Robinson as a sympathetic Dr. Zaius. Harrison and James Brolin played chimpanzees, which would become Zira and Cornelius in the movie. "The studio heads wanted to see if the makeup was doable," Linda says. "That was the purpose of this test. At that point, they hadn't green lighted *Planet of the Apes* yet. I remember that the makeup process took about three hours. I had to lay back and be perfectly still as they put this plaster mold on my face. After seeing the test, everyone was very enthusiastic about going ahead with making *Planet of the Apes*. But they felt the makeup needed a little more work and perfecting before it would look good on screen." Though Fox did go ahead with the film, Robinson backed out of playing Dr. Zaius. Because of his ill health, he didn't think he'd be able to endure the arduous makeup process.

In *Planet of the Apes* (skillfully directed by Franklin J. Schaffner), four astronauts, after hurdling through space for over 2,000 years, land on a planet where humans are mute and unintelligent and apes are their masters. Of the space travelers, only Charlton Heston as Taylor survives but he is shot in the throat by a band of gorillas who are hunting humans. Taylor is taken to Ape City (along with a woman he dubs Nova) where he tries to convince a sympathetic psychologist Dr. Zira (Kim Hunter) and her archeologist fiancé Cornelius (Roddy McDowall) of his intelligence. When he regains his speech, he proves his superiority but is thwarted by Dr. Zaius (Maurice Evans), who has always been aware of man's reputation as "the harbinger of death." The film climaxes in the Forbidden Zone with Taylor proving that the apes evolved from humans. He goes off with Nova only to discover the horrible truth—the planet of the apes is actually Earth, whose civilization was destroyed by man. "*Planet of the Apes* was an experimental kind of picture," comments Linda. "It tantalized us because we didn't know what was going to be next. We knew we were involved in something special. Also Dick was a very integral part of this movie. Creative genes are passed from one generation to another. In Dick's case, he had his father Darryl's and his own particular genius, which was defined in his ability to ignite talent and enthusiasm for this unusual and risky project."

Though Linda credits Zanuck for the success of *Planet of the Apes*, she also praises the vision of director Schaffner. "He was a very interesting, very quiet man," remarks Linda. "I remember Dick and I would have dinner with Bob Dovdell, the assistant director on the film. He and Dick were best friends from their Stamford days. Bob would tell us that nobody knows what the next shot will be because Schaffner keeps it in his back pocket. He would only tell his cameraman Leon Shamroy. But that lent itself to this kind of picture. It gave the actors a very interesting edge not knowing what to expect next. I think his directing style worked very effectively."

Planet of the Apes contains two surprising scenes that totally shock the audience. One comes near the beginning of the film when the audience first sees the gorillas on horseback as they beat the bushes and hunt the humans. Highlighted by Jerry Goldsmith's exciting score, which incorporates horns blown by the marauding gorillas, it is one of the film's most exciting sequences and sets the tone for the rest of the film. This scene was filmed on the 20th Century–Fox Ranch in Malibu Canyon (where they also built Ape City). "I remember it was extremely hot when we filmed this," recalls Linda. "Watching this scene now, I realize how arduous it was but I wasn't aware of it at that time. I had trust in the people in

Planet of the Apes (20th Century–Fox, 1968) starred Charlton Heston as lost astronaut Taylor and Harrison as Nova.

charge." The other scene is the film's final shot where Taylor kneels in front of the ruins of the Statue of Liberty and realizes that he has been on Earth all along. He yells, "You maniacs! You blew it up. God damn you! Damn you all to hell!"

Recalling her co-stars, Linda remarks, "Roddy McDowall, Kim Hunter and Maurice Evans were great people and fabulous troupers. I'm not just saying that, they were pros. They had a difficult time with all that makeup. And they had to report to the set at three A.M. As for Charlton Heston, he was an idol of mine since I was a teenager and saw him in *Ben-Hur* [1959]. I thought, 'My God, he is the most wonderful man in the world!' And then a few years later to be co-starring with him was delightful, to say the least. It wasn't in my nature to fawn over celebrities but I told Charlton that he was my idol. He was so nice and responded, 'Thank you very much.' He had a quiet quality about him and was very courteous with me. He encouraged me to favor the camera. I was a newcomer in many ways—which may have helped my character. I'm sure Heston had his doubts about me; however, he never showed them. He treated me more like a child than an adult and not much was discussed between us, in character or out. When you idolize someone like I did, you tend to submit rather than assert yourself. Again, this worked in our roles and the relationship between us, as Taylor and Nova."

Though Linda had appeared in two previous films, she received "and introducing Linda Harrison" in the film's credits. Zanuck wanted to draw attention to Linda because he felt this role would catapult her to stardom. And it did. Playing the mute Nova made Harrison stand out from the rest of the cast who for the most part were in monkey makeup. "They say playing a mute character is difficult but I think for me it was easier and the best way for me to go," says Linda. "Being a relatively new actress at 21 years old, I thought I had the right quality for the part. I can be a very introspective person or I can also be very extroverted. The role felt very comfortable for me. I think my best scene is when Heston and I were in the cage together. His character Taylor begins sharing things with Nova in a way to try to get her to understand him. He gets through to her on a certain level. I thought this scene was good."

With *Planet of the Apes* a critical and box office smash (*Variety* described it as being "a sociopolitical allegory, cast in the mold of futuristic science fiction" and "an intriguing blend of chilling satire"), Zanuck contacted Jacobs about doing a sequel to be called *Planet of the Apes Revisited*. The creators went through numerous scenarios before settling on Taylor and Nova discovering an underground city of mutant humans. Franklin Schaffner thought a sequel was a mistake and director Ted Post replaced him. Charlton Heston would only agree to a limited role because he too felt that a sequel was a bad idea. Paul Dehn then had to rewrite the script to accommodate Heston's absence during most of the film. James Franciscus was cast as astronaut Brent, who is sent to find Taylor and his crew. What he finds at first is a planet of angry apes ("The only good human is a dead human!") and Nova *sans* Taylor, who disappeared in the Forbidden Zone. As Brent and Nova venture beneath the planet, they discover the ruins of New York City inhabited by a race of masked telepathic human mutants who worship the Atom Bomb. After reuniting with the missing Taylor, Nova is gunned down by the invading apes. The battle between ape

Harrison and James Franciscus in *Beneath the Planet of the Apes* (20th Century–Fox, 1970) (courtesy of Linda Harrison).

and human ends with the world being blown to bits, killing everyone. (Or so it seemed. Two years later, *Escape from the Planet of the Apes* would hit the screen.) Unlike Heston, Linda had no problem with reprising her role of Nova in the sequel re-titled *Beneath the Planet of the Apes* (1971) because "I was to be featured more prominently in this so as an actress that suited me just fine. Nova also got to say her first word—'Taylor.' Nova was very loyal to him. They bonded and he was her knight in shining armor. That was an endearing quality about the character. She never forgot him.

"Making *Beneath the Planet of the Apes* was fun and physically challenging," continues Linda. "I had a lot more running and horseback scenes. But it wasn't like the first picture. Though Ted Post was a wonderful TV director, he did not have the same point of view as Franklin Schaffner. And James Franciscus was different, of course, from Charlton Heston. Charlton is a visionary kind of an actor. He inspired me while making *Planet of the Apes*. I felt Jim Franciscus was more of a cerebral kind of actor. He was an Ivy League school graduate and was more mental rather than intuitive. I liked him though. And I know that he felt thrilled to have the part. He was very dedicated to it."

After production wrapped on *Beneath the Planet of the Apes* in 1970, Linda married Dick Zanuck. She then was cast as one of a trio of starlets working at a movie studio in the TV series *Bracken's World*. She was the naïve one, Karen Jensen the ambitious one and Laraine Stephens the cold one. "I quickly agreed to do this series because I could be dressed beautifully and I could speak," says Linda with a laugh. "I finally had lines and could be more diversified. But I remember clearly having to go from *Beneath the Planet of the Apes* with essentially no lines to having lots of dialogue in *Bracken's World*. I was not prepared my first day of shooting and got a verbal reprimand from my producer. That entire weekend, Dick rehearsed my lines with me.

"Paulette was the least ambitious of the actresses. Here again it was art imitating real life. I also never had the drive to become a star. I was picked for Paulette because I had a lot of the qualities for the role in my own nature. Paulette was very vulnerable and gentle but at the same time she had a lot of emotional strength. When *Bracken's World* first began, she was very much in love with her boyfriend [Dennis Cole] and she had this pushy, controlling mother [Jeanne Cooper] who wanted her to become a star."

Bracken's World was cancelled in January 1971 after only a season and a half. Linda muses, "Had they done it like a continuing drama [à la *Peyton Place*] and focused on the regular characters, it would have lasted longer. NBC, however, wanted a one-hour contained show so they would stock each episode with a big guest star. And after a while, you run out of story." Soon after Linda's series was cancelled, Darryl Zanuck shocked the industry by firing his son as president of Fox. Linda was pregnant with their first

Publicity shot of Harrison as naïve starlet Paulette Douglas in the NBC-TV series *Bracken's World*.

child and she was let go also, as the studio did not pick up the option on her contract.

"What began to upset the apple cart was that Darryl was getting deeper involved with a young French actress named Genevieve Gilles. That troubled Dick. He was worried about his father's judgment because he had seen it happen before. These women [including Bella Darvi, Juliette Greco and Irina Demick] would come in and take control in very subtle but sometimes overt ways. Gilles became a major concern to Dick and David Brown, his partner. Dick tried keeping Darryl in balance but what can you do when a father is smitten? It's none of your business. So Gilles began demanding more power and getting it. Darryl and Dick's relationship became strained because of her and the declining movie revenues. Dick tried in a diplomatic way to stop his father's preoccupation with her. But Gilles wanted to star in a movie and Darryl said yes. She had no training and put the whole company in jeopardy when Darryl green-lighted this movie [*Hello-Goodbye*] at a time when Fox was in some financial straits. That began the wedge between the father and son. Dick and David tried to placate the father and run the business but it was interfering. It was time for the father to relinquish some of the power, but he wouldn't. He fired his own son at a board meeting! I felt it was a good omen because it was time for Dick to go on and not be under all that bureaucratic studio business. But it was difficult for Dick and his father. What's ironic was that three months after firing Dick, Darryl was forced out of Fox. Dick called his father upon hearing the news, something he had expected. They patched things up between them. I found this remarkable and quite endearing. Darryl then returned to his wife Virginia after many years of separation."

Professionally, at least, things worked out well for the Zanucks—Dick (along with David Brown) went off to Warner Bros. for a year as independent producers and then formed their own very successful production company. Personally things became rocky. After giving birth to her second son, the marriage between Linda and Richard began to disintegrate. "Above all, motherhood is my highest achievement but I needed another creative outlet called acting," reflects Linda. "Dick felt different about this. He had some accumulating fears about me working. It was very silly of him and this very attitude created a great conflict in our marriage. Real love is about encouraging one to do the thing that makes them happy. I didn't want a full-time career, just a part now and then. That would have gone a long way in helping our marriage."

A conflicted Linda then turned to a guru for spiritual guidance. She returned to acting in 1974 using the name "Augusta Summerland" because "the name was to signify a new beginning for me." Career-wise things were looking up for Linda when Dick suggested her for the role of the sheriff's wife in a little film called *Jaws* (1975), which he was producing for Universal. Linda lost out on the part because Universal executive Sid Sheinberg promised it to his wife Lorraine Gary. "I would have loved for Dick to have gone to bat for me," remarks Linda. "But by then I was deeply into spirituality with a questionable guru. The problem I had was that I thought he was a true guru when in fact he was a man with his own agenda. This was a great learning curve for me. It eventually destroyed my marriage."

Zanuck eventually found a role for Linda in *Airport 1975* as one of the all-star passengers trapped on a disabled airliner after a prop plane crashes into the cockpit, killing the crew. Though the film starred Charlton Heston, Harrison didn't have any scenes with him as she played the secretary to film star Gloria Swanson (who essentially played herself). "She was a prima donna," remarks Linda, smiling. "But I don't mean that in a bad way. Swanson was an actress of stature for many years and she carried that role off-camera. I think she enjoyed working with me because I was married to a Zanuck. She told me about her affair with Joe Kennedy. And she shared with me what it was like to be an actress in that era. It was interesting hearing her stories."

After divorcing Zanuck in 1978, Harrison abandoned acting to "regroup." Ironically, when she began pursuing acting again in the mid-eighties, it was Richard and his new wife Lili Fini who gave her a role as Wilford Brimley and Maureen Stapleton's doting daughter in their hit film *Cocoon* (1985), directed by Ronny Howard. "I liked working with Ron," exclaims Linda. "Ron has this natural directing style that encourages actors to be real. Not in the same sense as method acting but utilizing our unique mannerisms of speech and behavior that we use so freely in real life."

Today's Linda Harrison is still a strikingly beautiful, charming woman. She has re-settled back in hometown of Berlin, Maryland. Her sons Harrison Richard and Dean Francis are both following in the illustrious footsteps of their father and grandfather into the film business. As for Linda, she has been tending to her website (www.lindaharrison.com) and attends autograph shows and conventions across the country.

Linda Harrison in the early nineties (courtesy of Linda Harrison).

FILM APPEARANCES

1966 Way ... Way Out (20th Century–Fox) d. Gordon Douglas.
1967 A Guide for the Married Man (20th Century–Fox) d. Gene Kelly.
1968 Planet of the Apes (20th Century–Fox) d. Franklin J. Schaffner.
1970 Beneath the Planet of the Apes (20th Century–Fox) d. Ted Post.
1974 Airport 1975 (Universal) d. Jack Smight.
1985 Cocoon (20th Century–Fox) d. Ron Howard.
1988 Cocoon: The Return (20th Century–Fox) d. Daniel Petrie.
1996 Dunston Checks In (20th Century–Fox) [cameo] d. Ken Kwapis.
1999 Runaway Bride (Paramount) [cameo] d. Garry Marshall [scene deleted].

TELEVISION APPEARANCES

Batman "The Joker Goes to School" 3/2/66 ABC.

Bracken's World [series regular as Paulette Douglas] 9/19/69 to 1/1/71 NBC.
The Tonight Show Starring Johnny Carson [talk show guest] 11/16/69 NBC.
Barnaby Jones "Flight to Danger" 10/31/75 CBS.
Switch "Death Squad" 4/6/76 CBS.
Switch "Three for the Money" 3/6/77 CBS.
Barnaby Jones "The Damocles Gun" 10/20/77 CBS.
AMC Behind the Planet of the Apes—The Making (special) 9/98 AMC.
Hollywood Screen Tests: Take 2 (special) 11/99 AMC.

Also:
Men Against Evil (pilot).

Tisha Sterling

Beginning in 1967, when the alienated youth film replaced the beach movie as the type of fare aimed at the teenage audience, runaways, hippies, radicals and flower children began dominating the big screen. No actress personified these roles better than auburn haired Tisha Sterling. This beauty with the fragile features made her film debut as a bad girl in Bert I. Gordon's teen exploitation classic *Village of the Giants*. She then abandoned her blonde ingenue image to passionately play the rebel in a number of late sixties–early seventies films—a murderous waif in *The Name of the Game Is Kill*, a hippie who tangles with Clint Eastwood in *Coogan's Bluff*, a Greenwich Village kook in *Norwood*, a flower child–like alien in the science fiction film *Night Slaves* and a Brazilian street girl in *The Wild Pack*. "I was a rich little hippie girl who lived in Topanga Canyon," comments Tisha. "My life was like the Doors rock group." After taking a hiatus from acting to get her life in order, Sterling returned to the big screen in 1999 in the Bruce Willis film *Breakfast of Champions*.

Tisha Sterling was born Patricia Sterling on Dec. 10 in Los Angeles. Her parents, Hollywood stars Ann Sothern and Robert Sterling, divorced when Tisha was only three years old. "Growing up in Hollywood as the daughter of two famous people wasn't hard on me because when you are a child, whatever is happening seems to be the norm," remarks Tisha. "But in retrospect, I was extremely spoiled. I expected a lot from the world simply because that's what the world seemed to be. So when it didn't live up to those expectations it seemed dim to me." The rebellious Tisha was shuttled between schools in Hollywood, New York and Sun Valley. After being expelled from Marymount Junior School in Los Angeles, she attended public school only to return to Marymount in her junior year of high school ("I was only mildly chaotic the second time around").

Tisha never had the desire to act. It wasn't until she left home at age 17 that she realized she didn't know what to do to earn a living. "Acting seemed to be the only thing I knew how to do," says Tisha. "I did it and I was just so lucky. People were so good to me and gave me so many opportunities." Esteemed actress Margaret Leighton took Tisha to New York

Universal Pictures publicity photo of Tisha Sterling.

to co-star in Enid Bagnold's play *The Chinese Prime Minister*. However, Tisha was fired during tryouts in Toronto because at 17 she was deemed too young to play a sexy nymphomaniac ("They were absolutely right to let me go"). Undaunted, Tisha returned to Hollywood and quickly landed roles on *The Alfred Hitchcock Hour*, *Mr. Novak* and *The Donna Reed Show*, among others. When asked if she thought that her good fortune had to do with her famous parents, she reflects, "Being the daughter of Ann Sothern and Robert Sterling helped me to some extent, but I didn't use my mother and father's name ever. I was exposed to the business since I was a baby so I was familiar with aspects of show business. But I think it was harder for me in some ways because one doesn't want to think that they get jobs on the merit of their parents rather on themselves. I really don't think anyone that employed me gave me an acting job because of my mother. I believe I earned whatever role I got."

Tisha next auditioned and won a role in her first movie, Bert I. Gordon's *Village of the Giants* (1965). She co-starred with other famous Hollywood offspring Beau Bridges (son of Lloyd Bridges) and Tim Rooney (son of Mickey Rooney) as well as Tommy Kirk, Johnny Crawford, Joy Harmon and Bob Random. With her long blonde hair, Tisha looked every inch the ingenue but she played one of the teenage delinquents who grow to gigantic proportions in the film. Her scene where she tries to entice Tommy Kirk to reveal the whereabouts of the growth formula shows true acting promise. When told that Joy Harmon hated the opening scene with the teens dancing in the mud, Tisha says, "I guess I probably hated it too but I don't remember it very much. I just 'grinned and bared it.' I know we all had to just get into it and do it. I felt exploited throughout the whole movie. It was all tits and ass. But that's part of Bert Gordon's thing when making a movie. I thought Bert was very good at making these kinds of films.

"I really did have a good time making this film," continues Tisha. "Beau Bridges is great! He is a friend and I like him a lot. He is a very bright, funny and talented man. I became friendly with his first wife Julie and I think they were adopting children at the time. Joy Harmon is a very sweet girl. We really didn't do too much together after the film was over but we always kept in touch via other people. I would really love to find out what happened to Bob Random. His wife Ida became a costume or set designer. They were both fascinating people."

Tisha next guest-starred on two of the wackiest shows of the sixties, *Batman* and *Get Smart*. These zany series are ex-

Sterling and Tommy Kirk in *Village of the Giants* (Embassy, 1965).

tremely popular with audiences to this day, but when asked if they were fun to work on Tisha replies, "Each of them was just another TV show to me. I never thought working was particularly fun. To me it was *work*. I hated the waiting. I hated keeping my energy up over a ten- or twelve-hour period. I thought that was the hardest part about acting. It's very emotional—you just can't fake it—you have to be really there and it takes a tremendous amount of energy."

On *Batman*, she played Legs, the only daughter of criminal mastermind Ma Parker, played by the irascible Shelley Winters. She and her brood take over Gotham prison and strap the Dynamic Duo to electric chairs. "Shelley Winters was a bitch and was a holy terror to me," exclaims Tisha with a laugh. "She didn't want to be there—then she slipped and hurt her back on the set, which made her angry. After I became a much more serious actress and we re-connected [on the 1971 TV-movie *A Death of Innocence*], she loved me. And I still love her to this day. She's a marvelous teacher at the Actors Studio. And she is a very interesting, fabulous woman. I love her honesty and forthrightness. She's been known to be extremely hard to work with but it's just Shelley."

On *Get Smart*, Don Adams' Maxwell Smart becomes a judge at the Miss Galaxy Beauty Pageant so he can protect a scientist's daughter, Miss USA (Sterling), from KAOS kidnappers. "I played a bimbo," recalls Tisha chuckling. "They made me wear a really tight orange chiffon dress, which I remember just wanting to get out of it. Don Adams was terribly polite to me. He was very focused on his work. But he always had a quip or two and was very amusing on the set. Barbara Feldon was very sweet. I remember thinking how pretty she was."

In 1964, Tisha met actor Lal Baum at a party and they were married shortly thereafter. Their daughter Heidi was born on March 3, 1966. However, the marriage was rocky at best and it began affecting her work. It was reported that Tisha dropped out of *Journey to the Far Side of the Sun* due to "illness brought on by her marital problems." Star Roy Thinnes' then-wife actress Lynn Loring replaced her. By 1967, Tisha decided to get her life back on track and to get serious about her career. "Early on I was just given this wonderful opportunity," she says. "I didn't have to work that hard at it. But then I began to seriously study acting and became a member of the Actors Studio." She was seen there by Universal Pictures talent school coordinator Monique James, who offered Tisha a contract. Tisha reported to the studio with a new look. She had her long hair sheared off and let her natural auburn color grow in. ("I cut my hair because I decided I wanted a change. Mia Farrow did it first and we all followed suit!") She became part of the studio's acting school and her classmates included Kathryn Hays, Susan Clark and her good buddy Don Stroud, whom Tisha describes as being "a bad boy and I was kind of a bad girl—on the studio lot and everywhere else!"

Tisha's first film for her new studio was the 1968 western *Journey to Shiloh*. "I loved doing westerns—they were fun! I adore the costumes, the horses, and even the dirt." The film featured a number of hot, up-and-coming young actors including James Caan ("He's such a funny guy"), Michael Sarrazin, Don Stroud, Michael Burns, and Harrison Ford. The actors played young West Texans calling themselves the Concho County Comanches who ride out to volunteer for the Confederate Army during the Civil War. As they make their journey to Shiloh, Tennessee, they encounter perilous adventures along the way. Sterling portrayed Airybelle Sumner whom Tisha describes as "a dumb Southern belle. She really lived up to her name." According to Tisha, all her scenes were shot on a studio soundstage where they had to make it rain. "We were drenched in mud and manufactured rain for five days straight."

Tisha switched gears to play one of a trio of psychotic sisters in the twisted film *The Name of the Game Is Kill!* (1968), directed by former actor Gunnar Hellstrom. The movie has reached cult status due to the appearance of female impersonator T. C. Jones, who played the girls' crazy father pretending to be their murdered mother. In the film, Jack Lord (just before he landed *Hawaii Five-0*) played a Hungarian immigrant named Symcha Lipa who meets beautiful Susan Strasberg, the "normal" sister, while wandering the highways of Arizona. Susan operates a family-owned gas station and invites him to stay with her and her sisters: child-like, spider-loving Sterling and masculine Collin Wilcox, plus dear old mom Jones. All three sisters try to seduce and then kill Symcha.

The Name of the Game Is Kill! was beautifully filmed on location in Jerome, Arizona, by Vilmos Zsigmond. His remarkable cinematography and Stu Phillips's haunting theme "Shadows" (sung by the Electric Prunes) are the film's high points. "Making this film was an extremely wild experience for me," recalls Tisha. "I have never seen the film in its entirety and would love to see it one day.

Shelley Winters (*center*) as Ma Parker with her brood (including Sterling as Legs) plan to fry Batman (Adam West) and Robin (Burt Ward) on the ABC-TV series *Batman* in 1966.

It was a really hard shoot because we had to work long hours in this weird little town called Jerome—it was not much more than a ghost town. The temperature was close to 120 degrees and it was horrendous. We also all *hated* Gunnar Hellstrom. He was mean and we all wanted to mutiny. [*Laughs*] Anyway, I thought I did pretty well in this movie." *Variety* agreed: "Tisha Sterling is a marvel of witlessness and astonishing beauty. When those luminous eyes go blank revealing the nothingness behind them, it is a shocker of several dimensions."

"I worked with Jack Lord prior to working with him on this movie," continues Sterling. "Jack was really weird but he was a terrific fellow. He lived in the same building that I lived in. He was a very serious guy. He was always kind to

Hippie Sterling leads sheriff Clint Eastwood into an ambush in *Coogan's Bluff* (Universal, 1968).

me and looked after me like a father. Jack was also a very good artist and had a lovely wife who took care of him. Susan Strasberg was a Method actress so her technique would drive Jack crazy. T. C. Jones played our father. He was nice but also a bit weird. Collin Wilcox, on the other hand, was *wonderful*! We stayed friends for years after doing this movie. She introduced me to a macrobiotic diet. We lived close by to each other in Topanga Canyon."

Tisha ended 1968 with a star-making role. She played a duplicitous hippie in the stylish detective film *Coogan's Bluff*, the first collaboration between director Don Siegel and star Clint Eastwood. With this film, slack-jawed Eastwood made the leap from spaghetti western cowboy to cop. He portrayed Arizona deputy Coogan, who heads to New York City to extradite fugitive Don Stroud. While waiting for Stroud to recover from a bad LSD trip, Eastwood becomes involved with bland Susan Clark as a social worker and feisty Sterling as Stroud's conniving girlfriend. She helps Stroud escape and Clint roughs her up to find where he is hiding. In retaliation, she leads him to a pool hall where Stroud's cronies beat him up. The film climaxes high on the bluffs of the Cloisters. ("It was beautiful up there but it was freezing! It was a very cold winter that year.") The movie was the first to receive permission to film there. *Coogan's Bluff* received mixed reviews but Tisha won mostly good notices. Leonard Maltin commented, "Sterling is enjoyable as a hippie." *The New York Daily News* remarked, "Tisha Sterling makes an impression as the bad girl." Tisha credits her excellent performance to Siegel. "I loved working with Don and we had a marvelous rapport. I adored him and had an absolute blast doing this movie. He was a marvelously amusing, intelligent man."

When asked about the reported confrontations between Siegel and Eastwood while making this film, Tisha remarks, "Clint has very strong ideas about things. Don does too. So I'm sure they butted heads a lot. But at that time I don't think Clint was directing yet. They never argued in front of me, anyway. My relationship with Clint was very good. He is a sweet and darling man. Don Stroud and I were only rebellious a couple of times—not bad since we had a motorcycle and all of Manhattan to cause trouble in! [*Laughs*] Don and I became close buddies and we stayed that way for a long time. He is also a close friend with Stacy Keach. We were all together in Montana doing some horrific movie [*The Killer Inside Me*, 1976]. We were stuck there for three months."

Tisha was one of three women who become involved with restless Vietnam veteran Glen Campbell as he hit the highway for a series of unrelated adventures in *Norwood* (1970), directed by Jack Haley, Jr. The film is a pleasant road movie and is reminiscent of the Elvis Presley films, which is not too surprising since Hal B. Wallis produced it. Returning to his hometown after serving time in the Marines, Texas boy Campbell leaves his shiftless brother-in-law Dom DeLuise and his sister Leigh French to make it as a singer on the *Louisiana Hayride*. He's hired by shady Pat Hingle to transport two hooked-together cars to New York for auction as a way to get an audition. But after learning the cars are "hot and are about to burst into flames," he dumps them and his feisty driving companion Carol Lynley (amusing as a Southern ogress) in Illinois. He hitchhikes to New York City to hook up with Marine buddy Joe Namath but instead finds uptight

Greenwich Village beatnik Tisha Sterling. Sliding into her bathtub, she asks Norwood, "Does your guitar play underwater?" He replies, "No, but I do." Disappointed with New York despite his one nightstand with Tisha, Campbell heads back to Texas and meets a very pregnant Kim Darby on the bus. After her boyfriend abandons her, she and Campbell fall in love as Campbell finally makes his national televised singing debut.

Norwood was notable for reuniting *True Grit* co-stars Campbell and Darby and for featuring Broadway Joe in his film debut. However, Paramount lost faith in the film and released it after Namath's second film *C.C. and Company* (1970). As expected, the film was a hit with the drive-in crowd but not with audiences in the big cities. However, the *New York Times* liked Sterling and raved, "This beautiful girl is simply wonderful in her small role." Tisha remembers that "Jack Haley, Jr., was interesting to work with. He was my neighbor growing up. Carol Lynley and I did some promotion for the film together. Carol is very sweet and I like her a lot. When we came off the plane (I think somewhere in south Texas), these people started speaking Spanish to us. I didn't speak a word of it and all of a sudden Carol was conversing with them in Spanish. I was so impressed! I didn't know she was bilingual."

In *Coogan's Bluff* (Universal, 1968), Clint Eastwood forces Sterling to help him search the Cloisters where her boyfriend is hiding from the police.

Despite her good reviews in *Coogan's Bluff* and *Norwood*, Tisha wasn't able to capitalize on her success. She seemed to concentrate on working in television over film though she was extremely disappointed to lose the female lead to Lauren Hutton in the motorcycle drama *Little Fauss and Big Halsy* ("I wanted to work with *Robert Redford*!"). On television, Tisha could be seen playing a rebellious student on *CBS Playhouse*, a nuclear weapons protester on *The Name of the Game*, a pregnant heroin addict on *The Bold Ones: The Doctors* and a hippie prostitute on *Ironside*. Her most memorable made-for-TV film was the sci-fi hit *Night Slaves* (1971). This film reunited director Ted Post and actor James Franciscus from *Beneath the Planet of the Apes* (1970). The story involved a vacationing man (Franciscus) with a plate in his head who stops in a small town. He awakens in the middle of the night to see the hypnotized townspeople (including his wife Lee Grant) go off to a field to repair a disabled spaceship. Sterling played a beautiful alien. When asked if it was difficult to play a fantasy figure, she replies with a laugh, "No, because I think I *was* an alien back then."

Tisha continues, "I liked *Night Slaves* a lot. And I thought it turned out really well. We had a lot of fun doing this. We were up all night for days on end. I like Lee Grant. She was one of the best people I ever worked with. She is a fabulous actress and a fabulous woman. Lee was just an outspoken woman of the people—a defender of the underdog. James Franciscus was cool. And Ted Post was a good director—very together, very inventive and a very forward-thinking guy."

Sterling next traveled to South America to co-star in the feature *The Wild Pack* (1972) with Kent Lane (Rhonda Fleming's son) and John Rubinstein. Directed by acclaimed cinematographer Hall Bartlett, it was a semi-documentary look at a gang of street kids who have to steal, scavenge and beg to say alive in the slums of Brazil. Under its original title, *Sandpit Generals*, the film took first prize at the Moscow International Film Festival. "I think Hall was trying to show how horrendous it was for these teenagers growing up in Brazil but it was so beautiful—film-wise—that I don't think the audience really got how incredibly filthy and horrific life really is there," remarks Tisha. "The people were either impoverished or rich. There was no in between. Everybody is on the street. People live in cardboard boxes next to mansions. There is prostitution and leprosy. There is hardly any sanitation. It was horrendous. The military-type government is constantly pushing the people farther and farther away towards the water to live. They had these little shacks built over the water's edge on tiny bridges made literally from wood scraps. Though the people were very poor, they were friendly and very into their culture. You'd hear people playing music all day. Their religious beliefs are a combination of Christianity and voodoo. Being an American and being in a film, I was of course extremely privileged. But my heart went out to the people there."

As the seventies turned into the eighties, Tisha, like most of her contemporaries, found the number of feature film roles offered to her diminishing and she appeared in mostly made-for-TV movies. In 1981, Tisha moved to New York for awhile to try to land a part on a soap opera. It was there that she learned she had a gift for flower arranging. "I never knew I had this talent," Tisha says. "But I am an artist and I paint. I see something and recreate it."

Norwood (Paramount, 1970) featured Glen Campbell as a restless Vietnam vet and Sterling as a Greenwich Village bohemian.

After playing her mother's (Ann Sothern) character as a younger woman in the opening scene of the acclaimed film *The Whales of August* (1987), Sterling dropped out of acting because "I was so screwed up. I needed to go away and regroup. So that's what I did. I left Los Angeles and moved to Idaho. I wanted to get out of the city because I knew I would never get well if I stayed. I picked Idaho because I had come there since I was a child and always found it to be a really beautiful and healing place."

Tisha's wish to act again came true when a friend who was the casting director for Bruce Willis' movie *Breakfast of Champions* offered her a small role. The movie was being filmed in Idaho close to where Tisha resides. "I played a crazy novelist," says Tisha excitedly. "It has a fascinating cast playing all kinds of strange characters. I worked with Albert Finney. He is a wonderful actor. And Bruce Willis is a good guy. It was fun to have Hollywood come to Twin Falls, Idaho." Now that Tisha Sterling is living in Los Angeles again, this may be the first of many more films to come for her.

FILM APPEARANCES

1965 **Village of the Giants** (Embassy) d. Bert I. Gordon.
1968 **The Name of the Game Is Kill** (Fanfare) d. Gunnar Hellstrom.
 Journey to Shiloh (Universal) d. William Hale.

	Coogan's Bluff (Universal) d. Don Siegel.
1969	Big Daddy/Paradise Road (United Film Organization) d. Carl Hittleman.
1970	Norwood (Paramount) d. Jack Haley, Jr.
	Night Slaves (TV-movie) d. Ted Post.
1971	Powderkeg (TV-movie) d. Douglas Heyes.
	A Death of Innocence (TV-movie) d. Paul Wendkos.
1972	The Wild Pack/Sandpit Generals (AIP) d. Hall Bartlett.
1973	Snatched (TV-movie) d. Sutton Roley.
1974	Betrayal (TV-movie) d. Gordon Hessler.
1975	Crazy Mama (New World) [cameo] d. Jonathan Demme.
1976	Kiss Me ... Kill Me (TV-movie) d. Michael O'Herlihy.
	The Killer Inside Me (Warner Bros.) d. Burt Kennedy.
1977	In the Glitter Palace (TV-movie) d. Robert Butler.
1978	The Space-Watch Murders (TV-movie)
1981	The Coming/Burned at the Stake (International Films) d. Bert I. Gordon.
1987	The Whales of August (Alive Films) d. Lindsay Anderson.
1992	Dark Horse (Republic Pictures International) d. David Hemmings.
1999	Breakfast of Champions (Buena Vista) d. Alan Rudolph.

Television Appearances

The Ann Sothern Show "Loving Arms" 10/13/60 CBS.
The Alfred Hitchcock Hour "Change of Address" 10/12/64 NBC.
The Regis Philbin Show [talk show guest] 10/28/64 Synd.
Mr. Novak "Firebrand" 4/13/65 NBC.
The Donna Reed Show "Pop Goes Theresa" 9/16/65 ABC.
The Long Hot Summer "A Time for Living" 9/23/65 ABC.
The Long Hot Summer "A Stranger to the House" 9/30/65 ABC.
Slattery's People "Of Damon, Pythias and Sleeping Dogs" 11/12/65 CBS.
Frank Merriwell (pilot) 7/25/66 CBS.
Batman "The Greatest Mother of Them All" 10/5/66 ABC.
Batman "Ma Parker" 10/6/66 ABC.
T.H.E. Cat "Curtains for Miss Winslow" 12/2/66 NBC.
Get Smart "The Girl from KAOS" 2/4/67 NBC.
The Road West "Eleven Miles to Eden" 3/13/67 NBC.
Run for Your Life "It Could Only Happen in Rome" 12/20/67 NBC.
Bonanza "Star Crossed" 3/10/68 NBC.
It Takes a Thief "Birds of a Feather" 3/19/68 ABC.
The Name of the Game "Love-In at Ground Zero" 1/31/69 NBC.
The Name of the Game "The Bobby Currier Story" 2/21/69 NBC.
CBS Playhouse "The Experiment" 2/25/69 CBS.
The Bold Ones: The Doctors "What's the Price of a Pair of Eyes?" 10/5/69 NBC.
Insight "Exit" 4/27/69 Synd.
The Bold Ones: The Doctors "This Will Really Kill You" 9/20/70 NBC.
The Immortal "Paradise Bay" 12/10/70 ABC.
The Bold Ones: The Lawyers "The Hyland Confession" 1/31/71 NBC.
The Men from Shiloh "Flight from Memory" 2/17/71 NBC.
The Sixth Sense "Lady, Lady Take My Life" 1/29/72 ABC.
Insight "A Man Called Don" 2/2/72 Synd.
Medical Center "The Confession" 3/8/72 CBS.
Night Gallery "The Return of the Sorcerer" 9/24/72 NBC.
Ironside "Who'll Cry for My Baby?" 12/7/72 NBC.
Hawaii Five-0 "Little Girl Blue" 2/13/73 CBS.
Columbo "Candidate for Crime" 11/4/73 NBC.
ABC Wide World of Mystery "Death Is a Bad Trip" 7/23/74 ABC.
Caribe "The Assassin" 5/5/75 ABC.
Police Woman "Bait" 12/7/76 NBC.
McMillan "Coffee, Tea or Cyanide?" 1/30/77 NBC.
The Feather and Father Gang "Sun, Sand and Death" 3/14/77 ABC.
Charlie's Angels "Caged Angel" 10/31/79 ABC.
Charlie's Angels "Angels on the Line" 2/14/81 ABC.

More Groovy Gals

Pamela Austin

Best known for her series of Dodge car commercials as the Dodge Rebellion girl, pretty blonde Austin made her film debut (using the name Pamela Kirk) as one of the students guided around Hawaii by Elvis Presley in *Blue Hawaii* (1961). Signed to a contract with Warner Bros., Pamela changed her name but landed only small roles in *Rome Adventure* (1962) and *The Chapman Report* (1962). She had better luck at MGM and starred in the youth-oriented musical *Hootenanny Hoot* (1963) with Peter Breck. She was Elvis' hillbilly cousin Selena Tatum who vied with her sister Azalea (Yvonne Craig) for Elvis' attention in *Kissin' Cousins* (1964). The late sixties found Austin playing the dumb blonde on *Rowan & Martin's Laugh-In* before Goldie Hawn joined the cast. Her last known credit is the TV-movie *Evil Roy Slade* (1972).

Joan Blackman

The first Joan to star opposite Elvis Presley, this dark-haired beauty from San Francisco made a name for herself as the selfish wife of struggling actor Anthony Franciosa in *Career* (1959). She next co-starred with Jerry Lewis in *Visit to a Small Planet* (1960) before winning the role of Maile in the hit Elvis musical *Blue Hawaii* (1961) after Juliet Prowse was fired and Pamela Tiffin turned it down. She was rumored to be one of Elvis' least favorite co-stars, even though she played his love interest a second time in *Kid Galahad* (1962). But Blackman's film career seemed to happen in spurts. In the late sixties, she appeared with Richard Egan in the spy film *The Destructors* (1967) and with Lloyd Bridges in *Daring Game* (1968). And after being off the big screen for six years, she surprisingly turned up in *Macon County Line* (1974), *Moonrunners* (1975) (the forebear to the TV series *The Dukes of Hazzard*) and David Cronenberg's *Shivers* (1975).

Yvonne Craig

This former ballerina, who was discovered by producer Joe Pasternak, became a fixture on television from 1958 through the mid-seventies. Dark-haired and lovely, Craig appeared in the films *Eighteen and Anxious* (1957), *The Gene Krupa Story* (1959) and *High Time* (1960), among others, before being jilted by Elvis Presley early on in *It Happened at the World's Fair* (1963). As a mountain waif, Craig won the heart of the brunette Elvis while WAC Cynthia Pepper snagged his blonde hillbilly cousin (also Elvis) in *Kissin' Cousins* (1964). After joining the Beach gang as they headed to Sun Valley for a *Ski Party* (1965), Yvonne appeared in *In Like Flint* (1967) and TV's *The Man from U.N.C.L.E.* She also had the distinction of playing a mini-skirted scientist in the cult classic *Mars Needs Women* (1966). But Craig is best remembered for playing Barbara Gordon (a.k.a. Batgirl) on the last season of *Batman*. She added higher excitement to the series but not higher ratings and the show was cancelled in 1968. Yvonne continued acting in films (*How to Frame a Figg*, 1971) and on television but acting opportunities seem to have dropped off by the early eighties. She then became a very successful real estate agent. Today she is a regular at autograph shows and has written her autobiography titled *From Ballet to the Batcave and Beyond*.

SHELLEY FABARES

During the fifties, perky Shelley Fabares appeared in movies with John Saxon and Natalie Wood, and became a teen idol herself when she was cast as Mary Stone in the hit comedy series *The Donna Reed Show*. In the sixties, Shelley's popularity extended to the recording industry with the #1 single, "Johnny Angel." After leaving *The Donna Reed Show* in 1963, Fabares headed straight for the beach in *Ride the Wild Surf* (1964), co-starring Fabian, and was Elvis' leading lady in three of his films. In *Girl Happy* (1965) she played a mobster's daughter on vacation in Fort Lauderdale, secretly being chaperoned by Elvis and his band. *Spinout* (1966) featured Fabares as a spoiled heiress vying with Diane McBain and Deborah Walley for Elvis, who played a singer–race car driver intent on staying single. *Clambake* (1967) cast Fabares as a golddigger fighting off her attraction to poor water ski instructor Elvis while trying to snag rich playboy Bill Bixby. The joke was that Elvis was actually a rich Texan's son pretending to be poor. "I've made it a policy to say just a few things about Elvis and how I felt about him," remarks Fabares. "I've just always felt that, since he never talked about himself when he was here, it wouldn't be right for me to discuss him now. I will say that he was a wonderful person—kind, sweet and funny. Doing those pictures with him were some of the happiest experiences I ever had, professionally or personally. Even if the films weren't great—they were okay and perfect for what they were, at that time—the experience of doing them was extraordinary. I feel blessed and lucky that I was able to work with Elvis." After being idle in the late sixties, Fabares made a comeback as the wife of dying football player Brian Piccolo (played by James Caan) in the TV-movie *Brian's Song* (1971). She never had to fret for work again. During the seventies and eighties, Fabares shed her wholesome image to play a bitch on wheels, literally, on TV's *Forever Fernwood* and the devious, self-centered Francine on *One Day at a Time*. More recently, she spent nine seasons (and won two Emmy nominations) as TV anchorwoman Christine Armstrong on the hit sitcom *Coach* with Craig T. Nelson.

Shelley Fabares and Fabian in *Ride the Wild Surf* (Columbia, 1964).

MIMSY FARMER

This fragile-looking blonde began her career as the ingenue on television and on the big screen in *Spencer's Mountain* (1963) and *Bus Riley's Back in Town* (1965). She found more success playing a string of bad girls and misunderstood teenagers in such biker and alienated youth film classics as *Hot Rods to Hell* (1967), *Riot on Sunset Strip* (1967), *Devil's Angels* (1967) and *The Wild Racers* (1968). Farmer reached her pinnacle with *More* (1969), her first foreign film, which warned of the excesses of the counterculture as she played an American hippie who draws an innocent German (Klaus Grunberg) into the world of heroin and LSD on an island off of Spain. Farmer later relocated to Italy and worked steadily until the late eighties. She appeared in Dario Argento's *Four Flies on Grey Velvet* (1971), among many other European horror films. Her last known credit is Roger Vadim's *Safari* (1991) starring Peter McEnery.

ANNETTE FUNICELLO

Former Mouseketeer Annette Funicello was a Disney girl (1959's *The Shaggy Dog*, 1961's *Babes in Toyland*) and a recording artist ("Tall Paul") before she donned a bathing suit and joined Frankie

Small town girl Mimsy Farmer is terrorized by gang member Kip Whitman while biker chicks (Salli Sachse and Nai Bonet) look on in *Devil's Angels* (AIP, 1967).

Avalon in *Beach Party* (1963). They became the most popular surfing couple in film though neither of them looked as if they had ever laid a foot on the sand before. Even so, the chemistry between them was perfect for these types of films. *Beach Party* spawned a number of profitable sequels starring Frankie and Annette including *Muscle Beach Party* (1964), *Bikini Beach* (1964), *Beach Blanket Bingo* (1965) and *How to Stuff a Wild Bikini* (1965). When the Beach films began to wane, AIP teamed Annette with Fabian in two hot rod films, *Fireball 500* (1966) and *Thunder Alley* (1967). After making a cameo appearance in the Monkees' film *Head* (1968), Funicello wasn't seen on the big screen until she reteamed with Avalon and headed *Back to the Beach* in 1987. Unfortunately, ill health has kept her from working these past number of years.

LAUREL GOODWIN

This former model's only acting experience was summer stock when producer Hal B. Wallis saw her photograph in the Paramount studio publicity department and tapped her to play a lead role opposite Elvis Presley in *Girls! Girls! Girls!* (1962). Goodwin was cast as rich girl Laurel Dodge, who vies with sultry

Publicity shot of Annette Funicello and Frankie Avalon in *Muscle Beach Party* (AIP, 1964).

torch singer Stella Stevens for the attention of fisherman Elvis Presley. This was the King's second film set in Hawaii and it was a box office smash. Helping its success was a better-than-average soundtrack (including the hit "Return to Sender"), beautiful scenery and an entertaining performance from Goodwin. *Variety* raved, "The most striking thing about the picture is the introduction of Laurel Goodwin." Recalling the film, Goodwin says, "I first met Elvis on the set in makeup. I was a big fan of Elvis' music but meeting *Elvis Presley* did not knock me out. But he turned out to be charming and sweet. Elvis did not like this film. He was very uncomfortable with performing. He also felt very unsure of himself as far as acting went. He deferred to me continually because he felt I knew more about *acting*, whatever the hell that is. We got along beautifully throughout the entire shoot and spent a lot of time together. In fact, everybody was getting along wonderfully. Then Stella Stevens arrived in Hawaii. I met her for the first time when our limousine came to the hotel to take us on location. I came down that morning (and it was just a gorgeous, breathtaking day), the chauffeur opened the door, I got in and I said, 'Good morning, Miss Stevens. Welcome to Hawaii. I'm Laurel.' She said, 'Hello, I'm Stella.' I then said, 'It's a pleasure to meet you. How do you feel about being in Hawaii? It's just beautiful, isn't it?' She replied,

In *Girls! Girls! Girls!* (Paramount, 1962), Elvis Presley and Laurel Goodwin sail the open seas off the islands of Hawaii.

'Oh, God. This is just not my kind of place. I'm like a mushroom. I like dark, dank places.' I thought, 'Oh, what a pain in the ass!' [Laughs] I really wanted to like her and have admiration for her but Stella was over there under duress by Hal Wallis so she decided that she didn't like anything about it. She was very aloof to everybody—even to Elvis. They didn't have very much to say to each other. It wasn't even what I would call a professional relationship. Stella did not make any effort whatsoever to be pleasant or friendly to anyone and she was not well liked by any of the crew. I heard gossip and stories about her from wardrobe to makeup to hairdressing. They called her Madame Stella—she thought she was some great stellar star. And she wasn't really much of anything at that time."

Goodwin next appeared in the Jackie Gleason comedy *Papa's Delicate Condition* (1963) and the Sam Peckinpah–scripted Western *The Glory Guys* (1965). But her career never picked up steam. Goodwin remarks, "I was typecast as Beth the preacher's daughter, Beth the preacher's daughter and Beth the preacher's daughter. There weren't a whole lot of those roles but I got to do *all* the preachers' daughters. Also, the business began to change. Film output per studio dropped dramatically. There was very little work and an *awful* lot of competition. If I had been three inches shorter or two inches taller I would have gotten a lot more of those roles. I was hired twice and fired twice to play Gidget. At 5'7" I was deemed too tall." Though Goodwin gave it her all in her film appearances, she is remembered most for playing Ensign Colt in the original pilot for *Star Trek* (called "The Cage," starring Jeffrey Hunter). When *Star Trek* became a series with William Shatner, footage from the pilot was incorporated into the episode "The Menagerie." Goodwin retired from acting in the early seventies to spend more time with her husband Walter Wood, the noted film producer. Wood was also the first person to run the mayor's office for motion pictures and film in New York City and he is credited for revitalizing that industry in the Big Apple. Today the Woods are semi-retired and reside in Palm Springs.

Dolores Hart

They don't ask Dolores Hart where the boys are any more—she's now a nun. But before she took her vows, this talented brunette played Elvis Presley's sweet love interest in *Loving You* (1957) and *King Creole* (1958). She was a perfect contrast to the career-driven publicity agent Lizabeth Scott in the former and seductive gun moll Carolyn Jones in the latter. And it has been written that she and Elvis hit it off splendidly. Hart then was top-billed as one of the legions of college kids to descend on Fort Lauderdale during spring break in the first official Beach movie of the sixties, *Where the Boys Are* (1960). She played the sensible one, the girl her friends (Yvette Mimieux, Paula Prentiss and Connie Francis) go to for advice. Theater owners took notice and voted her a Star of Tomorrow in 1961. After playing a gold-digging flight attendant in *Come Fly with Me* (1963), Hart became Sister Judith and entered the Abbey of Regina Laudis (a cloistered order) in Connecticut. Today she is known as Mother Dolores and to raise money for their convent, she and her fellow nuns recorded a CD of chant music in 1998. She wrote, "Thank you so much for showing interest in my life in films. Your thought to include me is appreciated. However, I trust you will understand that it is not possible for me to participate."

Susan Hart

The dark-haired, shapely Susan Hart made her film debut as the heroine in the low-budget horror film *The Slime People* (1963) starring Robert Hutton. She spent the entire film carrying an over-sized pocketbook while being chased around Los Angeles (enclosed in a dome) by prehistoric, scaly creatures from the city's sewers. In 1964, she turned up in three Beach films. In *For Those Who Think Young* she was one of Pamela Tiffin's sorority sisters. *Ride the Wild Surf* cast her as a Hawaiian girl who falls in love with surfer Tab Hunter, much to her mother's chagrin. And in *Pajama Party* she played a curvaceous beauty whose sexy dancing causes flowers to melt and volcanoes to blow their tops. Her poise and talent snagged her a contract with American International Pictures. It also nabbed her a husband—the company's co-founder James H. Nicholson. In 1965, Hart appeared in two films with Vincent Price, *War-Gods of the Deep* and *Dr. Goldfoot and the Bikini Machine*. Her last film was *The Ghost in the Invisible Bikini* (1966): She and Boris Karloff were brought in after filming was complete to try to save the film. Hart played the title character who tries to prevent heirs Tommy Kirk and Deborah Walley from being swindled out of their inheritance by crooked lawyer Basil Rathbone. She wore a horrible blonde wig sprayed with

Susan Hart serves up a winner in *Pajama Party* (AIP, 1964).

sheep oil as most of her scenes were filmed against a black backdrop. In 1968, Hart retired from acting to raise her son and to concentrate on a singing career.

JOCELYN LANE

Austrian actress Jocelyn Lane appeared in a number of British films during the late fifties using her birth name of Jackie Lane. In 1964, she changed her name to Jocelyn and arrived in Hollywood. Almost immediately, this sexy petite blonde landed a lead role as a fitness instructor searching for her grandfather's hidden gold opposite Elvis Presley in *Tickle Me* (1965). Resembling Brigitte Bardot, Lane is considered by many to be Elvis' best-looking co-star. She followed up her success in *Tickle Me* with the Western *Incident at Phantom Hill* (1966) with Robert Fuller and the international comedy *How to Seduce a Playboy* (1967). She also played the photographer in the United Nations project *The Poppy Is Also a Flower* (1966), based on a story by Ian Fleming and featuring an all-star cast. And like her sixties contemporaries, she made guest appearances on all the top television programs of the day. In the cleverly titled biker flick *Hell's Belles* (1969), she played biker leader Adam Roarke's girlfriend and is kidnapped by good guy Jeremy Slate when Roarke steals his brand new chopper. Lane's last film was director Larry Buchanan's violent *A Bullet for Pretty Boy* (1970) starring

Fabian (billed as Fabian Forte) as the notorious gangster. Today, Jocelyn resides in England and does voiceovers for television commercials.

SUE ANE LANGDON

With her curvaceous figure and perky personality, Sue Ane Langdon played a variety of goofy dames throughout the sixties beginning with her short stint as Alice Kramden opposite Jackie Gleason on his variety series *American Scene Magazine*. After being let go after only a handful of episodes ("Jackie was not easy to work with"), Langdon turned her attention to the big screen. She began getting supporting roles in films aimed at the youth market including *When the Boys Meet the Girls* (1965) with Connie Francis, *Hold On!* (1966) with Herman's Hermits and two with Elvis Presley—*Roustabout* (1964) and *Frankie and Johnny* (1966). "I thought Elvis Presley was sweet and very nice," says Langdon. "But I almost didn't do *Roustabout* because doing an Elvis Presley movie was not really much of a stepping stone. I'm glad I did it because it is one of the main things I'm remembered for today. I enjoyed working with Elvis and can't say one bad thing about him. But I don't think he was that comfortable making movies. He was much more relaxed on stage." Langdon's comedic expertise allowed her to graduate from teenage movies to more adult fare. Typed as a kook with sex appeal (her der-

Voluptuous Sue Ane Langdon.

riere received a lot of press, especially after she bared it in 1965's *The Rounders*), Sue Ane appeared with some of Hollywood's top leading men including Walter Matthau in *A Guide for the Married Man* (1967) and Henry Fonda and James Stewart in *The Cheyenne Social Club* (1970). In *A Fine Madness* (1966), Sue Ane portrayed an office secretary who can't resist the charms of a carpet cleaner-cum-poet played by Sean Connery. ("Sean was a very confident actor and comfortable with his persona. I adored Sean. He was so cool! He was like a big bear but totally charming.") As the sixties came to an end, Langdon morphed into a dutiful housewife (and won a Golden Globe Award in the process) on the hit sitcom *Arnie*. She continued acting through the seventies and eighties. Her last film was *Zapped Again* in 1989 because "the parts I played in the sixties were fun and there is just not that kind of humor around any more. The innocence is gone from films today. The humor is harsh and it's not funny. Most of my roles were innocent, daffy women. These roles don't exist today. I don't miss acting an awful lot. I've done television, films and theater so I guess I got it all out of my system."

PATTY McCORMACK

Actress Patty McCormack recreated her Broadway role as the evil Rhoda Penmark, the 11-year-old homicidal monster from hell in the motion picture *The Bad*

Patty McCormack (*far right*) and fellow gang members (*left to right*) Diane McBain, Jeremy Slate and Sarah Marshall mourn the death of Ronnie Rondell in *The Mini-Skirt Mob* (AIP, 1968).

Seed (1956). McCormack was so good in the role that she received an Academy Award nomination. To soften her image, her next film role was as *Kathy O'* (1958). As Patty began to mature, she appeared mostly on television but did play a high school senior in the exploitation film *The Explosive Generation* (1961) in which William Shatner starred as a teacher who shocks a small town when he begins instructing his students in sex education. Patty remained off the big screen until 1968 when she co-starred in four alienated youth films including *The Mini-Skirt Mob* as a biker chick, *Maryjane* as a pot-smoking high school student and *Born Wild* as a student caught between two rival gangs (one Caucasian, the other Mexican) in a small Arizona town. The seventies found Patty working mostly on daytime soap operas (*The Best of Everything*, *As the World Turns*) although she made an appearance as one of the victims in *Bug* (1975), the last film produced by William Castle. Patty (now billed as Patricia McCormack) was back to her evil ways when she returned to the screen in 1995 in the surprise hit *Mommy*, the unofficial sequel to *The Bad Seed*.

MARY ANN MOBLEY

"Sweet as Southern pie," is the way former Miss America Mary Ann Mobley has been described by some of her co-stars.

Mary Ann Mobley and Elvis Presley share an Arabian adventure in *Harum Scarum* (MGM, 1965).

After honing her acting craft on television for a few years, Mobley snagged the lead in the teen musical *Get Yourself a College Girl* in 1964. But it was her performance as the thrill-seeking girlfriend of John Dillinger (Nick Adams) in *Young Dillinger* (1965) that won her kudos. She shared the Golden Globe Award for Most Promising Newcomers with Mia Farrow and Celia Kaye and was voted a Star of Tomorrow, placing higher on the list than Julie Christie. Mobley next co-starred with Elvis in *Girl Happy* (1965) as a Southern sexpot and in *Harum Scarum* (1965) as an Arab princess. To spy fans, she is remembered as the original Girl from U.N.C.L.E. on an episode of *The Man from U.N.C.L.E.* (When it was picked up as a series, Stefanie Powers replaced her because the producers felt that Mobley was too soft.) Happily married to actor Gary Collins since the late sixties, Mobley has since worked steadily on television, including replacing Dixie Carter as Conrad Bain's wife on the eighties sitcom *Diff'rent Strokes*. She stills acts today.

Nancy Sinatra

Beach Babe. Spy Gal. Biker Chick. Elvis Cutie. Nancy Sinatra appeared in all the sixties genres aimed at the youth audience though her film career lasted only from 1964 through 1968. For a time during the early sixties, Nancy was only known as the daughter of Frank Sinatra and the wife of teen heartthrob Tommy Sands. But in 1964, dark-haired Sinatra made her film debut in the beach film *For Those Who Think Young* as beatnik Bob Denver's girlfriend, followed by *Get Yourself a College Girl* (1964). She had talent and theater owners in *The Motion Picture Herald* voted her one of the top ten Stars of Tomorrow. After appearing with her father in the comedy *Marriage on the Rocks* (1965), she essayed the lead role in the mod spy spoof *Last of the Secret Agents?*, starring the comedy team of Marty Allen and Steve Rossi. She also sang the title tune. By this time, Nancy's singing career had overshadowed her acting. She had a #1 hit record with "These Boots Are Made for Walking" in 1966. The only reason she seemed to have showed up in *The Ghost in the Invisible Bikini* (1966) was to sing a couple of tunes, most notably "Geronimo." Sinatra's biggest movie hit though was *The Wild Angels* (1966), the film that revitalized the biker film for the sixties generation. It also helped change her image to a blonde-haired, leather-clad, tough mini-skirted chick. Some of Sinatra's other hit records included "Sugar Town," "Summer Wine" with Lee Hazelwood, and "Somethin' Stupid" with Frank Sinatra plus the theme songs from the films' *You Only Live Twice* and *Tony Rome* (both 1967). She ended her movie career with a role opposite Elvis Presley in *Speedway* (1968). She concentrated on her singing career before retiring in 1974 to raise her two daughters from a second marriage to Hugh Lambert. In 1989, Nancy made an

Publicity shot of Nancy Sinatra and Aron Kincaid in *The Ghost in the Invisible Bikini* (AIP, 1966).

appearance as herself on the hit TV drama series *China Beach,* set in Vietnam during the war. It was the start of a successful comeback, which included a new album with original songs and a national tour.

Deborah Walley

Deborah Walley was a theatre-trained actress doing Chekhov's *Three Sisters* in New York when Columbia talent scout Joyce Selznick spotted her. The talented redhead was brought to Hollywood and beat out numerous other actresses to succeed Sandra Dee as Gidget in *Gidget Goes Hawaiian* (1961). The film was a hit and made Walley a star. Her perky performance as the surfing sweetie won her the Photoplay Gold Medal Award for "Favorite Female Newcomer." But Walley did not want to be typecast as Gidget and had to fight hard to get varied roles. She made two films—*Bon Voyage* (1962) and *Summer Magic* (1963) for Walt Disney and gave a fine performance as a flaky coed in *The Young Lovers* (1964) starring Peter Fonda. However, in 1964 she signed a contract with AIP and her name became forever synonymous with beach movies. In *Beach Blanket Bingo* (1965) Walley unsuccessfully vied with Annette Funicello for the charms of Frankie Avalon. She had to settle for John Ashley (whom she married in real life) instead. Wally, however, did win Frankie in that same year's dumb service comedy *Sergeant Deadhead* and *Ski Party* (whose tag line proclaimed, "It's where the he's meet the she's on skis"). In *The Ghost in the Invisible Bikini* (1966) Walley had to survive a night in a haunted mansion along with heir Tommy Kirk and the rest of the beach gang to collect their inheritance. In between beach movies, Walley also found time to appear in the sci-fi cheapie *The Bubble* (1966) and compete with Shelley Fabares and Diane McBain for the charms of Elvis in *Spinout* (1966). She told author Kim Holston in the book *Starlet,* "Working with Elvis was wonderful, which was quite something because I really didn't think too much of him when I started the film *Spinout,* and we became fast friends during the filming." Her last beach movie was appropriately titled *It's a Bikini World* (1967), which reunited Walley with Tommy Kirk, this time playing rivals in a multi-event athletic contest. The film is notable, however, for the impressive lineup of rock acts—the Animals, the Castaways, the Toys, and the Gentrys. Walley took a respite from filmmaking to co-star on the sitcom *The Mothers-in-Law* (1967–1969) with Eve Arden and Kaye Ballard. She didn't return to the big screen until 1973's horror opus *The Severed Arm,* but her role as an inept thief in the low-budget comedy *Benji* (1974) was much more memorable and became one of that year's biggest surprise hits. Soon after, Walley retired to raise her family. Today she is the author of the children's book *The Last of the Blues* and recently appeared in an episode of *Baywatch*—an appropriate comeback vehicle for the sixties' ultimate beach babe.

Bibliography

Arkoff, Sam. *Flying Through Hollywood by the Seat of My Pants: From the Man Who Brought You "I Was a Teenage Werewolf" and "Muscle Beach Party."* Secaucus, NJ: Carol Pub. Group, 1992.

Beck, Calvin Thomas. *Scream Queens: Heroines of the Horrors.* New York: Collier Books, 1978.

Betrock, Alan. *The I Was a Teenage Juvenile Delinquent Rock 'n' Roll Horror Beach Party Movie Book.* New York: St. Martin's Press, 1986.

Brooks, Tim, and Earle Marsh. *The Complete Directory to Prime Time Network and Cable TV Shows, 1946–Present.* 4th ed. New York: Ballantine Books, 1995.

Cox, Stephen. *The Beverly Hillbillies.* Chicago: Contemporary Books, 1988.

_____. *The Hooterville Handbook: A Viewer's Guide to Green Acres.* New York: St. Martin's Press, 1993.

Crenshaw, Marshall. *Hollywood Rock.* New York: HarperPerennial, 1994.

Eisner, Joel. *The Official Batman Batbook.* Chicago: Contemporary Books, 1986.

_____, and David Krinsky. *Television Comedy Series: An Episode Guide to 153 TV Sitcoms in Syndication.* Jefferson, NC: McFarland, 1984.

Fonda, Peter. *Don't Tell Dad: A Memoir.* New York: Hyperion, 1998.

Gebert, Michael. *The Encyclopedia of Movie Awards.* New York: St. Martin's Press, 1996.

Gerani, Gary, and Paul H. Schulman. *Fantastic Television.* New York: Harmony Books, 1977.

Giankos, Larry James. *Television Drama Series Programming: A Comprehensive Chronicle, 1947–1959.* Metuchen, NJ: Scarecrow Press, 1978.

_____. *Television Drama Series Programming: A Comprehensive Chronicle, 1959–1975.* Metuchen, NJ: Scarecrow Press, 1980.

_____. *Television Drama Series Programming: A Comprehensive Chronicle, 1975–1980.* Metuchen, NJ: Scarecrow Press, 1981.

_____. *Television Drama Series Programming: A Comprehensive Chronicle, 1980–1982.* Metuchen, NJ: Scarecrow Press, 1983.

_____. *Television Drama Series Programming: A Comprehensive Chronicle, 1982–1984.* Metuchen, NJ: Scarecrow Press, 1987.

_____. *Television Drama Series Programming: A Comprehensive Chronicle, 1984–1986.* Metuchen, NJ: Scarecrow Press, 1992.

Goldberg, Lee. *Unsold Television Pilots, 1955 through 1988.* Jefferson, NC: McFarland, 1990.

Green, Joey. *The Get Smart Handbook.* New York: Collier Books, 1993.

Heitland, Jon. *The Man from U.N.C.L.E. Book: The Behind-the-Scenes Story of a*

Television Classic. New York: St. Martin's Press, 1987.

Hill, Tom, ed. *Nick at Nite's Classic TV Companion.* New York: Simon & Schuster, 1996.

Hirschhorn, Clive. *The Warner Bros. Story.* New York: Crown Publishers, 1979.

Holston, Kim. *Starlet.* Jefferson, NC: McFarland, 1988.

Horowitz, Murray. *TV 68.* New York: Media Books, 1967.

Hyatt, Wesley. *The Encyclopedia of Daytime Television.* New York: Billboard Books, 1997.

Inman, David. *The TV Encyclopedia.* New York: Pedigree Books, 1991.

Kesler, Susan E. *The Wild, Wild West: The Series.* Downey, CA: Arnett Press, 1988.

Krafsur, Richard P., ed. *The American Film Institute Catalog of Motion Pictures: Feature Films 1961–1970.* New York & London: R.R. Bowker, 1976.

_____. *The American Film Institute Catalog of Motion Pictures: Feature Films 1961–1970 Indexes.* New York & London: R.R. Bowker, 1976.

Lally, Kevin. *Wilder Times: The Life of Billy Wilder.* New York: Henry Holt, 1996.

Lentz, Harris M. *Science Fiction, Horror, and Fantasy Film and Television Credits.* Jefferson, NC: McFarland, 1983.

_____. *Science Fiction, Horror, and Fantasy Film and Television Credits, Supplement: through 1987.* Jefferson, NC: McFarland, 1989.

_____. *Science Fiction, Horror, and Fantasy Film and Television Credits, Supplement 2, through 1993.* Jefferson, NC: McFarland, 1994.

_____. *Television Westerns Episode Guide: All United States Series, 1949–1996.* Jefferson, NC: McFarland, 1997.

_____. *Western and Frontier Film and Television Credits, 1903–1995.* Jefferson, NC: McFarland, 1996.

Lichter, Paul. *Elvis in Hollywood.* New York: Simon and Schuster, 1975.

Lopez, Daniel. *Film by Genre.* Jefferson, NC: McFarland, 1993.

Luciano, Patrick, and Gary Coville. *American Science Fiction Television Series of the 1950s.* Jefferson, NC: McFarland, 1998.

McNeil, Alex. *Total Television: The Comprehensive Guide to Programming from 1948 to the Present.* New York: Penguin Books, 1996.

Malden, Karl, and Carla Malden. *When Do I Start?: A Memoir.* New York: Simon & Schuster, 1997.

Malo, Jean-Jacques, and Tony Williams, ed. *Vietnam War Movies.* Jefferson, NC: McFarland, 1994.

Maltin, Leonard. *Leonard Maltin's Movie and Video Guide 1995.* New York: Penguin Books USA, 1994.

Margulies, Edward, and Stephen Rebello. *Bad Movies We Love.* New York: Penguin Books USA, 1993.

Marill, Alvin H. *Movies Made for Television: The Telefeature and the Mini-Series, 1964–1984.* New York: New York Zoetrope, 1984.

Martindale, David. *Television Detective Shows of the 1970s: Credits, Storylines, and Episode Guides for 109 Series.* Jefferson, NC: McFarland, 1991.

Morris, Bruce. *Prime Time Network Serials: Episode Guides, Casts, and Credits for 37 Continuing Television Dramas, 1964–1993.* Jefferson, NC: McFarland, 1997.

Morton, Alan. *The Complete Directory to Science Fiction, Fantasy and Horror Television Series: A Comprehensive Guide to the First 50 Years 1946 to 1996.* Peoria, IL: Other world Books, 1997.

The Motion Picture Herald. January 1, 1958–December 31, 1972.

Noel, Chris, and Bill Treadwell. *Matter of Survival: The "War" Jane Never Saw.* Boston: Branden, 1987.

Oliviero, Jerry. *Motion Picture Players' Credits.* Jefferson, NC: McFarland, 1991.

O'Neill, James. *Terror on Tape.* New York: Billboard Books, 1994.

Parish, James Robert, and Vincent Terrace. *The Complete Actors' Television Credits, 1948–1988 Volume 2: Actresses.* Metuchen, NJ: Scarecrow Press, 1989.

Perry, Jeb H. *Screen Gems: A History of Columbia Pictures Television from Cohn to Coke, 1948–1983.* Metuchen, NJ: Scarecrow Press, 1991.

Phillips, Mark, and Frank Garcia. *Science Fiction Television Series: Episode Guides, Histories, and Cast and Credits for 62 Prime Time Shows, 1959 through 1989.* Jefferson, NC: McFarland, 1996.

Prouty, Howard H., ed. *Variety Television Reviews 1923–1988*. 15 volumes. New York: Garland, 1989.

Robertson, Ed. *The Fugitive Recaptured: The 30th Anniversary Companion to a Television Classic*. Los Angeles: Pomegranate Press, 1993.

Sinclair, Marianne. *Hollywood Lolitas*. New York: Henry Holt, 1988.

Stanley, John. *John Stanley's Creature Features Movie Guide Strikes Again*. Pacifica, CA: Creatures at Large, 1994.

Terrace, Vincent. *Encyclopedia of Television: Series, Pilots, and Specials*. New York: New York Zoetrope, 1985–1986.

_____. *Television Specials: 3,201 Entertainment Spectaculars, 1939–1993*. Jefferson, NC: McFarland, 1995.

Thomas, Tony, and Aubrey Solomon. *The Films of 20th Century–Fox*. Secaucus, NJ: Citadel Press, 1979.

Thompson, Howard, ed. *The New York Times Guide to Movies on TV*. Chicago: Quadrangle Books, 1970.

TV Guide. January 1, 1958–December 31, 1978. Weekly.

Variety Film Reviews 1907–1980. 16 volumes. New York: Garland, 1983.

Variety Portable Movie Guide. New York: Berkley Boulevard Books, 1999.

Waldron, Vince. *The Official Dick Van Dyke Show Book: The Definitive History and Ultimate Viewer's Guide to Television's Most Enduring Comedy*. New York: Hyperion, 1994.

Ward, Jack. *The Supporting Players of Television, 1959–1983*. Cleveland: Lakeshore West, 1996.

_____. *Television Guest Stars: An Illustrated Career Chronicle for 678 Performers of the Sixties and Seventies*. Jefferson, NC: McFarland, 1993.

Weldon, Michael. *The Psychotronic Encyclopedia of Film*. New York: Ballantine, 1983.

_____. *The Psychotronic Video Guide*. New York: St. Martin's Griffin, 1996.

West, Adam, and Jeff Rovin. *Back to the Batcave*. New York: Berkley Books, 1994.

Willis, John. *Screen World*. New York: Crown, annual.

Woolley, Lynn, Robert W. Malsbary, and Robert G. Strange, Jr. *Warner Bros. Television*. Jefferson, NC: McFarland, 1985.

Wood, Lana. *Natalie: A Memoir by Her Sister*. New York: Putnam, 1984.

Index

ABC Monday Night Football 219
ABC Wide World of Mystery 50
Absence of a Cello 138
Adams, Beverly 21, 134, 177, 229, 230
Adams, Don 273, 274
Adams, Nick 110, 293
The Addams Family 252
Adler, Stella 90, 129
Adventures in Paradise 10
Affliction 153
After the Fall 138
Agar, John 97, 160
The Agony and the Ecstasy 260
Airport 1975 165–166, 268
The Alamo 5, 31, 32
The Alaskans 41
Albertson, Jack 242
Albritton, Louise 148
Alda, Alan 138
Alexander, Jeff 97
The Alfred Hitchcock Hour 148, 272
Alice's Restaurant 26
All My Children 233
Allen, Corey 212
Allen, Debbie 221, 222
Allen, Elizabeth 252, 255
Allen, Irwin 5, 99, 207, 238, 240, 242, 243
Allen, Marty 293
Allen, Steve 109, 126
Almeda, Laurindo 61
Altered Ego 155
Altman, Robert 13
The Amazing Colossal Man 111

Ambition 207
American Scene Magazine 290
Amos Burke—Secret Agent 123
Amsterdam, Morey 20, 227
Anders, Merry 96, 160
Ando 166
Andress, Ursula 12, 200
Andrews, Edward 59
Andriane, Marayat 162
Angel in My Pocket 118
Angel Unchained 23
Angels Die Hard! 23
Animals 27, 173, 294
Ann-Margret 3, 18, 23, 34, 81, 84, 84, 85
Ansara, Michael 102
L'Archangelo 89
Arden, Eve 294
Argento, Dario 284
Arielle 207
Arkoff, Samuel Z. 19, 20, 44, 225
Arness, James 103
Arngrim, Stefan 239, 241
Arnie 2 91
Arnow, Max 237
Around the World Under the Sea 197, 199
Arthur, Maureen 123
As the World Turns 76, 292
Asher, William 5, 19, 138, 160, 225
Ashley, John 17, 20, 110, 205, 224, 226, 294
Askew, Luke 164, 165
Asner, Ed 96
Astaire, Fred 158
Astin, John 252
Astronauts 176

Attack of the Puppet People 111
Austin, Pamela 282
Avalon, Frankie 5, 20, 21, 31, 74, 75, 132, 137, 138, 138, 141, 160, 224–226, 228, 229, 237, 285, 286, 294
Avedon, Richard 90

B.L. Stryker 118, 181
Babes in Toyland 284
Baby Doll 40
Bacall, Lauren 86
Back to the Beach 285
The Bad Seed 291, 292
Bain, Conrad 293
Baker, Carroll 12, 40, 134
Baker, Joby 139, 140, 174
Baker, Joe Don 102
Baker, Tom 23, 74
Ball, Lucille 81
The Ballad of Andy Crocker 26, 67, 74
The Ballad of Josie 247, 250, 251
Ballard, Florence 176
Ballard, Kaye 294
Ballentine, Carl 148
Bancroft, Anne 160, 161
Barab, Nira 217
Bard, Mitchell vii, 76, 77
Bare, Richard L. 49
Barefoot in the Park (TV series) 216
Barich, Richard 129
Barrett, Majel 139
Barris, George 249
Barron, Baynes 98
Barry, Betty 125
Barry, Gene 59, 120, 124, 125

Barry, John 190
Barrymore, Drew 251
Barrymore, John Drew 251
Bartlett, Hall 279
Basehart, Richard 238
Basil, Toni 226
Bassey, Shirley 190
Batman 10, 11, 44, 45, 53, 64, 92, 98, 99, 99, 110, 118, 120, 126, 127, 128, 151, 211, 235, 237, 238, 261, 272, 273, 275, 283
Baum, Lal 274
Baxter, Les 48
Baywatch 294
Beach Ball 21, 22, 170, 175, 176, 247
Beach Blanket Bingo 20, 225, 228, 294
Beach Boys 19, 21, 186
The Beach Girls and the Monster 21
Beach Party 20, 21, 45, 83, 174, 175, 225, 247, 285
The Beachcomber 55
Beast of Blood 197, 205
Beatles 6, 18, 177, 186, 229
Beatty, Warren 151
Beau Brummels 112, 176
Bedi, Kabir 195
Bedroom Farce 76
Bedtime Story 95, 95
Bee, Molly 27
Bellamy, Earl 62
Bellini, Francesca 56
Ben Casey 134
Ben-Hur 265
Bender, Russ 98, 98
Beneath the Planet of the Apes 259, 266, 266, 267, 279
Benet, Brenda 175
Benji 294
Bergen, Edgar 113, 114, 243
Berle, Milton 187
Berlinger, Warren 46
Bernds, Edward 56, 58
Bernstein, Jay 179, 194
Berry, Halle 216
The Best of Everything (TV series) 292
Betz, Carl 43
Beulah 213
The Beverly Hillbillies 110, 120, 126
Beverly Hills, 90210 103, 132, 142, 143
Bewitched 10, 92, 93, 102, 110, 120, 126, 127, 176, 211, 213
Beymer, Richard 187, 188
Biano, Sollie 40
The Big Tease 104

Bikini Beach 20, 225, 227, 285
The Birdcage 90
Biroc, Joseph 21
Bisset, Jacqueline 260
Bixby, Bill 126, 283
Black and White 91
Black Gold 42
The Blackboard Jungle 17
Blackman, Joan 18, 282
Blodgett, Michael 205, 206, 206
Blondell, Joan 55
Blue Hawaii 18, 19, 84, 136, 174, 282
Bob & Carol & Ted & Alice 5, 13, 204
The Bob Crosby Show 27, 28
Bob Hope Chrysler Theatre 148, 237, 247, 251
The Bob Hope Show 125, 126, 126
Bogdonavich, Peter 13
Boland, Paul 64
The Bold Ones: The Doctors 279
Bon Voyage 294
Bonanza 132, 155, 189
Bonet, Nai 229, 285
Bonnie and Clyde 151
Boone, Brendon vii, 72, 256, 257, 257
Boone, Pat 81, 83
Borden, Lynn 220, 221
Borgnine, Ernest 148
The Born Losers 23
Born Wild 26, 116, 292
Born Yesterday 208
Boyd, Stephen 8, 148
Boyer, Charles 72
Bracken's World 207, 247, 252–255, 253, 255, 257, 267, 267
Brando, Marlon 92, 95, 95, 96
Breakfast at Tiffany's 56
Breakfast of Champions 271, 280
Breck, Peter 282
Brennan, Walter 75
Brian's Song 211, 219, 283
Bride of Satan 194
Bridges, Beau 17, 110, 112, 113, 272
Bridges, Jeff 165
Bridges, Lloyd 282
Brimley, Wilford 269
Britt, Mai 254
Broadside 53, 59, 61, 63
Broccoli, Cubby 190
Brolin, James 260, 262
Bronco 10
Bronson, Charles 72, 207
Brooks, Peter 186

Brothers 103
Brown, David 268
Brown, James 21
Brown, James B. 98, 98
Brown, Jim 165, 211
Brown, Nicole 180, 181
Brown, Oscar, Jr. 211
Brown, Peter 21
The Bubble 294
Buchanan, Larry 97, 289
Buchholtz, Horst 80, 80, 81, 90
Bug 292
A Bullet for Pretty Boy 289
Burke, Evan Andrew 50
Burke's Law 44, 53, 59, 72, 110, 120, 124–126, 132, 134, 176
Burns, George 249
Burns, Michael 274
Burns, Ronnie 249
Burton, Norman 190
Burton, Richard 40, 41
Bus Riley's Back in Town 284
Bus Stop 10, 234
Butch Cassidy and the Sundance Kid 15
Butler, Dick 193
Butterfield 8 148
Butterflies Are Free 76
Butterworth, Donna 20
Buttons, Red 126, 256
Buttram, Pat 49
Buzzanca, Lando 89
Byrne, Martha 76
Byrnes, Edd "Kookie" 10, 21, 22, 173, 175, 176

C.C. and Company 23, 278
Caan, James 219, 274, 283
Cabaret 71–73
Cafaro, Cheri 184, 190
Cage, Nicolas 104
La cage aux folles 90
Cagney, James 80, 81
Calder, Maury 238
Callan, Michael 15, 176
Cambridge, Godfrey 218, 220
Campbell, Glen 26, 277, 278, 280
Campo, Wally 229
Cannon 155
Cannon, Dyan 205
Cannon, Freddy 112
Cannon, J. D. 218
Cannon for Cordoba 13, 100, 101
Cape Fear 5, 53, 58, 59
Capitol 132, 141, 142, 195
Capri, Ahna 185
Caprice 158, 162–164, 164
Capshaw, Kate 167
Captain Nice 139

Index 301

Cardiff, Jack 74
The Cardinal 67, 71, 82
Cardinale, Claudia 62
Career 282
The Caretakers 42, 43
Carey, MacDonald 138
Carey, Michele 203, 204
Carey, Phil 42
Carmel, Roger C. 44, 45
Carrey, Jim 81
Carroll, Diahann 216
Carson, Johnny 103, 126
Carter, Dixie 293
Cash, Rosalind 221
Cassavetes, John 165, 229, 230, 238
Casselli, Mario 189
Castaways 294
Castle, William 212, 292
Cavell, Marc 229
CBS Playhouse 279
Cease Fire 181
Chamberlain, Richard 7, 8, 173, 175
Chambers, John 262
Chan, Peter 167
Chandler, Patti 224, 227, 229, 233
Change of Habit 19
Chapman, Eddie 200
The Chapman Report 282
Charles, Ray 177
Charlie's Angels 102
Charro! 19
Checker, Chubby 122
Cher 130
Cheyenne 10
Cheyenne Social Club 291
China Beach 181, 294
The Chinese Prime Minister 272
The Choppers 17
Christie, Julie 293
Chrome and Hot Leather 23
Cindy 213
Claire, Adele 113, 114
Clambake 19, 283
Clanton, Jimmy 121, 122
Clark, Fred 138, 200
Clark, Susan 274, 277
Clarke, Robert 94
Claudelle Inglish 40, 42
Cleopatra 159
Clifford, Mike 112
Clurman, Harold 88, 90
Coach 283
Cobb, Lee J. 67, 68, 152, 153, 219
Coburn, James 151–153, 152
Cocoon 269
Code: 99 207
Colbert, Claudette 42

Cole, Dennis 252, 255, 261, 267
Coleman, Dabney 146, 148, 155
Coleman, Randy 156
Collins, Gary 293
Collins, Joan 217
Columbo 118
The Comancheros 32
Come Blow Your Horn 109
Come Fly with Me 79, 82, 83, 288
Comrades: Almost a Love Story 167
Connery, Sean 5, 184, 190–193, 191, 192, 291
Connors, Chuck 194
Connors, Mike 134
Conrad, Robert 92, 101, 110, 251
Convy, Bert 73
Conway, Gary 124, 125, 239, 240, 241, 242
Conway, Tim 148, 149
Coogan's Bluff 271, 276, 277, 278, 279
The Cool and the Crazy 17
Cool Breeze 211, 220
Cool Hand Luke 5, 108, 109, 113–116, 115, 117
Cooper, Jeanne 255, 267
Coppola, Francis Ford 13
Corcoran, Noreen 185
Corday, Mara 12
Corcy, Wendell 160
Corman, Roger 5, 23, 153, 154, 205–207, 221, 229, 230
Cortland, Nicholas 220
Cosby, Bill 204, 216
Cotton Comes to Harlem 5, 13, 211, 218, 219, 220
Coughlin, Kevin 26, 46
Counter Measures 103
Cracking Up 94, 95
Craig, Yvonne 153, 226, 242, 282, 283
Crawford, Broderick 165
Crawford, Joan 8, 43
Crawford, Johnny 110, 112, 272
Cream 23
Crenna, Richard 96, 97
Crickets 186
Crime in the Streets 17
Cronenberg, David 282
Crosby, Bing 54, 126
Crosby, Bob 28
Crosby, David 229
Crosby, Gary 174
Crosby, Stills, Nash, & Young 232
The Crucible 234
Culp, Robert 204

Cummings, Bob 20, 227
Cummings, Jack 134
Curran, Pamela 97
Curse of the Swamp Creatures 92, 97
Curtis, Patrick 199, 200
Curtis, Tony 29, 30
Curtiz, Michael 32
The Cycle Savages 23

Dallas 50, 98, 141
Daly, Jonathan 21, 237, 249, 250
Daly, Tyne 23
Dalzell, Arch R. 48
Damien's Island 166
Damone, Vic 53, 55, 64
Dandridge, Dorothy 211, 216
Danon, Aurora 90
Danon, Echo Tiffin 90, 91
Danon, Edmondo 90
Danon, Marcello 90
Danova, Cesare 18, 56–58, 57
Darby, Kim 278
Darin, Bobby 81, 83
Daring Game 282
Dark Eyes 184, 194
Dark Shadows 256
Darren, James 19–21, 82, 83
Darvi, Bella 268
A Date with Chris 177
The Dating Game 222
Dave Clark Five 27, 173
Daves, Delmer 41
David, Saul 153
Davis, Ossie 218
Davis, Sammy, Jr. 254
Day, Doris 158, 162, 163, 250, 251, 255
Days of Our Lives 50, 103
Dead Wrong 195
Deaf Smith and Johnny Ears 89
Dean, James 151
Dean, Jimmy 190
A Death of Innocence 273
Death Valley Days 97
The Deathhead Virgin 50
Dee, Ruby 216, 218
Dee, Sandra 3, 19, 40, 81, 82, 147, 294
DeFoe, Willem 91
Dehn, Paul 265
DeLaurentiss, Dino 207
Delon, Alain 207
The Delta Factor 49
DeLuise, Dom 277
de Metz, Danielle 15, 57
Demick, Irina 268
Demon Rage 194
Deneuve, Catherine 12, 153
Denver, Bob 83, 293

Dern, Bruce 5, 23, 26, 230, 231, 242
The Destructors 282
Detour to Terror 179
Devil's Angels 23, 224, 228, 229, 230, 231, 284, 285
DeWilde, Brandon 71
DeWolfe, Billy 139, 140
Dexter, Maury 46, 48
Diamond, I.A.L. 81
Diamonds Are Forever 184, 190–194, 191, 192, 195
Dick Dale & His Del-Tones 19, 20, 225
The Dick Van Dyke Show 37, 53, 139
Diff'rent Strokes 293
Dimension 5 234, 237
Dinner at Eight 87
Dion 122
Dirty Sally 98
Disney, Walt 226, 294
The Disorderly Orderly 94, 95
A Distant Trumpet 40, 43
The Doberman Gang 141
Dr. Goldfoot and the Bikini Machine 5, 12, 21, 229, 234, 237, 288
Dr. Kildare 6, 10, 176, 185
Dr. Quinn, Medicine Woman 50
Dolenz, Mickey 116
The Doll Squad 92, 102, 103
Donahue, Jill 134
Donahue, Troy 15, 41–43, 41
Dondi 56
Doniger, Walter 255
The Donna Reed Show 272, 283
Don't Knock the Rock 17
Doors 19
Dormer, Mike 224
Douglas, Gordon 153
Douglas, Kirk 13, 71, 129
Dovdell, Bob 263
Dow, Tony 110
Down and Out in Beverly Hills 166
Dragstrip Riot 17
Dreyfuss, Richard 166
Drive, He Said 26
The Dry Season 76
Dudikoff, Michael 103
Duff, Howard 261
The Dukes of Hazzard 282
Dunaway, Faye 3, 151, 213
Dunn, Kathy 212
Dunnock, Mildred 160
Dylan, Bob 71
Dynasty 141

E se per Caso una Mattina 90
Earth vs. the Spider 111

Eastwood, Clint 72, 93, 271, 276, 277, 278
Easy Rider 23, 45, 76
Eaton, Shirley 229
Eden, Barbara 21, 100, 127
Edgington, Lyn 174, 174
Edmonds, Don 175
Edwards, Blake 30, 56
Egan, Richard 282
Eichelman, Fred R. 245
Eighteen and Anxious 283
Eisley, Anthony 113, 114, 178
Ekberg, Anita 12, 122
Ekland, Britt 195
Elder, Ann 187
Electric Prunes 274
Elliott, Sam 220, 221, 260
Elves 245
The Emperor Waltz 53
Escape from the Planet of the Apes 266
Evans, Maurice 263, 265
Eve 197, 200–202, 201, 202, 203, 204
Everett, Chad 37, 173, 236, 236
Everybody Loves Opal 146
Evil Fingers 90
Evil Roy Slade 282
Ewell, Tom 81
Exodus 5, 67, 69, 72
The Explosive Generation 292

Fabares, Shelley vii, 6, 18, 19, 21, 43, 44, 174, 174, 219, 283, 284, 294
Fabian 5, 21, 45, 46, 132, 137, 138, 283, 284, 285, 290
The Fall Guy 195
Family Affair 139
Family Man 104, 104
Farentino, James 148
Farmer, Mimsy 25, 230, 284, 285
Farrow, Mia 187, 230, 238, 274, 293
Faster Pussycat! Kill! Kill! 102
Father Knows Best 23
Fawcett, Farah 179
Faye, Alice 81
The F.B.I. 72, 134
Fee, Vicki 250
Feldon, Barbara 274
Felicia 148
Felker, Clay 81, 88
Felony Squad 189, 261
Fenneman, George 109
Ferrara, Abel 91
Ferrare, Christina 260
Ferrer, Jose 8
Field, Sally 15, 75, 110
Fielder, John 174
5th Dimension 212

Fimberg, Hal 153
A Fine Madness 291
Fini, Lili 269
Finney, Albert 280
Fireball 500 21, 132, 137, 138, 138, 141, 229, 285
Five the Hard Way 49
Flaming Star 18
Flanagan, Fionnula 194
Fleming, Rhonda 279
Flood, Curt 213, 222
Flood, Shawn Mitchell 222
Flower Drum Song 158
The Flying Nun 213
Follow That Dream 18
Fonda, Henry 13, 129, 291
Fonda, Jane 3, 181, 230
Fonda, Peter 5, 23, 25, 26, 225, 229–232, 232, 294
Fontaine, Joan 54
For Singles Only 170, 178, 180, 184, 187, 188
For Those Who Think Young 5, 20, 79, 82, 83, 288, 293
Ford, Glenn 93
Ford, Harrison 274
Ford, John 5, 160, 161, 184, 185
Ford, Tennessee Ernie 27
Forever Fernwood 283
The Fortune Cookie 213
Four Flies on Grey Velvet 284
4 for Texas 120, 122
Four Seasons 21, 175
Foxx, Redd 218
Franciosa, Tony 37, 84, 85, 85, 282
Francis, Anne 179
Francis, Connie 19, 173, 288, 290
Franciscus, James 265, 266, 267, 279
Frank, Joanna 23
Frankie and Johnny 290
Frederickson, Gray 235
Free Grass 26, 184, 187, 188
Freeman, Joan 59
French, Leigh 277
Fries, Chuck 207
Frogs 211, 213, 220, 221
From Russia with Love 73
Fuller, Robert 289
Fun in Acapulco 18, 84
Funicello, Annette 20, 21, 46, 137, 138, 224–228, 227, 247, 284, 285, 286, 294
Funny About Love 207
Funny Girl 200
Fury of the Succubus 194

Gaba, Marianne 12, 56, 227
Gaby: A True Story 208
Gardner, Ava 97

Garner, Ed 224
Garner, James 10
Garnett, Tay 49
Garrison's Gorillas 256
Garroway, Dave 109
Gary Lewis & the Playboys 21, 249
Gary, Lorraine 268
Gassman, Vittorio 79, 89
Gautier, Dick 46
Gaye, Marvin 177
Gaynor, Mitzi 120
Gazzara, Ben 193, 251
Geeson, Judy 100
The Gene Krupa Story 283
General Hospital 243
Gentle, Lili 261
Gentrys 294
George, Christopher 49
Gerber, David 207
Get Smart 120, 123, 126, 272, 273
Get Yourself a College Girl 5, 18, 28, 35–38, 36, 170, 173, 173, 293
Getting Straight 26
The Ghost and Mr. Chicken 5, 53, 61–64, 63
The Ghost in the Invisible Bikini 229, 288, 293, 293, 294
G.I. Blues 18
Gibbons, Leeza 209
Gibbs, Marla 221
Gidget 19
Gidget (TV) 110, 139
Gidget Goes Hawaiian 294
Gilardi, Jack 225
Gilberto, Astrud 27, 173
Gilford, Jack 73
Gilles, Genevieve 268
Gilliam, David 220, 221
Gilmore, Gail 110, 175
Giornata nera per l'Ariete 90
Girl Happy 18, 170, 173, 174, 174, 283, 293
The Girl in Lover's Lane 17
A Girl Named Tamiko 82
The Girls on the Beach 5, 21, 184–186, 186
Girls! Girls! Girls! 18, 84, 285–287, 287
Gish, Dorothy 71
Gleason, Jackie 171, 172, 287, 290
Glenville, Peter 84
The Glory Guys 287
The Glory Stompers 23, 170, 178, 179
Godzilla (1998) 50
Goetz, Bill 88
Gold, Ernest 68
Goldfinger 190

Goldsmith, Jerry 263
Golonka, Arlene 109
Gomer Pyle, U.S.M.C. 219
Good Morning, World 132, 139–141, 140
Good Times 216
Goodman, Benny 64
Goodman, John 208
Goodwin, Laurel vii, 18, 285–288, 287
Gordon, Anita 64
Gordon, Bert I. 17, 110–112, 271, 272
Gordon, Marianne 125
Gordy, Berry 219
Gore, Lesley 21, 186
Gorshin, Frank 110
Gossett, Louis, Jr. 219, 220
Gould, Sandra 127
Goulet, Robert 173
Gourson, Jeff 116
Grant, Cary 27, 29, 30, 254
Grant, Lee 279
Grateful Dead 19, 232
Graves, Peter 250
Gray, Charles 190
Grayeagle 193
Graziano, Rocky 121
Greco, Juliette 268
Green Acres 49, 219
The Green Berets 158, 164, 165
Grey, Joel 73
Grier, Pam 221
Grics, Tom 193
Griffith, Andy 118
Griffith, Melanie 208
The Group 13, 82
Grunberg, Klaus 284
Guardino, Harry 189
A Guide for the Married Man 108, 261, 291
Gunpoint 61
Gunsmoke 132, 134
Guys and Dolls 221

Hackett, Buddy 227
Hagen, Ross 48, 49
Hagman, Larry 50, 216, 217, 217
Hale, Jean vii, 8, 17, 146–157
Haley, Jack, Jr. 277, 278
Hall, Arch, Jr. 17
Hall, Jon 207
The Hallelujah Trail 79, 85
Hallick, Tom 194
Halsey, Brett 17
Hamilton, George 88
Hamilton, Guy 190, 193
Hamilton, Murray 212
Hamilton, Neil 45
Handle with Care 27, 28
Hanold, Marilyn 12

Happy Days 256
A Hard Day's Night 18
The Hard Ride 23
Hardly Working 243
Harlow (Baker version) 134
Harlow (Lynley version) 134
Harmon, Gay 108, 113
Harmon, Joy vii, 8, 17, 108–119, 272
Harper 79, 86, 86
Harris, Jonathan 99, 100
Harris, Julie 75
Harris, Neil Patrick 181
Harris, Richard 162
Harrison, Linda vii, 6, 7, 8, 252, 254, 255, 259–270
Hart, Dolores 19, 83, 84, 288
Hart, Susan 21, 83, 226, 237, 288, 289, 289
Harty, Patricia 176
Harum Scarum 293, 294
Harvey 54
Harvey, Laurence 31, 80
Haskell, Peter 252, 253, 253, 255
The Haunted House of Horror 5, 67, 68, 74, 75
Hawaii Five-0 7 2, 155, 274
Hawaiian Eye 10, 41
Hawkins, Jimmy 174
Hawn, Goldie 15, 139, 140, 282
Haworth, Jill vii, 26, 67–78
Hayes, Allison 96
Hays, Kathryn 274
Hazelwood, Lee 293
Head 285
Head, Edith 150–151
Heatherton, Joey 74, 177, 230
Hedison, David 238
Hedren, Tippi 49, 208
Hefner, Hugh 12, 55, 109, 189
Hello-Goodbye 268
Hell's Angels on Wheels 23
Hell's Belles 23, 289
Hell's Chosen Few 23
Hellstrom, Gunnar 274, 275
Helm, Anne 133
Hepburn, Audrey 56, 81
Herman's Hermits 290
Heston, Charlton 5, 166, 185, 262–267, 264, 269
Heyward, Louis M. "Deke" 229
High School Caesar 17
High School Confidential! 17
High Time 283
Hill, Marianna 19, 20, 136, 137
Hillyer, Sharon 59, 125
Hingle, Pat 277
Hold On! 290

Hollywood Screen Tests: Take 2 259
Home for the Holidays 74, 75
Hometown Jamboree 27
Homier, Skip 62
Hondells 175
Honeymoon Hotel 173
Hootenanny Hoot 282
Hope, Bob 126, 126, 129, 177, 178
Hope, Teri 12
Hopper, Dennis 5, 25, 178, 179, 230, 231
Hopper, Hedda 7
Horne, Lena 15, 211, 216, 222
The Horror of Party Beach 21
The Horror on Snape Island 74
Horten, Rena 249
Hot Potato 158, 166, 167
Hot Rod Gang 17
Hot Rod Rumble 17
Hot Rods to Hell 284
How to Frame a Figg 283
How to Seduce a Playboy 289
How to Stuff a Wild Bikini 20, 158, 160, 161, 224, 225, 227, 285
Howard, Ron 110, 269
Howard, Sandy 1
Hudson, Rock 8
Hughes, Kathleen 255
Hughes, Mary 224, 227, 233
Hugueny, Sharon 41, 42
Hunnicutt, Gayle 207
Hunter, Jeffrey 138, 185, 237, 288
Hunter, Kim 263, 265
Hunter, Tab 21, 288
Hustle 243
Huston, John 71
Hutton, Jim 85, 164, 173
Hutton, Lauren 279
Hutton, Robert 288
Hyde, Jimmy 213
Hyde, Johnny 213

I Dream of Jeannie 10, 116, 120, 126, 127, 213
I Love You Alice B. Toklas 252
I Sailed to Tahiti with an All-Girl Crew 49
I Spy 211, 216
Ice Palace 40
In Harm's Way 67, 71
In Like Flint 5, 12, 146, 151–155, 152, 155, 156, 283
In the Heat of the Night 46
Incident at Phantom Hill 289
The Incredible Hulk 243
Ireland, Jill 207
Iron Butterfly 23

Ironside 64, 216, 279
Irving, Holly 220
Isherwood, Charles 72
It! 67, 72, 73
It Happened at the World's Fair 18, 27, 34, 35, 283
It's a Bikini World 21, 294
It's Only Money 33, 33, 94, 133
Ito, Robert 160

Jackson, Sherry 12, 47, 48
Jacobs, Arthur P. 262
Jagger, Dean 41
Jailhouse Rock 18, 19
James, Monique 249, 274
James, Sheila 59
Jamison, Mikki 175
Jan and Dean 19, 21
Janssen, David 164
Jason of Star Command 92
Jaws 268
Jay & the Americans 176
Jefferson Airplane 19
The Jeffersons 216
Jensen, Karen vii, 13, 15, 21, 247–258, 267
Jergens, Diane 121
Jewison, Norman 213
The Joe Pyne Show 121
John Goldfarb, Please Come Home 160
Johnny Cool 59
Johnny Tiger 236
Johnson, Arte 179
Johnson, Candy 20
Johnson, Don 181, 208
Johnson, John 212
Johnson, Melodie 125
Jones, Carolyn 288
Jones, Christopher 25, 151, 213, 214, 214, 232
Jones, Dean 28
Jones, Jack 177
Jones, T.C. 274, 277
Joplin, Janis 19
Journey to Shiloh 274
Journey to the Far Side of the Sun 274
Joy in the Morning 8, 175
The Joy Luck Club 167
Julia 216
Jurow, Martin 171

Karloff, Boris 288
Kaszner, Kurt 239, 241, 242
Kathy O' 292
Katzin, Lee H. 256
Katzman, Leonard 98
Katzman, Sam 27, 173
Kauffman, Christine 67
Kaye, Celia 293
Keach, Stacey 277

Keaton, Buster 161, 227, 228
Keith, Brian 84, 85
Kelly, Gene 8, 261, 262
Kelly, Grace 103, 153
Kelly, Jim 158, 166
Kelly, John B. 103
Kendall, Kay 80
Kennedy, George 114–116, 115, 250
Kennedy, Jayne 221
Kenney, Wes 103
Kerr, Walter 73
Kersh, Kathy 127
Kid Galahad 282
The Killer Inside Me 277
Kincaid, Aron 175, 186, 189, 293
King, Zalman 219
King Creole 18, 19, 35, 288
King Dinosaur 111
Kirk, Tommy 21, 110–112, 226, 272, 273, 288, 294
Kiss Me, Stupid 120, 122, 123
Kiss the Other Sheik 87, 87
Kissin' Cousins 282, 283
Klugman, Jack 102
Knickerbockers 249
Knight, Shirley 42
Knotts, Don 5, 53, 61–63, 63
Koenig, Walter 199
Kohner, Frederick 19
Koster, Henry 159, 160
Kotto, Yaphet 213
Kovacs, Laszlo 25
Kraft Suspense Theatre 44, 148
Kruschen, Jack 162
Kwan, Nancy 158

Lacambre, Daniel 206
The Ladies' Man 53, 56
Lady Sings the Blues 219
Lai, Leon 167
Lamas, Lorenzo 179
Lambert, Hugh 293
Lancaster, Burt 79, 85
Lance, Leon 114
Land of the Giants 10, 92, 205, 216, 234, 237–243, 239, 240, 241, 245
Landis, Carole 57
Lane, Jocelyn 96, 96, 289, 290
Lane, Kent 279
Langdon, Sue Ane vii, 123, 290, 290, 291
Laredo 53, 64
La Rosa, Julius 108
Last of the Secret Agents? 293
Laugh? ... I'd Thought I'd Die 126
Law and Order 91
Lawford, Peter 67
Lawrence, Andre 84

Lawrence, John 21
The Lawrence Welk Show 37
Leave It to Beaver 110
Leder, Herbert J. 72
Lee, Bruce 44
Lee, Christopher 200, 202, 202
Lee, Spike 216
The Legend of Jesse James 151
Lehrer, Jim 88
Leigh, Suzanna 19, 20
Leighton, Margaret 271
Lembeck, Harvey 20, 137, 139, 212, 224, 225, 227
Lemmon, Jack 110, 185
Lenya, Lotte 73
Leonard, Sheldon 139
Leone, Sergio 193
Leslie, William 97
Let's Rock 108, 109
Levene, Sam 109
Lewis, Jerry 5, 27, 33, 53, 56, 62, 92, 94, 95, 132–134, 133, 198, 243, 245, 260, 282
The Lieutenant 10, 172
The Life and Times of Judge Roy Bean 97
Lisi, Virna 86
Little Fauss and Big Halsy 279
Little Ladies of the Night 193
Live a Little, Love a Little 19, 197, 203, 204, 204
The Lively Ones 53, 55
The Lively Set 11, 21, 79, 83
Lockhart, Calvin 218
Lockhart, June 99, 100
Lockwood, Gary 172, 173
Logan, Robert 175
Lois and Clark: The New Adventures of Superman 103
Lolita 71
Lom, Herbert 200, 202
Lombard, Carole 80
The Loner 237
The Long, Hot Summer (TV series) 186
Looking for Love 173
Lord, Jack 72, 274, 275, 277
Loren, Donna 224–226
Loring, Lynn 274
Los Amigos 89
Lost in Space 10, 92, 99, 238, 242
The Lost World (1960) 57, 238
Louis Armstrong—Chicago Style 256
Louise, Tina 30, 83, 184, 194
Love American Style 102, 116, 243, 254
The Love Boat 103
The Love-Ins 26
The Love Letter 167

Love Me Tender 18, 35
The Loved One 108, 110
Loving 129
Loving You 18, 288
Lumet, Sidney 13, 82
Lund, Deanna vii, 12, 18, 21, 234–246, 249
Luskin, Len 147
Lyman, Joni 134
Lynde, Paul 83, 227
Lynley, Carol vii, 12, 40, 71, 81, 82, 84, 84, 85, 110, 134, 207, 230, 277, 278
Lynn, Diana 53
Lyon, Sue 40, 151, 160, 237

McBain, Diane vii, 8, 10, 13, 18, 21, 23, 24, 40–52, 242, 283, 291, 294
McCallum, David 70, 71
McClory, Sean 56–58
McClure, Doug 21
McCoo, Marilyn 212
Macon County Line 282
McCormack, Patty 25, 46–48, 291, 291, 292
McCrea, Jody 2 0, 23, 178, 224, 226
McDowall, Roddy 72, 73, 98, 99, 99, 263, 265
McEnery, Peter 284
McHale's Navy 64, 148
McHale's Navy Joins the Air Force 146, 148, 150
McKay, Gardner 49, 85
McLaglen, Andrew V. 250
McNair, Barbara 12
McQueen, Neile Adams 185
McQueen, Steve 5, 162, 171, 172, 172, 185, 213
Mad Doctor of Blood Island 205
Mad Dog Coll 110
Madonna 123
Maibum, Richard 190
A Majority of One 120, 121
Majors, Lee 26, 74, 195
Make a Million 109, 134
Malden, Karl 42
The Male Animal 146
Malone, Dorothy 20, 187, 227
Mama's Family 103
A Man Called Dagger 120, 123, 124, 125
The Man from U.N.C.L.E. 10, 44, 97, 146, 158, 199, 283, 293
The Man in the Grey Flannel Suit 108
Mandoki, Luis 208
Manfredi, Nino 89, 90
Mankiewicz, Joseph L. 13, 129
Mankiewicz, Tom 190

Mann, Daniel 129, 148
Mannix 132, 134
Mansfield, Jayne 12, 30, 109, 200
Mantee, Paul 120, 123, 124, 125
Margotta, Michael 26, 46
Marilyn Is Alive 103
Marlise 64
Marlowe, Scott 103
Marriage on the Rocks 293
Mars Needs Women 283
Marsh, Sy 213
Marshall, Don 216, 239, 242
Marshall, Linda 185
Marshall, Peter 46
Marshall, Sandra 47, 291
Martin, Claudia 83
Martin, Dean 122, 123, 155
Martin, Dick 177
Martinson, Leslie H. 83
Marx, Groucho 109, 113
Mary, Mary 43
Maryjane 26, 40, 44–46, 46, 292
Mason, James 165
Mason, Marlyn 151
Massey, Daria 56
Mastroianni, Marcello 79, 86, 87
Matheson, Don 239, 241, 242, 243
Matheson, Michelle 245
Matthau, Walter 185, 261, 291
Maverick 10, 41
Mayer, Louis B. 134
Mazurki, Mike 160
Mazursky, Paul 166, 204
Meadows, Joyce 17
The Mechanic 207
Medavoy, Mike 259
Memo 138
Men Against Evil 260
Meredith, Burgess 71, 165
Mergers & Acquisitions 67, 76–77, 76
Merrill, Dina 30
Mickey Spillane's Mike Hammer (TV series) 195
Mickey Spillane's Mike Hammer (TV movie) 194
Midler, Bette 166
Midnight Kiss 207
Midnight Lace 56
Mikels, Ted V. 102, 103
Miles, Sherry 205, 206
Miles, Sylvia 148
Milland, Ray 220, 221
The Million Eyes of Su-Muru 229
Mimieux, Yvette 6, 19, 25, 40, 49, 175, 213, 288
Mineo, Sal 67, 68, 69, 73

The Mini-Skirt Mob 5, 23, 24, 40, 44, 47, 48, 50, 291, 292
Minnelli, Liza 71
Mission: Impossible 64
Mr. Jones 167
Mr. Novak 272
Mister Roberts 171
Mitchell, Don 216, 221, 222
Mitchell, Julia Pace 222
Mitchum, Robert 53, 58, 59
Mobley, Mary Ann 28, 37, 38, 110, 173, 173, 174, 178, 187, 292, 292, 293
The Mod Squad 15, 155, 216, 219
Moment to Moment 63
Mommy 292
Monkees 116, 118, 285
The Monkees 10, 116
Monroe, Marilyn 6, 8, 12, 103, 108, 170, 179, 213
Monteros, Rosenda 200, 201
Montgomery, Elizabeth 126, 127
Montgomery, George 27, 32
Moody, Lynne 194
Moonrunners 282
Moore, Gary 109
Moore, Michael 136, 162
Moore, Terry 123, 124
Moorehead, Agnes 102, 127
More 284
More, Kenneth 32
Morse, Eddie 94
Morse, Robert 173, 261
The Mothers-in-Law 294
Motorcycle Gang 17
Moxey, John Llewellyn 75, 194
Mulhare, Edward 162
Mumy, Bill 100
The Munsters 53, 64, 120, 126
Murphy, Audie 27, 32, 61, 62
Murray, Don 166
Murray, Jan 46, 123
Muscle Beach Party 20, 224, 225, 228, 285, 286
The Mutations 74
Mutiny in Outer Space 97
My Mother, the Car 176
My Three Sons 110, 139, 176

Nadel, Norman 73
Nader, George 229
Nader, Mike 224, 233
Nagy, Ivan 165
Namath, Joe 23, 198, 277, 278
The Name of the Game 279
The Name of the Game Is Kill 271, 274
Napoleon, Art 21
Napoleon, Jo 21

Nardini, Tom 127, 134
Neal, Patricia 71, 160
Needham, Hal 15
Negulesco, Jean 85
Neilson, John 256
Nelson, Craig T. 283
Nelson, Ozzie 197
Nelson, Ralph 171
Nelson, Ricky 197
Nero, Franco 79, 89, 90
Nesmith, Michael 116
Nettleton, Lois 83
Never Too Young (TV) 110, 116
A New Kind of Love 59
New Rose Hotel 91
Newman, Barry 247, 255, 256
Newman, Paul 5, 59, 67, 68, 79, 86, 89, 97, 114–116, 115, 205
Newmar, Julie 12, 97, 100
Nichols, Nichelle 216, 217, 221
Nicholson, Jack 23, 25, 26, 230
Nicholson, James H. 19, 20, 225, 226, 229, 288
Nielsen, Leslie 254, 255
Night Slaves 271, 279
The Night Stalker 75
Nightmare in Badham County 184, 193
Nimoy, Leonard 199
Nitzsche, Jack 111
Niven, David 72, 95, 96, 166
Nixon, Richard 198
Noel, Chris vii, 1, 7, 18, 21–23, 22, 37, 38, 122, 123, 125, 170–183, 187
Nolan, Jeanette 98
Nolan, Kathy 59
Nolte, Nick 166, 167
Nooney Rickett Four 134
Norwood 26, 271, 277–279, 280
La Notté 148
The Nutty Professor 5, 94, 95, 132, 133, 134, 197, 198
Nuyen, France 82, 237

Oakland, Simon 237
Oates, Warren 242
Ober, Philip 62
O'Brian, Hugh 83, 171
O'Brien, Edmond 186
O'Brien, Joan vii, 8, 18, 27–39, 173, 173
Occasional Wife 176
Ocean's Eleven 56
O'Connor, Carroll 55
The Odd Couple (TV) 102, 116
O'Donnell, Rosie 209

Oggi, domani e dopodomani 86
Oliver, Stephen 187
On Her Majesty's Secret Service 190
Once Upon a Coffeehouse 235
One Day at a Time 283
One Million, B.C. 57
One Million Years B.C. 200
One, Two, Three 79–81, 80
One Way Wahine 21, 108, 110, 112, 113, 114
O'Neal, Ryan 187, 189
O'Neill, Eileen vii, 1, 10, 11, 13, 15, 59, 120–131, 177
O'Neill, James 74
Opatoshu, David 68
Operation: Entertainment 129
Operation Petticoat 27–31, 29
Opie, Linda 225
Oppenheimer, George 73
Orr, Bill 10
The Oscar 8, 146–151, 147
Our Man Flint 146, 153
Out of Sight 5, 21, 234, 237, 247, 249, 250
The Outer Limits 70, 71
Ovitz, Mike 207
Oz 76

Pace, Judy vii, 6, 8, 9, 13, 15, 25, 26, 211–223
Page, Geraldine 80
Paige, Marvin 257
Pajama Party 21, 224, 226, 288, 289
Palmer, Peter 102
Pan, Hermes 158
Papa's Delicate Condition 287
Paper Tiger 158, 166
Paradise, Hawaiian Style 5, 19, 20, 132, 135–137, 137, 158, 161, 163, 164
Parker, Colonel Tom 19, 137, 162
Parker, Eleanor 75, 252, 255
Parkins, Barbara 187, 195
Parnell, Helen 200
Parrish 40, 41, 42
Parrish, Julie vii, 6, 18–21, 20, 132–145
Parsons, Louella 7, 12
Pasternak, Joe 282
Patterson, Lee 41
Pearce, Donn 116
Peck, Gregory 59, 108
Peckinpah, Sam 287
Penn, Arthur 151
Peplowski, Ken 64
Peppard, George 13, 100, 126
Pepper, Cynthia 283
Perrine, Valerie 90
Perry Mason 54, 176

Index

Pettet, Joanna 195
Petticoat Junction 219
Peyton Place (TV series) 10, 15, 186, 187, 211, 216, 219, 267
Phillips, Lee 17, 148, 149
Phillips, Sam 54
Phillips, Stu 274
Pierce, Arthur C. 97, 98, 158, 160
Pierson, Frank R. 116
Pine, Robert 62, 250
Pistols 'n' Petticoats 178
Pitts, ZaSu 121
A Place Called Today 184, 190
Planet of the Apes 5, 259, 260, 262–265, 264
Playboy magazine 12, 13, 53–55, 89, 109, 155, 171, 184, 189, 193
Pleasence, Donald 74
The Pleasure Seekers 6, 79, 84, 84, 85, 85
Pleshette, Suzanne 43
Poitier, Sidney 46
Polakof, James 195
Polanski, Roman 238
Pollack, Sidney 146
Ponti, Carlo 86
The Poppy Is Also a Flower 289
The Poseidon Adventure 207
Post, Ted 265, 267, 279
Poston, Tom 146
Powers, Stefanie 293
Preacher & Co. 257
Prelude 252
Preminger, Hope 69
Preminger, Ingo 256
Preminger, Otto 5, 67–69, 71, 82, 252
Prentiss, Paula 19, 71, 288
Presley, Elvis 1, 5, 6, 18–20, 20, 27, 34, 35, 43, 44, 59, 61, 84, 92, 96, 96, 132, 135–137, 137, 151, 158, 161–163, 163, 173–175, 174, 197, 203, 204, 204, 237, 277, 282, 283, 285–290, 287, 292, 293, 294
Previn, André 53
Price, Vincent 5, 21, 97, 237, 288
Priestley, Jason 143
Primo Baby 256
Prince, Hal 71–73
Prince, Steven Chester 76, 77
Provendie, Zina 134
Prowse, Juliet 34, 235, 282
Psych-Out 26
The Psychiatrist 75
Psychomania 5, 17, 146, 148, 149

Pyne, Joe 121
Pyramids 19

QB VII 193
Quantum Leap 118
Questal, Mae 33, 133
Quincy 160
Quinn, Anthony 89
Quintero, Jose 129

Rafelson, Bob 13
Raffin, Deborah 194
Rafkin, Alan 63
Randall, Tony 102
Randolph, Lillian 212, 213
Random, Bob 110, 113, 272
Rashad, Phylicia 222
Rasulala, Thalmus 211, 221
Rathbone, Basil 288
The Ravagers 26
Rawhide 72
Ray, Aldo 164
Ray, Fred Olen 103
Rebel Without a Cause 17
Red Fury 50
The Red Skelton Show 219
Redford, Robert 279
Reed, Robert 102, 194
Reefer Madness 46
Reese, Della 194
Reflections 134
Reform School Girl 17
Reiner, Carl 139, 261
Remick, Lee 85
Remington Steele 243
Return to Peyton Place (TV series) 132, 141
Reynolds, Burt 181, 182, 243
Reynolds, Debbie 43
Rhoades, Barbara 129
Rhue, Madlyn 30, 56
Richards, Aubrey 73
Richardson, Ralph 67
Richlin, Maurice 29
Richman, Peter Mark 187, 188
Rickles, Don 225, 227, 228
Ride the Wild Surf 21, 283, 284, 288
The Rifleman 61
Righteous Brothers 21, 175
Riley, Jeannine 102
Riot on the Sunset Strip 26, 284
Riptide 103
The Roaring Twenties 10
Roarke, Adam 23, 220, 221, 289
The Robe 41
Roberts, Lois 59
Robertson, Cliff 19, 64
Robertson, Dale 97
Robinson, Bill 251

Robinson, Edward G. 262, 263
Robson, Mark 252
Rock Around the Clock 17
The Rockford Files 141
Roddenberry, Gene 172
Rodrigues, Percy 216
Rogers, Linda 135
Rogers, Sheila 56
The Rogues 72
Roland, Gilbert 32
Rolle, Esther 221
Rolling Stones 232
Rome Adventure 282
Romero, Cesare 261
Romero, Eddie 205
Rondell, Ronnie 47, 48, 291
Rooney, Tim 110, 112, 272
Roots 216
Roots of Evil 245
Rose 90
Rosemary's Baby 238
Rosenberg, Stuart 114–116, 117
Ross, Diana 176
Rossi, Steve 293
Rothman, Stephanie 205, 206
The Rounders 291
Roustabout 18, 53, 59–61, 60, 61, 290
Rowan, Dan 177
Rowan & Martin's Laugh-In 139, 282
Rubin, Stanley 254
Rubinstein, John 279
Run for Your Life 72, 116, 247, 251
Run for Your Wife 235
Rush, Richard 23, 46, 123, 124
Russell, Rosalind 121

Sachse, Pete 224, 229
Sachse, Salli vii, 21, 23, 224–233, 285
Safari 284
Saint, Eva Marie 67, 68
St. Jacques, Raymond 164, 218
St. James, Susan 125
St. John, Jill 148, 177, 190
The St. Valentine's Day Massacre 146, 153–155, 154
Saltzman, Hary 190
The Salzburg Connection 247, 255, 256
Samar 32
The Sand Pebbles 162
The Sandpit Generals 279
Sands, Tommy 27, 83, 293
Sanford, Isabel 221
Sanford and Son 216
Santana, Tura 102
Sargent, Dick 61
Sarrazin, Michael 274

Index

Sassoon, Vidal 230
Satan's Mistress 194
Satan's Sadist 23
Saunders, Linda 185
Savage Season 50
The Savage Seven 23
Saxon, John 15, 187, 283
Schaffner, Franklin J. 263, 265, 267
Schell, Ronnie 139, 140
Schifrin, Lalo 116
Schiller, Lawrence 54, 55
Scorpio 207
Scorsese, Martin 13
Scott, Lizabeth 288
Scott, Sherry 194
Scott, Zachary 33
The Searchers 184, 185
Seberg, Jean 63
Secret File: Hollywood 92, 94
Seeds 26
Segal, Alex 175
Segal, George 129, 154, 154, 243
Selleck, Tom 260
Selznick, Joyce 294
Sergeant Deadhead 229, 294
Sergeant Was a Lady 94
Seven Women 160, 161
77 Sunset Strip 10, 44, 53
The Severed Arm 294
Sex and the Single Girl 43
The Shaggy Dog 284
Shake, Rattle, and Rock 17
Shamroy, Leon 163, 263
Shapiro, Stanley 29
Shatner, William 139, 199, 292
Shaw, Bobbi 161, 224, 229, 233
Shawlee, Joan 237
She 200
Sheets, Dale vii, 64
Sheinberg, Sid 268
Shelyne, Carole 249, 250
Sheridan, Ann 178
Shigeta, James 136, 158
Shivers 282
Shore, Dinah 32
The Sidehackers 49
Siegel, Don 277
The Silencers 146
Silverstein, Sheldon 197, 198, 199, 200, 201
Simmons, Jean 251
Simpson, O.J. 179–181
Sinatra, Frank 5, 122, 237, 238, 293
Sinatra, Nancy 19, 23, 28, 34, 37, 83, 173, 177, 229, 293, 293
Sing Along with Mitch 146
The Single Guy 158, 167
Six Black Horses 32

Ski Party 229, 283, 294
Skidoo 252
The Slams 211, 221
Slate, Jeremy 23, 47, 48, 289, 291
Slattery's People 96
Slezak, Walter 11, 127
The Slime People 288
Smedley, Richard 190
Smith, William 23
Smothers, Dick 128
Smothers, Tom 128
The Smothers Brothers Show 127
Snapdragon 167
Sokolov, Harry 260
Soldier in the Rain 171, 172, 175
something big 155
Sommer, Elke 12
Soo, Jack 164
Sothern, Ann 271, 272
Soulle, Olan 127
Soup or Salad? 76
Spaak, Catherine 86
Space Monster 92, 97, 98, 98
Speedtrap 184, 193
Speedway 19, 293
Spelling, Aaron 124, 125, 193
Spencer's Mountain 284
Spielberg, Steven 75, 76
Spinout 18, 40, 43, 44, 283, 294
Stack, Robert 42, 43
Stacy, James 21, 132, 134, 135
Staley, Chuck 54
Staley, Joan vii, 6, 8, 12, 15, 18, 53–66, 125
Stalmaster, Lynn 97
Standells 27
Stanley, Pat 56
Stanton, Harry Dean 47, 48
Stanwyck, Barbara 59
Stapleton, Maureen 269
Star Trek 10, 132, 138, 199, 216, 217, 288
Star Trek: Voyager 158, 167
State Fair (1962) 8, 64, 81
Steele Justice 167
Stefano, Joseph 75
Stephens, Laraine 207, 252–255, 253, 267
Sterling, Robert 271, 272
Sterling, Tisha vii, 17, 25, 88, 110, 112, 113, 271–281
Stern, Wes 216, 217
Stevens, Connie 3, 42, 81, 249
Stevens, Inger 261
Stevens, Stella 3, 12, 132, 134, 286, 287
Stewart, James 159, 291
Stick 243
Stockwell, Dean 26

Stone, Cliffie 27
Stone, Ezra 99
Storaro, Vittorio 90
Strasberg, Lee 129
Strasberg, Susan 26, 230, 274, 277
Strawberry Alarm Clock 26
The Strawberry Statement 26
Straziami ma di Baci Saziami 90
Streep, Meryl 15
A Streetcar Named Desire 234
The Streets of San Francisco 103
Streisand, Barbra 200
Stroka, Michael 256
Strong Medicine 76
Stroud, Don 23, 274, 277
Stump the Stars 243
The Stunt Man 123
Sturges, John 82, 85, 86
Sugarfoot 10, 41
Sullivan's Empire 247, 250
Summer and Smoke 79, 80
Summer Magic 294
Summerland, Augusta *see* Harrison, Linda
Supremes 21, 175, 176
Surf Party 21
Surfaris 19
Surfside Six 10, 41
The Survivors 88
Swanson, Gloria 268
Swartz, Charles S. 205
Sweet Sugar 206
A Swingin' Summer 21
The Sword of Ali Baba 158, 160

The Tab Hunter Show 53, 55
Taggart 148
Take Her, She's Mine 159
Takei, George 164
Tamblyn, Russ 187, 188
Tanasescu, Gino 155
Tarzan 211
Tashlin, Frank 33, 94, 133, 134, 163
Tata, Joey 142, 143
Tate, Sharon 12, 252
Taurog, Norman 34, 96, 204
Taylor, Elizabeth 148, 159
Taylor, Robert 236
Teacher, Lee 224
Teenage Doll 17
Teenage Millionaire 5, 17, 120–122
Tell It to Groucho 109, 110
Temple Houston 134
Tenney, Del 148
Tergesen, Lee 76
Terranova, Dan 110
Tewkesbury, Peter 151

That Girl 110
That's My Mama 216
There Was a Crooked Man 13, 129
Thinnes, Roy 75, 186, 274
The Third Day 120
13 Frightened Girls 212, 213
Thomas, Marlo 110
Thomas, Richard 254
The Thomas Crown Affair 213
Thompson, J. Lee 59
Three Coins in the Fountain 84
Three in the Attic 5, 25, 26, 211, 213–216, 214, 215
Three Sisters 294
Three the Hard Way 164–165
Thrett, Maggie 25, 213
Thunder Alley 21, 40, 44–46, 229, 285
Thurman, Glynn 216
Tickle Me 5, 95, 96, 96, 289
Tierney, Gene 85
Tiffin, Pamela vii, 6, 8, 11, 14, 20, 64, 79–91, 282, 288
Time Tunnel 238
Tiu, Vicky 34
Toback, James 91
Todd, Beverly 221
Todd, Mike 99
Tognazzi, Ugo 88, 90, 235
The Tonight Show Starring Johnny Carson 103, 126
Tony Rome 5, 234, 237, 238, 238, 293
Topper, Burt 97, 98
Tormé, Mel 64
The Tormentors 170, 178
Tors, Ivan 199
Towers, Harry Alan 197, 200–202
Toys 294
Transylvania Twist 245
Trikonis, Gina 212
The Trip 5, 26, 224, 225, 229–231, 232
Triple Cross 200
The Trouble with Girls 19, 151
True Grit 278
Trumbo, Dalton 72
Tryon, Tom 71
Tsu, Irene vii, 18–20, 136, 137, 158–169
Turner, Lana 31, 88
Turner, Tina 222
Turtles 21, 249
Twelve O'Clock High 72
Twist Around the Clock 17

Uncle Vanya 88
Under the Yum Yum Tree 108, 110
The Untouchables 37, 55

Up in the Cellar 26, 212, 213, 216, 217, 217
Uris, Leon 67
Ustinov, Peter 88, 93

Vadim, Roger 284
Valentine's Day 37
Valley of the Dolls 155, 252
Valley of the Dragons 15, 53, 56–58, 57
Van Ark, Joan 220
Van Doren, Mamie 30
Vander Ark, Brian 76
Vaughn, Robert 172, 173, 199
The Velvet Vampire 13, 197, 205, 206, 206
Vernon, Sherri 102
Vetri, Victoria 238
Il Vichingo venuto dal Sud 89
Vickers, Yvette 12
Village of the Giants 5, 17, 108, 110–112, 111, 113, 271, 272, 273
The Virginian 148
Visit to a Small Planet 282
Viva Las Vegas 18
Viva Max! 88
Voyage to the Bottom of the Sea 238
Voyage to the Bottom of the Sea (TV series) 165, 238

Wagner, Robert 86, 185
Walken, Christopher 91
Walker, Clint 10, 103
Walker, Nancy 146
Walker, Robert, Jr. 23, 200, 202, 202, 203
Walley, Deborah 43, 283, 288, 294
Wallis, Hal B. 18, 19, 79, 81, 82, 84, 135–137, 162, 277, 285
Walsh, Raoul 43
Walston, Ray 164
Walter, Jessica 75, 82
The Waltons 243, 254
War-Gods of the Deep 288
Ward, Burt 44, 99, 110, 127, 275
Warner, Jack 249
Warrick, Ruth 187
Way ... Way Out 260
Wayne, Aissa 32
Wayne, David 151
Wayne, John 5, 27, 31, 32, 71, 75, 79, 158, 164, 165, 178, 185
We Are in the Navy Now 32
Weinrib, Lennie 175, 249
Weisbart, David 252
Welch, Raquel 3, 8, 97, 177, 199, 200, 222, 261

Welcome Home, Soldier Boys! 26, 102
Weld, Tuesday 40, 81, 151, 171, 172, 175
Wellman, William, Jr. 134
Wells, Carole 178
Wendkos, Paul 236
Wendy and Me 249
West, Adam 11, 44, 110, 127, 151, 275
West, Martin 186
West Side Story 187, 188
The Whales of August 279
What's Happening 216
Where the Boys Are 19, 288
Whitney, Peter 97
Whorf, David 113, 114
Wicked, Wicked 49
Widmark, Richard 31
Wilcox, Collin 274, 277
The Wild Angels 23, 45, 224, 229, 230, 293
Wild in the Country 18
Wild in the Streets 5, 25, 229, 232
The Wild One 17
The Wild Pack 271, 279
The Wild Racers 284
The Wild Wild West 10, 44, 92, 98, 101, 189, 247, 251
Wild Wild Winter 21, 170, 176, 247
Wilder, Billy 5, 80–82, 90, 122, 213
Wilkinson, June 12
Williams, Billy Dee 219, 220
Williams, Clarence, III 216
Williams, Edy 49
Williams, Roger 64
Williams, Tennessee 80, 82
Williams, Van 41, 44
Willis, Bruce 271, 280
Wilson, Brian 225
Wilson, Earl 109, 166
Wilson, Jackie 122
Wilson, Mary 176
Winfrey, Oprah 209, 216
Wink Martindale's Dance Party 54
Winner, Michael 207
Winning 13, 205
Winter a-Go-Go 20, 132, 134, 135
Winters, David 226
Winters, Jonathan 88
Winters, Shelley 100, 273, 275
Wise, Robert 162
Witch Story 245
Women of the Prehistoric Planet 158, 160
Wonder, Stevie 21, 225
Wong, Linda 20, 136, 137

Wood, Lana vii, 12, 178, 184–196
Wood, Natalie 151, 178, 184, 185, 189, 204, 283
Wood, Walter 288
Woodbury, Woody 83
Woodward, Joanne 59
The World of Susie Wong 158

Yarnall, Celeste vii, 8, 13, 18, 19, 197–210
The Year of the Dragon 167
The Yin and Yang of Mr. Go 165
York, Dick 126
York, Francine vii, 13, 18, 92–107, 242
York, Susannah 100
You Bet Your Life 109
You Only Live Twice 293
Young, Heather 239, 242
Young, Loretta 31
Young, Terence 200, 207
Young Dillinger 110, 293
The Young Lawyers (TV movie) 219
The Young Lawyers (TV series) 211, 219
The Young Lovers 294
The Young Runaways 26

Zanuck, Darryl F. 162, 259, 261, 263, 267, 268
Zanuck, Dean Francis 269
Zanuck, Dick 6, 153, 154, 259–263, 262, 265, 267, 268, 269
Zanuck, Harrison Richard 269
Zanuck, Virginia 261, 268
Zapped Again 291
Zastupnevich, Paul 99, 240
Zitman, Jerry 249
Zsigmond, Vilmos 274

www.ingramcontent.com/pod-product-compliance
Ingram Content Group UK Ltd.
Pitfield, Milton Keynes, MK11 3LW, UK
UKHW050542150426
5217IPUK00026B/2038